Alexander the Great

Blackwell Sourcebooks in Ancient History

This series presents readers with new translations of the raw material of ancient history. It provides direct access to the ancient world, from wars and power politics to daily life and entertainment, allowing readers to discover the extraordinary diversity of ancient societies.

Published

Alexander the Great
Waldemar Heckel and J. C. Yardley

The Hellenistic Period
Roger Bagnall and Peter Derow

In Preparation

The Ancient Near East
Mark Chavalas

Bread and Circuses
Alison Futrell

Alexander the Great

Historical Sources in Translation

Waldemar Heckel and J. C. Yardley

Blackwell Publishing

BLACKWELL PUBLISHING
350 Main Street, Malden, MA 02148-5020, USA
9600 Garsington Road, Oxford OX4 2DQ, UK
550 Swanston Street, Carlton, Victoria 3053, Australia

First published 2004 by Blackwell Publishing Ltd

5   2008

Library of Congress Cataloging-in-Publication Data

Alexander the Great : historical sources in translation / edited by
Waldemar Heckel and J. C. Yardley.
    p. cm. – (Blackwell sourcebooks in ancient history)
Includes bibliographical references and index.
   ISBN 978-0-631-22820-2 (alk. paper) – ISBN 978-0-631-22821-9 (pbk. : alk. paper)
   1. Alexander, the Great, 356–323 B.C.   2. Greece–History–Macedonian Expansion, 359–323
B.C.–Sources.   3. Generals–Greece–Biography.   4. Greece–Kings and rulers–Biography.
I. Heckel, Waldemar, 1949- II. Yardley, John, 1942– III. Series.

DF234.A1 A45 2003
938'.07'092–dc21

2002153417

A catalogue record for this title is available from the British Library.

Set in 10 on 12.5 pt Stone Serif
by SNP Best-set Typesetter Ltd, Hong Kong

For further information on
Blackwell Publishing, visit our website:
www.blackwellpublishing.com

Contents

Plates

Abbreviations

AC	Acta Classica
AHB	Ancient History Bulletin
AJA	American Journal of Archaeology
AJAH	American Journal of Ancient History
AJPh	American Journal of Philology
AM	Ancient Macedonia/Archaia Makedonia
Anc. Soc.	Ancient Society
AncW	Ancient World
ANRW	Aufstieg und Niedergang der Römischen Welt
BICS	Bulletin of the Institute of Classical Studies, London
CA	Classical Antiquity
CJ	Classical Journal
CPh	Classical Philology
CQ	Classical Quarterly
CW	Classical World
FGrH	Die Fragmente der griechischen Historiker
GJ	Geographical Journal
G & R	Greece and Rome
GRBS	Greek, Roman and Byzantine Studies
HSCPh	Harvard Studies in Classical Philology
IA	Iranica Antiqua
IG	Inscriptiones Graecae
JHS	Journal of Hellenic Studies
JNES	Journal of Near Eastern Studies

LCM	*Liverpool Classical Monthly*
OLP	*Orientalia Lovaniensia Periodica*
PCPhA	*Proceedings of the Cambridge Philological Association*
PW	H. W. Parke and D. E. W. Wormell (1956), *The Delphic Oracle II: The Oracular Responses*
RFIC	*Rivista di filologia e istruzione classica*
RhM	*Rheinisches Museum für Philologie*
RSA	*Rivista storica dell'antichità*
SEG	*Supplementum Epigraphicum Graecum*
SO	*Symbolae Osloenses*
Syll.[3]	*Sylloge Inscriptionum Graecarum*
TAPhA	*Transactions of the American Philological Association*

Preface

Dan Quayle must have had a premonition when he made his famous gaffe about "Latin" America. This book began on a country road in Guatemala, in the back of a crowded and painfully slow-moving minivan bound from Tikal to Flores, with a man too long without a bathroom break to continue his journey in comfort. For this was my predicament in June 1999, when I began sketching the outline of an "Alexander sourcebook" in an attempt to divert my mind from what was quite literally a more pressing matter. John Yardley, wedged into the seat beside me and co-conspirator in this diversion, had come up with the idea for such a book several months before, but at that time there was no sense of urgency.

One year later, we rehearsed the project and discussed a grant application on yet another bus, this time careening through the dense morning mists of the Andes, somewhere between Alausi and Ingapirca. From an internet cafe in Cuenca, Ecuador, we contacted Al Bertrand of Blackwell Publishing to arrange the contract.

We should like to thank Laura Gagné and Nicole Bocci for reading the proofs; Pamela Arancibia for compiling the index; Iolo Davies for allowing us to reproduce, with minor changes, portions of his translation of the *Itinerary of Alexander*, and the Social Sciences and Humanities Research Council of Canada for supporting our work. Many friends and colleagues have helped us along the way: Lindsay Adams, John Atkinson, Liz Baynham, Brian Bosworth, Stan Burstein, Beth Carney, Kirk Grayson, Frank Holt, Konrad Kinzl, Daniel Ogden, Gordon Shrimpton, Larry Tritle, and Pat Wheatley. Most of all, we thank the tireless people at Blackwell Publishing – Al Bertrand, Angela Cohen and our copy-editor, Jack Messenger – who offered kind words of encouragement after every crack of the whip.

It is, of course, *de rigueur* for a scholar to thank wife and family for their patience, as if referring to some abnormal imposition: mine know full well that the completion of this book does not mean that I shall suddenly emerge from my study and become sociable. And for *this* I thank them.

Waldemar Heckel
Calgary, 22 July 2003

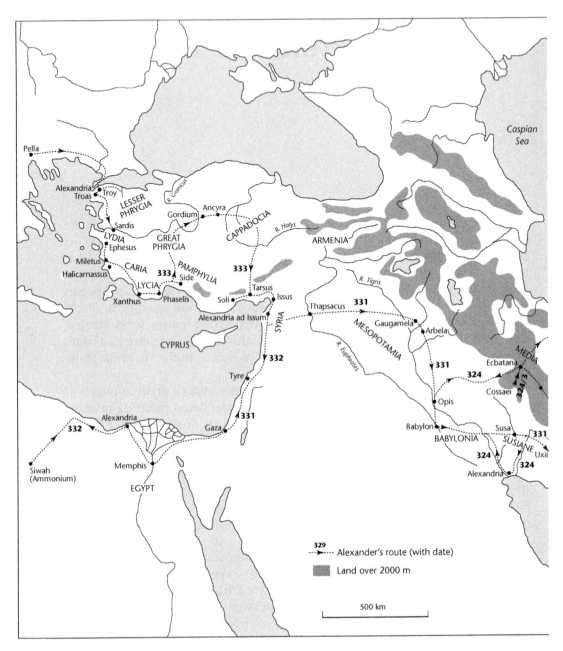

Alexander's campaigns, 334–323 BC

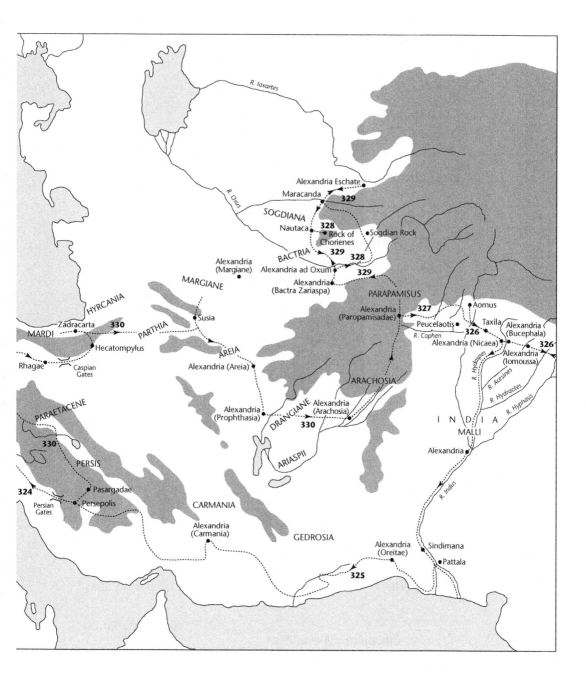

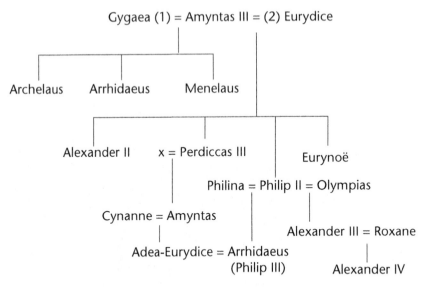

Stemma 1   The family of Philip II and Alexander

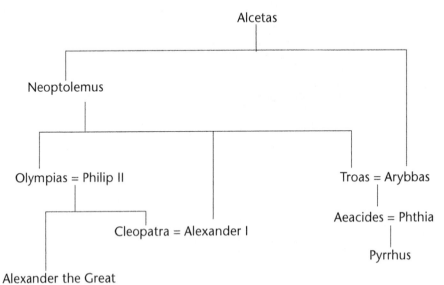

Stemma 2   The family of Olympias

Translator's Note

The texts of the major "Alexander authors" used for the translations are as follows:

Arrian: *Flavius Arrianus Alexandri Anabasis*, ed. A. G. Roos, revd. G. Wirth (Teubner: 1967)

Diodorus, Book 17: *Diodore de Sicile Bibliothèque Historique Livre 17*, ed. Paul Goukowsky (Budé: 1976)

Justin: *M. Iuniani Iustini Epitoma Historiarum Philippicarum Pompei Trogi*, ed. O. Seel (Teubner: 1972)

Metz Epitome/Liber de Morte: *Epitoma Rerum Gestarum Alexandri et Liber de Morte Eius*, ed. P. H. Thomas (Teubner: 1966)

Plutarch, *Alexander*: *Plutarchus Vitae Parallelae*, ed. K. Ziegler, 3 vols. (Teubner: 1964–73)

Quintus Curtius Rufus: *Quinte-Curce, Histoires*, ed. Henri Bardon, 2 vols. (Budé: 1947–8)

In places these works have suffered damage in the process of transmission (this is especially the case with the *Metz Epitome/Liber de Morte*) and I have indicated where the editors find the texts unsound, or where the text has been supplemented, with the following sigla:

† Text unsound at this point

⟨ ⟩ word(s) believed to have dropped out of text. Words found within such brackets are the editor's supposition of what must have been in the original.

J. C. Yardley

Introduction

Now there is one magnificent deed, as great as any other on Alexander's record, that I do not think should be allowed to fade into oblivion, whether it occurred in this land [i.e. the Gedrosian desert] or even earlier (as some have written) amongst the Parapamisadae. The army was advancing through sand and in by-now scorching heat – it was imperative that they reach water, and that lay some distance ahead of them. Alexander, overcome by thirst like the others, was having enormous difficulty leading the force, but he stayed on his feet just the same; for, as usually is the case in such situations, the rest of the men could more easily bear the hardships if the distress was shared.

[2] At that point a number of the light-armed troops left the main force in search of water. They found some gathered in a torrent-bed that was not deep – it was a meagre and miserable little supply. They scooped this up without difficulty and came eagerly to Alexander, believing they were bringing him some great present. As they were approaching they poured the water into a helmet and offered it to the king. [3] Alexander took the helmet and commended the men who had brought it. Then, as all looked on, he took the water and poured it out, and the entire army experienced such a surge of morale over this gesture that one might have suspected that every one of them had that very water that had been poured away by Alexander. This act of Alexander's, more than any other, I applaud as demonstrating the man's stamina and qualities of leadership.

Arrian, *History of Alexander* 6.26.1–3

The Conquest of the East

Classical Greek history ended in late summer or early autumn 336,[1] when Philip II of Macedon collapsed in the theatre at Aegae (Vergina), struck down by an assassin's dagger (see p. 26). He had staked his claim to military lead-

1 All dates, unless otherwise indicated, are BC. BC is also used occasionally to avoid ambiguity.

ership (*hegemonia*) on the battlefield of Chaeronea in 338, and seen it confirmed the following spring at Corinth. Here, too, was born an ambitious expedition against Persia, which Philip hoped to inaugurate with a splendid ceremony that followed the wedding of his daughter, Cleopatra, to her uncle Alexander I of Epirus (see stemma 2, p. xiv). But the ceremony and the king's life were cut short by Pausanias of Orestis. The motives of the assassin are at once simple and obscure: on a personal level, he was taking revenge for a sexual outrage that Philip had allowed to go unpunished; for the perpetrator was none other than the uncle of Philip's young bride.[2] Modern scholars have been reluctant to believe that Pausanias acted alone, and not as the instrument of powerful conspirators. Some have suspected the Lyncestians, the sons of Aëropus, acting either for personal gain or to place Amyntas IV, the son of Perdiccas III (see §I.1b and stemma 1, p. xiv) and, arguably, the rightful heir, on the throne. These at least were officially held responsible for the murder and executed by the new king. Others have pointed an accusing finger at the jilted queen, Olympias, Alexander's mother – and, indeed, there are even those who have thought the crown prince capable and guilty of the crime.

As a result of the act, Alexander became king, inheriting both the throne and Philip's expedition against Persia. Philip, as *hegemon* of the League of Corinth, had employed the Panhellenic slogans of Isocrates (see §V.1a–c) and revived the propaganda of the Athenian empire, which depicted Persia as the common enemy of Greece and – to use one of the buzz-words of modern scholarship – the "other" against which the Greeks measured themselves. Like the Achaean heroes of the Trojan War, whom the young king had admired since childhood and whose numbers included a mythical ancestor, Achilles, Alexander would lead a great expedition to the East. The Spartan king, Agesilaus (*regn.* 398–361), had attempted to play a similar role, only to be humiliated by the Boeotians, who overturned his sacrifices at Aulis. Once in Asia, Agesilaus' options were limited by a paucity of troops and a lack of support in European Greece; indeed, the machinations of enemy states, incited, as some claimed, by the gold of Persia, had necessitated his recall and preempted a strike against the heart of the Persian empire. Thus Xenophon, a great admirer of Sparta and the king, but the reality was far different.

Alexander, for his part, began with advantages that Agesilaus could only dream of. First, there was an army that had been reformed and hardened by almost a quarter century of training in the field; the phalangites (Alexander's *pezhetairoi* or "foot-companions") were drawn from rugged stock and a large Macedonian population, and they wielded their *sarissai* (lances of up to 18 feet in length) so as to smash the most courageous and efficient of hoplite armies and to paralyze with fear the reluctant barbarian levies. Then there was the political settlement that Philip had imposed upon Greece after his victory at Chaeronea, which combined with the age-old divisions of the Greeks to prevent serious uprisings in Alexander's absence. An attempt to

---

2 Also named Cleopatra. She was Philip's seventh and last wife (see §II.1a–c).

shake off the newly imposed yoke was frustrated by the speed of the young king, who left as a searing example of his power the destruction of Thebes and the enslavement of its population (see §V.2a–g); for the untried youth whom Athenian orators had despised as a "barbarian" was content to play the part, if terror would buy peace, and to follow this up with a show of clemency that elicited an equally insincere display of contrition. He did not need their love, only their obedience.

Hence, after a brief delay, Alexander and his mixed force of Macedonians and allies crossed the Hellespont in 334. In successive campaigning seasons, Asia Minor, the Levant, Egypt, and Mesopotamia fell to the conqueror. By the end of 331 he had occupied three of the Achaemenid capitals and threatened the fourth, Ecbatana. Here Darius, twice defeated in pitched battle, awaited reinforcements from the east, but these were slow to mobilize, and his courtiers and satraps urged a retreat into Central Asia. Finding their withdrawal slow and threatened by the relentless pursuit of the Macedonians, a faction led by Bessus and the chiliarch Nabarzanes deposed the king, clapping him in chains – allegedly of gold, as if to dignify the captive or mitigate the crime. On the verge of being overtaken by Alexander's advance column, which moved at rates that would tax even modern armies, the conspirators murdered Darius and left him dead by the roadway (see §IV.3a–c). Legend has it that Alexander found him still breathing and, after promising to avenge him, used his own cloak to cover the body. But this is nothing more than a noble fiction, promulgated much later by a victor who could afford such magnanimous gestures. In reality, although he may have been moved by the lifeless eyes of Darius, it was the spectre of Bessus, wearing the tiara upright and styling himself Artaxerxes V, that animated him. If Bessus could rally the semi-nomadic peoples of the Upper Satrapies, then the war would be prolonged.

This indeed came about, although Bessus was promptly arrested and extradited (see §IV.3d–j) in the hope that Alexander would turn his attention elsewhere. A succession of "rebels" – they would perhaps have called themselves "patriots" or "freedom fighters" – continued the resistance: Spitamenes, Catanes, Sisimithres, Oxyartes. In the end, it was political marriage rather than military force that won the peace; for Alexander took Roxane, the daughter of Oxyartes, as his bride in the winter of 328/7 (see §§VII.3d–e; VIII.6a–g). But the union was less popular with the Macedonians, who were offended by every manifestation of the king's orientalism. Already in the early stages of the campaign he had shown favour to defeated Persian officials, and in Babylon and Susa he had even reinstated them in their satrapies; in Egypt he had welcomed the pronouncements of the priests at Siwah, who acknowledged him as the son of Amun (see §IX.3a–d); and in Hyrcania he had begun to assume some of the trappings of Persian royalty (see §VII.1a–d). Now, as he set his sights on India, he attempted to introduce the Persian court protocol known as *proskynesis* (see §VII.2a–c). The practice, which required courtiers and subjects to abase themselves before the king, was doubly offensive to the Macedonians: first, it was thought that only gods deserved such veneration; and, second, they had become aware of the fact that their king no longer regarded himself as *primus inter pares* ("first among equals"). In the event, the experiment failed and Alexander gave in to pressure from his *hetairoi* (see glossary).

The king's orientalism was matched by a growing aloofness, an estrangement from his men and their traditions. Not surprisingly, the same period witnessed a series of conspiracies and confrontations, which were suppressed by judicially sanctioned execution or simple murder – Philotas and Parmenion (§X.3a–c), Alexander the Lyncestian (§X.2a–e), Cleitus (§X.4a–c), Callisthenes and the Pages (§X.5a–e). New commanders emerged, eager for advancement and reluctant to voice displeasure.

In India Alexander completed the annexation of the old Achaemenid empire, but the wheels of conquest bogged down in the monsoon-drenched lands of the Punjab. Porus at the Hydaspes (Jhelum) represented a more formidable opponent than Darius at Issus and Gaugamela, and the prospect of advancing beyond the Hyphasis (Beas) crushed the spirit of an already demoralized army. There was nothing to do but return to the West, though this would entail a detour, as the king followed the Indus river to its mouth and was rewarded with the sight of the ocean. He had indeed come to one of the limits of the world, even if this was not in the East.

The journey home, through the Gedrosia, where the privations of the army elicited one of the king's most noble acts, and through Carmania, where a Bacchic revel – dismissed by most modern scholars as a discreditable fiction – revived the army's spirit, led ultimately only to further confrontation, tragedy, and death. Back in the heartland of Persia, Alexander found that in his absence his administrators – Greeks, Macedonians, Persians – had succumbed to greed and lust for power. The so-called "reign of terror" amounted, in most cases, to little more than just punishment. Plans to integrate large numbers of eastern troops into the army were met with "mutiny" at Opis, and, although Alexander finally achieved a measure of concord, his own peace of mind was severely disturbed some time later when his dearest friend died at Ecbatana. The tragedy foreshadowed in style and suddenness the king's own death in Babylon in June 323, and this too was marked by controversy.

That Alexander was the victim of foul play, poisoned by Antipater and his faction, is a fabrication of the propaganda wars of the Successors. His death is almost certainly ascribable to natural causes, though the nature of these cannot be determined with certainty: malaria, typhoid, and alcoholism have all been proposed. His sudden death and lack of provision for a successor, although he had one illegitimate son living in Pergamum, and a wife who was six to eight months pregnant, set the stage for an era of civil wars that we call the Age of the Diadochoi ("Successors"). The permanence of the Hellenistic Kingdoms was not established until the years that followed the battle of Corupedium (282/1), when the last of Alexander's generals, Lysimachus and Seleucus, both of them septuagenarians, fought the last of the great wars of the Successors. The winner, it seemed, was prepared to unite Europe and Asia, but he fell victim to the man who would be known to history as "Ceraunus" ("The Thunderbolt").[3] So the adventure of Alexander, which had begun with the sharp blows of the assassin's dagger, ended in similar fashion with the passing of the last of Alexander's marshals, Seleucus Nicator.

The Historians of Alexander: Lost and Extant

Lost

From the very outset, Alexander had no shortage of writers to commemorate his achievements. Official records were kept in a *Royal Journal* (sometimes referred to as *Royal Diaries* or *Ephemerides*), compiled by Eumenes of Cardia (or Diodotus of Erythrae, though this may be a pseudonym). This work, insofar as one can characterize it on the basis of the surviving fragments, appears to have contained rather banal observations on the king's daily activities, with little of military or political value. At best, the *Ephemerides* served as an accurate record of the expedition's itinerary. Similar, though apparently more extensive, was the work of the king's chamberlain, Chares of Mytilene, probably published after Alexander's death but based on notes taken during the campaign. The "official" history was that of Callisthenes of Olynthus, written with the aim of glorifying the king, and of selling the Panhellenic expedition to the Greeks at home – for this reason, it seems to have been published in instalments. Hence Callisthenes was simultaneously war correspondent and propagandist; for then, as today, these responsibilities were easily blurred. Callisthenes' *Deeds of Alexander* – the title is revealing – ended abruptly, as the historian fell out of favor, first for his views on *proskynesis* and later for his part in the Hermolaus conspiracy. For the latter he paid with his life, though the nature of his death is not at all clear.

Two writers of Greek origin, who served with Alexander's fleet and were particularly interested in the wonders of India, wrote very soon after the king's death. Nearchus was allegedly already reading a version of his account to Alexander in his final days, and the published history claimed to correct the mendacities of Onesicritus of Astypalaea, a personal rival and helmsman of Alexander's ship, whom Strabo called the "chief pilot of the incredible."[4] If we assume that the pamphlet on the *Last Days and Testament of Alexander the Great* was published early, before 317 (Heckel 1988) or ca. 309/8 (Bosworth 2000), we must also conclude that Onesicritus wrote before that time; for, as the pamphlet indicates, the charge that Alexander was a victim of poisoning had already been made by Onesicritus, who would not name the conspirators for fear of reprisals. Nearchus must have written soon afterwards, since

---

3 Ptolemy, a son of Ptolemy I Soter of Egypt. He ruled Macedonia briefly but was soon killed by invading Galatians.
4 Strabo 15.1.28 C698.

he is last attested in 312 and, perhaps significantly, fails to appear as a fleet commander at the battle of Salamis (306), although he was a close friend of Demetrius and Antigonus the One-Eyed.

One other writer, Cleitarchus, who is now thought to have written fairly soon after Alexander's death, appears to have made use of both Onesicritus and Nearchus. Whether he himself accompanied Alexander's expedition is uncertain – most scholars believe that he did not – but, in Alexandria, he had access to eye-witnesses, veterans who fought on either side, and he was well informed about Persian affairs and customs, being the son of Dinon, the author of a work on *Persika*. Most important, however, was the fact that Cleitarchus wrote an entertaining, and somewhat sensational, account, which was in the late Roman Republic and early Empire by far the most popular, eclipsing the pedestrian narrative of Ptolemy and the blatantly apologetic history of Aristobulus of Cassandria. His style did not appeal to everyone, nor was his history free of factual error. But Cleitarchus also preserved much that would otherwise have gone unrecorded; for Ptolemy and Aristobulus alike were guilty of omissions, if not outright lies, of their own.

Ptolemy has long enjoyed a good reputation, although most would reject Arrian's naive remark that he had a greater claim to credibility since, as a king, it would be more shameful for him to tell lies! Only recently have scholars explored Ptolemy's bias and observed that he was as prepared to omit the achievements of his political enemies as to embellish his own. Nevertheless, the view that he wrote earlier rather than late, with the aim of maligning certain of the *Diadochoi*, is not compelling. Rather, his history appears to have been written in old age, probably after 285, when he shared the throne with his son, Ptolemy Philadelphus. Consequently, it is hard to differentiate between malice and forgetfulness, though both will have played a part in the shaping of the work.

Aristobulus' history is definitely late, and also the product of old age: Pseudo-Lucian says that he began writing his history at the age of 84. Certainly, Aristobulus claimed that the seer Peithagoras, brother of Apollodorus of Amphipolis, had predicted, in addition to the deaths of Hephaestion and Alexander, that of Antigonus at Ipsus in 301. Aristobulus had a fondness for geography and his numerous variant place-names suggest that he was either an insufferable pedant or obsessed with trivia. But most notably, he had a tendency to excuse even the king's most serious defects and his outright crimes, a trait that endeared him not only to Arrian but to several modern admirers as well.[5]

Extant

Of the extant historians of Alexander, five serve as the underpinnings of any modern narrative: Diodorus, Curtius, Plutarch, Arrian, Justin; and to these we

---

5   Most notably Tarn (1948, II: 39–42).

might add the *Metz Epitome*. The earliest of these surviving accounts was written in the second half of the first century BC: Diodorus Siculus discussed Alexander in the seventeenth book of his *Bibliotheca*, a world history from the mythical period to his own time. Book 17 is a particularly long one, despite the fact that a lacuna consumes the account of the events between mid-330 to early 326. Soon after Diodorus, a Romanized Gaul from Vasio (Vaison-la-Romaine) named Pompeius Trogus related the history of Alexander in the eleventh and twelfth books of a world history, the *Historiae Philippicae*. This work is, unfortunately, lost and we have only the uneven and error-filled epitome by a certain Marcus Junianius Justinus (Justin) to go by. It has been fashionable to dismiss Justin as worthless, and indeed his epitome has done much to tarnish the reputation of an otherwise worthy historian. But not everything in Justin is without merit, and one can learn a good deal about the popular Alexander tradition from comparing Justin's epitome with the works of Diodorus, Curtius, and others. Even Justin's own time of writing has been debated, though it now looks as if we can date him securely to the late second/early third century of our era.

Diodorus, Pompeius Trogus (Justin), and Quintus Curtius Rufus show unmistakable signs of basing their accounts on a common source, and that source can be identified with virtual certainty as Cleitarchus of Alexandria. More difficult to determine is whether these authors used Cleitarchus first-hand or through an intermediary. Diodorus appears to have used Cleitarchus directly and as his main source for Book 17, for it was his method to base each section of his world history on a particular primary source and, occasionally, to supplement this source with information from others. The extant books that deal with the Successors derive, beyond a doubt, from the work of Hieronymus of Cardia. About Trogus' method we can be less certain: some scholars believe that he consulted a large number of primary sources, and that for Books 11–12 he relied upon Cleitarchus; but it is equally possible that Trogus knew Cleitarchus through an intermediary, perhaps Timagenes of Alexandria. Quintus Curtius Rufus appears to have read Cleitarchus as well as Trogus, whence he may have derived the information that Timagenes, too, mistakenly claimed that Ptolemy son of Lagus saved Alexander's life at the Mallian town.

There was at one point great uncertainty about Quintus Curtius Rufus' time of writing: scholars have suggested various dates between the reign of Augustus and that of Septimius Severus. Today, it is generally believed that Curtius was a rhetorician and politician, who died in AD 53 while serving as proconsul of Africa. He is assumed to have written most of his history in the period between the fall of Sejanus and the accession of the emperor Claudius. Nevertheless, there are still those who favor Vespasian over Claudius, and it is perhaps a positive sign that the writer's time can be restricted to the first century of our era.

Curtius' *Historiae Alexandri Magni* comprised ten books and is thus the only full-length account of the Macedonian conqueror in Latin. The first two books, which included events up to Alexander's arrival in Celaenae (Phrygia), are lost, as are the end of Book 5 and the beginning of Book 6, as well as significant portions of Book 10. In addition to Cleitarchus and Trogus, Curtius appears to have made use of Ptolemy.

The *Metz Epitome* (discussed below), from which several passages in this volume have been taken, shows a close relationship to both Curtius and Trogus (Justin), as well as the occasional resemblance to Diodorus, but how these similarities are to be explained is still problematic.

Of the two remaining major sources, Plutarch and Arrian, it must be noted that the former, as a biographer, had very different aims from those of the historians. And, although he is eclectic in his use of sources, the narrative that forms the backbone of his story is almost certainly based on Cleitarchus. Arrian, by contrast, represents a totally different tradition and has until recently been the darling of Alexander scholars.

Arrian of Nicomedia died in AD 160, in his mid-70s, after a distinguished political and literary career. A Greek from Bithynia, he became a Roman citizen in the reign of Hadrian and served as consul in the time of Antoninus Pius. His works were modeled on those of Xenophon, and his *Anabasis of Alexander* – if that was, indeed, the true name of the history – owes much to Xenophon's account of the march of the younger Cyrus. Arrian selected as his "reliable" sources Ptolemy and Aristobulus, in the belief that their participation in the expedition made them trustworthy, while the fact that they wrote after the king's death rendered them less prone to flattery and distortion. The military narrative is notable for its clarity, due on the one hand to one of its primary sources and on the other to the personal experiences of Arrian himself. But the work has its share of errors, some textual, others the result of careless composition; and, of course, there is the matter of Arrian's "whitewashing" of Alexander.

Ancient authors other than the main Alexander historians

Other authors – geographers, tacticians, compilers of anecdotes, orators, and moralizing rhetoricians – offer glimpses of Alexander's life and accomplishments, and we have included selections from them. But, for the most part, the themes that we explore are developed through the evidence of the major historians mentioned above. The additional sources are listed below in alphabetical, rather than chronological, order.

Aelian

Aelian (Claudius Aelianus) was a Roman author of the late second and early third centuries AD who wrote in Greek. His "Historical Miscellany" (*Varia Historia*) is a compendium of anecdotes from the past, much of it drawn from earlier Greek authors.

Alexander Romance

The earliest manuscript of the *Alexander Romance*, often referred to as the work of Pseudo-Callisthenes (because several medieval manuscripts wrongly attributed its authorship to Callisthenes), dates to the third century AD. The work is a mangled collection of materials, historical and fictitious, that came together during the roughly 600 years that separate the time of Alexander from the earliest manuscript. As such it contains elements of the popular "Cleitarchean" tradition, collections of letters, exotic tales, and material from political pamphlets. Versions of the *Romance* exist in Greek, Latin, Armenian, Syriac, Arabic, and other oriental langages. See Stoneman (1991, 1994) and Baynham (1995b).

Aristotle (384–322)

From Stagira in the Chalcidic peninsula, Aristotle was the son of Nicomachus, court physician of Amyntas III, the grandfather of Alexander the Great. He was a student of Plato but, after his teacher's death (and perhaps because Speusippus was named as Plato's successor), he left Athens for Asia Minor. In 343 or 342 he became the tutor of the crown prince, Alexander. In 335 he went to Athens and founded his own school at the Lyceum, which was noted for its covered walkway (*peripatos*). His numerous works dealt with a wide range of subjects: ethics, metaphysics, politics, nature, and classification. The one quotation from Aristotle in this collection comes from the *Politics* (composed between 329 and 326) and deals with the death of Philip II. See Guthrie (1981).

Athenaeus of Naucratis in Egypt (ca. 200 AD)

Athenaeus' only work is the "Philosophers at Dinner" (*Deipnosophistae*), purportedly an intellectual "symposiastic" discussion (i.e., conducted during the post-dinner drinking) held by a number of leading people in such fields as medicine, law, and literature. It is very valuable for its citation of earlier authors now lost.

Cassius Dio

Like the most famous of the extant Alexander historians, Arrian, and Polyaenus (see below), the author of *Stratagems*, Dio (his praenomen was apparently Lucius) was born in Bithynia. He lived from ca. AD 164 to 235 and rose to high political rank, holding the consulship in 229, together with the emperor Severus Alexander. At first he compiled an account of Roman wars after Commodus, but then turned his hand to a complete history of Rome, from the city's founding to the year AD 229, in 80 books. Only Books 36–60 have survived virtually intact, though even these have numerous lacunae; the remainder are known only from extracts and abbreviated summaries by Zonaras and Xiphilinus.

Cicero (Marcus Tullius Cicero: 106–43)

A famous Roman orator and politician, Cicero was born in Arpinum and was the first in his family to be elected to the consulship and was thus a *novus homo* ("new man"). This was a great source of pride for Cicero, together with the fact that he attained the office *suo anno* (that is, in the first year in which he was eligible). A staunch defender of the Republic and of Senatorial authority, he was an enemy of Caesar and Antony, attacking the latter in bitter speeches known as *Philippics*. And it was at the hands of Antony's agents that he died. Cicero's political writings (he also wrote philosophical works) deal with contemporary Roman events, but he was knowledgeable about Alexander, having read, if nothing else, the work of Cleitarchus (Cicero, *Brutus* 42; *Laws* 1.7; *ad Fam.* 2.10.3).

Frontinus

Sextus Iulius Frontinus lived in the second half of the first century AD and died in 103 or 104. He wrote a work on aqueducts – not surprisingly, since he was the emperor Nerva's superintendent of aqueducts – and a collection of *Stratagems*. For his stratagems of Alexander the Great he appears to have drawn on the eleventh and twelfth books of the *Philippic History* of Pompeius Trogus, as can be determined from the similarities of language and content.

Heidelberg Epitome

The so-called *Heidelberg Epitome* is a collection of four excerpts of historical material dealing with the age of the Successors, found in the late nineteenth century in Codex Palatinus Graecus 129 in Heidelberg by Max Treu. The manuscript contains, in 141 pages, a vast number of excerpts on a variety of subjects. The date of composition and the name of the excerptor are unknown. The ultimate source of the historical material is also uncertain: the *Heidelberg Epitome* has many features in common with Diodorus Siculus, but Bauer (1914) ruled out Hieronymus of Cardia or Diodorus himself as the epitomator's original, suggesting instead Agatharchides of Cnidus and possibly also Timagenes of Alexandria. In most respects, the work is accurate and reminds the reader of Hieronymus; there is also a detectable bias in favor of Eumenes, Hieronymus' kinsman. Section IV, however, contains a serious error, claiming that Ptolemy married Cleopatra, the sister of Alexander, and identifying her as a daughter of Philip II's last wife, Cleopatra.

Historia Augusta

Historia Augusta is a late collection of *Lives* of Roman emperors, modeled to some extent on the work of Suetonius (see below). It begins with Hadrian and continues to AD 284. It purports to be the work of six different biographers, the *Scriptores Historiae Augustae,* even though stylistically it shows little of the variation that one would expect to find as one moved from author to author. Questions of authorship, date, authenticity, and purpose all remain unresolved.

Itinerary of Alexander (Itinerarium Alexandri)

The *Itinerarium Alexandri* is a work of anonymous authorship, written about AD 340 in the time of (and dedicated to) the emperor Constantius II, who was then undertaking a campaign against the Sassanian Persians. Inspired by Terentius Varro's work for young Pompey, when he set out for his war in Spain, the *Itinerarium* contained a summary of both Alexander's exploits against the Persians and those of the emperor Trajan in his Parthian expedition. Constantius II was to challenge the Persian empire in its third incarnation, that of the Sassanians. Only the portion dealing with Alexander has survived, and that in a single manuscript, which contained also the *Res Gestae Alexandri Magni* of Julius Valerius, a Latin version of the Greek *Alexander Romance.* Lane Fox (1997) has argued that Flavius Polemius (that is, Flavius Julius Valerius Alexander Polemius), consul in 338, was both the translator of the Greek *Alexander Romance* and author of the *Itinerary.* Like other summaries and collections of stratagems, the work is idiosyncratic, sketchy, and riddled with error. The bulk of the *Itinerarium,* however, deals with Alexander's campaigns from his accession to the invasion of India and corresponds, in places, closely with the material in the first four books of Arrian's *History of Alexander.* But the work can hardly be treated as an epitome of Arrian's history; for it contains numerous insertions inspired by other sources or attributable to the author's ignorance or imagination. All passages from the *Itinerary* included in this collection are taken, with the translator's permission, from Davies (1998).

Livy

Livy (Titus Livius) is perhaps the best-known, though not necessarily the best, historian of ancient Rome, and was born in 64 or 59 BC and died sometime after AD 14. His work *ab urbe condita* ("From the Foundation of the City") covered the history of Rome from its foundation to the early Principate in 142 books. Of these, only Books 1–10 and 21–45 have survived; short summaries of the books survive (the so-called *Periochae*), and an *Epitome* by Florus relies heavily on Livy, whom he often quotes verbatim, but uses other authors as well. We have used Livy to illustrate Roman attitudes towards Alexander.

Lucian

Lucian of Samosata (Syria) wrote in Greek during the second century AD, though he was not Greek in origin. His large body of works comprises various genres, and although he wrote a work entitled *How to write History*, he can hardly be considered a historian himself.

Metz Epitome

The *Metz Epitome* is an obscure epitome of a history of Alexander, contained in a single manuscript from Metz. This peculiar work was destroyed in a bombing raid during World War II. Fortunately, two transcriptions of the *Metz Epitome*, made in the nineteenth century, were in existence and formed the basis for a new text by Thomas (1966; see translator's note, above). Although the manuscript contained the *Liber de Morte* (now sometimes referred to as the "Last Days and Testament of Alexander the Great"), this work was entirely separate from the Alexander epitome. The epitome begins with the events after the death of Darius III and ends, abruptly, with Indian affairs (Alexander's descent of the Indus river system). It has much in common with the work of Curtius and Justin–Trogus and clearly belongs to the popular Alexander tradition. See Baynham (1995a).

Pausanias

Pausanias the Periegete was active in the middle of the second century AD (internal evidence suggests that he was still writing after 175). His *Description of Greece* covered ten books, and although it was not his aim to write history, the work contains much of historical value, including numerous references to events of the fourth century BC and the Hellenistic period. See Habicht (1985).

Pliny the Elder (Gaius Plinius Secundus: AD 23–79)

A Roman equestrian, Pliny the Elder (so-called to distinguish him from his nephew, Pliny the Younger, who also had literary pretensions) has the dubious distinction of having died as result of the eruption of Mount Vesuvius – he perished as a result of smoke inhalation, according to a letter written by his nephew to the historian Tacitus. His most famous work is the *Natural History*, a 37-volume treatise on geography and plant and animal life (and much more), dedicated to the emperor Titus.

Polyaenus

Born ca. AD 100 in Bithynia, Polyaenus was a Roman citizen of Macedonian background. At some point he moved to Rome and practiced law (he is attested there in 161); simultaneously he embarked upon a literary career. His work on *Stratagems* (*Strategica*) comprised eight books. The work was dedicated to the emperors Marcus Aurelius and Lucius Verus. Book 4 deals with the Macedonians and 4.3.1–32 specifically with Alexander the Great. See Krentz and Wheeler (1994).

Polybius of Megalopolis

Born ca. 200 BC, Polybius son of Lycortas was one of the greatest historians of antiquity. After a brief and arrested military and diplomatic career in the Achaean League, he was one of a thousand Achaeans who were taken to Italy after the Third Macedonian War. There he remained from 167 to 150, during which time he became the tutor of Scipio Aemilianus, who would in 146 destroy Carthage at the end of the Third Punic War. Polybius was thus knowledgeable in the affairs of both Greece and Rome, and ideally placed to write the history of the mid-Hellenistic world and middle Republic. He was critical of historians who lacked practical experience (i.e., did not know what they were writing about), directing his hostility against writers like Timaeus of Tauromenium, Phylarchus, and (as we see from the passage in this collection, §V.2f) Callisthenes of Olynthus, Alexander's "official" historian. Polybius' work ran to 40 books, of which only five survived intact; the rest are known from fragments, excerpts, and quotations. Polybius returned to Achaea after the sack of Corinth in 146. He died ca. 118. See Walbank (1972).

Pseudo-Callisthenes

See *Alexander Romance*.

Stephanus of Byzantium

Stephanus of Byzantium was a Greek grammarian and schoolteacher in Constantinople in the time of Justinian (sixth century AD). His main work was called *Ethnica*, an alphabetical lexicon of place-names that ran to 60 books but survives only in the form of an epitome (possibly as late as the tenth century). He is quoted in this collection (§XIII.1b) for his list of Alexandrias founded by the Macedonian king, which according to his survey numbered 18.

SHA

See *Historia Augusta*.

Strabo

Born ca. 64 BC, Strabo of Amaseia, a city on the Black Sea, compiled a *Geography* in 17 books, the most important surviving work on geography from the ancient world. Strabo made use of certain Alexander historians, especially for his descriptions of the Upper Satrapies and India: Cleitarchus, Aristobulus, Nearchus, and Onesicritus are all attested. He was also familiar with the great Hellenistic writer Poseidonius and his work. Strabo died sometime after AD 21.

Suetonius (Gaius Suetonius Tranquillus: ca. AD 70–ca. 130)

Suetonius is the Roman biographer of the Imperial age, best known for his work *de vita Caesarum*, generally referred to in English as *The Twelve Caesars*, which begins with the dictator Gaius Julius Caesar and ends with the emperor Domitian. In this collection we have quoted Suetonius to illustrate examples of *Alexandri imitatio*.

Valerius Maximus

Valerius Maximus is the Roman author of a nine-book work entitled "Memorable Deeds and Sayings" (*Factorum et Dictorum Memorabilium Libri 9*), written in the time of the emperor Tiberius. The work is one of illustrative examples, both Roman ("domestic") and foreign ("external"), drawn from earlier authors, especially Livy and Cicero, including some no longer extant, such as Pompeius Trogus.

Chronology

359	Accession of Philip II.
357	Marriage of Philip and Olympias.
356	Birth of Alexander the Great (July 20).
343	Aristotle becomes Alexander's tutor.
340	Alexander defeats the Maedians and founds Alexandroupolis.
338	Battle of Chaeronea.
336	Death of Philip II. Accession of Alexander.
335	Destruction of Thebes.
334	Beginning of the Asiatic campaign. Battle of the Granicus River. Capture of Sardis; Alexander's sieges of Miletos and Halicarnassus.
333	Alexander undoes the Gordian knot; battle of Issus. Alexander captures the family of Darius III; Parmenion takes Damascus.
332	Alexander takes Sidon and Tyre; siege of Gaza. Entry into Egypt.
332/1	Journey to Siwah; founding of Alexandria in Egypt.
331	Battle of Gaugamela. Surrender of Babylon and Susa; the Persian Gates, capture of Persepolis.
330	Destruction of Persepolis. Alexander advances to Ecbatana. Death of Darius III. Alexander moves into Afghanistan. Arrest and execution of Philotas; deaths of Alexander the Lyncestian and Parmenion.
330/29	Alexander crosses the Hindu Kush. Extradition and punishment of Bessus.
329/8	Campaigns in Bactria and Sogdiana. Macedonian defeat at the Polytimetus River. Death of Spitamenes.
328	Death of Cleitus.
328/7	Alexander marries Roxane, daughter of Oxyartes.

327	Conspiracy of Hermolaus. Death of Callisthenes. Alexander advances to India.
326	Battle against Porus at the Hydaspes (Jhelum); mutiny at the Hyphasis (Beas).
326/5	Descent of the Indus River system.
325	The Gedrosian campaign.
324	Alexander returns to Susa. Mutiny at Opis. Death of Hephaestion at Ecbatana.
323	Death of Alexander.
321/0	Alexander's funeral carriage is taken to Egypt. Perdiccas defeated in Egypt and assassinated by his own officers.

1 Macedonian Background

Early History of Macedonia

The details of Macedonian history before the fourth century BC are hazy: we have scattered references in Herodotus to Amyntas I (*regn.?*–498/7) and, although the activities of Alexander I Philhellene (498/7–454) are somewhat better documented, our knowledge of the reign of Perdiccas II (454–413) is also limited. Of the lives of Archelaus (413–399) and the ephemeral kings who intervened between his reign and that of Amyntas III, grandfather of Alexander the Great, we get only glimpses. The highly readable account of Casson (1926) was reprinted in 1968, only to be rendered obsolete by Hammond (1972) – and for the sixth to fourth centuries by Hammond and Griffith (1979). The best syntheses in English of early Macedonian history are those of Errington (1990) and Borza (1990); we have adopted the regnal dates given by the latter.

1(a)   Strabo, Geography *7.11ff. (fragments)*

Present-day Macedonia was earlier called Emathia, and took its name from Macedon, one of its early leaders (there was also a city Emathia, which was close to the sea). This land was inhabited by certain Epirot and Illyrian peoples, but mostly by the Bottiaei and the Thracians, the former being purportedly of Cretan descent and having Botton as their leader. As for the Thracian peoples, the Pierians lived in Pieria and the area around Olympus, and the Paeonians in the lands surrounding the River Axius[1] (a region thus called Amphixitis), while the Edonians and Bisaltae occupied the remainder of the territory as far as the Strymon. With regard to the last-named peoples, the Bisaltae are called simply that, while the Edonians are grouped into Mygdones, Edones, and Sithones.

---

1   The modern Vardar.

But over all the above-mentioned it was the tribe called the Argeadae who made themselves supreme, as did the Chalcidians in Euboea. In fact, the Chalcidians in Euboea actually invaded the land of the Sithones where they jointly founded some 30 cities (they were subsequently expelled from these, and most of them then came together into a single city, Olynthus) . . .

The River Peneus is the boundary of the southern part of Macedonia, which is towards the sea, dividing it from Thessaly and Magnesia. To the north the Haliacmon – along with the Erigon, Axius and a second system of rivers – forms the boundary with the people of Epirus and of Paeonia . . .

Now from where the Thermaic Gulf indents the coastline at Thessalonica, maritime Macedonia runs south towards Sunium in one direction, east towards the Thracian Chersonnese and in another, thus forming a triangular shape at the point of indentation. Since Macedonia stretches in both these directions, I should begin with the one I mentioned first. The first sector of this, that is that around Sunium, has Attica lying above it along with the land of Megara, as far as the Gulf of Crisa. After this comes the Boeotian coastline that faces Euboea, above which lies the rest of Euboea which runs westwards, parallel to Attica. Strabo also says that the Via Egnatia, coming from the Ionian Gulf, terminates at Thessalonica . . .

The River Peneus flows through Tempe, after rising in the Pindus range . . . and it demarcates Macedonia to the north from Thessaly to the south . . . Olympus lies in Macedonia, and Ossa and Pelion in Thessaly.

There is a city, Dium, at the foot of Olympus, and this has a village, Pimpleia, close by. It was there, they say, that Orpheus the Ciconian lived. He was a wizard who initially eked out a living by his music and prophecy, and from conducting ecstatic rites for the mysteries; but then, thinking he deserved better than that, he acquired a following and personal power. Some men happily embraced his teachings, but others, suspecting him of intrigue for violent ends, joined together and killed him . . .

Beyond Dium is the River Haliacmon which discharges into the Thermaic Gulf. The sector beyond this, that is the northern coastline of the Gulf running as far as the River Axius, is called Pieria, in which is situated Pydna, a city now called Citrum. Then come the cities of Methone and Alorus, and then the rivers Erigon and Loudias. The sailing distance from Loudias to the city of Pella is 120 stades, and Methone is 40 stades from Pydna, and 70 stades from Alorus. Pydna is a city of Pieria, and Alorus is in Bottiaea.

1(b) Justin 7.1–6

Macedonia was formerly called Emathia, after King Emathion, whose primitive heroism lives on to this day in those regions. [2] In keeping with its modest beginnings its territory was very restricted; [3] the inhabitants were called Pelasgians and the country Bottia. [4] Later, thanks to the valour of the kings and the enterprise of its people, it subjugated first its neighbours and then other peoples and tribes, extending its empire to the furthest limits of the

East. [5] Pelegonus, father of Asteropaeus (one of the most distinguished champions in the Trojan War, we are told), is said to have reigned in Paeonia, which is now part of Macedonia. [6] In another quarter, in Europa, a man called Europus occupied the throne.

[7] Caranus² also came to Emathia with a large band of Greeks, being instructed by an oracle to seek a home in Macedonia. Here, following a herd of goats running from a downpour, he seized the city of Edessa, the inhabitants being taken unawares because of heavy rain and dense fog. [8] Remembering the oracle's command to follow the lead of goats in his quest for an empire, Caranus established the city as his capital, [9] and thereafter he made it a solemn observance, wheresoever he took his army, to keep those same goats before his standards in order to have as leaders in his exploits the animals which he had had with him to found the kingdom. [10] He gave the city of Edessa the name Aegaeae and its people the name Aegeads³ in memory of this service. [11] Then, after driving out Midas – he, too, ruled part of Macedonia – and other kings, he supplanted them all as sole ruler, [12] and was the first to unify the tribes of different nations and make a single body of Macedonia, establishing a firm basis on which his expanding kingdom could grow.

2　The king after Caranus was Perdiccas,⁴ who was known both for his illustrious life and for his memorable final instructions, which resembled an oracular utterance. [2] When on his deathbed, the aged Perdiccas indicated to his son, Argaeus, the place where he wished to be buried, and gave orders that not merely his own bones but also those of his successors to the throne be laid in that spot, [3] declaring that the throne would stay in their family as long as the remains of their descendants were buried there. [4] It is on account of this piece of superstition that people believe that the line died out with Alexander, because he changed the place of burial. [5] Argaeus ruled with restraint and won the affection of the people. He left as his successor his son, Philip, who succumbed to an early death, appointing as his heir Aeropus, who was but an infant. [6] Now, the Macedonians were continually at war with the Thracians and Illyrians, and with these campaigns for their routine training they became so hardened that they began to alarm their neighbours with their illustrious military reputation. [7] Accordingly the Illyrians, with disdain for the tender years of the child monarch, launched an attack on the Macedonians. [8] The latter, defeated in battle, carried forward their king in his cradle, placed him to the rear of their battle line and renewed the fight with greater spirit, [9] imagining that the reason for their earlier defeat was that they had fought without the auspices of their king. [10] Now, however, they were going to win because from that superstition they had drawn the determination to do so. [11] At the same time they were gripped by pity for the child, since defeat would evidently

2　See Greenwalt (1985).
3　Perhaps Justin has misunderstood the origins of the Argeadae, whose capital was Aegae (Vergina) before the establishment of Pella. However, Hammond (Hammond and Griffith 1979: 12) accepts the reading.
4　For Caranus and the Macedonian king-list, see Greenwalt (1985).

make their monarch a prisoner. [12] So, once battle was joined, they routed the Illyrians with great slaughter and showed their enemies that what the Macedonians had lacked in the previous encounter was their king, not courage. [13] Aeropus was succeeded by Amyntas, who enjoyed particular renown both for his own merits and because of the outstanding character of his son, Alexander, [14] who was naturally endowed with all manner of superb abilities, to the extent that he even competed in the Olympic games in a variety of events.[5]

3   In the meantime Darius, king of Persia, after being driven from Scythia in ignominious flight, was concerned that he might be discredited everywhere because of his military losses. He therefore sent Magabasus[6] with some of his troops to conquer Thrace and the other kingdoms of that area, to which Macedonia would be added as a place of little importance. [2] Magabasus quickly executed the order of his king and sent an embassy to Amyntas, king of Macedonia, demanding to be given hostages as a guarantee of peace in the future. [3] The ambassadors were given a cordial reception but, becoming the worse for wine during the course of the dinner, they asked Amyntas to add to the magnificence of the feast the privileges of intimate friendship by inviting his daughters and wives to his banquet; for this, they said, was regarded amongst the Persians as a binding pledge of hospitality. [4] When the women arrived, the Persians began to fondle them in too familiar a manner, whereupon Amyntas' son, Alexander, asked his father to have regard for his dignity as an older man and leave the banquet, promising that he would moderate the exuberance of the guests. [5] When Amyntas left, Alexander also called the women away from the banquet for a short while, ostensibly to have them made up more attractively and bring them back more desirable.

[6] He put in their place some young men dressed as women and told them to use their swords, which they carried beneath their dress, to curb the forwardness of the ambassadors. [7] And so all the Persians were killed. When his embassy failed to return, Magabasus, not knowing what had happened, dispatched Bubares with part of his army to the area on what he thought would be an easy campaign of little significance; [8] he did not deign to go in person, for fear of demeaning himself by taking on such a contemptible people in battle. [9] Bubares, however, fell in love with Amyntas' daughter before war could commence and abandoned the campaign. He married her and, renouncing hostile intentions, entered into a regular family relationship with Amyntas.[7]

---

5   In order to compete in the Olympic games, one had to prove one's Greek blood. Hence, Alexander I, subsequently known as Philhellene (*regn.* ca. 498/7–454), established the Hellenism of the Macedonian royal house, tracing its descent through Temenus to Heracles (Hercules).

6   Megabazus (Herodotus 5.14).

7   The story of the murder of the Persian ambassadors (from Herodotus 5.18–21) was probably invented by Alexander Philhellene to deflect charges of collaborating with the Persians. The marriage of Bubares to Alexander's sister, Gygaea, shows that Macedon had entered into an alliance with Persia, albeit as a vassal of Darius I. See Burn (1984: 134).

4   After Bubares left Macedonia King Amyntas died. The family ties which his son and successor, Alexander, enjoyed with Bubares not only ensured him peace in the time of Darius but also put him on such good terms with Xerxes that when the latter swept through Greece like a whirlwind he granted Alexander authority over all the territory between Mt Olympus and Mt Haemus. [2] But Alexander extended his kingdom as much through his own valour as through Persian generosity.

[3] The throne of Macedonia then came by order of succession to Amyntas, son of Alexander's brother Menelaus.[8] [4] He, too, was remarkable for his energy and was possessed of all the qualities befitting a general. [5] He had three sons by Eurydice – Alexander, Perdiccas, and Philip, the father of Alexander the Great of Macedon – as well as a daughter, Eurynoë.[9] By Gygaea he had Archelaus, Arrhidaeus and Menelaus.[10] [6] Amyntas undertook difficult campaigns against the Illyrians and the Olynthians. [7] Moreover, Amyntas would have fallen victim to the treachery of his wife Eurydice (she had made a pact to marry her son-in-law,[11] undertaking to kill her husband and hand the crown to her lover) had their daughter not divulged her mother's liaison and criminal intentions. [8] After surviving all these dangers Amyntas died an old man, passing on the throne to his eldest son, Alexander.

5   Right at the start of his reign, Alexander averted further war with the Illyrians by agreeing to pay them tribute and giving them his brother, Philip, as a hostage. [2] Some time later he again used Philip as a hostage to re-establish peace with the Thebans, and it was this that most served to develop Philip's exceptional genius. [3] Kept as a hostage at Thebes for three years, Philip spent the earliest stages of his boyhood in a city characterized by old-fashioned austerity and in the home of Epaminondas, the great philosopher and general.[12] [4] Shortly afterwards, Alexander succumbed to the treachery of his mother Eurydice. [5] Although Eurydice had been caught red-handed, Amyntas had nevertheless spared her life for the sake of the children they had in common, unaware that she would one day prove their undoing. [6] Alexander's brother, Perdiccas, likewise became the victim of a treacherous

---

8   Justin, in the process of abbreviating the work of Pompeius Trogus (see introduction, p. xxii), has omitted some sixty years of Macedonian history. After the death of Alexander Philhellene, the kingship passed to his son Perdiccas II (452–413); Perdiccas was in turn succeeded by Archelaus (413–399). Archelaus was assassinated and a period of turmoil ensued, resulting in the accession of Amyntas III in 392. Although he was briefly driven out by the Illyrians, he endured in the kingship until his death in 369.

9   The MSS have Euryone, but Eurynoë is more likely to be correct.

10 For their role in the events that followed the death of Perdiccas III, see Ellis (1973).

11 Ptolemy of Alorus, who served as regent for Perdiccas III (368–365).

12 Epaminondas and Pelopidas were the greatest of the Thebans. Plutarch wrote lives of both of them, but only that of Pelopidas has survived. We do, however, have a brief life of Epaminondas by Cornelius Nepos, which is all the more valuable because the major surviving (contemporary) source for the early fourth century BC, Xenophon, was hostile to Thebes and tended to omit or downplay the achievements of her generals.

plot on her part.[13] [7] It was indeed a cruel blow that these children should have been murdered by their mother and sacrificed to her lust when it was consideration of these same children which had once rescued her from punishment for her crimes. [8] The murder of Perdiccas seemed all the more scandalous in that the mother's pity was not stirred even by the fact that he had an infant son. [9] So it was that for a long period Philip was guardian for the minor rather than king himself but, [10] facing the threat of more serious wars, and at a time when any assistance to be expected from the infant was too far in the future, he was constrained by the people to take the throne.

6 When he assumed power, everybody had great expectations of him both because of his natural ability, which held out promise of a great man, and because of the old prophecies concerning Macedonia [2] which had predicted that "Macedonia would enjoy great prosperity in the reign of one of Amyntas' sons." The wickedness of Philip's mother had left only Philip to realize that hope. [3] At the start of his reign the green youth of the novice was plagued by trouble: the murder of his brothers, so cruelly done away with; the large number of his enemies; the fear of treason; the poverty his kingdom suffered, exhausted by interminable warfare. [4] Then, too, there were wars brewing simultaneously in different quarters, as if many nations were conspiring to crush Macedonia. Philip could not take on these wars all at once, [5] and he decided they should be dealt with separately. Some he settled by negotiation and others by paying out money, while he attacked all the enemies who were easiest to conquer, so that by victory over these he might both strengthen his men's wavering resolve and also remove his enemies' disdain for him. [6] His first fight was with a contingent of Athenians; he defeated them in an ambush and, although he could have annihilated them, fear of a more serious conflict prompted him to let them go unharmed and without ransom. [7] After the Athenians, Philip shifted his attack to the Illyrians, killing many thousands of the enemy. [8] He next took Thessaly, where war was the last thing anyone expected, by a surprise attack, not because he wanted plunder but because he was eager to add the strength of the Thessalian cavalry to his own army. [9] He then amalgamated the cavalry and infantry to create an invincible army. He also captured the famous city of Larissa. [10] While these matters were proceeding successfully, he married Olympias, daughter of Neoptolemus, king of the Molossians; [11] the match was arranged by Arybbas, king of the Molossians, who was the girl's cousin and guardian and was married to her sister, Troas. This was the cause of Arybbas' downfall and of all his troubles. [12] For, while he was hoping to

13   This is untrue. Perdiccas died fighting the Illyrians in 360/59. Trogus' account may be based (directly or indirectly) on a source that was hostile to Eurydice, perhaps Theopompus of Chios; cf. *FGrH* 115 F 289. Flower (1994: 5–6), however, argues against Trogus' use of Theopompus. The inconsistencies that Flower sees may be explained by Trogus' possible use of Timagenes of Alexandria as an intermediary source.

increase his kingdom through his family ties with Philip, he was stripped of his own kingdom by the latter and grew old in exile.[14]

[13] After these achievements Philip was no longer satisfied with defensive campaigns but even went on the offensive against peaceful nations. [14] He was engaged in an attack on the city of Methone and was passing before its walls when an arrow fired from the defences struck out the king's right eye, [15] but the injury did not make him any the less effective in combat or more savage in his treatment of his enemies. [16] On the contrary, when, a few days later, the enemy sued for peace, he granted it, and showed not merely restraint but leniency in dealing with the defeated enemy.

Macedonians and Greeks: Language, Culture, Attitudes

It is clear from the extant Alexander historians that the lost sources made a clear distinction between Greeks and Macedonians – ethnically, culturally, and linguistically – and this must be an accurate reflection of contemporary attitudes. Alexander himself appears to have appreciated Greek culture and to have been conscious of Macedonian cultural inferiority, as is clear from §I.2a, below.

The vexed question of the ethnic background of the Macedonians has produced numerous discussions, many of them not entirely free of political bias; for the arguments concerning the ancient Greeks and Macedonians have been used to serve the nationalistic pretensions of contemporary politicians. The mere fact that Vlasidis and Karakostanoglou (1995) was distributed to all delegates at the *Sixth International Conference on Ancient Macedonia* in 1996 attests to modern concerns with the views of ancient historians; see also Tritle (1998) and Danforth (1995) for the contemporary issues; cf. Borza (1990: 90ff.). For the Macedonian language, see Hoffmann (1906), Hammond (1994b), and Badian (1982).

The Macedonian language

2(a)   *Plutarch*, Alexander *51.3–6*

Cleitus had spoken too freely. Alexander's companions stood up to face him and proceeded to shower him with abuse, while the older men attempted to calm the disturbance. [4] Turning then to Xenodochus of Cardia and Artemius of Colophon, Alexander said: "Don't you think Greeks walking amongst Macedonians are like demi-gods walking amongst wild animals?" . . .

[5] No longer able to control his temper, Alexander threw one of the apples within his reach at Cleitus and hit him, after which he looked round for his

---

14   There is considerable debate concerning when Philip deposed Arybbas and when Arybbas actually died. See Errington (1975) and Heskel (1988). The supporters of "Aryptaeus" who fought against Macedon in the Lamian War in 323/2 (Diodorus Siculus 18.11.1) may have been followers of the exiled Arrybas.

sword. [6] But Aristophanes, one of his bodyguards, got to it first and removed it. The others surrounded the king and begged him to stop, but he jumped to his feet and summoned his guards, loudly shouting *in the Macedonian tongue*,[15] which indicated that there was a serious crisis.[16]

2(b)   *Quintus Curtius Rufus 6.9.34–6*

Alexander fixed his gaze on [Philotas]. "The Macedonians are going to judge your case," he said. "Please state whether you will use *your native language* before them."

[35] "Besides the Macedonians", replied Philotas, "there are many present who, I think, will find what I am going to say easier to understand if I use the language you yourself have been using, your purpose, I believe, being simply to enable more people to understand you."

[36] Then the king said: "Do you see how offensive Philotas finds even his native language? He alone feels an aversion to learning it. But let him speak as he pleases – only remember that he is as contemptuous of our way of life as he is of our language."

2(c)   *Plutarch,* Eumenes *14.10–11*

When Eumenes heard this he came post-haste, hurrying on the men who were carrying him and, drawing back the curtains on both sides of the litter, he waved his hand in delight. [11] When the men saw him, they immediately saluted him in the Macedonian tongue. They then took up their shields, struck them with their sarissas, and let out a loud war cry to challenge their enemies – for now their leader was with them.

Was the Macedonian conquest a source of pride to all Greeks?

Plutarch, in two different *Lives*, discusses the effect on the Greeks of Alexander the Great seating himself on the Persian throne. In the first passage, from the *Alexander*, he records the words of Demaratus of Corinth, a pro-Macedonian and functionary of the League of Corinth. In the second passage, from the *Agesilaus*, Plutarch expresses his own views and what he regards as the views of most Greeks who were contemporary with these events. Alexander's delicate relations with the Greeks in this and other matters are discussed by Badian (1996).

---

15   *PSI* XII 1284, a fragment of Arrian's *History of the Successors*, mentions a certain Xennias, who is described as a "Macedonian-speaker."
16   For the significance of this passage see Hammond (1995a) and Bosworth (1996b). For Curtius' full account of the Cleitus episode, see §X.4c below.

2(d)   Plutarch, Alexander 37.6–7

Alexander wanted to reinvigorate his men, it now being wintertime, and remained there at Persepolis for four months. [7] It is said that, when the king first seated himself on the royal throne under the golden awning, the Corinthian Demaratus – a kindly man who had been a friend of Alexander's father – burst into tears, as old men do. Those Greeks had been deprived of a very pleasurable experience, he reportedly said, who had died before seeing Alexander seated on Darius' throne.

2(e)   Plutarch, Agesilaus 15.4

For, personally, I am not in agreement with the Corinthian Demaratus who claimed that the Greeks missed a very pleasurable experience in not seeing Alexander seated on Darius' throne. Actually, I think they might have had more reason to shed tears at the realization that the men who left this honour to Alexander were those who sacrificed the armies[17] of the Greeks at Leuctra, Coronea, and Corinth and in Arcadia.

The contest between Corrhagus the Macedonian and the Greek athlete, Dioxippus

The accounts of the duel between the Greek athlete Dioxippus and the Macedonian soldier Corrhagus (the text of Diodorus has Coragus; Horratas in Curtius) reveal the ethnic tension between Greeks and Macedonians, as well as the common disdain of soldiers for professional athletes. Diodorus' version places greater emphasis on the relationship between Macedonians and Greeks, and on Alexander's unsavory role in the "framing" of Dioxippus. In the brief account given by Aelian (*Varia Historia* 10.22), Dioxippus actually kills the Macedonian. See also Brown (1977).

2(f)   Diodorus Siculus 17.100.1–101.6

After recovering from his wound and sacrificing to thank the gods for his return to health, Alexander put on great banquets for his friends. During the drinking sessions there was one odd occurrence that is worth recording.

[2] There was a certain Macedonian called Coragus who had been accepted as one of the *philoi*. He was possessed of remarkable physical strength and

---

17 Or "generals." The places named here all witnessed battles in which the supremacy of Sparta was challenged in the decades after the Peloponnesian War; Leuctra (371) was the most famous and most devastating for Sparta.

had frequently performed courageous acts in battle. Under the influence of drink, Coragus challenged Dioxippus the Athenian, an athlete who had won the garland for the most prestigious victories in the games, to face him in single combat. [3] The other guests at the party spurred on the men's rivalry, as one might expect; Dioxippus accepted the challenge and the king fixed a date for the match. When the time for the contest arrived, men assembled in their tens of thousands to watch. [4] Being of the same race, the Macedonians and the king strongly supported Coragus, while the Greeks were behind Dioxippus. As the men came forward to the event, the Macedonian was equipped with splendid weapons; [5] the Athenian was naked and smeared with oil, and he carried an appropriately-sized club.

The physical strength and superb prowess of the two men provoked general admiration, and it was as though what was expected to take place was a contest between gods. The Macedonian aroused sheer amazement for his physical condition and dazzling arms, and some resemblance to Ares was noticed in him. Dioxippus, on the other hand, had the look of Heracles, being the superior of the two in strength and also because of his athletic training – and still more because of the identifying characteristic of the club.

[6] As they advanced on each other, the Macedonian, at an appropriate remove, hurled his javelin, but the other man swerved slightly and avoided the blow that was aimed at him. Then Coragus went forward holding his Macedonian *sarissa* before him but, as he approached, Dioxippus struck the *sarissa* with his club and broke it. [7] Having thus encountered two set-backs, the Macedonian was now reduced to fighting with the sword; but just as he was about to draw the weapon Dioxippus moved first and jumped at him. As Coragus was drawing the blade, Dioxippus grabbed his sword-hand with his own left hand and with the other pulled his rival off balance and made him trip over. [8] His antagonist thrown to earth, the Greek set his foot on the man's neck, held up his club, and turned his gaze to the spectators.

101 The crowd was in uproar over this unexpected turn of events and display of extraordinary bravado. The king ordered the man's release, terminated the spectacle and left, furious at the Macedonian's defeat. [2] Releasing his fallen antagonist, Dioxippus went off with a notable victory, and with a garland presented to him by his countrymen for having brought to the Greeks a glory that they all shared. But Fate did not permit the man to pride himself on his victory for long.

[3] The king's attitude towards Dioxippus became increasingly hostile, and the *philoi*[18] of Alexander, and all the Macedonians attached to the court, resented his fine qualities. They therefore persuaded the man in charge of the king's domestic arrangements to slip a golden cup under Dioxippus' pillow. At the next drinking-party they accused him of theft and pretended to have found the cup, and thus brought him into discredit and disgrace. [4] Dioxippus could see he had a cabal of Macedonians against him. He there-

---

18   *Philoi* = *hetairoi*. See glossary s.v. *asthetairoi* and *pezhetairoi*.

fore left the party, and on entering his own quarters a little later he wrote Alexander a letter about the plot hatched against him, entrusted the letter to his own people for delivery to the king, and committed suicide. He had acted unwisely in accepting the challenge to single combat, but far more foolishly in putting an end to his life, [5] and so, many of his critics, rebuking him for his stupidity, said that it was a cruel thing to have great physical strength and little intelligence.

[6] After reading the letter the king was very upset at Dioxippus' death and often regretted the loss of his good qualities. He had not used his services when they were available to him, and now he felt sorry when they were gone; and from the malice of his detractors he came to recognise, when it served no purpose, the good and noble character of the man.

2(g) Quintus Curtius Rufus 9.7.16–26

One person present at the banquet was the Athenian Dioxippus, a former boxer whose superlative strength had made him well known and well liked by Alexander. Jealous and spiteful men would make cutting remarks about him, partly in jest, partly in earnest, saying that they had along with them a useless, bloated animal and that, while they went into battle, he was dripping with oil and preparing his belly for a banquet. [17] Now at this feast the Macedonian Horratas, who was already drunk, began to make the same type of insulting comment to Dioxippus and to challenge him, if he were a man, to fight a duel with him with swords the next day. Only then, said Horratas, would Alexander be able to decide whether *he* was reckless or Dioxippus a coward. [18] Dioxippus accepted the challenge, contemptuously scoffing at the soldier's bravado. The next day the two men were even more insistent in their demands for the contest and, since Alexander could not deter them, he allowed them to carry out their plan. [19] A huge crowd of soldiers, including the Greeks, supported Dioxippus. The Macedonian had equipped himself with regular weapons: he held a bronze shield and a spear, which they call a *sarissa*, in his left hand and a javelin in his right, while he also had a sword at his side – as if he were going to fight a number of men simultaneously. [20] Glistening with oil and wearing a garland, Dioxippus grasped a purple cloak in his left hand and a stout, knotty club in his right. The equipment itself generated tense expectation in the whole crowd, for it appeared sheer lunacy rather than recklessness for a naked man to take on one in armour.

[21] The Macedonian hurled his javelin, certain his adversary could be killed at a distance. Dioxippus avoided it by leaning slightly to the side and, before Horratas could transfer the spear to his right hand, he sprang at him and broke the weapon in two with his club. [22] With both missiles gone, the Macedonian had now started to draw his sword, but Dioxippus caught him in a bear-hug, quickly kicked his feet from beneath him and smashed him to the ground. Then, grabbing the sword, he set his foot on the neck of the prone

Macedonian and, lifting his club, would have battered his defeated foe to death had he not been stopped by the king.

[23] The outcome of the show dismayed Alexander, as well as the Macedonian soldiers, especially since the barbarians were present, for he feared that a mockery had been made of the celebrated Macedonian valour. [24] So it was that the king's ears were opened to accusations made by envious men. A few days later a golden cup was deliberately set aside during a banquet and the servants came to the king pretending to have lost what they had, in fact, themselves removed. [25] Often one shows less presence of mind in an embarrassing situation than when really guilty. Dioxippus could not bear the eyes that all turned on him and marked him out as the thief. On leaving the banquet he wrote a letter which was to be delivered to the king and then fell on his sword. [26] Alexander was pained by his death, which he thought indicated resentment rather than remorse on Dioxippus' part, especially when the excessive jubilation of the men jealous of him revealed the falseness of the accusation against him.

The King, Aristocracy, and Macedonian Institutions

Macedonian veneration of the king

The Macedonian state was ruled by a king from a royal house known as the Argeadae, which claimed descent from the legendary Hercules through Temenus of Argos. Alexander I Philhellene (*regn.* ca. 498/7–454) evinced his Greek ancestry and thus gained admission to the Olympic games. Although the kingship was restricted to the Argead house, the king was nevertheless regarded as first among equals, his powers curtailed considerably by a body of aristocrats known as the *hetairoi*, or "Companions." From their numbers, the king drew his military commanders and advisers. Many of the regional troops, especially the infantry from Upper Macedonia, were commanded by members of the princely families of the various cantons. By the time of Philip II the position of the king *vis-à-vis* the aristocracy had been strengthened, and Alexander the Great established a far more autocratic form of rule than the Macedonians had been used to.

3(a)   Quintus Curtius Rufus 3.6.17–20

The Macedonians have a natural tendency to venerate their royalty, but even if one takes that into account, the extent of their admiration, or their burning affection, for this particular king is difficult to describe. [18] First of all, they thought his every enterprise had divine aid. Fortune was with him at every turn and so even his rashness had produced glorious results. [19] His age gave added lustre to all his achievements for, though hardly old enough for undertakings of such magnitude, he was well up to them. Then there are the things generally regarded as rather unimportant but which tend to find greater approval among the soldiers: the fact that he exercised with his men, that he made his appearance and dress little different from an ordinary citizen's, that he had the energy of a soldier. [20] These characteristics, whether they were natural or consciously cultivated, made him in the eyes of his men as much an object of affection as of awe.

3(b)   Quintus Curtius Rufus 10.3.1–4

Who would have believed that a gathering fiercely hostile moments before could be paralysed with sudden panic [2] at the sight of men being dragged off for punishment whose actions had been no worse than the others? [3] They were terror-stricken, whether from respect for the title of king, for which people living in a monarchy have a divine reverence, or from respect for Alexander personally; or perhaps it was because of the confidence with which he so forcefully exerted his authority. [4] At all events they were the very model of submissiveness: when, towards evening, they learned of their comrades' execution, so far from being infuriated at the punishment, they did everything to express individually their increased loyalty and devotion.[19]

The royal pages

The sons of Macedonian nobles were educated at Pella along with the crown prince and his brothers. Thus they came to be known as *syntrophoi*, or "foster brothers," of the king's sons. At the court they also served the king, protecting him while he slept, and accompanying him on the hunt. Like the youths at the Persian court, they learned "both how to rule and to be ruled" (Xenophon, *Anabasis* 1.9), and at the same time they served as hostages for the good behaviour of their fathers and elder kinsmen. But their early associations with the crown prince often paid important dividends later in their careers. See Heckel (1986; 1992a: 237ff.) and Hammond (1989a: 53–8; 1990); cf. Kienast (1973).

3(c)   Quintus Curtius Rufus 5.1.42

Amyntas brought[20] also fifty grown-up sons of Macedonian noblemen to serve as a bodyguard. These act as the king's servants at dinner, bring him his horses

---

19   For the historical context of this passage see §X.8a–b.
20   To Alexander, who in 331 was in Mesopotamia.

when he goes into battle, attend him on the hunt and take their turn on guard before his bedroom door. Such was the upbringing and training of those who were to be great generals and leaders.

3(d)   Diodorus Siculus 17.65.1

And from Macedonia there came 50 sons of the king's *philoi*. These had been sent by their fathers to serve as the king's bodyguard.

3(e)   Quintus Curtius Rufus 8.6.2–6

As was observed above [see I.3.c], it was customary for the Macedonian nobility to deliver their grown-up sons to their kings for the performance of duties which differed little from the tasks of slaves. [3] They would take turns spending the night on guard at the door of the king's bedchamber, and it was they who brought in his women by an entrance other than that watched by the armed guards. [4] They would also take his horses from the grooms and bring them for him to mount; they were his attendants both on the hunt and in battle, and were highly educated in all the liberal arts.[21] [5] It was thought a special honour that they were allowed to sit and eat with the king. No one had the authority to flog them apart from the king himself. [6] This company served the Macedonians as a kind of seminary for their officers and generals, and from it subsequently came the kings whose descendants were many generations later stripped of their power by the Romans.

3(f)   Arrian 4.13.1

From Philip's time it was customary for the sons of high-ranking Macedonians to be assigned to attend the king when they were reaching puberty. These were given the responsibility of generally seeing to the king's personal needs and also guarding him while he slept. And whenever the king went riding they would receive the horses from his grooms and bring them to him. They would then help him mount in the Persian manner[22] and join the king in the competition of the hunt.

---

21   At this time (in 328/7) the pages would have been educated by Callisthenes, just as many of Philip's pages in the 340s received instruction, along with Alexander, from Aristotle.

22   Possibly the institution of the pages was itself modelled on Persian practice: see Kienast (1973).

The Somatophylakes and Hetairoi

The *hetairoi* have already been mentioned. If they did not command individual units, they served in most cases in the Macedonian "Companion Cavalry" and/or as members of the king's council. The closest of the king's *hetairoi* dined with him and were, in theory, permitted to voice their opinions freely. The *Somatophylakes* were a select body of seven, whose function it was to protect the king on and off the battlefield. Membership in this body may originally have been restricted to certain families or have had some sort of geographic representation. But this too appears to have changed as Alexander's power grew. Our knowledge concerning the unit is enhanced by the fact that the historian (and later king of Egypt) Ptolemy son of Lagus was a member of that body. For full discussion, see Heckel (1992a: 237ff.) and Hammond (1989a: 53–8).

3(g)   Arrian 6.28.3–4

He enrolled Peucestas as an additional Somatophylax; [4] . . . up to this time Alexander's bodyguards numbered seven: Leonnatus son of Anteas, Hephaestion son of Amyntor, Lysimachus son of Agathocles, Aristonous son of Pisaeus, all from Pella, Perdiccas son of Orontes from Orestis, Ptolemy son of Lagus and Pithon son of Crateuas from Eordaea. Now an eighth was added, Peucestas, who had given Alexander protection with his shield.[23]

3(h)   Quintus Curtius Rufus 9.6.4

It was customary for Alexander's principal friends and his bodyguards to keep watch before the king's quarters whenever he had fallen ill.

The army assembly

Granier (1931) is the seminal work on the question of whether the Macedonian army acted as an assembly that had to be consulted by the king on important matters (for example, kingship, treason) and as a lawcourt. Recently Granier's conclusions have been challenged by Errington (1978), Lock (1977a), and Anson (1985, 1991); cf. Hammond (1989a: 60ff.) and Polo (1993).

---

23 In the Mallian campaign. See §III.6d (where Peucestas' role is curiously omitted).

3(i) Quintus Curtius Rufus 6.8.25

In capital cases, it was a long-established Macedonian practice for the king to conduct the trial while the army (or the commons in peace-time) acted as jury, and the position of the king counted for nothing unless his influence had been substantial prior to the trial.

3(j) Justin 11.1.7–10

Alexander's arrival remedied the situation: [8] he addressed the entire host in an assembly, offering them such timely consolation and encouragement as to eliminate the anxiety of the fearful and inspire hope in them all. [9] He was twenty years old, at which age he demonstrated great promise, but he did so with such restraint that he seemed to have still more in reserve than was then apparent. [10] He exempted the Macedonians from all obligations except military service, and this won him the unanimous support of the people, so much so that they said they had exchanged their king's identity, not his merits.

The traditional form of execution

The Macedonian method of public execution was stoning, but it is noteworthy that where crimes against Persian symbols of power were concerned – Bessus' murder of Darius III (see §IV.3a–j) and assumption of the royal title; the Macedonian Poulamachus' desecration of the tomb of Cyrus the Great – Alexander resorted to crucifixion or impalement.

3(k) Quintus Curtius Rufus 6.11.10

The general feeling was that Philotas should be stoned to death according to Macedonian custom . . . [cf. Curtius 6.11.38].

3(l) Arrian 4.14.3

[According to some authors] Hermolaus and the men arrested with him were then stoned to death by those present.

3(m) Quintus Curtius Rufus 7.2.1

While Amyntas was making this speech, there chanced to arrive men bringing back in chains his fugitive brother Polemon . . . whom they had overtaken. The assembly was in an ugly mood and could barely be restrained from stoning Polemon immediately, after their usual custom . . .

A law concerning treason?

Tarn (1948, II: 270–2) is probably right in suggesting that what Curtius presents as a law (*lex*) must have been no more than customary practice (*mos*) and that the alleged existence of such a law does not excuse Alexander's murder of Parmenion, as some modern scholars have tried to argue. In fact, the very nature of the Macedonian aristocracy was such that, because of the extensive network of intermarriages, a complete purge of the relatives of convicted traitors would lead to the virtual annihilation of the ruling class.

3(n)   Quintus Curtius Rufus 6.11.20

In the meantime word of the torture of Philotas had got around, and this spread panic among the cavalry, the men from the best families and especially those closely related to Parmenion. What they feared was *the Macedonian law which provided the death penalty also for the relatives of people who had plotted against the king*. Some, therefore, committed suicide and others fled into remote mountains and desert wastes as sheer terror spread throughout the camp. Finally the king learned of the consternation and proclaimed that he was suspending the law relating to the punishment of relatives of the guilty.

Macedonian marriage custom

Renard and Servais (1955) demonstrate that the marriage of Alexander and Roxane, as described by Curtius (below), follows Macedonian rather than Persian practice. The wedding was commemorated in a painting by Aëtion (described by Lucian, §VIII.6e); the original is lost, but the description inspired the painting in the Villa Farnesina in Rome by Giovanni Antonio Bazzi, "Il Sodoma."

3(o)   Quintus Curtius Rufus 8.4.27–9

Roxane's father was transported with unexpected delight when he heard Alexander's words, and the king, in the heat of passion, ordered bread to be brought, in accordance with their traditions, for this was the most sacred symbol of betrothal among the Macedonians. The bread was cut with a sword and both men tasted it. [28] I presume that those responsible for establishing the conventions of their society used this modest and readily available food because they wanted to demonstrate to people uniting their resources how little should be enough to content them. [29] Thus the ruler of Asia and Europe married a woman who had been introduced to him as part of the entertainment at dinner – to produce from a captive a son to rule over her conquerors.

II Philip II, Father of Alexander the Great

Amyntas III had three sons: the first, Alexander II, ruled briefly (369-368) and was assassinated while witnessing a "weapons" dance called the *telesias*; at the time of his death, the second son, Perdiccas, was still in his teens and his brother-in-law, Ptolemy of Alorus, exercised the regency from 368 to 365 – it was at this time that the youngest son, Philip, was a hostage in Thebes – until Ptolemy too was murdered and Perdiccas ascended the throne. Finally, in 360/59, Perdiccas III was killed in battle against the Illyrians, leaving a very young crown prince, Amyntas, whose claims were swept aside in the midst of this national emergency in favour of Philip II. Although he is best known as the father of Alexander the Great, Philip was the man who forged the powerful kingdom of Macedon and the army that was to be the mainstay of Alexander's might. Between 359 and 338 he brought Macedon from the brink of disaster to domination of the North and then virtually of the whole of European "Greece." The decisive victory at Chaeronea in 338 put an end to all thoughts of resistance and paved the way for the creation of the League of Corinth, which was to elect Philip as its *hegemon* or military leader, in particular of a great expedition against the traditional enemy of the Greeks, Achaemenid Persia.[1] However, when Philip returned to Pella in spring or summer 337, he diverted his attention to marriage, taking his seventh bride and, in the process, destroying what harmony he enjoyed with the most dominant of his wives, the Epirot Olympias, mother of the crown prince Alexander. Philip's marriage, as our sources make clear, was not made for political reasons but was a love match; nevertheless, it had unintended political implications. These led, both directly and indirectly, to instability at the court and, ultimately, to Philip's assassination in 336 and the accession of Alexander the Great. For general literature, see Ellis (1976) and Cawkwell (1978). For the Macedonian background, see Borza (1990) and Errington (1990).

---

1   That is, the Persian empire established in the middle of the sixth century BC by Cyrus I. For the situation in Persia at this time, see §IV.1a–e.

Philip's Marriages

Philip married at least seven times, almost always for political reasons. The last marriage, to the Macedonian Cleopatra (whom Arrian calls Eurydice), although it was clearly a love match, created political chaos at the court and played no small part in the estrangement of Philip and Alexander, and, apparently, in the conspiracy to murder the king. For the marriages themselves, see Green (1982), Ogden (1999: 17–29), and Carney (2000a: 51–81); cf. Tronson (1984) on the Satyrus passage.

1(a) Athenaeus 13.557b–e = Satyrus, The Life of Philip

Philip of Macedon did not, like the Darius who was overthrown by Alexander, take women along on his campaigns. When Darius was actually fighting a war in which he had everything at stake, he led around with him 360 concubines, according to Dicaearchus[2] in the third book of his *Life of Greece.*

Philip had a fresh wedding with every campaign. In his *Life* of Philip Satyrus states: "In the twenty-two years of his rule [557c] Philip married the Illyrian Audata, by whom he had a daughter, Cynnane,[3] and he also married Phila, sister of Derdas and Machatas. Then, since he wished to extend his realm to include the Thessalian nation, he had children by two Thessalian women, Nicesipolis of Pherae, who bore him Thessalonice, and Philinna of Larissa, by whom he produced Arrhidaeus.[4] In addition, he took possession of the Molossian kingdom by marrying Olympias, by whom he had Alexander and Cleopatra, [557d] and when he took Thrace the Thracian king Cothelas came to him with his daughter Meda and many gifts. After marrying Meda, Philip also took her home to be a second wife along with Olympias. In addition to all these wives he also married Cleopatra, with whom he was in love; she was the daughter of Hippostratus and niece of Attalus. By bringing her home as another wife alongside Olympias he made a total shambles of his life. For straightaway, right at the wedding ceremony, Attalus made the remark 'Well, now we shall certainly see royalty born who are legitimate and not bastards'. Hearing this, Alexander hurled the cup he had in his hands at Attalus, who in turn hurled his goblet at Alexander.

[557e] After that Olympias took refuge with the Molossians and Alexander with the Illyrians, and Cleopatra presented Philip with a daughter who was called Europa."

---

2   Mentioned also in §X.8c. Dicaearchus was a student of Aristotle and wrote a work entitled *Bios Hellados* ("Life of Greece," which calls to mind Peter Ackroyd's *London: The Biography*), but little else is known about him.
3   See §III.2a–d.
4   See §III.2e–j.

1(b)   Justin 9.7.3–4

As for Alexander, it was believed that he feared a brother born to his step-mother as a rival for the throne, and that this had occasioned his quarrelling at a banquet, first with Attalus and then with Philip himself, [4] so acrimoniously that Philip lunged at him with sword drawn and was only just prevailed upon not to kill his son by the entreaties of his friends.

1(c)   Plutarch, Alexander 9.5–10

But the malaise that reigned in the women's quarters because of Philip's marriages and love affairs in some way infected the realm, and the domestic upsets occasioned numerous reproaches and bitter antagonisms. (These were further exacerbated by the bad nature of Olympias, a jealous and resentful woman, who would spur Alexander to anger.) [6] A very clear case of this phenomenon was provided by Attalus at the wedding of Cleopatra, a young woman whom Philip was marrying – for he was in love with the girl, despite his age. [7] Attalus was Cleopatra's uncle, and becoming tipsy during the drinking he invited the Macedonians to beg the gods that from Philip and Cleopatra a successor to the throne should be born who was legitimate.

Stung by the remark, Alexander declared: "And me, you swine, what do you think I am – a bastard?" and he threw his goblet at Attalus. [9] At this Philip drew his sword and got up, advancing on Alexander. Luckily for the two of them he tripped and fell, thanks to the combination of his anger and the wine. [10] "Look, gentlemen," said Alexander, mocking his father, "this is the man who is preparing to cross from Europe to Asia. He's fallen on his face crossing from one couch to another!"

Philip's Death

Philip's death in late summer or early autumn 336 may have been the result of a personal grievance on the part of Pausanias of Orestis, but the likelihood of its being the culmination of a plot devised by those who coveted the throne is great. Whether those involved were Olympias and Alexander, who felt threatened by Attalus and his ward Cleopatra, Philip's seventh and last wife, or by the Lyncestians, the sons of Aëropus – either for their own gain or to place Amyntas son of Perdiccas on the throne – cannot be determined. Various theories have been proposed by modern scholars, and these cover the entire spectrum of possibilities. See Badian (1963), Hamilton (1965), Bosworth (1971a), Ellis (1971), Prandi (1998), Fears (1975), Heckel (1981a), Develin (1981), Fredricksmeyer (1990), and Carney (1992). The problem of the so-called "Tomb of Philip II" at Vergina and its burgeoning literature cannot be discussed here. For an overview, see Borza (1999: 69–74).

2(a) Justin 9.5.8–7.14

[8] At the onset of spring Philip sent ahead three generals into Persian territory in Asia: Parmenion, Amyntas and Attalus, [9] whose sister[5] he had recently married after repudiating Olympias, the mother of Alexander, because he suspected her of adultery.[6]

6 In the meantime, as the auxiliary troops from Greece were assembling, Philip celebrated the marriage of his daughter Cleopatra to that Alexander whom he had made king of Epirus.[7] [2] The day was remarkable for its sumptuous preparations which befitted the greatness of the two kings, the one giving away a daughter and the other taking a wife. [3] There were also splendid games. Philip was hurrying to see these, flanked by the two Alexanders, his son and his son-in-law, without bodyguards,[8] [4] when Pausanias, a young Macedonian nobleman whom nobody suspected, took up a position in a narrow alleyway and cut Philip down as he went by, thus polluting with funereal sorrow a day set aside for rejoicing. [5] In the early years of puberty Pausanias had been sexually abused by Attalus and to that indignity had been added a further outrage: [6] Attalus had taken him to a banquet, made him drunk and subjected him not only to his own carnal desires but, like a prostitute, to those of his fellow-diners as well, so making the boy an object of universal ridicule amongst his peers. [7] Outraged by this treatment, Pausanias had frequently complained to Philip, only to be put off by various excuses, not without ridicule as well, while he could at the same time see his enemy honoured with the rank of general. He then directed his rage against Philip himself, and exacted from the unfair judge the vengeance he could not exact from his enemy.

7 It was also believed that Pausanias had been suborned by Olympias, mother of Alexander, and that Alexander himself was not unaware of the plot to murder his father. [2] For Olympias was thought to have felt no less resentment over her repudiation and the fact that Cleopatra had been preferred to her than Pausanias felt over his sexual abuse. [3] As for Alexander, it was believed that he feared a brother born to his stepmother as a rival for the throne,[9] and that this had occasioned his quarrelling at a banquet, first with Attalus and then with Philip himself, [4] so acrimoniously that Philip lunged at him with sword drawn and was only just prevailed upon not to kill his son

5 Cleopatra was Attalus' niece.
6 Thus Pompeius Trogus (whom Justin is epitomizing), who wrote in the Augustan age, when adultery was an important political issue.
7 Philip had ousted Olympias' uncle, Arybbas, in 342 and replaced him with her brother, Alexander.
8 That is, the hypaspist guard. Philip was trying to show his Greek visitors that he had no need of a bodyguard in his own kingdom (see §II.2b, below).
9 This (potential) brother was never born: Cleopatra's child was a daughter, Europa (see §II.1a). For the fictitious Caranus, see Heckel (1979).

by the entreaties of his friends. [5] That was why Alexander had gone with his mother to his uncle in Epirus, and after that to the kings of Illyria, [6] and he was with difficulty reconciled with his father, when Philip recalled him, and barely persuaded to return by the entreaties of his relatives. [7] Olympias was also trying to induce her brother Alexander, the king of Epirus, to go to war, and she would have succeeded if Philip had not forestalled him by giving him his daughter in marriage. [8] It is thought that Olympias and her son, their wrath stimulated by these exasperations, incited Pausanias to proceed to so heinous a crime while he was making his complaints about the abuse going unpunished. [9] At all events, Olympias had horses ready for the assassin's getaway. [10] Afterwards, when she heard of the king's murder, she came quickly to the funeral, ostensibly doing her duty; and on the night of her arrival she set a golden crown on Pausanias' head while he still hung on the cross, something which no one else but she could have done while Philip's son was still alive. [11] A few days later, she had the murderer's body taken down and cremated it over the remains of her husband; she then erected a tomb for him in the same place and, by inspiring superstition in the people, saw to it that funerary offerings were made to him every year. [12] After this she forced Cleopatra, for whom Philip had divorced her,[10] to hang herself, having first murdered her daughter in the mother's arms, and it was from the sight of her rival hanging there that Olympias gained the vengeance she had accelerated by murder. [13] Finally she consecrated to Apollo the sword with which the king was stabbed, doing so under the name Myrtale, which was the name that Olympias bore as a little girl.[11] [14] All this was done so openly that she appears to have been afraid that the crime might not be clearly demonstrated as her work.

2(b)   Diodorus Siculus 16.91–4

During the archonship of Pythodorus[12] at Athens, the Romans elected as their consuls Quintus Publius and Tiberius Aemilius Marcus, and the 111th Olympic games were held, at which Cleomantis of Cleitor won the sprint. [2] It was during this year that King Philip, who had been appointed commander-in-chief by the Greeks and had commenced hostilities against the Persians, sent Attalus and Parmenion ahead to Asia, according them a portion of his forces and instructing them to free the Greek cities. Philip himself was eager to embark on the war with the good will of the gods, and

---

10 Since the Macedonian kings were polygamous, there was no need to divorce one woman *for* another.
11 For the significance of Olympias' names, see Heckel (1981b) and Carney (2000a: 62–3).
12 The correct form is Pythodelus, archon in 336/5. Diodorus is attempting to reconcile Athenian archon years with those of Roman consuls, who at this time took office on 15 March.

he put a question to the Pythia,[13] asking her if he would defeat the king of Persia. The Pythia gave back the following oracular response:

The bull has been wreathed, it is finished, the man to perform the sacrifice is here.

[3] It was a cryptic response, but Philip took the oracle as being in his favour, assuming that it was a prophecy foretelling that the Persian would be sacrificed like a sacrificial victim. The truth of the matter was otherwise. It meant, on the contrary, that Philip would be slaughtered, wearing a wreath like the bull, during a festival and sacrifices to the gods. [4] But the fact was that the king assumed that the gods would be fighting on his side, and was delighted at the prospect of Asia becoming a captive of Macedon.

Accordingly, he immediately issued orders for the holding of lavish sacrifices to the gods and celebrated along with them the wedding of Cleopatra, his daughter by Olympias, whom he gave in marriage to Alexander, king of Epirus, legitimate brother of Olympias. [5] Along with showering honours on the gods, he also wanted as many Greeks as possible to take part in the festivities, and he began to organise spectacular music contests and sumptuous banquets for friends and *xenoi* [guest-friends].[14] [6] He therefore sent for his personal friends from all over Greece and instructed his own courtiers to invite as many of their own acquaintances from abroad as they could. It was his earnest endeavour to treat the Greeks kindly and repay them for the honours bestowed on him in connection with his supreme command by providing them with appropriate social events.

92   Eventually large numbers of guests poured in to the festival from all parts, and the contests and marriage were held in tandem at Aegae in Macedonia. Philip was crowned with golden wreaths that were given to him not only by individual men of distinction but also by most of the important cities, including Athens. [2] When this particular wreath was being announced, the herald added a final comment that anyone involved in a plot against the king who sought asylum in Athens would be extradited. By this chance remark heaven was letting Philip know almost by some divine forewarning that a plot was afoot. [3] In the wake of this came certain other utterances, apparently divinely-inspired, that foretold the king's undoing.

At the royal drinking party, in fact, the tragic actor Neoptolemus, whose vocal power and reputation were second to none, was told by Philip to deliver some pieces of poetry that had achieved popularity, and particularly pieces relevant to his campaign against the Persians. The performer judged that his poetic recitation would be considered pertinent to Philip's crossing and he meant to denounce the Persian king's opulence, great and much-celebrated

---

13   The Pythian priestess of Delphi. See Fontenrose (1978: 337, Q213 = PW266).
14   This institution had its origins in the earliest times and involved reciprocal hospitality between aristocratic members of different communities. See Konstan (1997).

though it was, as being liable to a reversal of fortune. The following was the piece of poetry that he began to recite:

> Your proud thoughts soar higher than the upper air, encompassing huge, culti-vated plains, and when you envisage houses you go beyond houses, arranging in folly your life ahead. But he who crawls the path of darkness catches the swift of foot, and suddenly approaches unseen, taking from mortals their long-term hopes – much-labouring Hades.[15]

He continued in this vein, everything he said centring on the same idea. [4] Philip was delighted with the assurance he was given, and was utterly and completely focused on the notion of the downfall of the Persian king. He kept in mind, too, the oracle from the Pythia which contained the same message as the words uttered by the tragic actor.

[5] Eventually the drinking party broke up, and the games were due to start the next day. It was still dark when the crowds moved hastily to the theatre, and at daybreak the procession took place in which Philip put on display, along with all the other paraphernalia, statues of the twelve gods, superbly crafted and amazingly decked out in rich splendour. But with these he also displayed a thirteenth image that was appropriate for a god, one of Philip himself – the king was actually showing himself seated along with the twelve gods![16]

93   The theatre filled up and Philip himself came in wearing a white cloak. He had given orders for his bodyguards to follow him at some remove, for he was showing the world that he had the universal goodwill of the Greeks to safeguard him and needed no protection from bodyguards. [2] While he was basking in such success and while everybody was showering praise and con-gratulations on the man, there suddenly appeared on the scene – unexpect-edly and completely out of the blue – a plot against the king, and his death. [3] To elucidate my account of these events, I shall preface it with the reasons for the plot.

Pausanias was a Macedonian by birth who came from the area that is called Orestis. He was a bodyguard of the king, because of his good looks, he had become Philip's lover.[17] [4] When Pausanias saw another Pausanias – the man

---

15   Possibly an Aeschylean ode.

16   Just what Philip intended by this gesture is uncertain, although contemporaries must have considered it hubristic. Since Philip claimed descent from Heracles, he may have been alluding to that hero's apotheosis and status as a thirteenth Olympian and thereby appro-priating some measure of divinity. He depicted himself as *isotheos*: "a mortal in many respects equal to the gods, but always known to differ from them, not least by his acknowl-edged mortality" (Badian 1996: 15).

17   Pausanias of Orestis – and the same will have been true of the other Pausanias, if there is any truth to the story – was presumably one of the "pages" (*paides basilikoi*) and it appears that homosexual relations between them, as well as a certain amount of pederasty at the court, were relatively common. For Philip's alleged relationship with Alexander of Epirus, see Justin 8.6.5–8; for the pages, see §X.5a–b.

had the same name as him – receiving Philip's amorous attentions, he used insulting language to him, saying that he was effeminate and ready to submit to sex with anyone who wanted him. [5] The fellow could not stand such malicious abuse, but for the moment he held his tongue. Then he communicated to Attalus, one of his friends, what he was going to do and committed suicide in an extraordinary manner. [6] For, a few days later, when Philip was in combat with king Pleurias of Illyria,[18] this second Pausanias stood before the king and on his own body took all the wounds aimed at the king, dying in the act.

[7] The event gained notoriety. Then Attalus, who was one of Philip's courtiers and had great influence with the king, invited Pausanias to dinner, and there he poured large quantities of neat wine into him and handed him to his muleteers for them to abuse his body in a drunken orgy. [8] When Pausanias sobered up after the drinking bout he was deeply hurt by the physical outrage and brought a charge against Attalus before the king. Philip was also angered by the enormity of the deed, but he was unwilling to show his disapproval because of his close ties with Attalus and the fact that he needed his services at that time. [9] Attalus, in fact, was the nephew[19] of the Cleopatra who had become the king's new wife, and he had been chosen as commander of the force that was being sent ahead into Asia – he was a man of courage in the military sphere. Accordingly, the king preferred to mollify Pausanias' legitimate anger over what he had suffered, and he bestowed on him substantial gifts and promoted him to positions of honour in the bodyguard.

94   The resentment of Pausanias, however, remained unchanged, and he passionately longed to take his revenge not only on the perpetrator of the deed but also on the man who would not exact punishment for him. The sophist Hermocrates also greatly helped him in his decision to act. Pausanias had studied under Hermocrates, and during his schooling had asked him how one could gain great fame. The sophist replied that it was by killing a man who had accomplished great deeds, since the person who brought off the killing would become part of posterity's memory of the man. [2] Pausanias took the remark in the context of his personal indignation and, his anger brooking no delay in the plan, scheduled his coup for the upcoming games. It went as follows. [3] Placing horses at the city gate he came to the entrance to the theatre with a Celtic dagger concealed on his person. Philip had told the friends who were with him to go ahead to the theatre, and his bodyguards were separated from him. Pausanias, seeing the king all alone, ran up to him and, with a dagger thrust that went clean through his ribs, left him dead on the ground. He then ran to the gate and the horses[20] that had been prepared for his getaway. [4] Immediately some of the bodyguards rushed to the king's body while others – Leonnatus, Perdiccas and Attalus amongst them – poured

18   Probably in early 337.
19   Uncle.
20   The plural is curious. Many scholars have questioned why Pausanias would need more than one horse if he acted alone.

out in pursuit of the murderer. Pausanias had a head start on his pursuers and would have mounted his horse before they caught him had he not fallen when his sandal became entangled in a vine. As he was getting up, Perdiccas and his group caught up with him and stabbed him to death.

2(c)   Aristotle, Politics 5.10.16 1311ᵃ39

The plot hatched by Pausanias against Philip arose from the latter's allowing Pausanias to be sexually assaulted by Attalus and his men.

2(d)   Valerius Maximus 1.8. ext. 9

King Philip of Macedon was warned by the same oracle to safeguard himself against injury from a four-horse chariot. He therefore had chariots unyoked throughout his kingdom and always kept clear of the place in Boeotia called Quadriga.[21] He did not, nevertheless, escape a danger of the kind to which he had been alerted – Pausanias had an engraving of a four-horse chariot on the handle of the sword with which he killed him.[22]

2(e)   Valerius Maximus 8.14 ext. 3–4

. . . those who in their pursuit of everlasting fame have not hesitated to resort even to crime to gain notoriety.

4   I wonder if Pausanias should not be set at the head of these. He asked Hermocles[23] how he could gain instant celebrity, and Hermocles replied that if he killed some well-known individual that man's renown would rub off on him. Thereupon Pausanias immediately assassinated Philip, and so gained his end, making himself as well known to posterity by his murderous act as Philip did by his valour.

2(f)   Plutarch, Alexander 10.4–5

Of Alexander's other companions Philip banished from Macedonia Harpalus and Nearchus, as well as Erigyius and Ptolemy.[24] Later on Alexander recalled them and conferred on them the highest honours.

---

21   The word means "Four-horse Chariot." *Quadriga* is Latin; hence there would be no Boeotian town of the name. The reference is to Harma (the name means "Chariot"), which forms part of the "Four Villages" (Tetrakomia) near Tanagra (Strabo 9.2.14 C405).
22   Cf. Aelian, *Varia Historia* 3.45.
23   Diodorus 17.94.1 (§II.2b) calls him Hermocrates.
24   For their part in persuading Alexander to meddle in the negotiations conducted by Philip with the Carian satrap, Pixodarus.

[5] When Pausanias was sexually assaulted at the instigation of Attalus and Cleopatra and failed to gain redress, he assassinated Philip. Most of the responsibility for this was attributed to Olympias, who was reckoned to have encouraged and egged on the resentful young man, but aspersions were cast on Alexander, too.

A Comparison of Philip and Alexander

3(a)   Justin 9.8.1–21

Philip died at the age of 47 after a reign of 25 years.[25] [2] By a dancer from Larissa he had a son, Arrhidaeus, who was king after Alexander,[26] [3] and he also fathered many other children from the different wives which he had, as kings do. Some of these died of natural causes, others violently. [4] He was a king with more enthusiasm for the military than the convivial sphere; [5] in his view his greatest treasures were the tools of warfare. [6] He had a greater talent for acquiring wealth than keeping it, and thus despite his daily pillaging he was always insolvent. [7] His compassion and his duplicity were qualities which he prized equally, and no means of gaining a victory would he consider dishonourable. [8] He was charming and treacherous at the same time, the type to promise more in conversation than he would deliver, and whether the discussion was serious or light-hearted he was an artful performer. [9] He cultivated friendships with a view to expediency rather than from genuine feelings. His usual practice was to feign warm feelings when he hated someone, to sow discord between parties that were in agreement and then try to win the favour of both. [10] Besides this he was possessed of eloquence and a remarkable oratorical talent, full of subtlety and ingenuity, so that his elegant style was not lacking fluency, nor his fluency lacking stylistic elegance.

[11] Philip was succeeded by his son Alexander who surpassed his father both in good qualities and bad. [12] Each had his own method of gaining victory, Alexander making war openly and Philip using trickery; the latter took pleasure in duping the enemy, the former in putting them to flight in the open. [13] Philip was the more prudent strategist, Alexander had the greater vision. [14] The father could hide, and sometimes even suppress, his anger; when

---

25   Cf. §II.1a (Satyrus, *Life of Philip*) where he is given 22 years. The use of inclusive reckoning by Justin (Trogus) does not explain the discrepancy; rather Satyrus' 22 years may reflect the likelihood that Amyntas son of Perdiccas was nominally king in the first years after his father's death; but see Griffith (Hammond and Griffith 1979: 209 n.2).

26   He reigned as Philip III (323–317), together with Alexander IV, son of Alexander the Great and Roxane. The charge that his mother was a dancer (= prostitute) is pure slander: she was, in all likelihood, a woman of the Aleuadae, the Larissan aristocracy. For more on Arrhidaeus, see §III.2e–j below.

Alexander's had flared up, his retaliation could be neither delayed nor kept in check. [15] Both were excessively fond of drink, but intoxication brought out different shortcomings. It was the father's habit to rush straight at the enemy from the dinner-party, engage him in combat and recklessly expose himself to danger; Alexander's violence was directed not against the enemy but against his own comrades. [16] As a result Philip was often brought back from his battles wounded while the other often left a dinner with his friends' blood on his hands.[27] [17] Philip was unwilling to rule along with his friends; Alexander exercised his rule over his. The father preferred to be loved, the son to be feared. [18] They had a comparable interest in literature. The father had greater shrewdness, the son was truer to his word. [19] Philip was more restrained in his language and discourse, Alexander in his actions. [20] When it came to showing mercy to the defeated, the son was temperamentally more amenable and more magnanimous. The father was more disposed to thrift, the son to extravagance. [21] With such qualities did the father lay the basis for a worldwide empire and the son bring to completion the glorious enterprise.

---

27 A rhetorical plural. Only the murder of Cleitus in 328 is meant.

III Alexander's Family, Youth, Appearance, and Character

Alexander's Parents and Mythical Ancestors

1(a) Diodorus Siculus 17.1.5

Alexander's ancestry went back to Heracles on his father's side, while through his mother he was related to the Aeacids.

1(b) Plutarch, Alexander 2.1–2

As for Alexander's family, it is firmly established that he was descended from Heracles through Caranus on his father's side and from Aeacus through Neoptolemus on his mother's. [2] The story goes that Philip was initiated into the mysteries at Samothrace along with Olympias. She was an orphan and he was still a very young man; he fell in love with her, and on the spur of the moment became betrothed to her after gaining the blessing of her brother Arybbas.

1(c) Justin 11.4.5

Cleadas even appealed to the king's personal devotion to Hercules, who was born in their city[1] and from whom the clan of the Aeacidae[2] traced its descent, and to the fact that his father Philip had spent his boyhood in Thebes.

1(d) Justin 7.6.10–12

While these matters were proceeding successfully, Philip married Olympias, daughter of Neoptolemus, king of the Molossians; [11] the match was arranged

1 Thebes.
2 This should read "Argeadae." The error may originate with Justin rather than Trogus.

by Arybbas, king of the Molossians, who was the girl's cousin and guardian and was married to her sister, Troas. This was the cause of Arrybas' downfall and all his troubles. [12] For, while he was hoping to increase his kingdom through his family ties with Philip, he was stripped of his own kingdom by the latter and grew old in exile.

1(e)   Theopompus of Chios
(FGrH 115 F355 = Tzetzes, ad Lycophr. 1439)

Olympias traced her line all the way back to Pyrrhus son of Achilles and Helenus son of Priam, according to Theopompus and Pyrander. Pyrrhus' line goes back to Aeacus . . .

1(f)   Pausanias, Description of Greece 1.9.8

For Alexander was an Epirot, and related to the Aeacids on his mother's side . . .

1(g)   Plutarch, On the Fortune of Alexander 1.10 = Moralia 332a

[Plutarch, in a fictitious passage, puts these words into Alexander's mouth]: Forgive me for following the footsteps of Dionysus, divine founder and forefather of my line.

Alexander's Siblings: A Warlike Half-Sister and
a Mentally Defective Half-Brother

Alexander's siblings are named in Athenaeus 13.557b–e (see §II.1a above). Only one brother is attested: the mentally deficient Arrhidaeus (who later became King Philip III, *regn.* 323–317/16); see below. There were four sisters: Cleopatra, Cynnane, Thessalonice, and Europa. Of these, Europa was murdered soon after her birth; Cleopatra married her uncle, Alexander I, and became queen of Epirus; Cynnane was given by Philip to Amyntas IV, and contrived to put her daughter Adea-Eurydice on the throne as the queen of Philip III; Thessalonice eventually married (perhaps against her will) Cassander son of Antipater. The career of Cynnane is described below. See Heckel (1983–4) and Carney (1988; 2000a: 69–70, 129–31). Justin speaks of a half-brother named Caranus: see Tarn (1948, II: 260–2) and Heckel (1979) *contra* Unz (1985).

Cynnane: Warrior princess

2(a)   Arrian 1.5.4

Langarus was generally held in great honour by Alexander and, in particular, he received from him such gifts as are considered the greatest at the court of the king of Macedon. Alexander also agreed to give him his sister Cyna in marriage if he came to Pella. Langarus, however, died of an illness on his return home.

2(b)   Polyaenus, Stratagems *8.60: "Cynnane"*[3]

Philip's daughter Cynnane used to undergo military training, lead armies and face enemies in battle. When she faced the Illyrians she brought down their queen with a well-timed blow to the neck and killed large numbers of Illyrians as they fled. She married Amyntas son of Perdiccas, but soon lost him, and could not face the prospect of taking a second husband. Instead, she gave similar military training to the one daughter she had by Amyntas, Eurydice. When Alexander died in Babylon and the successors were in violent conflict, Cynnane took the risk of crossing the Strymon. Antipater tried to stop her, but she overpowered the forces blocking her way and crossed the river. Then, defeating those in her path, she crossed the Hellespont, for she wished to join up with the Macedonian army. Alcetas confronted her with his forces, but when the Macedonians recognised the daughter of Philip and the sister of Alexander they felt ashamed and had a change of heart. Cynnane rebuked Alcetas for his ingratitude, and was daunted neither by the number of his men nor the extent of his armament. She nobly submitted to a bloody death, preferring to lose her life rather than see the line of Philip driven from the throne.

2(c)   Arrian, Events after Alexander *1.22–3*

Not much later, there also occurred the death of Cynane, which Perdiccas and his brother, Alcetas, engineered. Cynane had the same father as Alexander, namely Philip. Her mother was Eurydice, and she was the wife of Amyntas, whom Alexander killed pre-emptively at the time that he crossed to Asia.

---

3   The Teubner edition has "Kyna" (Cyna), as in Arrian 1.5.5, but the MSS read Kynnane, which is correct: this form is epigraphically attested and was used by Duris of Samos, the source of this passage: cf. Athenaeus 13.560f (§III.3d). The various spellings – Cyna, Cynane, Cynnane – are Latinized versions of the Greek forms found in the individual texts.

Amyntas was the son of Perdiccas, and Perdiccas was the brother of Philip – so that the murdered Amyntas was Alexander's cousin. [23] Cynane brought her daugher Adea, who was later renamed Eurydice, to be Arrhidaeus' wife. Arrhidaeus did, in fact, marry her later, through the efforts of Perdiccas, who wanted to terminate the discord of the Macedonians. This had flared up at the death of Cynane and was growing serious.

2(d)   Duris of Samos
(FGrH 76 F 52 = Athenaeus 13.560f)

Duris of Samos also states that the first war of women was that fought between Olympias and Eurydice. In this, he claims, Olympias advanced in Bacchic fashion, to the sound of drum-beats, while Eurydice went forward armed in the Macedonian manner; for she had received a military training from Cynnane the Illyrian.

Arrhidaeus: Philip III

2(e)   Plutarch, Alexander 10.1–2

Pixodarus the satrap of Caria was trying to worm his way into an alliance with Philip through a family tie, and he wished to give the eldest of his daughters in marriage to Philip's son, Arrhidaeus. He therefore sent Aristocritus to Macedonia to broach the subject. At this, some snide comments began to come to Alexander from his friends and his mother: Philip, they said, was trying to facilitate Arrhidaeus' succession to the throne by a glittering marriage of great political significance. [2] Disturbed by these remarks, Alexander sent the tragic actor Thessalus to Caria to discuss the matter with Pixodarus and tell him that he should forget about the illegitimate idiot and instead establish a marriage tie with Alexander.

2(f)   Plutarch, Alexander 77.7–8

For it was Perdiccas who immediately found himself in the position of greatest power, towing Arrhidaeus behind him almost as a mute representative of the monarchy. Arrhidaeus was the child of Philip by Philinna, a woman of no distinction and of common birth, and he was of impaired mental faculties because of a physical disorder, but not one that struck him from natural causes or was congenital. [8] They say, rather, that when he was a boy the character that shone through was refined and not lacking in nobility, but that he was later disabled by drugs given him by Olympias and that this was how his mind was destroyed.

2(g)   Heidelberg Epitome 1

Alexander's courtiers were at odds over the question of the throne, and it was arranged that the king would be Arrhidaeus (later also named Philip), the half-brother of Alexander on his father's side. He was to rule until Alexander's son reached the appropriate age. However, since Arrhidaeus was mentally retarded, and epileptic to boot, Perdiccas was chosen as a trustee and caretaker of the affairs of court.

2(h)   Justin 13.2.11, 3.1

[11] Ptolemy rejected Arrhidaeus' claim to the throne, not only because of his low birth on his mother's side – he was purportedly the son of a prostitute from Larissa – but also because of the serious disability from which he suffered, which might mean a regent holding the real power while he was king in name only.

3   [1] . . . the infantry were furious at being left no say in the matter, so they declared Alexander's brother Arrhidaeus king, appointed guards for him from amongst their own number and issued orders that he be addressed by his father's name, Philip.

2(i)   Quintus Curtius Rufus 10.7.2

[Meleager addresses the officers in Babylon:] "you are forgetting Philip's son, Arrhidaeus, brother of our late king Alexander; recently he accompanied the king in performing our religious ceremonies and now he is his sole heir."

2(j)   Plutarch, On the Fortune of Alexander 2.5 = Moralia 337d–e

But who could have made a great man of Arrhidaeus? He was no different from a child when Meleager set him on Alexander's throne, except that his baby clothes were royal purple. Meleager did well, though, to show in a matter of days how men can be kings by their merits and how they can also be kings by pure chance. For to succeed a man who was a real champion on the throne Meleager brought in an actor, or (to put it more accurately) a mute diadem, so to speak, passed across the stage of the inhabited world.

Alexander's Education

That Alexander was educated by Aristotle is well known (but see Chroust 1964). The effects of Aristotle's teaching were not always what might have been imagined, and there was some fall-out from the king's confrontation with, and eventual execution of, his kinsman Callisthenes. Alexander was also influenced by his earlier teachers, Leonidas of Epirus and Lysimachus the Acarnanian. Indeed, Olympias, his mother, had played no small role in selecting his tutors in the early years. On Aristotle, see Guthrie (1981: 35–45).

3(a) Plutarch, Alexander 5.7–8

There were, not surprisingly, a large number of nurses, pedagogues and teachers appointed to supervise Alexander's rearing, all of them under the direction of Leonidas, a man of stern character and a relative of Olympias.[4] He did not refuse the title "pedagogue", since the position was an important and honourable one, but to everyone else, because of his standing and kinship, he was known as "Alexander's tutor" or "the professor". [8] It was Lysimachus, an Acarnanian by nationality, who assumed the formal role and title of pedagogue. He was not a man of distinction in general, but he attained popularity and held second place to Leonidas because he would call himself Phoenix, Alexander Achilles and Philip Peleus.[5]

3(b) Plutarch, Alexander 7.1–4

Philip could see that Alexander had an inflexible nature that resisted coercion but could be easily led by reason to what needed to be done, and so he would try persuasion rather than an authoritarian approach. [2] He had little confidence in the average teachers of arts and science to give the boy direction and training . . . and so he sent for the best known and most erudite of the philosophers, Aristotle,[6] to whom he paid a handsome and appropriate fee. [3] Aristotle hailed from Stageira, which had been destroyed by Philip. The king now resettled it, bringing back those of its citizens who had been exiled or enslaved.

[4] For their periods of instruction and study Philip assigned to the two a place close to the *nympheum* of Mieza where, down to this day, the stone benches and shaded walkways are on display for the visitor.

---

4 For Leonidas and his discipline, see §VIII.1e.
5 Peleus was the father of Achilles, whom Phoenix tutored.
6 Aristotle's father, Nicomachus, was the court physician of Philip's father, Amyntas III.

3(c)   Plutarch, Alexander 8.2–4

Alexander was by nature fond of learning and reading. He regarded the *Iliad* as a guide-book to military excellence, and called it such; and, according to Onesicritus' history,[7] he took with him Aristotle's revised version – the so-called "casket copy" – which always lay under his pillow along with his dagger. [3] Finding access to other books difficult in the interior of Asia, he instructed Harpalus to send him some. Harpalus sent him the books of Philistus, numerous tragedies by Euripides, Sophocles and Aeschylus, and the dithyrambs of Telestes and Philoxenus.[8]

[4] Initially he had a great regard for Aristotle, whom he loved no less than his father, as he used to say – thanks to the one he had life, and thanks to the other he knew how to live well. Later, however, he regarded Aristotle with some suspicion, not enough to want to do him harm, but the fact that his familiarity with him lacked its former intensity and warmth indicated a rift in their relationship.

Alexander's Body

General appearance

Despite the immense interest in him in antiquity, very few securely identified portraits of Alexander have survived. Nevertheless, we have the Azara herm, the Alexander Mosaic from Pompeii, and various coins of the Successors that depict Alexander – often in the style of Heracles – on the obverse. Furthermore, the Alexander Sarcophagus depicts two Alexanders, one in the great battle scene (where he wears a lion headdress), the other a rider wearing the diadem in the hunting scene. But most "Alexanders" are so identified for stylistic reasons; for they exhibit the famous tilt of the head and the shaggy mane-like hair. See Nielsen (1993), Stewart (1993: 9–41 for literary testimonia, and 42–70 for actual images); cf. Schwarzenberg (1976) and Kiilerich (1988, 1993).

4(a)   Plutarch, Alexander 4.1–7

Alexander's physical features are best depicted in those statues of him made by Lysippus, the only artist by whom Alexander felt he should be sculpted. [2] As a matter of fact, the features which most of the successors and Alexander's friends later tried to affect have been accurately caught by the artist: the angle of the neck, slightly inclined to the left, and the languishing

---

7   For Onesicritus, see the Introduction, p. xx.
8   See Brown (1967).

glance of the eyes. [3] Apelles, however, in painting him wielding the thunderbolt, failed to capture his complexion, making it too dark and swarthy. In fact, Alexander was fair-skinned, they say, but his pale coloration became ruddy, in the chest area particularly but also in the face. [4] I have read in the *Memoirs* of Aristoxenus that an agreeable odour emanated from his skin and that his breath and whole physique had a fragrance that pervaded his clothes. [5] This was possibly the result of his temperament, which was hot and fiery, for in Theophrastus' view fragrance is a result of the action of heat on the moist humours. [6] This is why the arid and very hot tracts of the world produce spices in the greatest number and of the best quality – the sun draws off the moisture, the corrupting agent, as it were, that lies on the surface of bodies. [7] In Alexander's case it would seem that it was the heat of his temperament that made him fond of drink and quick-tempered.

4(b)   Aelian, Varia Historia *12.14*

They say that Alexander, son of Philip, enjoyed natural good looks, with curly, fair hair, but they add that there was something in his appearance that aroused fear.

4(c)   Aelian, Varia Historia *2.3*

When Alexander saw at Ephesus the portrait that Apelles had made of him he did not give the picture the praise it warranted. Then his horse was brought to the spot, and it proceeded to neigh at the horse in the picture, thinking that it, too, was real, at which point Apelles remarked: "Your Majesty, the horse is evidently a better judge of painting than you are."

4(d)   Itinerary of Alexander *6*

He himself was of sharp expression and had a somewhat aquiline nose; his forehead was almost all bare, though quite thickly fringed from exercise because of the speed at which he would ride; he let this be the deciding factor here, and as a result he had made his hair curl upwards and lie back and away from his face. He used to say that this was more becoming for a soldier than if his hair were to hang downwards. He was a young man medium in stature, somewhat shrivelled in his limbs – though they were not such as to make him any the slower when his blood was up, a fact which aided him in action even if it did not benefit his appearance. Knotted indeed as his body was, with a good number of protruding muscles, it was with remarkable co-ordination of the sinews that his strength was exerted. Tireless in running at any goal he chose, he was vehement in attacking his threatened victim; excessive in the convulsive effort of hurling a spear, he was still skilled in aiming at his target. Hot-blooded in his onrush where boldness was called for, resolute in taking on a confident adversary, he was certain of his intention when at a distance from the enemy, and full of violence at close quarters; on horseback he lacked foresight, and was quite wild – on foot, fearless and unrelenting in combat. He seemed to be everywhere to give orders in difficult situations, yet he laid an even heavier burden on his men by the incentive of the personal example he set them; for he thought it shameful to be outdone by anyone in some valiant piece of work, as he energetically demanded of his body the due contribution of its youthful strength.[9] He himself looked somewhat rough with his pointed beard; the rest of his face was clean-shaven. As for the care which anyone would quite rightly take of himself, he would wish this for himself, certainly either in his role as general or merely as a soldier. Now that I have given you a portrait of Alexander, it is for you to look to yourself, for flattery has not been my intention, and I refuse to seem pleasing to your ears when all your men may make judgment of you with their eyes.

His alleged shortness

There is general agreement in modern accounts that Alexander was of less than average height, even though the ancient evidence for this is scant. What the sources do say about the king's size is mainly comparative or based on a misunderstanding; the only explicit statement is both absurd and comes from a late and unreliable source. We have, however, come to equate Alexander with Napoleon, who, as one writer has recently pointed out, "was about 5 ft. 6 in. tall, certainly not exceptionally short even by today's standards": thus Baynham (2001: 117 n.15).

4(e)   Quintus Curtius Rufus 3.12.16–17

While [Hephaestion] was the king's age, in stature he was his superior, [17] and so the queens took him to be the king and did obeisance before him after their manner. Whereupon some of the captive eunuchs pointed out the real Alexander, and Sisigambis flung herself at his feet apologizing for not recognizing him on the ground that she had never before seen him. Raising her with his hand, Alexander said, "My lady, you made no mistake. This man is Alexander too."

4(f)   Diodorus Siculus 17.66.3

The king had a strange experience when he took possession of the treasure. He sat on the royal throne and found this was too large for his own physical

---

9   This passage appears to be particularly corrupt.

dimensions. One of the pages saw that Alexander's feet were far from reaching the footstool for the throne, and so he brought Darius' table and slipped it under his feet as they dangled in the air.

4(g)   Quintus Curtius Rufus 6.5.29

Thalestris looked at the king, no sign of fear on her face. Her eyes surveyed a physique that in no way matched his illustrious record – for all barbarians have respect for physical presence, believing that only those on whom nature has thought fit to confer extraordinary appearance are capable of great achievements.

4(h)   Alexander Romance 3.4

Porus was pleased with this and undertook to fight a duel with Alexander; for he saw that in physical size Alexander was no match for him. Porus was five cubits tall,[10] and Alexander not even three.

Alexander's Attitude towards Sex

Tarn (1948, II: 319–26) devoted an entire section of his "Sources and Studies" to this topic, and it is perhaps a sign of the times that this very question is regarded as one of the important ones (cf. Davidson 2001: 10). One must allow for the possibility that Alexander, like T. E. Lawrence, was perhaps not greatly interested in sex, or at least inclined to avoid sexual encounters.[11]

5(a)   Athenaeus 10.435a

In his *Letters* Hieronymus[12] says that Theophrastus claims Alexander had little appetite for sexual activity. And Olympias, at any rate, had the Thessalian

---

10 From the Latin word for elbow (*cubitum*), the cubit represents the distance from the elbow to the fingertips, roughly 18 inches. Hence Porus' height, according to the *Alexander Romance*, would have been about $7\frac{1}{2}$ feet, whereas Alexander was 4 ft 6 ins!

11 It is perhaps pointless to discuss sexual attitudes outside their cultural contexts, and one cannot find anything in Alexander's upbringing that would have approximated the Victorian and Christian education, which shaped Lawrence's social behavior, or the incident at Deraa, which tortured him emotionally. But both individuals displayed an indifference to sexual encounters that has left their biographers uneasy or perplexed. Nor is this a matter that ought to be treated with a corresponding indifference. As Mack (1998: 416) notes: "The biographer's justification for exploring the sexual (or any other intimate aspect of the life of the person being studied) is his belief that it is vitally related to his public life, that understanding it is essential to understanding the subject's character in general."

12 Hieronymus of Rhodes: third-century BC philosopher, whose patron was Antigonus Gonatas (cf. Tarn 1913: 328ff. for Antigonus and the philosophers in Athens).

hetaira Callixena, who was very beautiful, go to bed with him (and Philip was her accomplice in this); for they wanted to make sure that he was not effeminate. Olympias often begged him to have sex with Callixena.

5(b)   Aelian, Varia Historia *12.34*

We have been left on record many love-affairs of the ancients, not the least of which are the following. Pausanias was in love with his own wife, and Apelles with the concubine of Alexander called Pancaste, a native of Larisa. (They also say that Pancaste was the first woman with whom Alexander had sexual relations.)

5(c)   Plutarch, Alexander *67.7–8*

When he reached the royal palace of Gedrosia, Alexander once again gave the army some recreation by arranging a festival. [8] The story goes that he was drunk while watching some dancing competitions, and that Bagoas, whose lover he was, won a dancing-prize, came through the theatre in his finery and seated himself next to the king. Seeing this, they say, the Macedonians clapped in applause and loudly called for Alexander to kiss him, until eventually the king took him in his arms and gave him a kiss.

5(d)   Plutarch, Alexander *22.1–6*

Philoxenus, governor of the coastal areas, informed Alexander by letter that a certain Theodorus of Tarentum was with him, and that the man had two exceedingly good-looking boys to sell. He asked Alexander if he wanted to buy the boys. This angered the king, who time and again cried out to his friends asking them what moral failing Philoxenus had ever seen in him to make him waste his time procuring such vile creatures. [2] In a letter to Philoxenus he roundly berated him and ordered him to tell Theodorus to go to hell along with his wares. [3] Alexander also came down heavily on Hagnon who, with youthful exuberance, had told him in a letter that he wanted to purchase Crobylus, famed in Corinth for his good looks, and bring him to the king.
[4] When he was apprised that the Macedonians Damon and Timotheus, who were serving under Parmenion, had debauched the women of some mercenaries, the king sent written orders to Parmenion that, if the men were found guilty, he should punish them with execution as being wild animals born to destroy human beings. [5] In this letter he also has this to say about himself (and I quote): "In my case it would be found that, so far from looking upon the wife of Darius or wishing to look upon her, I have not even per-

mitted people to talk of her beauty." [6] And he would state that his awareness of his mortality arose most from sleeping and the sexual act, as if to say that tiredness and pleasure derived from the same weakness in nature.

5(e)   Justin 11.10.2–3

. . . now, too, he began to fall in love with the prisoner Barsine because of her beauty [3] (by her he later had a son whom he named Hercules).[13]

His relationship with Hephaestion

Several *syntrophoi* and drinking companions of Alexander are attested in the sources, but Hephaestion stands out as his closest personal friend, to whom he confided his innermost secrets. To some extent Hephaestion's military advancement was based on nepotism, and on at least one occasion Alexander may have questioned his own judgement (see §X.7a, below). See also Heckel (1992a: 65–90) and Reames-Zimmerman (1999, 2001).

5(f)   Plutarch, Alexander 39.8

Olympias often included such remarks in her letters and Alexander would keep what she wrote secret. Once, however, when Hephaestion followed his usual practice of reading along with Alexander – and it was a letter of hers that had been opened – Alexander did not stop him. Instead, he took off his ring and put the seal to Hephaestion's lips.

5(g)   Aelian, Varia Historia 12.7

Alexander placed a wreath on the tomb of Achilles and Hephaestion placed one on that of Patroclus, hinting thereby that he was the beloved of Alexander as Patroclus was the beloved of Achilles.

5(h)   Valerius Maximus 4.7 ext 2

After taking possession of Darius' camp, which contained all the king's relatives, Alexander came to address these latter, with his dear friend

---

13 Barsine had been captured by Parmenion at Damascus soon after the battle of Issus (late 333). Hercules was born in 327. Tarn (1921a) dismisses him as unhistorical, but Brunt (1975) has effectively refuted his arguments. For Hercules' fate, see Wheatley (1998).

Hephaestion at his side. Darius' mother, encouraged by his visit, lifted her head from the ground where she had prostrated herself, and in the Persian fashion did obeisance to Hephaestion and saluted him as Alexander, since he was the superior of the two in height and good looks. Apprised of her mistake, she became extremely agitated and was searching for words of apology when Alexander said to her: "Your confusion over the name is unimportant, for this man is also Alexander."

5(i)   Aelian, Varia Historia 7.8

When Hephaestion died, Alexander hurled arms onto his funeral pyre, and along with the body melted down gold and silver, burning also clothing that was highly valued amongst the Persians. In addition, he sheared off his own locks, a Homeric gesture of grief and imitating that poet's Achilles. However, some of Alexander's actions were more violent and impetuous than Achilles' – he sheared Ecbatana of its citadel and stripped it of its city wall. As far as his hair is concerned, it seems to me that his behaviour was typically Greek, but in assaulting the walls Alexander was already reacting to grief in a barbarian manner, and he also changed his mode of dress, completely succumbing to rage, passion and tears.

5(j)   Arrian 7.14.4

Others say he spent all day and all night prostrate beside the corpse, and yet others that he hanged the doctor, Glaucias, for being in error when he gave Hephaestion a drug or (according to some) for overlooking the fact when he saw him soused with wine. That Alexander cut off his hair over the body I do not think implausible for a number of reasons, but especially because of his emulation of Achilles with whom he had been in competition since he was a boy.

Alexander's Drinking, Personal Habits, and Health

Alexander's fondness for drink has always been a topic of interest. In antiquity there were several contemporary sources which attributed his death to excessive drinking (Ephippus of Olynthus, *FGrH* 126, and a certain Nicoboule, *FGrH* 127). O'Brien (1980, 1992) has argued that Alexander was an alcoholic and that this may have contributed to his death (see also XI.1a–d, below). Alexander's illness near Tarsus, after dipping in the cold waters of the Cydnus River, may have been a case of malaria (see Engels 1978b, and §III.6c, below). Furthermore, Alexander's numerous wounds appear to have had an impact on his behavior – some would see him as suffering from post-traumatic stress disorder (PTSD) – and it is worth noting that many of his most cruel acts and bloody reprisals were preceded by wounds sustained in battle.

6(a)   Aelian, Varia Historia 3.23

The following is not admirable conduct on Alexander's part. On the fifth day of the month of Dius, so they say, he was drinking in Eumaeus'[14] quarters. Then, on the sixth, he slept as a result of the drinking, his awareness extending only so far as getting up to confer with his officers on the matter of the next day's march, which he said would start early. On the seventh he dined in Perdiccas' quarters, drank once more and then slept on the eighth. On the fifteenth of the same month he was drinking again, and his behaviour the next day followed his usual after-drinking pattern. He had dinner with Bagoas on the twenty-seventh – Bagoas' house lay 10 stades from the palace – and slept on the twenty-eighth. We have, therefore, only two explanations. Either Alexander did himself a lot of harm from drinking for so many days in the month or else the authors recording these events are lying. One can tell from their work that those authors do produce stories of this kind on other occasions as well, Eumenes of Cardia being one of them.

6(b)   Aelian, Varia Historia 12.26

The greatest drinkers, so they say, were Xenagoras the Rhodian, whom they called "The Jar", the boxer Heraclides, and Proteas, son of Lanice, who was brought up with King Alexander. In fact, Alexander himself is said to have exceeded all men in his drinking.

6(c)   Itinerary of Alexander 12

Alexander rode into Tarsus begrimed with sweat and dust, an impressive military figure with this proof of labour along with his royal insignia. He caught sight of the river Cydnus flowing through the middle of the city, its banks thronged with the assembled citizens; it was lovely in appearance, the water piercingly cold as it flowed all-too strongly with its swift current between grassy banks. Delighted by such a sight of the watery element – or perhaps overcome by the boiling heat of the day and longing for coolness, or again wishing to display his own fortitude to the vast audience of citizens whose gaze was fixed on him – he ascended, with a leap, the bridge spanning the river, and with his shield and breastplate (or, as some accounts relate, his spear and helmet) he moved with another swift leap and threw himself headlong into the stream and, keeping hold of his arms, swam right across. Thus indeed is it one of the qualities of a king's fortitude to set in his own person a pattern for his soldiery and show them how they should conduct themselves. Less vigorous than his spirit, however, was his physical capacity for resisting

14 Eumaeus is otherwise unknown and may be a corruption of Eumenes or Ptolemaeus (Ptolemy).

injury: for his whole body had been full of heat and vapour and he had taken a draught of the river's coldness that was all the deeper for the burden of arms he carried. He now ran so violent a fever accompanied by contraction of the sinews, with his very vitals unmanned by the force of the chill, that his doctors were giving up hope of his recovery, except that their devotion to him had increased their diligence.

6(d) Plutarch, On the Fortune or the Virtue of Alexander 1.2 = Moralia 327a–b[15]

My own body bears many marks to prove that Fortune has fought against me and not been my ally! First of all, amongst the Illyrians, I was struck on the head with a stone, and on my neck with a club. Then, at the Granicus, I had my head split open with a barbarian dagger, and at the Issus my thigh slit by a sword. At Gaza, too, I received an arrow in the ankle and dislocated my shoulder when I fell from my saddle, and at Maracanda I had my shin-bone split open by an arrow. On top of all that, there were the blows I received from the Indians, and the savagery of wild animals that I endured. I was shot in the shoulder with an arrow amongst the Aspasians, in the leg amongst the Gandridae. Amongst the Mallians I had an arrow fixed in my breast deep enough to cover the metal head, and received a club-blow to the neck when the scaling-ladders set against the wall were broken down. And on that occasion fortune set me all on my own, and cheerfully made my opponents in such a great exploit not a distinguished people, but insignificant barbarians. And had it not been for Ptolemy setting his shield over me; had it not been for Limnaeus standing before me and facing the enemy hordes till he fell; and had not the Macedonians with spirit and sheer force torn down that wall . . . then that barbarian village of no account would have had to serve as Alexander's tomb!

6(e) Plutarch, Alexander 45.5–6

Apart from everything else he had recently received an arrow-wound to the calf which left his tibia broken and dislocated, and he had also been struck on the neck by a stone which darkened his vision for quite some time. [6] And despite this he would not stop putting himself at risk at every turn. In fact, after he had crossed the River Orexartes,[16] which Alexander actually thought was the Tanais, and had routed the Scythians, he pursued the latter over a distance of a hundred stades, suffering from dysentry though he was.

15 In this philosophical work, Plutarch imagines what Alexander might say in response to the claims of Fortune that his successes were her work. Although the speech is fictitious many of the details of Alexander's wounds are correct.

16 The Iaxartes (modern Syr-Darya).

Alexander's Character, Intellect, and Moderation

7(a)   Plutarch, Alexander 5.1–3

When Philip was once away on a journey Alexander entertained some ambassadors from the Persian king and became quite familiar with them. He captivated them with his cordiality, and also by asking no immature or inconsequential questions, [2] for he inquired instead into the length of the roads, into how one made the journey inland, into the king's military qualities [3] and into the fighting ability and strength of the Persians. The ambassadors were duly impressed, and considered Philip's celebrated cunning to be nothing in comparison with his son's enthusiasm and ardour for great exploits.

7(b)   Quintus Curtius Rufus, 3.12.18–21

Had he been able to maintain this degree of moderation to the end of his life, I would certainly consider him to have enjoyed more good fortune than appeared to be his when he was emulating Father Liber's triumph on his victorious march through all the nations from the Hellespont right to the Ocean. [19] For then he would surely have overcome the defects he failed to overcome, his pride and his temper; he would have stopped short of killing his friends at dinner, and he would have been reluctant to execute without trial men who had distinguished themselves in battle and had conquered so many nations along with him. [20] But good fortune had not as yet overwhelmed him: while it was on the increase, he bore it with self-restraint and abstinence, but eventually he failed to control it when it reached its peak. [21] At this particular time, certainly, his actions were such that he outshone all previous kings in self-control and clemency.

Alexander and Bucephalas

One of the best-known stories from the life of Alexander is that of the precocious youth breaking and riding Bucephalas, an episode that illustrated both the daring and intelligence of the prince. Alexander's devotion to the animal, which endured until Bucephalas' death from old age in 326, is evinced by his anger at the Mardians who stole the horse in 330 and by the founding of a city on the banks of the Hydaspes that he named Bucephala. See Anderson (1930; 1961: 20ff.).

8(a)   Plutarch, Alexander 6

The Thessalian Philoneicus once brought Bucephalas to Philip – he wanted to sell him for thirteen talents – and the men went down to the plain to put the horse through his paces. The animal seemed difficult and altogether unmanageable; he would not allow anyone to mount him, nor would he heed the voice of any in Philip's entourage, rearing up against all of them. [2] Philip was annoyed, and ordered the horse taken away because it was completely wild and ungovernable, but Alexander, who was there, said: "What a horse they are losing simply because they are too inexperienced and too spineless to be able to handle him!"

[3] At first Philip kept quiet, but when Alexander murmured this a number of times and became quite upset, he said: "Is it because you know more than them, or can better handle a horse, that you are criticising your elders?"

[4] "I could at least handle *this* horse better than any of them," replied Alexander.

"And if you do not, what penalty will you take for your impulsiveness?"

"I'll pay the price of the horse, by God."

[5] There was laughter at this, and then the financial terms of the bet were settled between the two. Alexander ran to the horse, took the reins and turned him towards the sun, for he had apparently noticed that he was greatly agitated by the sight of his shadow that fell and danced about in front of him. [6] Alexander ran beside the animal for a short while and patted him while he saw he was fiery and panting; then, gently setting aside his cloak, he leapt up and firmly mounted him. [7] He used the reins to put some gentle pressure on the bit, and took control of the horse without hurting or tearing his mouth. Then, seeing that he had dropped his menacing demeanour and was raring to gallop, he gave him some rein and drove him on, now with a firmer tone of voice and a kick of his foot.

[8] At first an anxious silence fell over Philip's entourage, but when Alexander turned and came back truly pleased with himself and exultant, they all shouted out in noisy applause and the father, it is said, burst into tears of joy. He supposedly kissed Alexander on the head when he dismounted and said to him: "Son, look for a kingdom that matches your size. Macedonia has not enough space for you."

The theft of Bucephalas

8(b)   Plutarch, Alexander 44.3–5

There a number of the barbarians came unexpectedly upon the men leading Alexander's horse, Bucephalas,[17] and captured the animal. [4] The king's anger knew no bounds. He sent a herald and threatened to put every one of the barbarians to death, along with their children and their wives, unless they sent him back his horse. [5] In fact, when they came bringing his horse, and

---

17   "Ox-head." The name was that of a breed of horses from Thessaly, branded with the head of an ox; but there is a story that the horse was black with a white mark on the forehead that resembled an ox's head (see §III.8e).

also putting their cities in his hands, he treated them all charitably and paid a ransom for the horse to the men who had taken him.

8(c)   *Quintus Curtius Rufus 6.5.18–21*

In their ignorance of the area, however, many lost their way and some were captured, and the captured included the king's horse, whom they called Bucephalas, prized above all other animals by Alexander. (The horse would not allow another man to sit on him and, when the king wished to mount, he would of his own accord bend his knees to receive him, so it was thought that he was aware of his rider's identity.) [19] Alexander's anger and grief surpassed the bounds of propriety. He ordered that the horse be traced and a proclamation issued through an interpreter that failure to return him would result in no Mardian being left alive. Terrified by this warning, the Mardians brought up the horse and other gifts, too, [20] but even this failed to appease Alexander. He gave orders for the woods to be felled and for earth to be hauled from the mountains and heaped on the flat ground where the branches formed the barrier. [21] When the work had reached a considerable height the barbarians abandoned hope of holding their position and capitulated. The king took hostages from them and put them under Phradates.[18]

8(d)   *Diodorus Siculus 17.76.5–8*

Alexander was putting the countryside[19] to the torch, while the pages who led the royal horses at some distance from the king, when some of the barbarians swooped down and made off with the very best one of these animals. [6] This horse was a gift from the Corinthian Demaratus, and had been present with the king at all his battles in Asia.

Unharnassed it would allow itself to be mounted only by its groom, but once in its royal trappings it would then accept not even him. It was only for Alexander that he was compliant at this stage, and for him alone he would lower his body to be mounted.

[7] Infuriated at the loss of a horse of such calibre, Alexander ordered the land to be totally shorn of trees and the word put out to the natives, by men speaking their language, that unless they surrendered the horse they would see their land entirely devastated and all the inhabitants put to death. [8] These threats were promptly put into effect and the terrified natives returned the horse, sending with it gifts of the greatest value. Furthermore, in their desire

---

18   Autophradates, the satrap of the Tapurians, who was permitted to retain his office after surrendering to Alexander.
19   Of the Mardians.

to gain the king's forgiveness, they also sent along fifty men, and Alexander took the foremost of these as hostages.

8(e)   Arrian 5.19.5–6

In earlier days Bucephalas had faced many of Alexander's ordeals and dangers with him, and had been ridden exclusively by the king because he refused all others who tried to mount him. His dimensions were large, his spirit noble, and his distinguishing characteristic was the brand of an ox-head, for which they say he had the name Bucephalas (some, however, claim that, though black, he had on his head a white mark that resembled an ox-head more than anything else).

[6] This horse was lost in Uxian territory,[20] and Alexander had it proclaimed throughout the land that he would kill all the Uxians unless they returned his horse to him – and the return followed hard on the heels of the proclamation. Such was Alexander's attachment to the horse, and such the barbarians' fear of Alexander. This is all I have to say in praise of Bucephalas, and I have done it for the sake of Alexander.

Bucephalas' death and the foundation of Bucephala

8(f)   Arrian 5.14.4

Some claim that the Indians arriving with the son of Porus also fought a battle against Alexander, and the cavalry with him, at the point where they landed. In fact, these people say that Porus' son actually arrived with a greater force; that Alexander himself was wounded by him; and that Bucephalas, the horse that Alexander loved most, was killed after also receiving a wound from the son of Porus. But Ptolemy, son of Lagus, gives a different version, with which I am in agreement.

8(g)   Arrian 5.19.4

At the point where the battle took place – which was also his point of departure for the crossing of the River Hydaspes – Alexander founded two cities, calling one Nicaea to commemorate his victory over the Indians, and the other Bucephala, in honour of his horse Bucephalas, who died there. The

---

20   Arrian is alone in placing the theft in the land of the Uxians. Bosworth (1995: 314–15) attributes the confusion to the fact that there were two peoples named Mardians, one of whom lived south of the Uxians, the other in the Caspian region. But Curtius' reference to the satrap of the Tapurians (see §III.8c and note 18) shows that the Mardians in question lived near the Caspian.

horse had not been wounded by anyone, but was worn out from the heat of the sun and old age (he was about thirty years old).

8(h)   Metz Epitome 62

There were also many horses killed, including Alexander's, Bucephalas by name, on whose back he had always been victorious in all his battles. Accordingly, Alexander founded a town in that place bearing the horse's name, which today is called Bucephala. Afterwards he ordered the customary burial of the dead, his own and the bravest of the enemy.

8(i)   Plutarch, Alexander 61.1–3

After the battle with Porus Bucephalas also died, not immediately afterwards but a little later. Most say he died while being looked after for his wounds, but according to Onesicritus it was because he was worn out with age, dying as he did at thirty.

[2] Alexander was terribly upset, thinking the loss to be no less than that of a companion or friend, and in honour of him he founded a city on the banks of the Hydaspes, which he called Bucephalia. [3] It is also said that there was a dog called Perita that Alexander brought up and loved, and that when he lost it he founded a city that he named after it. Sotion claims that he got this information from Potamon of Lesbos.

Plate 1　Bust of Alexander known as the Azara Herm. Musée du Louvre, photo © RMN/Hervé Lewandowski.

Plate 2　Alexander with lion headdress from the battlescene on the Alexander Sarcophagus. Istanbul Museum/photo Art Archive/Dagli Orti.

Plate 3 Hephaestion; from a hunting scene on the Alexander Sarcophagus. Istanbul Museum/photo Art Archive.

Plate 4 The Alexander Mosaic from the House of the Faun, Pompeii. The inspiration appears to have been the painting of Alexander's battle of Issus done by Philoxenus of Eretria for Cassander. Museo Nazionale, Naples/SCALA.

Plate 5 Coin showing Alexander with lion headdress (Nickle Arts Museum, Calgary).

Plate 6 Coin showing Alexander with elephant headdress (Nickle Arts Museum, Calgary).

Plate 7 Coin showing Alexander with horns of Amun (Ammon) (Nickle Arts Museum, Calgary).

Plate 8 The Marriage of Alexander and Roxane from fresco by "Il Sodoma." Palazzo della Farnesina, Rome/SCALA.

IV The Persians and their Empire

The Empire before Alexander's Accession

The years that preceded Philip II's death and the accession of Alexander to the throne of Macedon were also turbulent ones for the Persian empire. There, Artaxerxes III (Ochus) had been murdered in late 338 by his chamberlain, the elder Bagoas, who engineered the accession of Ochus' son Arses (Artaxerxes IV). But Arses, too, was soon removed and the kingship devolved upon Darius III, who in the first year of his reign appears to have been forced to deal with an uprising in Egypt. See Olmstead (1948), Cook (1983), and Briant (1996); cf. Ruzicka (1997). A good discussion of the Persian army can be found in Sekunda and Chew (1992).

1(a)   Diodorus Siculus 17.5.3–6.2

While Philip was still on the throne, Ochus was king of Persia, and his rule over his subjects was brutally harsh. Ochus was detested for his callousness, and his chiliarch Bagoas – he was, physically, a eunuch but had a villainous and aggressive nature – did away with him by poison, through the agency of a certain doctor. Bagoas then put the youngest of Ochus' sons, Arses, on the throne. [4] He also did away with the new king's brothers, who were still at a very early age, so that the young man's isolation would make him more compliant to him. The young man, however, was outraged by Bagoas' lawless conduct and made it clear that he was going to punish the perpetrator of these crimes, whereupon Bagoas struck before he could implement his plans, murdering Arses, along with his children, when he had been king for two years.

[5] The royal house was now without an heir and there was no descendant to succeed to power, and so Bagoas picked out one of the courtiers, Darius by name, and helped him gain the throne. Darius was the son of Oarsanes, who

was himself the son of Ostanes, and Ostanes was the brother of Artaxerxes,[1] a former king of the Persians.

[6] There was a curious incident involving Bagoas that is worth recording. With his usual bloodthirstiness he attempted to murder Darius with poison. Information concerning the plot reached the king, who issued an invitation to Bagoas on some pretext of sociability. He then gave him the cup and obliged him to drink the poison.

6 Darius was considered fit to rule because of his reputation for surpassing all Persians in courage. Once, when King Artaxerxes was at war with the Cadusians, one of the Cadusians, who was noted for strength and courage, issued a challenge to single combat to any of the Persians willing to accept. Nobody dared take up the challenge apart from Darius, who alone faced the danger and killed the challenger, for which he was honoured by the king with sumptuous gifts and gained amongst the Persians unrivalled prominence for his courage. [2] It was on account of this brave showing that he was considered worthy of the throne, and he took power about the time that Alexander succeeded to his kingdom on the death of Philip.

1(b)   Justin 10.3.1–6

The kingdom now passed to Ochus who, fearing a similar conspiracy, filled the palace with his kinsmen's blood and with the slaughter of his most prominent citizens. Nothing moved him to compassion: not family ties, not sex, not age – evidently he meant to appear more guilty than his murderous brothers. [2] After thus purifying his kingdom, as it were, he made war on the Cadusians. [3] In this campaign, one of the enemy issued a challenge to single combat and a certain Codomannus[2] went forward to face him, cheered on by the whole army. The Persian dispatched his adversary and restored to his countrymen both the victory and their glorious reputation which they had almost lost. [4] For this noble feat Codomannus was made satrap of Armenia. [5] Then, some time later, King Ochus died, and because the memory of Codomannus' exploit of old still lived on he was appointed king by the people and given the name Darius so that his royal status would be complete. [6] He fought a protracted war against Alexander the Great with varying success and great courage but, finally, defeated by Alexander, and murdered by his kinsmen, he died along with the Persian Empire.

1(c)   Quintus Curtius Rufus 10.5.23

Amid such reflections, Sisigambis was reminded of how her eighty brothers had all been butchered on the one day by the most barbarous of kings,

1   Artaxerxes II Mnemon. See Plutarch, *Artaxerxes* 1.1.
2   The origin and meaning of Codomannus are unknown. His real name was Artashata.

Ochus, and how the slaughter of so many sons was augmented by that of their father . . .

1(d)   *Valerius Maximus 9.2 ext 7*

More overt and loathsome was the brutality of the other Ochus, who had the surname Artaxerxes. He buried alive his sister, who was also his mother-in-law, placing her head downwards; and he speared to death his uncle along with more than a hundred of the man's sons and grandsons. It was not that he had been spurred to do this by any harm they had done him; rather he could see that they enjoyed the acclaim of the Persians for their integrity and courage.

1(e)   *Strabo,* Geography *15.3.24 C736*

The line of succession from Darius ended with Arses, whom the eunuch Bagoas murdered and instead placed on the throne another Darius who was not of royal blood. This Darius Alexander overthrew, and himself reigned for ten or eleven years. After that sovereignty over Asia was split between a plurality of successors and their descendants and then was lost. Persian rule lasted some 250 years. These days the Persians are a united body, but have kings that are subject to other kings – Macedonian earlier on, but Parthian now.

Persian Wealth and Displays of Opulence

2(a)   *Quintus Curtius Rufus 3.3.8–25*

It is a tradition among the Persians not to begin a march until after sunrise, and the day was already well advanced when the signal was given by trumpet from the king's tent. Above the tent, so that it would be visible to all, a representation of the sun gleamed in a crystal case. [9] The order of the line of march was as follows: in front, on silver altars, was carried the fire which the Persians called sacred and eternal. Next came the Magi, singing the traditional hymn, [10] and they were followed by 365 young men in scarlet cloaks, their number equalling the days of the year (for in fact the Persians divide the year into as many days as we do). [11] Then came the chariot consecrated to Jupiter, drawn by white horses, followed by a horse of extraordinary size, which the Persians called "the Sun's horse". [12] Those driving the horses were equipped with golden whips and white robes. Not far behind were ten carts amply decorated with relief carvings in gold and silver, [13] and these were followed by the cavalry of twelve nations of different cultures, variously armed. Next in line were the soldiers whom the Persians called the "Immortals", some 10,000 in number.[3] No other group were as splendidly bedecked in barbarian opulence: golden necklaces, clothes interwoven with gold, long-sleeved tunics actually studded with jewels. [14] After a short interval came the 15,000 men known as the "the king's kinsmen". This troop was dressed almost like women, its extravagance rather than its fine arms catching the eye. [15] The column next to these comprised the so-called *Doryphoroe*, the men who usually looked after the king's wardrobe,[4] and these preceded the royal chariot on which rode the king himself, towering above all others. [16] Both sides of the chariot were embossed with gold and silver representations of the gods; the yoke was studded with flashing gems and from it arose two golden images (each a cubit high) of Ninus and Belus respectively. Between these was a consecrated eagle made of gold and represented with wings outstretched.

[17] The sumptuous attire of the king was especially remarkable. His tunic was purple, interwoven with white at the center, and his gold-embroidered cloak bore a gilded motif of hawks attacking each other with their beaks. [18] From his gilded belt, which he wore in the style of a woman, he had slung his scimitar, its scabbard made of precious stone. [19] His royal diadem, called a "cidaris" by the Persians,[5] was encircled by a blue ribbon flecked with white. [20] 10,000 spearmen carrying lances chased with silver and tipped with gold followed the king's chariot, [21] and to the right and left he was attended by some 200 of his most noble relatives. At the end of the column came 30,000 foot-soldiers followed by 400 of the king's horses.

[22] Next, at a distance of one stade, came Sisygambis, the mother of Darius, drawn in a carriage, and in another came his wife. A troop of women attended the queens on horseback. [23] Then came the fifteen so-called *armamaxae*[6] in which rode the king's children, their nurses and a herd of eunuchs (who are not at all held in contempt by these peoples). [24] Next came the carriages of the 360 royal concubines, these also dressed in royal finery, and behind them 600 mules and 300 camels carried the king's money, with a guard of archers in attendance. [25] After this column rode the wives of the king's relatives and friends, and hordes of camp-followers and servants. At the end, to close up the rear, were the light-armed troops with their respective leaders.

3 So called because the strength of the unit was never allowed to drop below 10,000, whereas other units had nominal strengths but their actual numbers often fell short of these.
4 *Doryphoroe* are "spear-bearers" and the term is commonly used of a king's (or tyrant's) bodyguard. Looking after the king's wardrobe is certainly not one of their functions. The text may originally have read *dorophoroe* ("gift-bearers"); see Heckel (1992b).
5 It was actually the tiara, worn upright and surrounded by the diadem, that was called the cidaris or kitaris.
6 *Harmamaxai*. These were covered wagons used for transporting women and children. See Xenophon, *Anabasis* 1.2.16; Arrian 3.19.2; Plutarch, *Artaxerxes* 5.3 (Stateira, the wife of Artaxerxes II, won the approval of her subjects by raising the curtains of her carriage and making herself approachable).

Persian spoils deposited and captured in Damascus

Before the battle of Issus (late 333; see §VI.2c–f), Darius sent Cophen son of Artabazus to convey the bulk of the personal property, as well as the relatives, of prominent Persians to Damascus for safe-keeping; his own family, however, accompanied him to the battlefield. The vast sums of money and the numbers of individuals (including foreign ambassadors) who were sent to Damascus suggest that Darius envisioned a longer campaign in the west, using that city as a temporary base. After the Persian defeat at Issus, Damascus could not be saved and fell into Macedonian hands. Among the captives was Barsine, who was to become Alexander's mistress.

2(b) Diodorus Siculus 17.32.3

Darius wanted to lighten his force and so sent his pack-animals and non-combatants to Damascus in Syria. He then learned that Alexander had seized the high ground and, thinking he would not dare do battle in the plain, he took a short-cut and marched towards him.

2(c) Arrian 2.15.1

Alexander then learned that the moneys that Darius had sent off to Damascus had been captured, and that those Persians left in charge of them had also been taken, along with all the other royal appurtenances. He gave orders for Parmenion to take everything back to Damascus and put it under guard.

2(d) Quintus Curtius Rufus 3.13.12–16

Now they reached those who had been the first to flee. Several women were dragging their little children along with them as they went, and among these were the three unmarried daughters of Ochus,[7] who had been king before Darius. Once before a revolution had brought them down from the lofty station their father enjoyed, but now fortune was more cruelly aggravating their plight. [13] The same group contained the wife of Ochus, the daughter of Darius' brother, Oxathres,[8] and the wife of Artabazus, Darius' chief courtier, as well as Artabazus' son, whose name was Ilioneus. [14] The wife and son of Pharnabazus (the man whom Darius had given supreme command over the

---

7   One of them, Parysatis, later married Alexander in Susa in 324. See §VII.3b, below.
8   Her name was Amestris: she married Craterus, Dionysius of Heraclea Pontica, and finally Lysimachus.

coastal area) were also taken, as were the three daughters of Mentor, and the wife and son of the renowned general Memnon.[9] Scarcely any courtier's household was unaffected by the catastrophe. [15] Also captured were the Lacedaemonians and Athenians who had broken their oath of allegiance to Macedon and joined the Persians. By far the best known among the Athenians because of their pedigree and reputation were Aristogiton, Dropides and Iphicrates, and among the Lacedaemonian prisoners were Pasippus and Onomastorides, along with Onomas and Callicratides; these also enjoyed distinction in their home city.

[16] The coined money taken amounted to 2,600 talents, and the weight of wrought silver was equivalent to 500 talents. Thirty thousand men were also captured, together with 7,000 pack-animals and their burdens.

2(e) Justin 11.10.1–3

When, after this, Alexander looked upon the treasures and extravagant riches of Darius, he was overcome with awe at such splendour. [2] It was now that he first started to hold sumptuous banquets and splendid dinners. [3] Now, too, that he began to fall in love with the prisoner Barsine because of her beauty (by her he later had a son whom he named Hercules).

The Persian capitals: Babylon, Susa, and Persepolis

Alexander's reception in Babylon appears to have involved an old ritual of kingship and transfer of power: see Kuhrt (1987: 48–52). His treatment of Persepolis has received considerable attention: see Borza (1972), Balcer (1978), Hammond (1992b), Sancisi-Weerdenburg (1993), and Bloedow and Loube (1997). For the city and its treasury, see Cahill (1985); cf. Schmidt (1953–70).

2(f) Cleitarchus, FGrH 137 F11

Alexander the Great had Thais, the Attic *hetaira*, with him, did he not? Of her Cleitarchus says that she was responsible for the burning of the palace in Persepolis.

---

9   This wife is Barsine, who became Alexander's mistress (cf. §IV.2e, below). The daughter of Artabazus and his Rhodian wife, Barsine was the wife of Mentor and, after his death, of his brother Memnon. Curtius appears to have omitted her name deliberately, since, in the preceding chapter (3.12.21–3), he has just praised Alexander for his *continentia*. It would have stultified his argument if he had recorded how Alexander fell in love and had sexual relations with another captive: see Heckel (1994: 71–2). For Barsine's life, see Carney (2000a: 101–5, 149–50).

2(g)   Justin 11.14.6–10

It was with this engagement that he seized control of Asia, in the fifth year after his accession to the throne, [7] and his triumph was so complete that none dared rebel thereafter, while the Persians, after so many years of dominion, submissively accepted the yoke of enslavement. [8] The men were rewarded and granted thirty-four days' rest, after which Alexander made an inventory of the spoils and [9] discovered a further 40,000 talents in the city of Susa. [10] He also captured the Persian capital, Persepolis, a city which had enjoyed many years of renown and which was filled with spoils from all over the world (though these only came to light at its demise).

2(h)   Quintus Curtius Rufus 5.1.17–27

Moving on to Babylon Alexander was met by Mazaeus, who had taken refuge in the city after the battle. He came as a suppliant with his grown-up children to surrender himself and the city. Alexander was pleased at his coming, for besieging so well-fortified a city would have been an arduous task [18] and, besides, since he was an eminent man and a good soldier who had also won distinction in the recent battle, Mazaeus' example was likely to induce the others to surrender. Accordingly, Alexander gave him and his children a courteous welcome. [19] Nevertheless, he put himself at the head of his column, which he formed into a square, and ordered his men to advance into the city as if they were going into battle.

A large number of Babylonians had taken up a position on the walls, eager to have a view of their new king, but most went out to meet him, [20] including the man in charge of the citadel and royal treasury, Bagophanes. Not to be outdone by Mazaeus in paying his respects to Alexander, Bagophanes had carpeted the whole road with flowers and garlands and set up at intervals on both sides silver altars heaped not just with frankincense but with all manner of perfumes. [21] Following him were his gifts – herds of cattle and horses, and lions, too, and leopards, carried along in cages. [22] Next came the Magi chanting a song in their native fashion, and behind them were the Chaldaeans, then the Babylonians, represented not only by priests but also by musicians equipped with their national instrument. (The role of the latter was to sing the praises of the Persian kings, that of the Chaldaeans to reveal astronomical movements and regular seasonal changes.) [23] At the rear came the Babylonian cavalry, their equipment and that of the horses suggesting extravagance rather than majesty.

Surrounded by an armed guard, the king instructed the townspeople to follow at the rear of his infantry; then he entered the city on a chariot and went into the palace. The next day he made an inspection of Darius' furniture and all his treasure, [24] but it was the city itself, with its beauty and antiquity, that commanded the attention not only of the king but of all the

Macedonians. And with justification. Founded by Semiramis[10] (not, as most have believed, Belus, whose palace is still to be seen there), [25] its wall is constructed of small baked bricks and is cemented together with bitumen. The wall is thirty-two feet wide and it is said that two chariots meeting on it can safely pass each other. [26] Its height is fifty cubits and its towers stand ten feet higher again. The circumference of the whole work is 365 stades, each stade, according to the traditional account, being completed in a single day. The buildings of the city are not contiguous to the walls but are about a juger's width[11] from them, [27] and even the city area is not completely built up – the inhabited sector covers only 80 stades – nor do the buildings form a continuous mass, presumably because scattering them in different locations seemed safer. The rest of the land is sown and cultivated so that, in the event of attack from outside, the besieged could be supplied with produce from the soil of the city itself.[12]

2(i)   Arrian 3.16

From the battle Darius headed along the Armenian mountains straight for Media, and with him in his flight were the Bactrian cavalry, who had been deployed at his side in the battle, and a number of Persians (the king's relatives and a small number of the so-called *melophoroi*). [2] During the retreat he was further joined by some 2,000 foreign mercenaries led by Patron the Phocian and Glaucus the Aetolian. Darius' flight was headed for Media because he thought that, from the battle, Alexander would take the route for Susa and Babylon. The whole of that area was populated, and the road was not a difficult one for the pack-animals, while at the same time Babylon and Susa stood out clearly as the prizes of war. The route towards Media, however, was not an easy one for a large army to negotiate.

[3] Darius was not wrong in his judgment. On setting out from Arbela Alexander immediately took the road towards Babylon. He was not far away from Babylon, and was leading his forces along in battle order, when the Babylonians came to meet him in a body, accompanied by their priests and leaders. They brought gifts, and surrendered to him the city, with its citadel, and its wealth.

10   The legend of a voluptuous warrior queen attached itself to an otherwise obscure Assyrian queen, Sammu-ramat, who in the late ninth century BC may have been regent for her son, Adad-Nirari IV, in his minority. For her legend, see Capomacchia (1986).
11   The *iugerum* is normally an area measurement (28,000 sq. ft. or 240 ft. × 120 ft.). Curtius perhaps uses it as an equivalent to the Greek *plethron* which is both a measure of length (100 ft.) and of area.
12   The same practice was later to prove the salvation of Constantinople on numerous occasions.

[4] On entering Babylon, Alexander instructed its inhabitants to rebuild the temples that Xerxes had torn down, especially the temple of Bel, the god the Babylonians honour most of all. He designated Mazaeus satrap of Babylon, and Apollodorus[13] of Amphipolis commander of the troops the king was leaving there with Mazaeus; and Asclepiodorus, son of Philon, he made collector of taxes. [5] In addition, he sent Mithrenes to Armenia as satrap (it was he who surrendered to Alexander the citadel at Sardis). In Babylon, too, Alexander met the Chaldaeans. He followed all their advice regarding religious offerings in Babylon, and in particular sacrificed to Bel following the prescriptions they gave him.

[6] Alexander now set off for Susa, and en route was met by the son of the satrap of Susa and a messenger from Philoxenus (Alexander had sent Philoxenus to Susa right after the battle). In the letter from Philoxenus was the information that the people of Susa had surrendered the city to Alexander, and that all the city's wealth was secured there for him. [7] Alexander reached Susa after a 20-day journey from Babylon, and on entering the city he took possession of the treasury, which amounted to some 50,000 talents of silver, and the rest of the king's personal accoutrements. There was a lot more taken there, too, things that Xerxes had brought back from Greece, and in particular some bronze statues of Harmodius and Aristogeiton.[14] [8] These Alexander sent back to the Athenians, and the statues now stand in the Cerameicus in Athens on the way up to the acropolis, right across from the Metroon and not far from the altar of the Eudanemi. Anyone who has received initiation in the mysteries of the two goddesses knows the altar of Eudanemus, which lies on the plain.

[9] At Susa Alexander offered sacrifice in the traditional manner, and staged a torch-race and athletic competitions. Then, setting off into Persia, he left behind Abulites, a Persian, as satrap of Susiana, Mazarus (one of the *hetairoi*)[15] as garrison commander in the citadel of Susa, and Archelaus son of Theodorus as overall commander. He sent Menes to the coast to be governor of Syria, Phoenicia and Cilicia. [10] He gave Menes about 3,000 talents to transport to the coast, and he was to send to Antipater as much of that sum as Antipater required for the campaign against the Spartans. It was here, too, that Amyntas son of Andromenes reached the king with the troops he was bringing from Macedonia. [11] The cavalrymen amongst these Alexander allocated to his Companion cavalry, and the infantry he attached to the other regiments, basing the distribution on nationality. There had previously been no cavalry companies, but now he established the principle of there being two such units

13   He reappears in the accounts of Alexander's death (see §XI.1a).
14   The so-called *Tyrannicides*. Harmodius and Aristogeiton organized a conspiracy against the tyrant Hippias and his brother Hipparchus in 514. In the event, they managed only to kill Hipparchus, but the name of "Tyrant Slayers" nevertheless stuck.
15   Mazarus was probably the Persian garrison commander who was replaced. The name of the Macedonian commander who replaced him – probably Xenophilus (see Heckel 2002b) – has apparently dropped out of the MSS.

per squadron, and as company commanders he appointed those of his *het-airoi* judged outstanding in courage.

2(j)   Plutarch, Alexander 38

It transpired after this that, when Alexander was about to march against Darius, he put himself at the disposal of his companions for some drunken amusement, the kind of party at which women participated in the carousing, coming on a *komos* to join their lovers.[16] [2] Amongst these women the best known was Thais, an Athenian who was mistress of Ptolemy, the future king. She was partly paying Alexander elegant compliments and partly teasing him, but in her tipsy state she was eventually induced to make a statement that suited the character of her native state, but was too grand for her personal situation. [3] She said that she was that day receiving payment for all her hardships in her wanderings over Asia, basking in pleasure as she was now in the haughty palace of Persian kings. [4] But, she said, it would be even more pleasurable to go on a *komos* and torch the house of Xerxes (who burned down Athens), personally lighting the fire as King Alexander looked on. In this way, she added, word might spread amongst men that the women with Alexander inflicted greater punishment on the Persians on behalf of the Greeks than had all those famous admirals and generals of his. [5] At these words there were noisy cries of applause from the *hetairoi*, who competed with each other in urging on the king; and he, complying, jumped up and led the procession, wearing his wreath and carrying a torch. [6] The rest of them followed in a noisy *komos* and stood around the palace, while those other Macedonians who saw what was happening also came running up joyfully with torches. [7] These men were hoping that burning and destroying the palace were indications of Alexander's mind being set on affairs back home and of an intention not to remain abroad.

[8] Some authors say that this was how events unfolded, others that the deed was premeditated, but there is agreement that Alexander quickly regretted what he had done and ordered the fire extinguished.

2(k)   Quintus Curtius Rufus 5.6.19–7.11

On the thirtieth day after setting out from Persepolis, Alexander returned to it, [20] and then awarded his friends and the other men gifts proportionate to

---

16   The *komos* was a regular feature of Greek (and subsequently Roman) social life and literature. After a dinner-party, young men would sometimes take to the streets, still wearing the garland that they wore at the dinner and carrying a torch to light their way. In a noisy group, they would make for the house of a mistress or a favorite boy, or sometimes another dinner-party (like Alcibiades in Plato's *Symposium*). The disreputable nature of the scene here is underlined by the fact that it is women who are on the *komos* coming to *their* lovers. Alexander's subsequent use of garland and torch in this passage is also to be explained by this Greek custom.

their individual merit, distributing virtually everything he had taken in the city.

7 Alexander had some great natural gifts: a noble disposition surpassing that of all other monarchs; resolution in the face of danger; speed in undertaking and completing projects; integrity in dealing with those who surrendered and mercy towards prisoners; restraint even in those pleasures which are generally acceptable and widely indulged. But all these were marred by his inexcusable fondness for drink. [2] At the very time that his enemy and rival for imperial power was preparing to resume hostilities, and when the conquered nations, only recently subdued, still had scant respect for his authority, he was attending day-time drinking parties at which women were present – not, indeed, such women as it was a crime to violate, but courtesans who had been leading disreputable lives with the soldiers.

[3] One of the latter was Thais. She too had had too much to drink, when she claimed that, if Alexander gave the order to burn the Persian palace, he would earn the deepest gratitude among all the Greeks. This was what the people whose cities the Persians had destroyed were expecting, she said. [4] As the drunken whore gave her opinion on a matter of extreme importance, one or two who were themselves the worse for drink agreed with her. The king, too, was enthusiastic rather than acquiescent. "Why do we not avenge Greece, then, and put the city to the torch?" he asked.

[5] They were all excited by the wine, and so they got up, when drunk, to burn the city which they had spared when under arms. Alexander took the lead, setting fire to the palace, to be followed by his drinking companions, his attendants and the courtesans. Large sections of the palace had been made of cedar, so they quickly took flame and spread the conflagration over a large area. [6] The army, encamped not far from the city, caught sight of the fire and, thinking it accidental, came running in a body to help. [7] But when they reached the palace portico, they saw their king himself still piling on torchwood, so they dropped the water they had brought and began throwing dry wood into the blaze themselves.

[8] Such was the end of the palace that had ruled all the East. From it in bygone days law had been sought by so many nations; it had been the birthplace of so many kings; it had struck unparalleled terror into the land of Greece, constructing a fleet of 1,000 ships and an army that flooded Europe after bridging the sea and digging through mountains to make a marine canal.[17] [9] Not even in the long period following its destruction did it rise again; the Macedonian kings took up residence in other cities, which are now occupied by the Parthians. Of Persepolis there would be no trace were its location not marked by the Araxes. This had flowed close to the walls, and according to people living nearby – though it is a matter of belief rather than knowledge – the city was 20 stades from it.

17   The canal was dug at Sane, on the Athos peninsula. Traces of this are still visible at the modern site of Nea Roda. Xerxes' invasion occurred in 480–479, although the king himself returned to Persia after the Greek naval victory at Salamis in the summer of 480.

[10] The Macedonians were ashamed that a city of such distinction had been destroyed by their king during a drunken orgy, so the whole episode was given a serious explanation and they convinced themselves that this was the most appropriate method of destruction for it. [11] As for Alexander, it is generally agreed that, when sleep had brought him back to his senses after his drunken bout, he regretted his actions and said that the Persians would have suffered a more grievous punishment at the hands of the Greeks had they been forced to see him on Xerxes' throne and in his palace.

2(l)   Arrian 3.18.11–12

To the satrapy of Persis Alexander appointed Phrasaortes, son of Rheomithres, but he also burned down the palace of Persepolis. Parmenion advised the king to let the palace stand. Apart from anything else, he said, it was not a good thing to destroy what was now his own property. Also, this was not the way to win the allegiance of the Asians, who would suppose that his intention was not to maintain a stable rule over Asia, but simply to conquer and move on. [12] Alexander, however, insisted that he wished to punish the Persians for razing Athens to the ground and burning down its temples during their invasion of Greece, and that he was also exacting retribution for all the other wrongs they had done the Greeks. But in my opinion Alexander was not wise in doing this, and this was no punishment for Persians who had lived long before.

2(m)   Itinerary of Alexander 29

Alexander took possession of the treasures of Cyrus, and of Xerxes, too, which had been laid up there as though in complete security; he took also all the pleasances of the court. Nevertheless the palace he destroyed by fire out of hatred for the injury inflicted on Greece by Xerxes; as for the pleasure gardens, he destroyed these also, despite their now being his own. Evidently his motive was to repay, for his own part, the damage, and exact the deserved recompense, of the destruction which Xerxes had visited on the Greeks.

Death of Darius III

For the most part, Darius III is not a sympathetic character: there was at least one strand of the tradition that depicted him as cowardly and susceptible to the bad advice of his courtiers; the courage of his young son, Ochus, and the fighting spirit of his brother Oxathres (cf. later on the example of Porus at the Hydaspes, §VI.2j–l below) form a sharp contrast. On Darius in general, see Seibert (1987), Nylander (1993), and Badian (2000a). The passages that follow recount the last days of a ruler betrayed by his courtiers and generals, and the punishment inflicted upon the regicide Bessus, first by the Persians who betrayed him and then by Alexander.

Arrest and murder of Darius

3(a)   *Quintus Curtius Rufus 5.13.15–25*

Bessus and his fellow-conspirators came to Darius' wagon and started urging him to mount a horse and flee to escape his enemy. [16] Darius, however, declared that the gods had come to avenge him and, calling for Alexander's protection, refused to go along with the traitors. At this they were furious. They hurled their spears at the king and left him there, run through many times. [17] They also maimed his animals to prevent them advancing any further, and killed the two slaves accompanying the king. [18] After this crime, to disperse the traces of their flight, Nabarzanes made for Hyrcania and Bessus, with a small retinue of cavalry, for Bactria. Deprived of their leaders, the barbarians scattered wherever hope or panic directed them, and a mere 500 cavalry remained massed together, still unsure whether resistance or flight was the better idea. [19] When Alexander discovered that his enemy was terrified, he sent Nicanor on with some cavalrymen to check their flight and he himself followed with the rest. Some 3,000 who offered resistance were cut down and the others were now being herded along like cattle, but without injury since the king's orders were to avoid bloodshed. [20] None of the captives was able to identify Darius' cart and, though the wagons were individually searched as the Macedonians overtook them, there was no indication of where the king had fled. [21] As Alexander sped along, barely 3,000 of the cavalry kept up with him, but into the hands of those following him at a slower pace fell whole columns of fleeing Persians. [22] It is an incredible fact that the captives outnumbered their captors – so completely had their misfortune deprived these terrified men of their senses that they had no clear perception of the enemy's small numbers and their own multitude.

[23] Meanwhile, since they lacked a driver, the animals pulling Darius had left the main road and after wandering around for four stades had come to a stop in a certain valley, exhausted as much by the heat as by their wounds. [24] There was a spring close by. This had been pointed out to the Macedonian Polystratus by people who knew the area, and he now came to it because he was tormented with thirst. While he drank the water from his helmet, he caught sight of the spears stuck in the bodies of the dying animals [25] and, surprised at their being wounded rather than driven off, . . . [was shocked by the cries] of a man only half alive . . .[18]

3(b)   *Justin 11.15.1–15*

Meanwhile, in the Parthian village of Thara, Darius was bound in shackles and chains of gold by his own kinsmen, who wished to conciliate the victor.

---

18   The text breaks off at this point and we must turn to Justin (below) for the remainder of the story.

[2] It was, I suppose, the decision of the immortal gods that the Persian Empire should come to an end in the land of those destined to succeed to it![19] [3] Moving at a rapid pace, Alexander arrived there the following day, only to discover that Darius had been removed at night in a covered carriage. [4] Accordingly, he told the main body to follow behind and pressed on after the fugitive with 6,000 cavalry, fighting many hazardous battles on the way. [5] After covering many miles and finding no trace of Darius, he gave the horses a breathing space, and it was then that one of his men, making for a nearby spring, came upon Darius in his carriage. The king had been stabbed several times but was still breathing. [6] A captive was brought and from his speech Darius recognized him to be a fellow-countryman. Darius said that this at least brought him some consolation in his present misfortune since he would now be talking to someone who would understand him, and not uttering his final words in vain. [7] He then ordered that the following message be taken to Alexander: that though he had done the Macedonian no favours he now died indebted to him for the greatest services, since in the case of his mother and children he had found Alexander's character to be that of a king rather than an enemy, and that he had been luckier in the enemy fate had allotted him than he had been in his relatives and kinsmen. [8] For, Darius explained, his wife and children had been granted their lives by that enemy, whereas he himself had now been deprived of his by his relatives, men to whom he had granted both their lives and their kingdoms. [9] And for this act they would now receive the recompense which Alexander as victor decided to give them. [10] To Alexander he showed his gratitude in the only manner a dying man could, by his prayers to the gods above and below, and to the patron deities of royalty, that he achieve the conquest and dominion of the whole world. [11] For himself he asked a favour that was just and easily granted – burial. [12] As for revenge, the reason for exacting it was no longer just Darius; now it was a question of precedent and the common cause of all kings – and for Alexander to ignore this would be dishonourable as well as dangerous, since it was a matter both of his sense of justice, on the one hand, and expediency, on the other. [13] To which end he gave the soldier his right hand, as the supreme guarantee of the kingly trust that he was to take to Alexander. He then stretched out his hand and died. [14] This was reported to Alexander and when he saw the body he wept at the thought of Darius' succumbing to a death so unworthy of his exalted position. [15] He ordered that the body be given a royal burial and his remains set in the tombs of his ancestors.

19 In the middle of the third century BC people known as the Parni settled in what was the Persian satrapy of Parthia and came to be known as the Parthians. They played no small part in the decline of the Seleucid kingdom and soon clashed with Rome. They were a factor in Middle Eastern politics until the mid-third century AD. See Colledge (1967).

3(c)   Itinerary of Alexander 30

Alexander pressed on in pursuit, by now a mere day's march behind, only to learn from a deserter that Darius' companions had wearied of the latter's flight and, as if to ingratiate themselves with the one who was stronger, were holding Darius in irons, while Bessus (a courtier of the king) had assumed his insignia. Alexander's desire lent him wings and the hope of achieving that desire fired him to use an all-too-rough short-cut on his way (the toil which this involved was the price he paid for shortening the delay); he took Bessus by surprise. The latter showed fight and his troops were scattered with heavy loss, being forcibly dislodged; but Bessus himself took refuge in flight and slipped away. At the site of the battle Alexander's men found Darius the king slain by his own followers, who had then fled along with Bessus. Therefore Alexander ordered that Darius' body, at least, be treated with the honour befitting a king, and be laid to rest in the tombs of his forebears.

Arrest and punishment of Bessus

3(d)   Itinerary of Alexander 34

No one dared resist their passage [of the Oxus River]; indeed, as they proceeded through a terrain now more level, word came that Bessus had been arrested by his own men in that district and was being held prisoner by way of an indemnity on behalf of his fellow-fugitives for the guilt they all shared. This made Alexander travel with more patience than he was wont; but he sent forward Ptolemy son of Lagus to take up Bessus and bring him to his presence. There was no delay; Bessus was brought, in chains, and with that Alexander's wrath was extinguished like a flame. He reproached Bessus for his slavish and wicked treachery and had him flogged on that account, then ordered him kept in custody for the present for full punishment to be inflicted in due time. As for the rest of Bessus' party, he granted them a generous amnesty.

3(e)   Diodorus Siculus 17.83.7–9

After declaring himself king, Bessus sacrificed to the gods and then invited his friends to the sacrificial feast. There, during the drinking, he had words with one of his companions whose name was Bagodaras. As feelings became more heated, Bessus lost his temper and was all for putting Bagodaras to death, abandoning the idea only at his friends' urging. [8] Bagodaras, however, sought to escape this perilous situation and fled to Alexander during the night. When he was granted a safe haven and promised gifts by Alexander, the most important of Bessus' officers were also won over, and these put their heads together, seized Bessus and brought him to Alexander. [9] The king honoured the men with fine gifts and delivered Bessus to Darius' brother and his other relatives for punishment. After subjecting him to all manner of abuse and torture, these chopped his body into little bits and scattered the pieces.

3(f)   Metz Epitome 5–6

When Spitamenes, who was Bessus' closest associate, heard that Alexander was coming, he called together Dataphernes, Catanes and Darius' other kinsmen and, declaring to them that the time had come to avenge Darius and work their way into Alexander's friendship, urged them to arrest Bessus so they could surrender him to Alexander at the earliest opportunity. It took little effort or time to persuade them, for every day they missed Darius more and their animosity towards Bessus increased. [6] So Spitamenes, because he was very close to Bessus, easily got rid of the guards from the tent; they all then entered in a body, tied Bessus up, stripped him of his royal trappings and set out for Alexander. When he caught sight of them arriving unexpectedly with Bessus in chains, Alexander was absolutely delighted and he dismissed those who had brought him only after showering them with praise and gifts.

3(g)   Metz Epitome 14

Then Alexander led the army through the territory of Sogdiana, from which he advanced into Bactria. Here he had Bessus brought to him, hung him up and stoned him to death in Persian fashion. Then, eleven days later, he reached and crossed the river Ochus, after which he came to the river Oxus.

3(h)   Plutarch, Alexander 43.6

When he found Bessus later on, Alexander had him dismembered. He had part of Bessus' body tied to each of two straight trees that were bent over to the same point. Then he released the two, and the force as each tree sprang back to its position took with it the part of the body attached to it.

3(i)   Quintus Curtius Rufus 7.5.36, 40–1, 43

Alexander advanced from there to the river Tanais,[20] where Bessus was brought to him, not only in irons but entirely stripped of his clothes.

---

20   The Iaxartes (modern Syr-darya).

Spitamenes led him with a chain around his neck, a sight that afforded much pleasure to the barbarians as to the Macedonians . . .

[40] Alexander told Darius' brother Oxathres (who was one of his body-guards) to approach him, and had Bessus put in his charge. Bessus was to be hung on a cross, his ears and nose cut off, and the barbarians were to shoot arrows into him and also protect the body from the carrion birds. [41] Oxathres promised to take care of everything but added that the birds could be kept off only by Catanes, whose superb marksmanship Oxathres wished to put on display. Catanes, in fact, was so accurate at hitting what he aimed at that he could pick off birds . . . [43] Gifts were then awarded by Alexander to those responsible for bringing in Bessus, but his execution was postponed so that he could be killed in the very spot where he had himself murdered Darius.

3(j)   Arrian 3.29.7–30.5

Alexander sent Ptolemy son of Lagus ahead with orders to march speedily against Spitamenes and Dataphernes. Ptolemy was to take with him three squadrons of the cavalry of the Companions, all the mounted javelin-throwers, the battalion of Philotas, one chiliarchy of hypaspists, all the Agrianes and half the bowmen. Following his orders, he covered in four what was usually a ten days' march and reached the camp where Spitamenes and his barbarians had bivouacked the day before.

30 There Ptolemy learned that Spitamenes and Dataphernes were not firmly committed to the surrender of Bessus. Accordingly, he left his infantry with orders to follow him in formation and, riding ahead himself with the cavalry, came to a village where Bessus was located with only a few of his sol-diers – [2] Spitamenes and his men had already departed, ashamed to be per-sonally involved in the surrender of Bessus. Ptolemy encircled the village with his cavalry (there was a wall of some kind around it, and gates in the wall), and sent a herald to report to the barbarians in the village that, they would be released unharmed if they surrendered Bessus to him. These then let Ptolemy's troops into the village, [3] and Ptolemy seized Bessus and left again.

After this Ptolemy sent ahead to Alexander to ask about the manner in which he was to bring Bessus into the king's sight. Alexander instructed him to fasten the man, naked, in a wooden collar, and bring him like that, setting him on the right-hand side of the road along which Alexander and the army would be coming. Ptolemy did as he was instructed.

[4] When Alexander caught sight of Bessus, he halted his chariot and asked him why he had seized Darius in the first place and taken him around in irons, and later murdered him – Darius was his king and at the same time his relative and benefactor. Bessus replied that he was not alone in deciding on this course of action; he had taken it in conjunction with the men who were Darius' courtiers at the time, in order to be spared punishment by Alexander. [5] Alexander ordered him to be flogged for this, and further instructed a herald

to call out during the punishment those very acts for which Alexander reproached Bessus when he questioned him. After being tortured in this manner Bessus was sent to Bactra for execution.

Such is Ptolemy's version of Bessus, but Aristobulus says that it was Spitamenes' and Dataphernes' men who brought Bessus to Ptolemy and they who fastened him naked in a wooden collar and delivered him to Alexander.

V Alexander and the Greeks

The Panhellenic Crusade

Xenophon attributed Panhellenic sentiments to both Callicratidas (Xenophon, *Hellenica* 1.6.1–7) and Agesilaus (*Hellenica* 3.4) and there must surely have been many in the Greek world who regarded the Persians as the "common enemy of the Greeks" (cf. Demosthenes 14.3). Isocrates in the *Panegyricus* and *Philip* preached a Panhellenic war of vengeance on Persia, and it appears that both Philip and Alexander were happy to make use of such propaganda to give some purpose to the newly-created League of Corinth. See Flower (2000).

1(a) Aelian, Varia Historia *13.11*

It has been reported to me that it was the rhetorician Isocrates who was responsible for the servitude that the Macedonians imposed on the Persians. For the fame of the speech *Panegyricus*, which Isocrates delivered to the Greeks, spread to Macedonia, and it was this that first stirred Philip's animosity towards Asia. When Philip died, the speech provided the incentive for his son Alexander, heir to his father's estate, to keep up Philip's momentum.

1(b) Arrian 1.16.7

Alexander sent to Athens three hundred full suits of Persian armour as a votive offering to Athena on the Acropolis, with orders for the following inscription to accompany them:

> An offering from Alexander, son of Philip, and the Greeks, apart from the Spartans, taken from the barbarians who live in Asia.

1(c)   Plutarch, Alexander 16.17–18

To make the Greeks partners in his victory, Alexander sent the Athenians a special gift of three hundred shields taken from the enemy and, for the Greeks in general, had a very proud inscription carved on the other spoils: [18] "An offering from Alexander, son of Philip, and the Greeks, apart from the Spartans, taken from the barbarians who live in Asia."

Alexander's Punishment of those Greeks who Opposed Him

Thebes

Alexander's destruction of Thebes in 335 was an act of terror, intended as a warning to any other Greek state that might wish to rebel against Macedon. The Thebans had also had a long history of "medism" (i.e., collaboration with the Persians) and they were at this time calling upon their fellow Greeks to throw off the Macedonian yoke with the help of the Great King of Persia (Diodorus Siculus 17.9.5). Since Thebes was a city with a long and distinguished history, and the actions of the Macedonians were excessively brutal, it was convenient to argue that the decision was made by a Greek council, which included many bitter enemies of the Thebans. This is, in fact, a prominent feature of all accounts. There may be some truth in it, but the final decision was Alexander's, and there may have been other considerations. Thebes had intervened in Macedonian affairs during the reigns of Alexander II, Ptolemy of Alorus, and Perdiccas III, during some of which time Alexander's father, Philip, had been a hostage in the city.

2(a)   Justin 11.3.6–4.8

Next he directed the army towards Thebes, intending to show the same mercy if he met with similar contrition. [7] But the Thebans resorted to arms rather than entreaties or appeals, and so after their defeat they were subjected to all the terrible punishments associated with a humiliating capitulation. [8] When the destruction of the city was being discussed in council, the Phocians, the Plataeans, the Thespians and the Orchomenians,[1] Alexander's allies who now shared his victory, recalled the devastation of their own cities and the ruthlessness of the Thebans, [9] reproaching them also with their past as well as

---

1   The Phocians were traditional enemies of Thebes, and they had been engaged in a bitter struggle during the Sacred War; the last three were Boeotian states, which had been dominated by Thebes through the Boeotian League. This league had voted, in the summer of 364, to raze the city of Orchomenus after killing its adult males and selling its women and children into slavery (Diodorus Siculus 15.79.3–6). See Buck (1994), Buckler (1980), and Munn (1997).

their present support of Persia against the independence of Greece. [10] This, they said, had made Thebes an abomination to all the Greek peoples, which was obvious from the fact that the Greeks had one and all taken a solemn oath to destroy the city once the Persians were defeated. [11] They also added the tales of earlier Theban wickedness – the material with which they had filled all their plays – in order to foment hatred against them not only for their treachery in the present but also for their infamies in the past.

4   Then one of the captives, Cleadas, was given permission to speak. The Thebans had not defected from the king, he said – for they had been told he was dead – but from the king's heirs. [2] Whatever wrong they had done must be blamed on their gullibility, not disloyalty, and for this they had already paid a heavy price with the loss of their young warriors. [3] All that was left to them now was an enfeebled and harmless population of old men and women, who had themselves been subjected to violence and outrage more bitter than anything they had ever experienced. [4] Their entreaties, he continued, were no longer for their fellow-citizens, of whom so few remained, but for the harmless soil of their fatherland and for a city which had given birth not only to men but to gods as well. [5] Cleadas even appealed to the king's personal devotion to Hercules, who was born in their city and from whom the clan of the Aeacidae traced its descent, and to the fact that his father Philip had spent his boyhood in Thebes. [6] He asked Alexander to spare a city which worshipped his ancestors born within it as gods and which had also witnessed the upbringing of the most eminent of kings. [7] But anger prevailed over entreaties. The city was destroyed, its lands divided among the victors, [8] and the prisoners were auctioned off, their price being pushed up not by the bidders' desire to make a bargain, but by the intensity of the hatred for an enemy.

2(b)   Plutarch, Alexander 11.1–12

And so, at the age of twenty, Alexander took over the realm, which was in every quarter fraught with bitter jealousies, and deadly enmities and dangers. [2] For the barbarian tribes who were his neighbours would not accept their subjugation and yearned for the independent kingdoms of their ancestors. In addition, although Philip had defeated Greece in armed conflict, he had not had sufficient time to completely subdue and tame her. All he had done, in fact, was bring change and confusion and then, with people unused to the new circumstances, leave behind him a state of restlessness and turmoil.

[3] The Macedonians were fearful of this predicament and felt Alexander should completely abandon the Greek situation and apply no further pressure there. They thought he should use gentle means to bring back into line the barbarians who had defected, and use conciliation to check unrest at its first appearance. [4] Alexander, however, started from a position diametrically opposed to this; he set out to establish security and safeguards for his realm

with action and a heroic spirit, assuming that all would descend upon him if he were seen to waver in his resolve. [5] The uprisings amongst the barbarians and the wars in those areas he terminated with a swift military incursion that went as far as the Ister,[2] where in a mighty battle he defeated Syrmus, king of the Triballians. [6] Then, when told of the defection of the Thebans and the support voiced for them by the Athenians, he immediately led his forces through Thermopylae. Demosthenes, he said, had called him a child while he was amongst the Illyrians and Triballians, and a young whippersnapper when he was in Thessaly; and now he wanted to look like a man before the walls of Athens.

[7] Approaching Thebes, Alexander still gave its people the chance to show contrition for what had been done; he demanded only the surrender of Phoenix and Prothytes, and he proclaimed that any who went over to him would be pardoned. [8] However, the Thebans in turn demanded that Alexander surrender to them Philotas and Antipater[3] and proclaimed that those wishing to join in the liberation of Greece should stand at their side. At this point the king sent his Macedonians into combat. [9] The Theban defence was conducted with courage and spirit, above and beyond their actual strength, in a struggle against an enemy that outnumbered them many times over. [10] But when the Macedonian garrison left the Cadmea and also fell on them from behind, most of their men found themselves surrounded and went down fighting. The city was then taken, sacked and razed to the ground. [11] For the most part this measure was prompted by Alexander's expectation that the Greeks would be shocked by a disaster of such proportions and thus frightened into inaction. But the king also prided himself on responding to the complaints from his allies, for both the Phocians and the Plataeans had condemned the conduct of the Thebans. [12] Making an exception of priests, all those with ties of hospitality to the Macedonians, the descendants of Pindar, and people who had opposed the decision to revolt, he sold them all into slavery, some 30,000 souls. The number of those who died there was in excess of 6,000.

2(c)   Arrian 1.9.9–10

Alexander turned over the decision of what was to be done with Thebes to the allies who participated in the military action. These decided to secure the Cadmea with a garrison, but to raze the city to the ground and distribute amongst the allies whatever lands were not sacred. Women and children, and any surviving Theban men, they would sell into slavery, with the exception

---

2   The Danube.
3   These names are very common in Macedonia and, in this case, do not refer to well-known individuals. Diodorus Siculus 17.8.7 names a certain Philotas (not the famous son of Parmenion) as *phrourarchos* ("garrison commander") of the Cadmea; Antipater may have been one of his subordinates; cf. Hamilton (1969: 30).

of priests and priestesses, and any people who had enjoyed ties of hospital-ity with Philip or Alexander, or had been *proxenoi* of the Macedonians. [10] They say Alexander preserved the house of the poet Pindar, as well as his descendants, because of his veneration of for Pindar.

2(d)   Diodorus Siculus 17.14.1–4

The Theban dead numbered more than 6,000, and the men taken prisoner upwards of 30,000. The amount of money that was taken as plunder was beyond belief.

The king saw to the burial of the more than 500 Macedonian dead. He then convened the delegates of the Greeks and put before their full council the question of how they should deal with the city of Thebes. [2] When the delib-erations began, men who were ill-disposed towards the Thebans proceeded to advocate subjecting them to most cruel punishment, and pointed out that they had espoused the barbarian cause against the Greeks. They observed that in the time of Xerxes the Thebans had allied themselves with Persia and actu-ally fought against Greece, and that they were the only Greek people to be honoured as benefactors by the Persian kings, with the ambassadors from Thebes assigned privileged seating before the kings. [3] By recounting numer-ous other instances of this sort they inflamed the feelings of the delegates against the Thebans, and these eventually voted to demolish the city, to sell the prisoners of war, to have the Theban exiles liable to arrest throughout Greece, and permit no Greek to harbour a Theban. [4] In conformity with the will of the council, the king demolished the city and thereby instilled terri-ble fear in those of the Greeks liable to defect. He sold off the prisoners of war and by that accumulated 440 talents of silver.

2(e)   Cleitarchus
(FGrH 137 F1 = Athenaeus 4.148d–f)

In his detailed account of the matter in the first book of his *History of Alexan-der* Cleitarchus also says that the Thebans' entire wealth was brought to light after the destruction of the city by Alexander, and it amounted to 440 talents.

Greek mercenaries who fought against Macedon

2(f)   Arrian 1.16.6

The mercenaries that he took prisoner, however, he clapped in irons and shipped off to Macedonia for forced labour. His reasoning was that they, as Greeks, had infringed an accord made in common by the Greeks by fighting for the barbarians against Greece.

2(g)   Arrian 1.29.5–6

An Athenian deputation also reached Alexander at Gordium. Its members requested that he release into their custody the Athenian prisoners of war who had been captured at the River Granicus while fighting for the Persians and who were at that moment being kept in irons in Macedonia along with the two thousand captives. [6] In fact, the ambassadors left disappointed for the moment with regard to the Athenian prisoners, for Alexander did not consider it a safe move, while a state of war still existed with Persia, to relax his intimidation of Greeks who did not balk at fighting for the barbarians against Greece. When the time was right, he replied, they could send another deputation on the prisoners' behalf.

2(h)   Arrian 3.6.1

At Tyre Alexander made a second sacrifice to Heracles, and staged athletic and music contests. It was there that the *Paralus*[4] reached him from Athens. It brought Diophantus and Achilles as ambassadors, but the entire crew of the *Paralus* also served as part of the embassy with them. In fact, these obtained the goals for which they were sent, and in particular Alexander released to the Athenians those Athenian prisoners of war taken at the Granicus.

Greek Ambassadors to the Great King Captured by Alexander

Despite the formation of the League of Corinth, the punishment of Thebes, and Alexander's insistence that Greeks who fought as mercenaries for the Great King were traitors to the Greek cause, Athens, Sparta, and Thebes continued to send ambassadors to the Persian king. Alexander's treatment of such envoys as fell into his hands varied depending on their cities of origin and the progress of the campaign. The names of certain ambassadors vary from source to source and there is some confusion over when and where they were captured. See Atkinson (1980: 462–5).

3(a)   Quintus Curtius Rufus 3.13.15

Also captured[5] were the Lacedaemonians and Athenians who had broken their oath of allegiance to Macedon and joined the Persians. By far the best known among the Athenians because of their pedigree and reputation were Aristogiton, Dropides and Iphicrates, and among the Lacedaemonian prisoners

---

4   One of the Athenian state ships sent out for special ambassadorial missions.
5   At Damascus.

were Pasippus and Onomastorides, along with Onomas and Callicratides; these also enjoyed distinction in their home city.

3(b)   Arrian 2.15.2–3

The king also learned of the capture of the envoys who had reached Darius before the battle,[6] and these he ordered to be sent to him. The envoys were the Spartan Euthycles; Thessaliscus, son of Ismenias, and the Olympic victor Dionysodorus both Thebans; and the Athenian Iphicrates, son of the general Iphicrates. [3] When these men came to Alexander, he immediately turned loose Thessaliscus and Dionysodorus, Thebans though they were. He did this partly because he felt sorry for the Thebans, and partly because the men's actions struck him as pardonable – their country had been enslaved by Macedon, and they were merely trying to find any help they could for them-selves and their homeland from the Persians and Darius. He was fair in his estimate of both men, but in private he said that he was releasing Thessalis-cus out of respect for his family – Thessaliscus being a member of the Theban nobility – and Dionysodorus because of his victory in the Olympic games. Because of his friendly relations with the city of Athens, and his regard for the reputation of Iphicrates' father, he kept Iphicrates in his retinue, showing him the utmost respect, and on his death from an illness sent his bones back to his relatives in Athens. Euthycles he initially kept under house arrest. He was a Spartan and his city was openly hostile to Alexander at that time; and the king could find no adequate justification for condoning his actions as a private citizen. Later on, however, as Alexander's successes mounted, he released Euthycles as well.

3(c)   Plutarch, Alexander 40.3

Alexander accordingly put even greater effort into his military campaigns and hunting, exposing himself to hardships and danger, to the point that a Spartan ambassador who was with him when he brought down a huge lion observed: "That was good fight you put up against the lion, Alexander, to see which of you would be king."

3(d)   Arrian 3.24.4

Alexander now returned to the camp from which he had begun his expedi-tion into the land of the Mardians. Here he found the Greek mercenaries already arrived in the camp, along with Spartan representatives who were on

---

6 Of Issus.

a diplomatic mission to King Darius: Callistratidas, Pausippus, Monimus and Onomas, and with them Dropides from Athens. These Alexander arrested and imprisoned, but the envoys from Sinope he released. The Sinopeans were not members of the Greek League but subject to the Persians, and Alexander felt there was nothing untoward about their sending representatives to their king.

Resistance to Alexander in his Absence

For more on resistance to Alexander, see Bosworth (1988a: 187–228) and Heckel (1997); for the anti-Macedonian party in the Peloponnese, see McQueen (1978).

Agis III of Sparta

The Spartans had refused to join Philip's League of Corinth in 337; nor did they reconsider when Alexander renewed the alliance (note Alexander's dedication of the spoils after the Granicus, which pointedly excluded the Lacedaemonians: §V.1b–c, above). Nevertheless, their king, Agis III, intrigued with the Persian commanders in Asia Minor and in 331 attacked the Macedonian forces at Megalopolis. After winning a minor victory over the Macedonian general, Corrhagus, he was defeated and killed by a larger army led by Antipater. Although Alexander disparaged the event as a "war of mice" (see §V.4c, below), the activities in the Peloponnese had caused him considerable anxiety and affected his prosecution of the war against Darius III. For Agis' war and the thorny question of chronology, see Badian (1967a, 1994), Cawkwell (1969), Borza (1971), Lock (1972), and Bosworth (1988a: 198–204).

4(a)   Quintus Curtius Rufus 6.1.1–21

Agis threw himself into the thick of the fighting and, cutting down those putting up any determined resistance, drove most of the enemy before him. [2] The winning side now began to run and, until they brought their over-enthusiastic pursuers down to level ground, they were falling without striking back; but the moment they reached a position where they could make a stand they fought on equal terms. [3] Among all the Spartans their king was conspicuous not only for his fine physique and weapons but even more for his magnificent and unsurpassable courage. [4] He was under attack from all directions, both at long and short range. For a long time he kept up the fight on different sides, parrying missiles with his shield or avoiding them with an agile movement, until his thighs, transfixed by a spear and bleeding heavily, gave way as he fought. [5] His attendants placed him on his shield and swiftly carried him back to camp, scarcely able to bear the violent jarring of his wounds.

[6] The Lacedaemonians did not abandon the fight, however. As soon as they could gain a position which favoured them more than the enemy, they closed ranks and withstood the assault of the enemy line which came at them like a flood. [7] That there never was a more violent conflict is a matter of record: the armies of the two nations with the greatest military reputations were fighting an evenly matched battle. [8] The Spartans reflected on their prestige of old, the Macedonians on their prestige of the present, the former fighting for liberty and the latter for power, the Spartans lacking a leader and the Macedonians fighting space. [9] Moreover, the constant change of fortunes on that day alternately increased the confidence and anxieties of each side, as if Fortune deliberately kept even the clash between these men of supreme valour. [10] However, the narrow terrain to which the fighting had been confined would not permit a full-scale engagement of the two forces, so there were more spectators than combatants and those beyond the range of missiles shouted encouragement to their respective sides.

[11] Eventually the Spartan line began to tire, the men hardly able to hold their weapons which were slippery with sweat, and then to give ground. [12] When an enemy thrust made the Spartan retreat more pronounced, the victor started exerting pressure on his disordered foe and, swiftly covering all the ground previously occupied by the Spartans, started in pursuit of Agis. [13] The latter, seeing his men on the run and the enemy vanguard approaching, gave orders that he be put down. He tried his limbs to see if they could respond to his inner determination, [14] but found that they failed him. He sank to his knees, swiftly put on his helmet and, using his shield to cover his body, started brandishing his spear in his right hand, actually daring any of the enemy to strip the spoils from him as he lay there. [15] No one would risk hand-to-hand combat with him. They attacked him at long range with spears, which he flung back at his enemy until a lance lodged in his exposed chest. He pulled it from the wound, momentarily rested his bowed and failing head on his shield, and then collapsed dead upon his arms, blood and breath flowing from him together. [16] Five thousand three hundred Lacedaemonians fell, and no more than 1,000 Macedonians, but hardly anyone returned to camp unwounded.

The victory shattered the spirit not only of Sparta and her allies but of all who had kept a speculative eye on the war's fortunes. [17] Nor was Antipater unaware that the expression of those congratulating him belied their true feelings, but his desire to finish the war obliged him to tolerate such deception. Though pleased with the success of the campaign, he nonetheless feared an envious reaction because in his achievements he had exceeded the scope of a subordinate officer. [18] In fact, though Alexander wanted his enemies defeated, he actually expressed his displeasure that the victory had gone to Antipater, for he felt that anything redounding to another's credit detracted from his own. [19] Accordingly Antipater, being well acquainted with Alexander's vanity, did not presume to arrange the terms of the victory himself but left them to the discretion of the Greek council. [20] This only granted the Lacedaemonians permission to send ambassadors to the king, while the Tegeans, with the exception of the ringleaders, won pardon for their rebellion, and orders were issued for the Achaeans and Eleans to give 120 talents to the people of Megalopolis, whose city had been under siege from the rebels.

[21] So ended the war. It had started suddenly, but it was concluded before Darius' defeat by Alexander at Arbela.

4(b)   Justin 12.1.4–11

In the meantime, the king received despatches from Antipater in Macedonia containing news of the war against the Spartan king, Agis, in Greece, and of the war fought by Alexander, king of Epirus, in Italy, and also of the operations of his governor Zopyrion in Scythia. [5] The tidings inspired mixed emotions in him, but his elation on learning of the deaths of his two royal rivals outweighed his distress at the loss of the army with Zopyrion. [6] For after Alexander's departure virtually the whole of Greece had rushed to arms to seize the opportunity of recovering independence, [7] following the lead of the Spartans who had been alone in repudiating the peace of Philip and Alexander and in rejecting their conditions. The leader of this campaign was Agis, King of Sparta. [8] Antipater concentrated his forces and put down the insurrection right at its outbreak, [9] though there were heavy casualties on both sides. [10] When King Agis saw his forces take to their heels he discharged his bodyguard – to show himself second to Alexander only in luck, not in courage – and wrought such havoc amongst his enemies that, at times, he drove back whole companies of men. [11] He was finally overcome by their superior numbers, but in glory he defeated them all.

4(c)   Plutarch, Agesilaus 15.6

. . . Alexander even added a joke when he was told of the war waged by Antipater against Agis. "Men," he said, "it appears that while we were in the process of vanquishing Darius, there was a battle of mice over there in Arcadia."

Greeks in the upper satrapies

The difficult campaign in Bactria and Sogdiana required the establishment of numerous garrisons in the region (see §XIII.1d–f). This network of forts not only secured Macedonian control but it allowed Alexander to rid himself of large numbers of Greek mercenaries, many of whom were of questionable loyalty, and of veterans who were no longer fit for military service (apomachoi); cf. Thomas (1974). In time, the Greeks began to long for their homeland, and reports of Alexander's death, even if premature (in 326/5), inspired them to consider emulating the famous Ten Thousand and marching home – though the distances were far more imposing. See Holt (1988: 82–91).

4(d)   Quintus Curtius Rufus 9.7.1–11

While this was taking place in India, unrest had arisen among the soldiers recently settled by the king in colonies around Bactria, and they had revolted against Alexander, less out of hostility towards him than from fear of punishment. [2] After murdering some of their compatriots, the stronger party began to contemplate armed insurrection. Occupying the citadel of Bactra, which had been rather carelessly guarded, they had also compelled the barbarians to join the uprising. [3] Their leader was Athenodorus, who had even assumed the title of king, though his desire was not so much for power as for returning home with men who acknowledged his authority. [4] A certain Biton, who was his countryman but hated Athenodorus because of personal rivalry, hatched a plot against him, and through the agency of a Bactrian called Boxus invited him to a banquet and had him murdered at the table. [5] Calling a meeting the next day, Biton persuaded most of the people that Athenodorus had actually been plotting against his life, but there were others who suspected Biton of treachery and this suspicion gradually began to spread. [6] Accordingly, the Greek soldiers took up their arms and would have killed Biton, if they had been given the chance, but their leaders appeased the anger of the mob.

[7] Unexpectedly rescued from imminent danger, Biton shortly afterwards conspired against those responsible for saving him. His treachery was discovered, however, and the Greeks arrested both him and Boxus. [8] They decided that Boxus should be executed immediately, but that Biton should be tortured to death. As the torture-irons were already being applied to his body, the Greeks for some unknown reason rushed to arms like madmen [9] and, when those who had been ordered to torture Biton heard the uproar, they abandoned their task, fearing that the cries of the rioters were intended to stop them. [10] Stripped as he was, Biton came to the Greeks and the pitiful sight of the man under sentence of death brought about a sudden transformation of their feelings. So they ordered his release. [11] Twice reprieved in this manner, Biton returned home with the others who had deserted the colonies allotted them by the king. Such were the events in the area of Bactra[7] and the Scythian borders.

4(e)   Diodorus Siculus 17.99.5–6

The king was under treatment for several days. Now the Greeks who had been resettled in Bactria and Sogdiana had long been dissatisfied with living amongst the barbarians and, when word reached them at this time that the king had died of his wounds, they defected from Macedon. [6] They formed a

---

7   Curtius often uses Bactra (the town) and Bactria (the region) interchangeably.

group of some 3,000 people, but experienced many difficulties as they journeyed homewards; and later on, after Alexander's death, they were slaughtered by the Macedonians.

4(f)   Diodorus Siculus 18.7.1–9

The Greeks who had been settled in the so-called 'Upper Satrapies' by
Alexander sorely missed the Greek culture and way of life, cast away as they
were in the furthest corners of the realm. While the king still lived they tolerated the situation through fear, but on his death they rebelled. [2] They considered the matter together and, choosing the Aenianian Philon as their
commander, they put together a substantial force. They had more than 20,000
infantry, and 3,000 cavalry, all men who had frequently been put to the test
in the trials of warfare and were noted for their valour.

[3] When Perdiccas was informed of the rebellion of the Greeks, he selected
by lot from the Macedonians 3,000 infantry and 800 cavalry. He chose as
leader of the entire force Pithon, who had been one of Alexander's bodyguards, a man of spirit and capable of taking command, and he put under
him the troops drawn by lot. He also gave Pithon letters addressed to the
satraps, and these contained orders for them to supply Pithon with fighting
men amounting to 10,000 infantry and 8,000 cavalry. Perdiccas then sent him
out to tackle the rebels.

[4] Pithon was a man with great ambitions. He was happy to take on the
commission because he had it in mind to enlist the support of the Greeks by
treating them with indulgence and then strengthen his force by forging an
alliance with them. After that he would go his own way and make himself
ruler of the Upper Satrapies. [5] Perdiccas, however, suspected that this was
Pithon's design and so gave him a direct order to put to death all the rebels
once he had defeated them and to distribute the spoils amongst the soldiers.

Pithon moved off with the soldiers that had been given to him and took
on, as well, the allied troops from the satraps. He then proceeded against the
rebels with his entire force. Using the services of a certain Aenianian, he
bribed Letodorus, who been given command of 3,000 men in the rebel force,
and completely outmatched his enemy. [6] When the pitched battle began and
the victory hung in the balance, the traitor abandoned his allies and, along
with his 3,000 soldiers, made an unexpected retreat to a certain hill. The
others thought these men had begun to flee and, losing their composure, they
themselves turned and ran. [7] After winning the battle Pithon sent a herald
to the defeated rebels to tell them to put down their weapons and to return
to their various homes after being given guarantees.

[8] Oaths to secure the guarantees were then taken and the Greeks were
merged in with the Macedonians. This made Pithon very happy, since things
were developing according to plan; but the Macedonians remembered
Perdiccas' instructions and, with no thought for the oaths they had taken,

broke their compact with the Greeks. [9] They made a surprise attack on them, catching them off their guard, brought them down with their spears and plundered their possessions. Deceived in his hopes, Pithon returned to Perdiccas with the Macedonians. Such were developments in Asia.

Harpalus, the Exiles' Decree, and the Lamian War

In 324 Alexander had returned to the West to find the centre of his empire in disarray: political malfeasance, embezzlement, and corruption were the order of the day. Many satraps and other officials, including the imperial treasurer, Harpalus, had acted in the most lawless and immoral fashion, disregarding also the wishes of Alexander – as if he would never return from the East. What followed has been characterized by some scholars as a reign of terror: the punishments the king meted out were indeed severe, and the victims numerous, but this is not to say that they were unmerited or excessive.

Harpalus, for his part, had anticipated the king's arrival, slipping away first to Tarsus in Cilicia and then to Athens (see §X.8a–d). Here he offered generous bribes to politicians in the hope of inciting a war against Macedon. Hostility to Alexander was mounting in the city, which had only recently learned of the king's plans to proclaim the Exiles' Decree, which restored political exiles to their cities and would deprive Athens of its control of Samos; but the Athenians gave in to pressure from Alexander's agent Philoxenus, and Harpalus was ordered out of the city. Some politicians, however, were tainted by association with Harpalus and the belief that they had taken money from him. Most notable amongst these was Demosthenes. And although Harpalus failed in his scheme to foment war – in fact, he was murdered soon afterwards by some of his own followers – the unrest in Greece resurfaced after the news of Alexander's own death, triggering the so-called Lamian War.

For Harpalus' flight see Badian (1961), Jaschinski (1981), Worthington (1986; cf. 1992: 41–77; 1994a), and Blackwell (1999). On the Exiles' Decree, see Bosworth (1988a: 220–8), and for the Lamian War, see Ashton (1983) and Worthington (1994b).

4(g)   Diodorus Siculus 17.108.6–8

On his return from India Alexander executed large numbers of satraps against whom charges had been brought, and Harpalus consequently feared punishment himself. So, putting together 5,000 talents of silver and recruiting 6,000 mercenaries, he left Asia and sailed to Attica. [7] No one giving him a welcome, he left his mercenaries near Taenarum in Laconia while he himself took some of the money and made himself a suppliant to the Athenian people. His extradition was now sought by Antipater and Olympias, and after having distributed large sums of money amongst orators who spoke publicly on his behalf he slipped away and put in at Taenarum to rejoin his mercenaries. [8] From there he sailed to Crete, only to be murdered by one of his friends, Thibron. The Athenians undertook a reckoning of Harpalus' funds, and they found

Demosthenes and a number of other orators guilty of having taken money from the man.

4(h)　Pausanias, Description of Greece 2.33.4–5

Harpalus fled from Athens, crossing by ship to Crete, and not long afterwards died at the hands of the slaves who were attending on him (though there are some who claim that he was treacherously murdered by Pausanias, a Macedonian). The treasurer who looked after his money sought refuge in Rhodes, and there he was arrested by the Macedonian Philoxenus, who had also demanded the extradition of Harpalus from Athens. When he had the slave in his hands, Philoxenus kept on interrogating him until he had a full account of all those who had been in the pay of Harpalus, and after he acquired this information he sent a letter to Athens. [5] In the letter he listed the names of those who had taken money from Harpalus and the sums each had taken, but he made no reference at all to Demosthenes, although the man was anathema to Alexander and Philoxenus himself had had a personal quarrel with him.[8]

4(i)　Justin 13.5.1–8

While these things were going on in the East, in Greece the Athenians and the Aetolians were devoting all their energies to the war which they had started when Alexander was still alive. [2] What had prompted the hostilities was a letter written by Alexander on his return from India which restored those exiled from all the cities with the exception of condemned murderers. [3] The letter was read out at the Olympic festival, at which all of Greece was gathered, and caused a great uproar [4] because large numbers of the exiles had been expelled not by due process of law but by political factions made up of prominent citizens who now feared that the exiles, if recalled, would gain greater political power than the authorities themselves. [5] As a result, many cities angrily and openly proclaimed at the time that they would assert their independence by military means, [6] but foremost among them were the Athenians and Aetolians. [7] When news of this was brought to Alexander, he had given instructions for 1,000 warships to be levied from the allies to conduct the war in the West and he had intended making an expedition with a powerful force to destroy Athens. [8] The Athenians accordingly raised a force of 30,000 men and 200 ships and now opened hostilities against Antipater, who had received Greece in the allocation.

---

8 It is tempting to see as the ultimate source of this information Demochares, Demosthenes' nephew, who wrote a history of this period and undoubtedly sought to exculpate his uncle.

4(j)   *Diodorus Siculus 17.109.1*

In the period of the Olympic games, Alexander had a proclamation made at Olympia that all exiles should return to their native lands, apart from those guilty of sacrilege or murder.

4(k)   *Diodorus Siculus 18.8.2–5*

For, a short time before his death, Alexander decided to recall all the exiles in the Greek cities. He did this to boost his reputation, and at the same time because he wanted to have in each city numerous individuals sympathetic to him to counter the revolutionary and subversive activities of the Greeks. [3] So, since the Olympic games were approaching, he gave a decree concerning the recall to Nicanor of Stagira and sent him to Greece with orders to have the decree read out to the crowds assembled at the festival by the victorious herald.[9] [4] Nicanor did as he had been told, and the herald took the letter and read it out. It went as follows:

> A message from King Alexander to the exiles from the Greek cities. Though we are not responsible for your exile, we shall nevertheless assume responsibility for your return to your various homelands, except in the case of those with curses on their heads. We have given Antipater written instructions in the matter; he is to use force in the case of cities refusing to accept the recall.

[5] When this announcement was made the crowd loudly applauded, those attending the festival showing their joyful appreciation for the king's gift and responding to his benefaction with shouts of praise. All the exiles had assembled for the festival and there were more than twenty thousand of them.

4(l)   *Quintus Curtius Rufus 10.2.1–7*

So, with thirty ships, they crossed to the Attic promontory of Sunium, having decided to make for the port of Athens from there. [2] On learning this, the king was equally incensed with Harpalus and the Athenians. He ordered a fleet to be mustered for an immediate journey to Athens but, while he was privately considering this plan, a letter arrived. Harpalus, it said, had entered Athens and had won the support of leading citizens by bribery, [3] but soon an assembly of the people was held which ordered him to leave the city. He had come to the Greek troops who arrested him and, at the instigation of a friend of his, treacherously murdered him. [4] Pleased with the news, Alexander dropped his

---

9   A contest of heralds opened the Olympic games.

plan of crossing to Europe. However, he ordered the restoration of exiles (except those with the blood of citizens on their hands) by all the cities which had expelled them. [5] The Greeks dared not disobey his order, despite their belief that it constituted the first step towards the collapse of their laws, and they even restored what remained of their property to the condemned men. [6] Only the Athenians, champions of everybody's cause and not just their own, were reluctant to tolerate such a hotchpotch of classes and individuals, for they were used to government based on law and tradition, not a king's command. [7] Accordingly, they barred the exiles from their territory and were prepared to suffer anything rather than admit what was once the scum of their city and subsequently the scum of their places of exile.

Alexander and the Greek Cities of Asia Minor

Letter to the people of Chios

When Alexander set out to conquer Asia Minor in 334, he went as *hegemon* of the League of Corinth and as avenger of the Greeks, and he resorted to Panhellenic propaganda. For the Greeks of Asia Minor, liberation was a mixed blessing: they were at the same time "conquered" by the Macedonian army and subject to the will of its king. That they became members of the League of Corinth is undocumented and, indeed, unlikely. Alexander's grants of autonomy were accompanied by the imposition of "protective" garrisons; oligarchies were, as a rule, overthrown and replaced by democracies; bloody retribution was visited upon the former ruling parties and their adherents; and Alexander could – and did – interfere in their affairs at will and with impunity. The selections translated below are meant as examples, to illustrate the nature of the problems in these cities and their relationship with Alexander.

General Reading: Heisserer (1980) and Bosworth (1988a): 250–6. For *Chios* see Tod (1948) no. 192, pp. 263–7; Heisserer (1980) 79–83; cf. Austin (1981) no. 5; Bagnall and Derow (1981) no. 2: Harding (1985) no. 106. For *Priene* see Heisserer (1980) 145–56; cf. Harding (1985) no. 106. For *Mytilene* see *IG* IX.2, 6; Heisserer (1980) 118; Harding (1985) 113.

5(a)   Syll.³ 283

From King Alexander to the People of Chios, written in the Prytany of Deisitheos:[10] All those exiled from Chios are to return, and the constitution on Chios is to be democratic. Drafters of legislation are to be selected to write and emend the laws so as to ensure that there be no impediment to a democratic constitution and the return of the exiles. Anything already emended or drafted is to be referred to Alexander. The people of Chios are to supply twenty triremes, with crews, at their own expense, and these are to sail for as long as

---

10   334 BC, according to Heisserer (1980: 83–95).

the rest of the Greek naval force accompanies us at sea. With respect to those men who betrayed the city to the barbarians, all those who escaped are to be exiled from all the cities that share the peace, and to be liable to seizure under the decree of the Greeks. Those who have been caught are to be brought back and tried in the Council of the Greeks. In the event of disagreement between those who have returned and those in the city, in that matter they are to be judged by us. Until a reconciliation is reached among the people of Chios, they are to have in their midst a garrison of appropriate strength installed by King Alexander. The people of Chios are to maintain the garrison.

Letter to Priene

5(b)　Tod (1948: no. 185, lines 1–15)

From King Alexander. Such people of Priene as are living in Naulochus are to be autonomous and free. They are to be the owners of the land and all the dwellings in the city, just like the people in Priene . . . But with respect to the land of the Myrselaioi and Pedieis, that and its surrounding countryside I declare to be mine, and all living in these villages are to pay the tribute. I release from obligation to pay taxes the city of Priene and the garrison . . .[11]

Restoration of the Mytilenean exiles

5(c)　Tod (1948: no. 201)

. . . and let the chief officers [basileis] support the returnee on the grounds that the man earlier resident in the city is guilty of fraud. And should anyone fail to abide by these settlements let him no longer receive any property from the city or come into possession of any of the assets granted him by those people earlier resident in the city.[12] Instead, let those of the people earlier resident in the city who granted them to him possess them, and let the magistrates [strategoi] transfer back the assets to the man earlier resident in the city on the grounds that the returnee has not been reconciled. And let the chief officers [basileis] support the man earlier resident in the city on the grounds that the returnee is guilty of fraud. And should anyone bring legal action concerning these issues, the circuit judges [peridromoi] are not to introduce it in court, nor the judges [dikaskopoi] or any other civil servant.

Should everything not follow the provisions laid down in the decree, this is to be the concern of the magistrates [strategoi], the chief officers [basileis], the circuit judges [peridromoi], the judges [dikaskopoi] and the other civil ser-

11　The last seven lines of the inscription are too fragmentary to permit a meaningful translation.
12　I.e., one of those who remained during the period of exile of those now returning and, presumably, holding property that was not right fully his own.

vants. They must condemn the man who violates any of the regulations set down in the decree so that the returnees may have no quarrel with those earlier resident in the city. Thus they may all live in the city in harmony and reconciled with each other, without treacherous dealings, and thus they may adhere to the terms written into this statute and the settlement provided in this decree.

The assembly of the people [*demos*] is to choose twenty men, ten of them returnees, ten of them men earlier resident in the city. These must be zealously alert and see to it that nothing should ever stand between the returnees and those earlier resident in the city. They must see that, in the case of disputed assets, the returnees, ideally, become reconciled both with those earlier resident in the city and with each other. Failing that, they must see that they behave with utmost fairness, and all adhere to the settlement clauses that the king has approved in the statute, living in the city and the country in concord with each other. They must see to it that the finances to effect the reconciliation are as great as can be, and consider the oath that the citizens are to take. In all these matters the chosen representatives must report to the assembly of the people [*demos*] whatever agreement they have reached amongst themselves. Having heard this, the assembly [*demos*] must, if it deems it expedient, debate the ratification of those things agreed amongst themselves as being expedient, repeating the process used for the decision earlier taken by the popular assembly [*demos*] in the case of those returning in the prytany of Smithinas.

Judgment in the case of any omission in the decree is to lie with the executive council [*boule*]. The decree once ratified by the popular assembly [*demos*], all the people [*demos*] are to pray to the gods, on the twentieth of the month that follows the sacrifice, that the reconciliation of the returnees and those already living in the city provide safety and prosperity for all the citizens. All civic priests and priestesses are to open the temples and the people [*demos*] are to gather for prayer. The chief officials [*basileis*] are to give to the gods each year the sacrificial victims that the people [*demos*] promised in a vow when they sent the messengers to the king. All the people [*demos*] are to attend the sacrifice, as are the messengers sent to the king, who were chosen from those already living in the city and from the returnees. After inscribing this decree on a stone stele, the treasurers [*tamiai*] are to set it up in the temple of Athena.

VI The Army and War

General introductions to the military aspects of Alexander's campaigns can be found in Milns (1976), Warry (1991), Hanson (1999: 135ff.), and Heckel (2002a); for greater detail see Fuller (1958). On Macedonian warfare, see Adcock (1957) and Sage (1996: 181–96); see also Hammond (1981). The best modern account in English is Bosworth (1988a).

Financial Resources and Military Strength

Financial resources

Although Philip II acquired mines that yielded gold and silver in the region of Mount Pangaeus, near which he founded the city of Philippi, he was clearly not fiscally responsible. When Alexander became king in 336 he found the treasury depleted, and although he augmented it with booty taken in the North and at Thebes (see §V.2d–e), he relied on the wealth of Asia to meet the expenses of his campaigns. The captured wealth of Persia (in the camp of Issus, at Damascus, and later in the Achaemenid centers of Babylon, Susa, Persepolis, and Ecbatana) remedied the Macedonians' financial woes, but in the early stages the army was undoubtedly hard-pressed. See also IV.2c–m; X.8a–d. Further discussion can be found in Bellinger (1963: 35–80); see also Montgomery (1985) on Philip's economic practices; cf. Austin (1986) for Hellenistic economies.

1(a)   *Plutarch*, On the Fortune of Alexander
1.3 = Moralia *327d*

Philip's financial resources were depleted, and he was also encumbered with a debt of 200 talents, according to Onesicritus' history.

1(b)   Arrian 7.9.6

[Alexander speaking to his men at Opis].[1] "My inheritance from my father consisted of a few gold and silver drinking-cups and less than sixty talents in the treasury. There were also about 500 talents' worth of debt contracted by Philip. I myself borrowed another 800 in addition to this, and then, launching forth from a country that was failing to sustain you properly, I immediately opened up a way through the Hellespont for you, despite Persian supremacy at sea at the time ..."

1(c)   Quintus Curtius Rufus 10.2.24

[Alexander addressing his men at Opis]. "This was the smart equipment you had when I took you on, together with a debt of 500 talents, when the entire royal assets were no more than sixty talents – such was the basis for the great achievements to come ..."

1(d)   Plutarch, Alexander 15.2

To maintain such forces Aristobulus claims Alexander had no more than 70 talents. Duris says he had enough to maintain them for 30 days and Onesicritus that he also had a debt of 200 talents.

1(e)   Plutarch, On the Fortune of Alexander
1.3 = Moralia 327e

The munificent and splendid provisions stockpiled for him by Fate amounted to 70 talents. Duris, however, says it was enough to keep him supplied for only 30 days.

Military strength

Engels (1976) is still the best starting point for any consideration of army numbers, reinforcements, distances, march rates, and other logistical problems (see particularly "Appendix 5: Statistical Tables," pp. 144–58); cf. also Brunt (1976) 526–32. For the officers and command structure, see Heckel (1992a). On the question of casualties and reinforcements later in the campaign and the effects of the war on Macedonian manpower, see Bosworth (1986; 2002: 64–97) and Hammond (1989b).

---

1   For the context of the following remarks, see §X.9c.

1(f)   Diodorus Siculus 17.17.3–5

It was found that, in terms of infantry, there were 12,000 Macedonians, 7,000 allies and 5,000 mercenaries. These were all under the command of Parmenion. [4] The Odrysians, Triballians and Illyrians accompanying him numbered 7,000, and there were a thousand archers and so-called Agrianes, so that the infantry totalled 32,000. Cavalry numbers were as follows: 1,800 Macedonians,[2] commanded by Parmenion's son Philotas; 1,800 Thessalians, commanded by Callas,[3] the son of Harpalus; from the rest of Greece a total of 600 under Erigyius; and 900 Thracian guides and Paeonians, with Cassander as their commander. This made a total of 4,500 cavalry [actually, 5,100: ed.].

Such was the strength of the army that crossed to Asia with Alexander. [5] The number of soldiers left behind in Europe, who were under Antipater's command, totalled 12,000 infantry and 15,000 cavalry.

1(g)   Plutarch, Alexander 15.1

As for the numerical strength of the army, those giving the lowest figures record infantry numbers as 30,000 and cavalry as 4,000, while those giving the highest place infantry at 43,000 and cavalry at 5,000.

1(h)   Plutarch, On the Fortune of Alexander
1.3 = Moralia 327d

Alexander had the nerve to aspire to Babylon and Susa; or, rather, he took it into his head to rule all mankind. And for this he was relying on the 30,000 infantry and 4,000 cavalry that he had with him; for such, Aristobulus says, was their total number. According to King Ptolemy, however, the number was 30,000 infantry and 5,000 cavalry; according to Anaximenes 43,000 infantry and 5,500 cavalry.

1(i)   Frontinus, Stratagems 4.2.4

With 40,000 men who had already been trained by his father, Philip, Alexander of Macedon launched an attack on the world and vanquished enemy forces without number.

---

2   The Companion Cavalry.
3   The correct spelling is probably Calas (see §VI.2b, below); he may have been an uncle or cousin of the famous treasurer (on whom see §X.8a–d).

Major Battles

The Granicus River

In 336 Alexander fought his first major battle with the Persians in Hellespontine (or Lesser) Phrygia at the River Granicus, which flows into the Propontis (Sea of Mamara) west of Zelea. It was at this town that the satraps of Asia Minor had planned their strategy, rejecting in the process the advice of the Greek mercenary captain, Memnon of Rhodes. Instead of implementing a "scorched earth" policy, they chose to confront the Macedonians with their combined satrapal armies on the banks of the Granicus. Distrustful of their Greek mercenary troops, they placed them at the rear of the army, where they could provide little help to the Persian forces, who were duly routed by Alexander's army. See Devine (1986a, 1988), Foss (1977), Green (1991: 489–512), and McCoy (1989).

2(a)   Plutarch, Alexander 16.3–11

Alexander plunged into the river with thirteen cavalry squadrons. [4] He was now driving into enemy projectiles and heading towards an area that was sheer and protected by armed men and cavalry, and negotiating a current that swept his men off their feet and pulled them under. His leadership seemed madcap and senseless rather than prudent. [5] Even so, he persisted with the crossing and, after great effort and hardship, made it to the targeted area, which was wet and slippery with mud. He was immediately forced into a disorganized battle and to engage, man against man, the enemies who came bearing down on them, before the troops making the crossing could get into some sort of formation.

[6] The Persians came charging at them with a shout. They lined up their horses against those of their enemy and fought with their lances and then with their swords, when the lances were shattered. [7] A large number closed in on the king, who stood out because of his shield and the crest on his helmet, on each side of which there was a plume striking for its whiteness and its size. Alexander received a spear in the joint of his cuirass, but was not wounded. [8] Then the Persian generals Rhoesaces and Spithridates came at him together. Sidestepping the latter, Alexander managed to strike Rhoesaces, who was wearing a cuirass, with his spear, but when he shattered the spear he resorted to his sword. [9] While the two were engaged hand-to-hand, Spithridates brought his horse to a halt beside them and, swiftly pulling himself up from the animal, dealt the king a blow with the barbarian *kopis*. [10] He broke off Alexander's crest, along with one of the plumes, and the helmet only just held out against the blow, the blade of the *kopis* actually touching the top of the king's hair. [11] Spithridates then began to raise the weapon for a second blow, but Cleitus (the Black) got there first, running him

through with his spear. At the same moment Rhoesaces also fell, struck down by a sword-blow from Alexander.

2(b) Arrian 1.14–16

With these words, Alexander sent Parmenion to take charge of the left wing while he himself went over to the right. Philotas son of Parmenion he had already stationed before the right, at the head of the cavalry of the Companions, the archers and the Agrianian javelin-throwers. Beside Philotas Alexander placed Amyntas son of Arrhabaeus, who commanded the *sarissophoroi*, the Paeonians and the squadron of Socrates. [2] Next to these were ranged the hypaspists of the *hetairoi*, under the command of Nicanor son of Parmenion, and beyond them the heavy infantry of Perdiccas son of Orontes, followed by that of Coenus son of Polemocrates. Then came the infantry of Amyntas son of Andromenes, followed by that under the command of Philip son of Amyntas.

[3] On the left were stationed, in the first place, the Thessalian cavalry under Calas son of Harpalus. Next to these were the allied cavalry led by Philip son of Menelaus, with the Thracians under Agathon beyond them. Beside these were the infantry – the troops of Craterus, Meleager and Philip – extending to the middle of the line.

[4] The Persian cavalry numbered about 20,000, the foreign mercenary infantry slightly fewer than that. They were deployed with the cavalry along the bank of the river in a long phalanx, with the infantry behind them; and the land sloped upwards away from the bank. They concentrated their cavalry squadrons on the bank at the point where they could see Alexander himself, opposite their left flank; for the brilliance of his arms, and the frenzied activity of the attendants around him, made him easily recognizable.

[5] For a while the two armies remained motionless at the river's edge, apprehensive of what lay ahead, and a deep silence fell on both sides. The Persians were waiting for the Macedonians to begin their crossing, intending to fall on their enemy as they emerged from the water. [6] Alexander, however, leaped on his horse and urged his entourage to follow him and show their courage. He then ordered the mounted skirmishers to enter the river first, and with them the Paeonians under Amyntas son of Arrhabaeus and a single cavalry squadron. The latter was preceded by that of Socrates under Ptolemy son of Philip – this squadron happened to have the overall command of the cavalry that particular day. [7] Alexander himself took charge of the right wing, entering the stream as the trumpets sounded and shouts went up to Enyalius.[4] He kept the troops extended across the river, angled in the direction of the flow,

---

4 The war god, Ares.

to prevent a Persian flank attack as he emerged, and so that he himself could engage the enemy with as compact a formation as possible.

15   The troops with Amyntas and Socrates reached the bank first and that was the spot at which the Persians directed their fire from above. Some of them hurled down javelins into the river from a point where the bank was higher, and others went down the more gently sloping terrain to the level of the stream. [2] The two cavalry forces were pushing and shoving, one side trying to get out of the river, the other trying to prevent them from getting out, and javelins were discharged in large numbers by the Persians, while the Macedonians fought with their lances.

Greatly outnumbered, the Macedonians were in serious trouble at the first clash. They were not fighting on firm ground, and at the same time they were defending themselves at a point in the river below their enemy, while the Persian attack was coming from a dominant position on the bank. Most importantly, however, this was where the crack Persian cavalry was stationed – where Memnon's sons and, along with them, Memnon himself were facing the hazard of combat. [3] The first Macedonians to engage were cut down by them as they put up a magnificent display of courage, the only survivors being those falling back to join the approaching Alexander. For Alexander was already at hand, bringing with him the right wing, and he led the attack on the Persians, at the point where the cavalry was concentrated and the chief officers of the Persians were positioned. [4] Around Alexander a violent battle commenced, and meanwhile the Macedonian regiments were crossing the river one after the other, this now posing less of a problem. The battle was fought on horseback, but it looked more like an infantry engagement. In the fray horses were enmeshed with horses and men with men, as one side – the Macedonians – tried to dislodge the Persians definitively from the bank and push them onto level ground, while the other – the Persians – attempted to stop their enemy from landing and to push them back into the river again. [5] But by this time the troops with Alexander were getting the upper hand: their strength and experience were showing, but what especially counted was the fact that they were combatting light spears with lances of cherry-wood.

[6] It was at that point that Alexander's lance was shattered in the action, and he asked Aretes, a royal groom, for another. But Aretes was under pressure himself and had also had his lance broken, and he was fighting creditably with one half of his broken weapon. He showed this to Alexander and bade him ask someone else, at which Demaratus, a man of Corinth who was one of the *hetairoi*, gave the king his own lance. [7] Alexander took it, and then caught sight of Darius' son-in-law Mithridates riding far ahead of the others and bringing with him a wedge-shaped formation of cavalry. The king charged out ahead of his men, drove his lance into Mithridates' face and brought the man to the ground. Meanwhile Rhoesaces charged at Alexander and struck him on the head with his sword. He sliced off a section of Alexander's helmet [8] which, nevertheless, withstood the blow. Alexander brought

down Rhoesaces, as well, delivering a lance-thrust to the chest that pierced his cuirass. By this point Spithridates had raised his sword to strike Alexander from behind, but Cleitus son of Dropides got there first, slashing Spithridates' shoulder with his *kopis* and lopping it off. In the meantime the cavalry that had successfully negotiated their way downstream kept on appearing to swell the forces around Alexander.

16 The Persians were now being badly beaten in every quarter. Lances were being driven into their faces and those of their mounts; they were being pushed back by the cavalry; and they were also incurring heavy casualties from the light-infantry interspersed amongst the cavalry. They began to give ground, starting at that point where Alexander was risking his life in the front line. But when their centre buckled and the cavalry were broken on each wing, there was flight on a massive scale. [2] About a thousand of the Persian cavalry were killed, but the pursuit was not of long duration because Alexander turned on the foreign[5] mercenaries. These were still massed together in the spot where they had been positioned at the start, more from bewilderment at the unexpected turn of events than from any reasoned assessment of the situation.

Alexander brought his phalanx down on them and ordered his cavalry to attack them on every side. He then proceeded to cut them down, encircled as they were in a confined space, with the result that none escaped – except by going unnoticed amongst the dead – and about 2,000 were taken prisoner. [3] The following Persian officers fell in the battle: Niphates, Petenes, and Spithridates, satrap of Lycia; Mithrobouzanes, hyparch of Cappadocia; Mithridates, son-in-law of Darius; Arbupales, son of that Darius who was the son of Artaxerxes;[6] Pharnaces, brother of Darius' wife; and Omares, commander of the mercenaries. Arsites made good his escape from the battle to Phrygia and there, they say, he committed suicide because in the eyes of the Persians he was responsible for the defeat on that day.

[4] As for the Macedonians, about 25 of the Companions lost their lives in the first onslaught, and bronze statues of these men are set up in Dium; these Alexander commissioned from Lysippus – the only person chosen by the king to sculpt him. Of the rest of the cavalry more than sixty died, and about thirty infantry. [5] These men Alexander buried the day after the battle along with their weapons and the rest of their equipment. To their parents and children he accorded immunity from taxation on their land, from personal services and from property taxes. In the case of the wounded he was scrupulously attentive, visiting each of them in person, examining his wounds, asking how he was wounded and affording him the opportunity to talk about, and brag about, his exploits.

---

5 That is, foreign to the Persians. They were Greeks.
6 This Darius was the eldest son of Artaxerxes II; he was executed on a charge of conspiring against his father (Plutarch, *Artaxerxes* 26–9).

[6] Alexander buried the chief officers of the Persians as well as the Greek mercenaries who fell fighting alongside the enemy. The mercenaries that he took prisoner, however, he clapped in irons and shipped off to Macedonia for forced labour. His reasoning was that they, as Greeks, had infringed an accord, made in common by the Greeks, by fighting for the barbarians against Greece. [7] He also sent to Athens three hundred full suits of Persian armour as a votive offering to Athena on the Acropolis, with orders for the following inscription to accompany them:

An offering from Alexander, son of Philip, and the Greeks, apart from the Spartans, taken from the barbarians who live in Asia.

Issus

The failure of the satrapal coalition to defeat Alexander at the Granicus River required Darius III to take the field himself, this time with a considerably larger army (October–November 333). Although at first he intended to meet the Macedonian invader on the plains of Mesopotamia, where his superior numbers could be used to great advantage, Darius was misled by Alexander's delay at Tarsus – where he had been stricken with illness (probably malaria) – into thinking that the Macedonians would remain in the secure confines of Cilicia. Therefore, he crossed the Amanus range to the north just as Alexander was preparing to leave Cilicia via the Belen Pass, which led past the Pillar of Jonah. Suddenly, to the surprise of both leaders, the positions of the two armies were reversed, with the Persians to the north, astride Alexander's line of communications, and the Macedonians to the south, where the path lay open to Babylon in the east. Alexander then redeployed his troops and led them onto the coastal plain near the River Pinarus, where Darius' troops were stationed. The sea and the hills served effectively to negate the numerical superiority of the Persian army. See further Devine (1980, 1984, 1985a, 1985b) and Murison (1972); cf. Miltner (1933).

2(c)   Arrian 2.8.1–11.10

At that point Alexander ordered the men to take their meal, but he also sent a few horsemen and archers to the gates to examine the road they would have to take back. After darkness fell the king himself went with the entire army to seize the gates once more. [2] When, around midnight, he was again in control of the pass,[7] he allowed the army the remainder of the night for rest on the rocks, and set sentry posts at strategic points. About dawn he went

---

7   The Belen Pass and the Pillar of Jonah, by which one moves from the Cilician coast into Syria.

down from the gates along the road. As long as the terrain was restricted to a narrow defile, he led the force in a column, but when it opened up he widened the column, up to the range of hills on the right, and to the sea on the left, by bringing hoplites forward, one company after another.

[3] During the march, Alexander's cavalry had been positioned behind the infantry, but when they came to the open terrain he drew the army up in battle formation. On the right wing (towards the hills) he placed, as his first infantry battalions, the *agema* and the hypaspists, led by Parmenion's son, Nicanor, and beside these the battalion of Coenus, after which came Perdiccas' troops. These extended from the right wing to the centre of the hoplites. [4] On the left wing there was, first, the battalion of Amyntas, then that of Ptolemy, next to which was that of Meleager. Command of the infantry troops on the left wing had been assigned to Craterus, but the left wing as a whole was in the charge of Parmenion. To prevent an encircling movement by the barbarians – who could easily outflank them, thanks to their superior numbers – Parmenion was under orders not to move back from the sea.

[5] When the news was brought to him that Alexander was moving forward to do battle, Darius sent some 30,000 of his cavalry across the River Pinarus, together with about 20,000 light infantry, so that he could marshal the rest of his force in his own time. [6] In terms of heavy-armed troops, he placed first, facing the phalanx of the Macedonians, his Greek mercenaries, about 30,000 strong. Next to these, and on both sides of them, he set some 60,000 of the so-called Cardaces, who were also heavy-armed. These were all that the topography would permit to be drawn up in a line. [7] Darius also positioned about 20,000 men on the hillside on his left, facing Alexander's right, and some of these found themselves to the rear of Alexander's army. For the range of hills parted where they were stationed to leave some flat ground, which was like a bay in the sea; then bending at an angle it placed those posted in the foothills to the rear of Alexander's army. [8] The remainder of his army, light and heavy armed, was drawn up by nationality, and was situated to the rear of the Greek mercenaries and the barbarians supporting them in the line, and was so deep as to render it ineffective. The entire army with Darius reportedly totalled about 600,000 soldiers.

[9] As Alexander advanced, the terrain widened a little and he brought up to the front his cavalry – the so-called Companions, the Thessalians [and the Macedonians].[8] He positioned them on the right wing, where he himself was, and sent the troops from the Peloponnese and the other allied forces to Parmenion on the left wing.

[10] When his heavy infantry had been set in place, Darius recalled with a signal the cavalry that he had posted at the river for the purpose of giving cover for the deployment of his forces. Of these he placed the majority on the right wing on the side of the sea, facing Parmenion – the ground there

---

8   These words should be deleted from the text. The Macedonians *are* the Companions.

was somewhat better for riding – but some he also put on the left towards the hills. [11] But as they were ineffectual in that position because of the lack of space, he ordered most of them to ride across to the right wing. Darius himself took the centre of the whole army, which was the traditional position for the kings of Persia. Xenophon son of Gryllus has given an account of the rationale of this battle order.[9]

9 Alexander could see meanwhile that all the Persian cavalry had gone over to his left, on the seaward side, and that he had only his Peloponnesians and other allied cavalry drawn up in that position. Accordingly, he swiftly despatched his Thessalian horse to the left, under orders not to ride across before the entire army but to pass unobtrusively behind the phalanx, so that their crossing would not be observed by the enemy. [2] Before the cavalry on the right he stationed the *prodromoi*, led by Protomachus, and the Paeonians, led by Ariston; and in front of the infantry he set the archers, who were under the command of Antiochus. The Agrianes, led by Attalus, and some of his cavalry and archers, he placed at an angle to the mountain range to his rear, so that on his right wing his force was arranged in two separate bodies. One of these was oriented towards Darius and all the Persian troops across the river, and the other towards those who had been positioned on the rising ground to the Macedonians' rear. [3] On the left before the infantry were stationed the Cretan archers and the Thracians, led by Sitalces, and in front of these were the cavalry of the left wing. The whole line was supported by foreign mercenary troops.

Alexander's phalanx appeared to him insufficiently solid on his right, and it seemed probable that the Persians would considerably outflank him there. He therefore ordered two squadrons of his Companions – the one from Anthemus whose commanding officer was Peroedes son of Menestheus, and the so-called Leugaean that was led by Pantordanus son of Cleander – to move unobserved across to the right. [4] He also brought the archers, a contingent of the Agrianes, and some of the Greek mercenaries over to the right wing, stationing them in front, and thus he extended the phalanx beyond the wing of the Persians. In fact, the Persians stationed on the hillside did not come down to the plain. Then, on Alexander's orders, a charge was conducted against them by the Agrianes, and by a few of the archers, and they were easily pushed out of the foothills, after which they fled to the heights of the range. Alexander at that point decided to add numbers to the phalanx by also using the men who had been drawn up to cover these enemy units; he was content to leave 300 horse in position against them.

10 After arranging his troops in this manner, Alexander led them forward with occasional halts, so that his advance appeared to be at a leisurely pace. As for the barbarians, Darius did not lead them out against the enemy once he had set out his battle line, but remained in his original position on the banks of the river. In many places the banks were sheer, but at points he had

9 Xenophon, *Anabasis* 1.8.21–2

extended a palisade along them where access seemed too easy. It thus became immediately clear to Alexander's troops that this was a man whose spirit had been broken.

[2] When the armies were now closing in on each other, Alexander rode the whole length of the line calling on his men to show courage. He addressed by name, and with appropriate honours and titles, not just the generals, but squadron leaders, company commanders and any of the foreign mercenaries that had some reputation for their superior rank or their courage. And the cry came back to him from every quarter – he should lose no time now in making his attack on the enemy. [3] Even so Alexander continued to lead them forward, in battle order, at a measured pace, despite now having Darius' force in view; he did not want to have any component of his phalanx become distended through too swift a march and so cause it to disintegrate. But when they were within javelin range, Alexander's entourage and Alexander himself (he was positioned on the right) charged to the river ahead of the others, intending to strike alarm into the Persians with a lightning attack and to minimize damage from the archers by coming swiftly to hand-to-hand combat.

And things conformed to Alexander's expectations. [4] As soon as the battle became hand-to-hand combat, the units drawn up on the left of the Persian force were pushed back, and in this quarter Alexander and his entourage won a stunning victory. [5] However, while Alexander had charged swiftly across the river, had taken on the Persians posted there hand-to-hand, and was now pushing them back, the Macedonians in the centre did not engage with equal speed. And at many points they found the banks precipitously steep, and were unable to preserve a united front to their formation. The Greek mercenaries on Darius' side saw a widening breach in the phalanx, to the right, and it was just at this point, where they saw the most serious break in the phalanx, that they concentrated their attack. [6] The struggle here was a fierce one. The mercenaries were trying to push the Macedonians back into the river and to recover the victory for their comrades who were already in flight; the Macedonians were eager not to fall short of Alexander's already-apparent success or tarnish the reputation of the phalanx, until then proclaimed invincible. [7] And there was also in play something of a rivalry between the Greek and Macedonian races. It was here that Ptolemy son of Seleucus met his end after a display of bravery, along with some 120 distinguished Macedonians.

11   When they saw the Persians who were positioned opposite them already defeated, the battalions stationed on the right wing now turned on the foreign mercenaries of Darius – the point where their comrades were under pressure – and drove them back from the river. They then outflanked the shattered section of the Persian army to swoop down on the wings, and were soon cutting down the foreign troops. [2] The Persian cavalry drawn up facing the Thessalians did not stay in place beyond the river, either, once this action got under way; they came charging across to make a spirited attack on the Thessalian squadrons. Here a furious cavalry engagement ensued, and the

Persians did not give ground until they were aware that Darius had fled and until their mercenaries had been thoroughly beaten and cut off by the phalanx. [3] But at that point it was a total rout, and it was clear to see. The horses of the Persians were also under severe pressure in the retreat, carrying as they were heavily armed riders. And the horsemen, negotiating narrow roads in large numbers as they retreated in terrified disorder, suffered heavy casualties, being trampled underfoot by each other as much as by the pursuing enemy. In addition, the Thessalians were relentless in their pursuit, and there was as much slaughter of the cavalry in the flight as there was of infantry.

[4] As soon as his left wing was repulsed by Alexander and he observed that it was severed from the rest of the army, Darius, in his chariot, lost no time and was amongst the first to flee. [5] While the ground he came upon in his flight was even he was secure in the chariot, but when he encountered gullies and other difficult terrain he abandoned it, casting off his shield and his cape, and also leaving his bow in the chariot. He then mounted a horse and fled, and it was the imminent onset of darkness that saved him from capture by Alexander. [6] For while there was daylight Alexander kept up a vigorous pursuit, but when it grew dark and seeing what was before him became impossible he turned back again to the camp. He did, however, take with him Darius' chariot along with his shield, cape and bow. [7] In fact, time had been lost in his pursuit because he had turned back at the moment when the phalanx began to break formation, and did not take up the chase until he saw the foreign mercenaries and the Persian cavalry pushed back from the river.

[8] Amongst the Persian dead were Arsames, Rheomithres, and Atizyes, who had been cavalry commanders at the Granicus; and Sauaces, the satrap of Egypt, and Bubaces, both members of the Persian nobility, also lost their lives. Some 100,000 common soldiers, including more than 10,000 cavalry, were killed. Consequently, according to Ptolemy son of Lagus, who accompanied Alexander on the campaign, the men who were along with them in pursuit of Darius came to a ravine during the chase and made their way over it on Persian bodies.

[9] The camp of Darius was immediately taken by storm, and with it were also taken Darius' mother, his wife (who was also his sister) and his infant son. Two daughters were also captured, and a few noble Persian ladies waiting on them. The rest of the Persians had actually sent their women and their baggage to Damascus, and [10] Darius, too, had sent to Damascus most of his money, plus all the other appurtenances that go along with the Great King to support his extravagant life-style, even when he is on campaign. As a result no more than 3,000 talents were taken in the camp. In fact, the money in Damascus was also captured a little later by Parmenion, who had been sent there for this purpose. Such was the end of that battle. It took place when Nicocrates was archon in Athens, in the month of Maimacterion.[10]

10   Late October or November 333.

2(d)   *Quintus Curtius Rufus 3.8.16–11.27*

Darius now struck camp and crossed the river Pinarus, intending to stick to the heels of what he believed was an enemy in flight. But the men whose hands he had amputated[11] reached the Macedonian camp bearing the news that Darius was following them with all the speed he could muster. [17] This was hard to believe; so Alexander sent his scouts ahead with orders to investigate the coastal areas and find out whether Darius was there in person or whether one of his subordinates had been trying to create the impression that the Persian army was coming in its entirety. [18] When the scouts were on their way back, a huge body of men was sighted in the distance. Then fires began to flare up throughout the plains, and the whole area appeared to be alight almost with one continuous blaze; for the Persian hordes were not in formation and were unusually spread out because of the pack animals. [19] Alexander ordered his men to pitch camp just where they were; he was delighted that the issue was to be decided there, in the pass, something he had desired in all his prayers.

[20] However, as usually happens when a critical moment is approaching, his confidence gave way to worry. Fortune itself, whose favour had granted him so much success, he now began to fear. As he considered its past gifts to him, not surprisingly he began to reflect on how changeable it was, and how only a single night now separated him from such a critical event. [21] Then again it would occur to him that the rewards outweighed the risks and that, while victory might be in doubt, one thing was quite certain, that he would die an honourable death which would bring him great praise. [22] So he ordered his soldiers to refresh themselves and to be ready and under arms at the third watch. Alexander himself climbed to the top of a high ridge and by the light of several torches sacrificed to the tutelary gods of the area in traditional manner.

[23] The men had now been given the specified third trumpet call and they were ready to march as well as to fight. They were instructed to advance briskly and, as day broke, they reached the narrow defile which they had determined to occupy. [24] The advance detachment informed Alexander that Darius was 30 stades away, so at this point he ordered the line to halt and, taking up his arms, arranged the battle order.

News of the enemy's approach was brought to Darius by terrified peasants, and he could hardly believe that he was really being confronted by the troops he thought were fleeing before him. [25] As a result considerable alarm swept over all the Persians – they were actually better prepared for a march than for a battle – and they hurriedly seized their weapons. However, their feverish

---

11   The sick had been left behind near Issus. Darius, when he came upon them, had them mutilated and shown the Persian army. Then he released them so that they would reach the Macedonians and spread fear through their condition and news. Thus Curtius 3.8.13–15; Arrian 2.7.1 speaks of the mutilation but says the men were then killed.

haste, as they ran this way and that calling their comrades to arms, only served to increase their panic. [26] Some had slipped away to a hilltop to get a view of the enemy; most were putting bridles on their horses. Variously occupied and not observing one command, their individual consternation had brought about general confusion. [27] Darius at first decided to occupy a hilltop with a detachment, intending to make an encircling movement around his enemy, both in the front and in the rear, and he was also going to send forward other troops on the side of the sea (which offered protection to his right wing) to press Alexander hard from all directions. [28] In addition he had sent forward a force of 20,000, supplemented by a troop of archers, with orders to cross the river Pinarus (which separated the two armies) and make a stand opposite the Macedonian forces. If they were unable to manage that, they were to fall back onto the hills and, without being detected, encircle the rear of the enemy forces. [29] His sound strategy, however, was shattered by fortune, which is more powerful than any calculation. Some of the Persians were too frightened to carry out their orders, others obeyed them to no effect – for when the parts give out, the entire structure collapses.

9 Darius' army was ordered as follows: Nabarzanes held the right wing with his cavalry and a supplementary force of some 20,000 slingers and archers. [2] On the same wing was Thimodes who was in command of the Greek mercenary infantry, 30,000 strong. This was unquestionably the strongest element of the army, Darius' counterpart to the Macedonian phalanx. [3] On the left wing stood the Thessalian Aristomedes with 20,000 barbarian infantry, and in reserve Darius had placed his most warlike tribes. [4] The king himself intended to fight on the same wing and was accompanied by 3,000 select cavalry (his usual bodyguard) and 40,000 infantry. [5] Then there were the cavalry of the Hyrcanians and Medes, and next to them the cavalry of the other races, positioned beyond them to the right and left. This force, ordered as described, was preceded by 6,000 javelin-throwers and slingers. [6] Every accessible area in the defile was packed with his troops, and the wings stood on the mountains on one side and on the seashore on the other. They had placed the king's wife and mother and a crowd of other women in the centre of the force.

[7] Alexander set his phalanx – the strongest element in the Macedonian army – at the front. Parmenion's son, Nicanor, held the right wing and next to him stood Coenus, Perdiccas, Meleager, Ptolemy[12] and Amyntas, all leading their respective units. [8] On the left wing, which reached as far as the sea, were Craterus and Parmenion, but Craterus had been instructed to take orders from Parmenion. The cavalry was deployed on both wings, the Macedonians reinforced by Thessalians to the right, the Peloponnesians on the left. [9] Before this force, Alexander had positioned a company of slingers interspersed with archers, and the Thracians and Cretans, who were also light-armed, preceded

---

12 Not the famous Ptolemy (son of Lagus), the future king of Egypt, but Ptolemy son of Seleucus. He was killed in this engagement.

the main army as well. [10] Alexander placed the Agrianes who had recently arrived from Thrace opposite those troops which Darius had sent ahead to occupy the hilltop. Parmenion he had ordered to extend his column as far as he could towards the sea so as to separate the line further from the hills held by the barbarians. [11] The latter, in fact, not daring to offer resistance to the Macedonians as they came up or to surround them after they had passed, took to their heels in a panic, especially at the sight of the slingers. It was this that guaranteed safety to Alexander's flank, which he had feared would be under attack from the high ground.

[12] The Macedonians advanced in rows of thirty-two armed men, for the narrows would not admit a wider line. Then the defiles of the mountain gradually began to widen and open up more room so that the infantry could not only advance in their usual order but could also be given cavalry cover on the flanks.

10   When the two armies were already in sight of each other but still out of javelin range, the Persian front raised a wild, fierce shout. [2] The Macedonians returned it, the echo from the mountain tops and vast forests making them sound more numerous than they were ... [3] Alexander went ahead of his front standards and kept motioning his men back with his hand so that they would not hurry too much in their excitement and be out of breath when they entered battle. [4] Riding up to the line, he would address the soldiers with words that suited their dispositions. The Macedonians, who had won so many wars in Europe and who had set out to conquer Asia and the furthest lands of the East as much at their own instigation as his – these he reminded of their long-standing valour. [5] They were the liberators of the world; they would one day traverse the bounds set by Hercules and Father Liber to subdue not only the Persians but all the races of the earth. Bactria and India would be Macedonian provinces. What now lay before their eyes was minimal, he said, but victory gave access to everything. [6] It would not be fruitless labour on the sheer rocks and crags of Illyria and Thrace: they were being offered the spoils of the entire East. And they would scarcely need their swords: the whole enemy line, wavering in panic, could be driven back just by their shields. [7] Alexander also referred to his father, Philip, the conqueror of the Athenians, and recalled to their minds the recent conquest of Boeotia and the annihilation of its best-known city. He reminded them of the river Granicus, of all the cities they had stormed or which had capitulated, of the territory that now lay behind them, all of it subdued and trampled under their feet. [8] Approaching the Greeks, he would remind them that these were the peoples who had inflicted wars upon Greece, wars occasioned first by Darius and then Xerxes, when they insolently demanded water and earth ... [9] He reminded them that these were the men who had demolished and burned their temples, stormed their cities, violated all the laws of gods and men.

Since the Illyrians and Thracians usually made their living by looting, Alexander told them to look at the enemy line agleam with gold and purple

– equipped with booty not arms! [10] They were men, he said, so they should advance and seize the gold from this cowardly bunch of women. They should exhange their rugged mountain-tops and barren hill-trails permanently stiff with frost for the rich plains and fields of the Persians.

11   They had now come within javelin range when the Persian cavalry made a furious charge on the left wing of their enemy; for Darius wanted the issue decided in a cavalry engagement since he presumed that the phalanx was the main strength of the Macedonian army. An encircling movement around Alexander's right wing was also in progress. [2] When the Macedonian saw this he ordered two cavalry squadrons to maintain a position on the ridge while he promptly transferred the rest to the heart of the danger. [3] Then he withdrew the Thessalian cavalry from the fighting line, telling their commander to pass unobtrusively behind the Macedonian rear and join Parmenion, whose instructions he was to carry out energetically.

[4] The troops sent forward into the midst of the Persians were now totally surrounded and were stoutly defending themselves. But, being densely packed and virtually locked together, they could not effectively hurl their javelins which, simultaneously discharged, became entangled with one another as they converged on the same targets; so that the few which fell on the enemy did so gently and without inflicting injury, while the majority fell ineffectually to the ground. Thus, obliged to fight hand-to-hand, they swiftly drew their swords. [5] Then the blood really flowed, for the two lines were so closely interlocked that they were striking each other's weapons with their own and driving their blades into their opponents' faces. It was now impossible for the timid or cowardly to remain inactive. Foot against foot, they were virtually engaging in single combat, standing in the same spot until they could make further room for themselves by winning their fight: [6] only by bringing down his opponent could each man advance. But, exhausted as they were, they were continually being met by a fresh adversary, and the wounded could not retire from the battle as on other occasions because the enemy were bearing down on them in front while their own men were pushing them from behind.

[7] Alexander was as much a soldier as a commander, seeking for himself the rich trophy of killing the king. Riding high in his chariot, Darius cut a conspicuous figure, at once providing great incentive to his men to protect him, and to his enemies to attack him. [8] His brother, Oxathres, saw Alexander bearing down on Darius and moved the cavalry under his command right in front of the king's chariot. Oxathres far surpassed his comrades in the splendour of his arms and in physical strength, and very few could match his courage and devotion to Darius. In that engagement especially he won distinction by cutting down some Macedonians who were recklessly thrusting ahead and by putting others to flight. [9] But the Macedonians fighting next to Alexander, their resolve strengthened by mutual encouragement, burst with Alexander himself into the line of Persian cavalry. Then the carnage truly took on cataclysmic proportions. Around Darius' chariot lay his most famous generals who had succumbed to a glorious death before the eyes

of their king, and who now lay face-down where they had fallen fighting, their wounds on the front of the body. [10] Among them could be recognized Atizyes, Rheomithres and Sabaces,[13] satrap of Egypt – all generals of mighty armies – and heaped around these were a crowd of lesser-known infantrymen and cavalrymen. The Macedonians' dead were not numerous, but they were the most courageous of them, and among the wounds received was a sword graze to Alexander's right thigh.

[11] By this time Darius' horses had been pierced by lances and were distracted with pain; they had begun to toss the yoke and were on the point of hurling the king from his chariot. Frightened that he might fall into his enemy's hands alive, Darius jumped down and mounted a horse which had followed his chariot for this very purpose. He even stooped to throwing off his royal insignia so that they would not betray his flight. [12] The rest of his men now scattered in fear. They broke out of the fighting wherever they could find an escape route, throwing down the weapons which shortly before they had taken up to protect themselves – thus does panic engender fear even of the things that help.

[13] Some horsemen whom Parmenion had despatched were hard on the heels of the fleeing Persians, who by chance had all fled towards that wing. On the right, however, the Persians were pressing hard against the Thessalian cavalry, [14] and one squadron had already been trampled down in the attack. Now the Thessalians wheeled their horses round vigorously, split up and then returned to the attack, inflicting great slaughter on the barbarians who, confident of victory, had broken ranks and were in total disarray. [15] The Persian horses as well as their riders were weighed down by their rows of armour-plating, and so they were severely handicapped by the manner of fighting which especially calls for speed. Indeed, the Thessalians had been able to attack them without suffering casualties while they were wheeling their horses about.

[16] Alexander had not previously ventured to pursue the barbarians, but when he was brought word of this successful engagement and was now victorious on both wings he proceeded to give chase to the fugitives. Not more than 1,000 horsemen accompanied the king, while huge numbers of the enemy were in retreat – [17] but who counts troops in a time of victory or of flight? So the Persians were driven on like cattle by a mere handful of men, and the fear that drove them to flee also impeded their flight. [18] On the other hand, the Greeks who had fought for Darius (they were led by Amyntas, a lieutenant who had deserted from Alexander) had managed to get away, because they were cut off from the main force, without even appearing to be in flight. The barbarians took very diverse escape routes. [19] Some followed a course leading directly into Persia; others, taking a more circuitous path, headed for the high ground and sequestered mountain passes; a few made for

13 The same names are given in corrupt form in Diodorus 17.34.5: "Antixyes, Rheomithres and Tasiaces."

the camp of Darius. [20] But the camp, filled with all manner of riches, had already been entered by the victors. Alexander's men had made off with a huge quantity of gold and silver (the trappings of luxury, not war) and, since they pillaged more than they could carry, the paths were littered everywhere with the meaner articles which they had greedily cast aside after comparing them with superior goods.

[21] Now they came to the women, and the more these prized their jewels, the more violently they were robbed of them. Not even their persons were spared the violence of lust. [22] They filled the camp with all manner of lamentation and screaming in reaction to their individual misfortunes, and villainy of every shape and form manifested itself as the cruelty and licence of the victor swept through the prisoners irrespective of rank or age. [23] Then a true illustration of fortune's caprice was to be seen. The men who had formerly decorated Darius' tent and fitted it out with all kinds of extravagant and opulent furnishings were now keeping back the very same things for Alexander, as if for their old master. That tent, in fact, was the only thing the Macedonian soldiers left untouched, it being their tradition to welcome the conqueror in the tent of the conquered king.

[24] However, it was Darius' mother and his wife, now prisoners, who had attracted to themselves everybody's gaze and attention. His mother commanded respect for her age as well as for her royal dignity, his wife for a beauty that even her current misfortune had not marred. The latter had taken to her bosom her young son, who had not yet turned six, a boy born into the expectation of the great fortune his father had just lost. [25] In the lap of their aged grandmother lay Darius' two grown-up but unmarried daughters, grieving for their grandmother as well as for themselves. Around her stood a large number of high-born women, their hair torn, their clothes rent and their former gracefulness forgotten. They called upon their "queens" and "mistresses", titles formerly appropriate but no longer applicable. [26] They forgot their own plight and kept asking on which wing Darius had stood and how the battle had gone, claiming that they were not captives at all if the king still lived. But Darius' flight had taken him far away with frequent changes of horses.

[27] A hundred thousand Persian infantry and 10,000 cavalry were killed in the action. On Alexander's side about 504 were wounded, a total of 32 infantrymen were lost, and 150 cavalrymen died. At so small a cost was huge victory secured.

2(e)   Justin 11.9.1–2, 9–12

Darius meanwhile advanced to offer battle with 400,000 infantry and 100,000 cavalry. [2] The enemy numbers disturbed Alexander when he considered the smallness of his own; but he also reflected on what brilliant victories he had won with that same small force and what powerful nations he had defeated . . .

[9] After this the battle began, a furious one in which both kings were wounded, and the outcome remained in doubt until the moment when Darius took flight. [10] What followed was a slaughter of the Persians: 61,000 infantry and 10,000 cavalry fell, and 40,000 prisoners were taken. Of the Macedonians 130 infantrymen were lost and 150 cavalrymen. [11] In the Persian camp large quantities of gold and other treasures were found, [12] and among the prisoners taken in the camp were the mother of Darius, his wife (who was also his sister) and his two daughters.

2(f)   Polybius 12.17–20, 22 (commenting on Callisthenes, FGrH 124 F35)

I do not wish to give the impression of lightly dismissing the credibility of men of stature, and shall cite in evidence a single engagement, one that is especially famous and also not far removed from us in time. And, most importantly, it is one at which Callisthenes was present.

I refer to Alexander's battle against Darius in Cilicia. Here Callisthenes says that Alexander was already marching beyond the defile – the so-called Gates of Cilicia – when Darius, who had been following the route through the so-named Amanid Gates, came down into Cilicia with his force. Callisthenes claims that Darius learned from the local people that Alexander was ahead of him and making for Syria, and he began to follow him. Then, as he approached the defile, he encamped at the River Pinarus. From the sea right to the foothills, according to Callisthenes, the terrain here does not exceed a width of 14 stades, and through it the river mentioned above flows at an angle. As the river emerges from the hills it is flanked by ravines, and as it proceeds through the level country its banks are sheer and impossibly difficult. Callisthenes gives these details. He then says that, when Alexander turned and marched towards the Persians, Darius and his officers decided to deploy their entire infantry right in the camp in the original order, and to use the river as cover since it actually flowed past the camp. After that he declares that the Persians set their cavalry along the seashore, the mercenaries next to them along the river, and beside these the peltasts, whose formation extended to the hills.

18   But how Darius positioned these troops before his infantry is difficult to see, if the river flowed right past the camp and especially when the numbers were so great. For there were 30,000 cavalry according to Callisthenes' own account, and 30,000 mercenaries . . .

So, over what area was the mass of the mercenary troops deployed? Obviously they were behind the cavalry. But that is not what Callisthenes says. Instead he says these led the attack on the Macedonians. From this one must conclude that the cavalry held half the terrain – the seaward half – while the companies of mercenaries held the half that lies toward the hills. From this information one can easily calculate the depth of the cavalry and the distance of the river from the camp. Callisthenes then goes on to say that, when the enemy drew near, Darius, who was himself in the middle of his formation, called over to him the mercenaries from the wing . . .

Finally, he says the cavalry on the right wing came forward and made an assault on the contingent with Alexander, and this, resolutely facing the charge, counter-attacked and put up a sterling fight. But it has slipped his mind that the river – which he has only just described – lay between them.

19   The situation is much the same with regard to Alexander. Callisthenes claims that the king made the crossing to Asia with 40,000 infantry and 4,500 cavalry, and that a further 5,000 infantry and 800 cavalry joined him as he was about to invade Cilicia. Take away 3,000 infantry and 300 cavalry – assuming the highest estimate for absences for special duties – and one will still be left with 42,000 infantry and 5,000 cavalry.

Such are the relevant figures. Callisthenes then says that Alexander learned of Darius' arrival in Cilicia when he was 100 stades away from the Persian king and had already passed the defile. Wheeling around, he retraversed the defile, keeping the phalanx at the head of the column, followed by the cavalry, and with the baggage at the rear. On first coming out into open territory, he deployed his force, ordering all his men to reform the phalanx to give it a depth of 32 ranks, which he then dropped to 16 and then, finally, as it approached the enemy, eight.

The errors here are more egregious than those mentioned earlier. Suppose that one stade accommodates 1,600 men when they are spaced for marching, and that they were proceeding six-ranks deep with the men keeping a distance of 6 feet from each other. It is obvious that 10 stades will accommodate 16,000 men and 20 stades twice that number. From this it is easy to see that, at the time that Alexander gave a depth of sixteen ranks to his force, he needed an area 20 stades deep, and he would still be over the mark by a margin of all his cavalry and ten thousand infantry.

20   Callisthenes then says that, when he was some 40 stades distant from the enemy, Alexander was leading his troops lined up for a frontal attack. It would be difficult to imagine a blunder worse than this. For where – and especially in Cilicia – could one find such terrain that would enable him to lead a phalanx lined up for a frontal attack, and carrying the *sarissa*, over a space 20 stades wide and 40 stades deep? There are so many things impeding such a deployment and such a movement that one would have difficulty enumerating them. Just one of the statements made by Callisthenes himself suffices to demonstrate what I mean. He observes that the torrents running down from the mountains create ravines so large that they say most of the Persians perished in such gullies during their flight. One might object that Alexander wanted to be prepared when the enemy appeared; but what is less prepared than a phalanx that is loosely formed and twisted at the front? . . .

22   It would take too long to list all the errors alongside these in Callisthenes' account – I limit myself to a very small number. He says that

Alexander, in making his troop disposition, was eager to be fighting against Darius himself, and that Darius initially entertained the same wish with regard to Alexander, but subsequently had a change of heart. But Callisthenes says absolutely nothing about how the two men knew where the other's position was in his respective army, and where Darius took up his alternate position.

Also, how did a force of heavy-armed men climb an embankment that was sheer and covered with thorn-bushes? That too is absurd. It is universally agreed that Alexander received practice and training in military science from childhood, and one should not attribute to him this sort of foolishness. Rather, one should attribute it to the historian, whose ignorance renders him incapable of distinguishing what is possible from what is impossible in such circumstances.

Gaugamela

The battle of Gaugamela (331), often named after Arbela, the nearby town to which Darius fled when he was defeated, constitutes the second and decisive battle between Alexander and the armies led by the Great King himself. Unlike Issus, where the terrain neutralized the numbers and mobility of the Persian forces, Gaugamela was distinctly advantageous to the Persian side, and there were moments in the battle when it appeared that the scales had been tipped in favour of the defenders. But it is also a tribute to the military genius of Alexander, and the steady discipline of commanders like Parmenion and Craterus, that the outcome of the engagement was a complete rout of the barbarian forces, one which opened the path for Alexander to the rich Achaemenid capitals of Babylon, Susa, and Persepolis. See Griffith (1947), Marsden (1964), and Devine (1975, 1986b, 1989).

2(g)   Arrian 3.11.1–15.7

Darius and the army under his command maintained the original battle order throughout the night – they had no regular fortified camp around them, and at the same time they feared an enemy night attack. [2] More detrimental than anything else to the Persian cause at this juncture was the long period spent standing under arms and the fear that normally precedes great ventures, a fear not spontaneously arising from the immediate situation but one incubated over a long period until it dominated their minds.

[3] Darius' troop deployment was as follows (in fact, according to Aristobulus, a written account of how Darius formed up his force was subsequently captured):

The Bactrian cavalry were on his left wing, and with them were the Dahae and Arachosians. Beside these were placed the Persians, cavalry and infantry intermixed; the Susians were next to the Persians, and next to the Susians were the Cadusians. [4] Such was the constitution of the left wing up to the centre of the entire force.

On the right wing were drawn up the forces from Hollow Syria and Mesopotamia. Further along to the right were the Medes, with the Parthyaeans and Sacae next to them; then the Topeirians and Hyrcanians; then the Albanians and Sacesinians. This formation extended to the centre of the entire army.

[5] In the centre, where King Darius was in position, the king's relatives were posted along with the *melophoroi*, the Indians, the so-called "transplanted Carians,"[14] and the Mardian bowmen. The Uxians, Babylonians, the peoples dwelling on the Red Sea and the Sittacenians were placed to the rear of these in deep formation.

[6] Ahead of the left wing, and facing Alexander's right, were posted the Scythian cavalry, about a thousand Bactrians and a hundred scythed chariots. The elephants were placed next to the royal squadron of Darius along with some fifty chariots. [7] Ahead of the right the Armenian and Cappadocian cavalry had been deployed, along with fifty scythed chariots. The Greek mercenaries were drawn up flanking Darius and his Persian troops on both sides and facing the Macedonian phalanx – they alone were considered a match for it.

[8] Alexander's army was arranged in the following order. His right was made up of the cavalry of the Companions, with the *ile basilike* in front, under the command of Cleitus son of Dropides. Next to this was the squadron of Glaucias, followed by (in order) the squadrons of Ariston, of Sopolis son of Hermodorus, of Heraclides son of Antiochus, of Demetrius son of Althaemenes and of Meleager. The last of the squadrons was that commanded by Hegelochus son of Hippostratus. The cavalry of the Companions was under the overall command of Philotas son of Parmenion.

[9] After the cavalry came the Macedonian phalanx with, in first place, the *agema* of the hypaspists and, next to them, the other hypaspists. These were under the command of Nicanor son of Parmenion. Beside these was the battalion of Coenus son of Polemocrates, followed by the battalions of Perdiccas son of Orontes, of Meleager son of Neoptolemus and of Amyntas son of Philip, the latter being led by Simmias because Amyntas had been despatched to Macedonia to mobilize troops.

[10] On the left of the Macedonian phalanx was the battalion of Craterus son of Alexander, and Craterus also had overall command of the infantry on the left wing. Beside these were the allied cavalry, commanded by Erigyius son of Larichus, and next to them, on the left wing, the Thessalian cavalry, under Philip son of Menelaus. Overall command of the left wing lay with Parmenion son of Philotas, and around him units of the Pharsalian cavalry, the best and strongest of the Thessalian horse, were in operation.

12   Such was the arrangement of the front made by Alexander, but he also put in place a second line, giving his army two fronts. The officers of those

---

14   Carians who had, at an unknown time, been resettled in Mesopotamia. Cf. Diodorus 17.110.3 and Briant (2002: 719).

drawn up in the second line had orders to wheel round and take the barbarian charge if they saw their own troops being encircled by the Persian army. [2] In case it became necessary to extend or close up the phalanx, half the Agrianes, under Attalus, and with them the Macedonian archers, under Brison, were placed on the right wing next to the *ile basilike*, but obliquely, and next to the archers were the so-called "Old Mercenaries" and their leader, Cleander. [3] Stationed before the Agrianes and the archers were the mounted skirmishers and the Paeonians, led by Aretes and Ariston, and right at the front were the mercenary cavalry under Menidas. Before the royal squadron and the rest of the Companions the other half of the Agrianes and archers were deployed, along with the *akontistai* of Balacrus, all these facing the scythed chariots. [4] Menidas and his troops had instructions to wheel about and attack the enemy on the flanks should he encircle their wing. Such was the configuration of Alexander's right wing.

On the left, the Thacians, under the leadership of Sitalces, were stationed in an oblique formation, with the allied cavalry under Coeranus next to them, followed by the Odrysian horse under Agathon son of Tyrimmas. [5] Ahead of all of these, on this side, were deployed the cavalry of foreign mercenaries led by Andromachus son of Hieron. The infantry from Thrace were detailed to guard the pack animals. Alexander's army totalled about 7,000 cavalry and around 40,000 infantry.

13   The two armies were now approaching each other, and Darius and the troops around him came into view. The latter comprised the Persian *melophori*, the Indians, the Albanians, the "transplanted Carians" and the Mardian bowmen, and they were so positioned in order to face Alexander himself and the royal squadron.

Alexander led his force towards the right, and the Persians countered the movement, greatly outflanking him on their left in doing so. [2] By now the Scythian cavalry, riding along the front, were coming into contact with the troops at the head of Alexander's line, and Alexander still kept moving to the right. He was close to the point of leaving the terrain that had been trodden and made passable by the Persians, and Darius was now afraid that a Macedonian advance onto rough ground would make it impossible for him to use his chariots. He therefore ordered the troops in advance of his left to ride around the Macedonian right, where Alexander was at the head of his men, to prevent the Macedonians from extending that wing any further. [3] When that was happening, Alexander ordered his mercenary cavalry, led by Menidas, to launch an attack on them, but the Scythian horse, and the Bactrians who were formed up with the Scythians, counter-attacked. The mercenaries were few, and with their greatly superior numbers the Scythians drove them back. Alexander then ordered the Paeonians of Ariston and the mercenaries to mount an attack on the Scythians, and with that the barbarians gave ground. [4] The rest of the Bactrians now bore down on the Paeonians and the mercenaries, turning back to the battle those of their side who were already in flight and setting in motion a real cavalry engagement. Casualties amongst Alexander's men were higher: they were in difficulties because of the barbarian numerical superiority and also because the Scythians – both the soldiers and their mounts – had armour offering more effective protection. Even so, the Macedonians withstood their onslaught and, with forceful attacks made by one squadron after another, drove them out of formation.

[5] Meanwhile the barbarians unleashed their scythed chariots in the direction of Alexander himself, thinking that they would break up his phalanx. In this they were very wrong. First, as soon as the chariots began their attack, they were showered with spears by the Agrianes and the *akontistai* under Balacrus who were posted ahead of the cavalry of the companions. Also, these men grabbed the reins, pulled the drivers from the vehicles and, crowding around them, cut down the horses. [6] A number did in fact manage to pass through the Macedonian ranks, for these, following their instructions, parted where the chariots attacked. As a result the chariots passed through intact, and without harm to the men at whom they were aimed, but the grooms in Alexander's army and the royal hypaspists overpowered these chariots as well.[15]

14   By now Darius was attacking all along the line, and Alexander instructed Aretas to charge those Persians who were riding around the Macedonian right wing in an attempt to encircle it. [2] For a time Alexander kept leading his men in column. Then the horsemen who had gone out to assist those being encircled on the right wing made some headway in breaking the front of the barbarian line, and at this point the king veered towards the gap in the line. Forming into a wedge the cavalry of the Companions, and the part of the phalanx deployed in that quarter, he proceeded to lead them against Darius himself at running pace and raising the battle cry.

[3] For a short time there was hand-to-hand combat. Then the cavalry with Alexander, and the king himself, made a vigorous thrust, pushing the Persians and striking at their faces with their lances, while the Macedonian phalanx, in close order and bristling with spears, had already also begun attacking them. To Darius, who had long been in a state of panic, it was an utterly frightening sight, and he was the first to turn and run. The Persians attempting to ride around the Macedonian wing were also seized with panic when Aretas' troops made a spirited charge on them.

[4] In this quarter the Persians were in full flight, and the Macedonians were chasing and cutting down the fugitives. Simmias and his battalion, however, could no longer keep pace with Alexander in the pursuit. Instead, they halted the phalanx and fought on the spot, for word was brought that the Macedonian left was under severe pressure. [5] In fact, the Macedonian line had been broken in this sector, and some of the Indians and some of the Persian cavalry were forcing their way through the breach, to the point of reaching the pack animals. There the action was now hot. The Persians were

---

15   This is presumably an error for the *paides basilikoi* (i.e. the "Pages"), who are elsewhere associated with the *hippokomoi*, or grooms (see Arr. 4.13.1 = §1.3f), and who would have occupied a less dangerous position on the battlefield.

confidently attacking men for the most part unarmed, and who had not expected anyone to get through to them (which meant cutting through a double line of troops). In addition, when the Persians made their charge, the barbarian prisoners of war also joined them in attacking the Macedonians in the fray. [6] However, the commanders of the troops drawn up as a reserve force to the first phalanx were informed of the incident. They wheeled about to form a new front, in accordance with their orders, and attacked the Persians from behind, killing them in large numbers as they crowded around the pack animals (though some beat a retreat and escaped). The Persians on the right wing, meanwhile, were not yet aware of Darius' flight. They had ridden around Alexander's left and were attacking Parmenion's troops.

15   At that point the Macedonians found themselves for the first time under attack from two sides, and Parmenion swiftly despatched a message to Alexander to tell him that his situation was precarious and that he needed help. When the message reached Alexander, he gave up further pursuit, wheeled round and came at a gallop to the barbarian right with the cavalry of the Companions. Here he first of all charged those of the enemy cavalry who were in flight: the Parthyaeans, a number of the Indians, and the Persians, who represented the most numerous and the strongest section of the enemy. [2] This was the hardest cavalry fighting of the entire engagement. The barbarian configuration was a deep one, as they were in squadrons, and they clashed with Alexander's men head-on, eschewing the conventional tactics of the cavalry fight with its javelin-throwing and equestrian manoeuvres. Instead, it was a matter of each man trying to force his own way through, this being his only hope of saving himself, and of blows without number delivered and received – they were fighting now not for another man's victory but for their own survival. In that spot some sixty of Alexander's Companions fell, and Hephaestion himself was wounded, along with Coenus and Menidas. Even so, Alexander prevailed here as well.

[3] Those Persians who broke through Alexander's line were now in full flight, and Alexander was close to engaging with the right wing of the enemy. In the meantime the Thessalian cavalry had been performing brilliantly in an action in which they were not outclassed by Alexander – indeed, the barbarians on the right wing were already fleeing the field when Alexander engaged them. The king therefore turned from them and recommenced his pursuit of Darius, chasing him as long as there was daylight. Parmenion's troops followed in pursuit of the enemy with whom they had been engaged.

[4] After crossing the River Lycus,[16] however, Alexander pitched camp to give his men and the horses something of a respite, and Parmenion took the barbarian camp with its baggage, elephants and camels.

[5] Alexander gave his horsemen a rest until midnight, and then went on again at a rapid pace to Arbela where he thought he would seize Darius, his

---

16   The Greater Zab, which flows in a southerly direction to join the Tigris and separates Gaugamela from Arbela.

treasury and the other royal paraphernalia. He reached Arbela the following day after covering a total of something like 600 stades since the battle. He did not, however, catch Darius in Arbela, for the king was fleeing without stopping at all; but his treasury was taken and all his equipment. The chariot of Darius was once more captured; and taken for the second time, too, were his shield and bow and arrows.

[6] About a hundred of Alexander's men lost their lives and more than a thousand horses perished from wounds and exhaustion suffered in the pursuit (about half of them belonging to the Companions). The count of the barbarian corpses was reportedly around 300,000, but prisoners taken far outnumbered the dead, and the elephants and chariots not destroyed in the battle were also taken.

[7] Such was the end of this engagement. It took place during Aristophanes' archonship at Athens, in the month of Pyanepsion.[17] And the prophecy of Aristander – that the battle and victory of Alexander would take place in the same month as a lunar eclipse – came true.

2(h)　Quintus Curtius Rufus 4.12.1–16.9

Darius immediately despatched an advance unit of 3,000 horse under Mazaeus to secure the roads the enemy would take. [2] Alexander, on the completion of the last rites for Darius' wife, left all the more cumbersome appendages to his army in the fortified camp under a small garrison and hastened to meet the enemy. [3] He had split his infantry into two bodies, giving cavalry cover to the flanks on both sides, and the column was followed by the baggage. [4] Then he sent ahead Menidas and 200 horse with orders to determine Darius' whereabouts, but since Mazaeus had taken up a position close by, Menidas did not dare advance beyond him, reporting to Alexander that he had heard nothing but the noise of men and the neighing of horses. [5] On sighting the scouting party in the distance, Mazaeus also pulled back to the Persian camp with news of the approach of the enemy, and Darius, who wanted to settle the issue in the open plains, accordingly ordered his men to arms and drew up his battle line.

[6] On the left wing were about 1,000 Bactrian horse, the same number of Dahae and 4,000 Arachosians and Susians. These were followed by 100 scythed chariots, next to which stood Bessus with 8,000 horse, also Bactrian. [7] Two thousand Massagetae completed the cavalry detachment. Alongside these Darius had added the infantry contingents of several races, not indiscriminately mixed but each contingent attached to the cavalry of its respective race. Then came Persians, Mardians and Sogdianians led by Ariobarzanes and Orontobates. [8] These two commanded units of the force, but supreme command rested with Orsines, who was descended from one of the seven

17　Arrian's date is out by one month, probably as a result of incorrectly converting from Macedonian to Attic (Athenian) months. Plutarch, *Alexander* 31.8 (cf. *Camillus* 19.5) says the battle occurred in the Attic month Boedromion, thus placing it in late September 331.

Persians and also traced his line back to the renowned King Cyrus. [9] These were followed by other tribes unfamiliar even to their own allies and then came Phradates with a mighty column of Caspii at the head of fifty chariots. Behind the chariots were Indians and other residents of the Red Sea area, who provided nominal rather than real support, [10] and this detachment was completed by another group of scythed chariots to which Darius had attached his foreign troops. These were followed by the so-called lesser Armenians, themselves followed by Babylonians, and after both came the Belitae and the inhabitants of the Cossaean mountains. [11] Next were the Gortuae, a people of Euboean stock who had once returned with the Medes and now had degenerated to total ignorance of their original culture. Next to them Darius had positioned the Phrygians and the Cataonians, and the entire column was brought up by the Parthyaei, a race living in the areas which are today populated by the Parthians who emigrated from Scythia. Such was the appearance of the left wing.

[12] The right was composed of people from greater Armenia, Cadusia, Cappadocia, Syria and Media, and these also had fifty scythed chariots. [13] The total for the whole army amounted to 45,000 cavalry and 200,000 infantry. Drawn up as described, they advanced 10 stades and when the order was given to halt awaited their enemy under arms.

[14] For no apparent reason alarm permeated Alexander's army. The men were panic-stricken as fear swept imperceptibly through all their breasts. Intermittent flashes in the bright sky, of the type seen on hot summer days, had the appearance of fire; the Macedonians believed that they were flames gleaming in Darius' camp, and that they had negligently advanced among enemy outposts. [15] Now if Mazaeus, who was guarding the road, had struck while they were still panicking, a terrible disaster could have been inflicted on the Macedonians, but in fact he sat inactive on the that hill he had occupied, content not to be under attack. [16] Alexander, learning of the consternation among the troops, ordered that a halt be signalled and that his men lay down their arms and rest. He told them the sudden panic was completely unjustified, that the enemy still stood a long way off, [17] so, finally pulling themselves together, they simultaneously recovered their confidence and took up their weapons. Even so Alexander believed that in the circumstances the safest plan was to establish a fortified camp on the spot.

[18] Mazaeus had positioned himself with a select cavalry unit on a high hill overlooking the Macedonian camp, but the next day he returned to Darius, either because he panicked or because his mission had been limited to gathering intelligence. [19] The Macedonians then occupied the hill which he had abandoned, for it was safer than the flat ground and it also afforded a view of the enemy battle line then being deployed on the plain. [20] But the humid atmosphere of the hills had diffused a mist over the area and, while this did not prevent a general view of the enemy, it did render it impossible to see how their forces were divided and organized. The Persian horde had flooded the plains, and the noise from the myriads of soldiers had filled the ears even of those a long way off.

[21] The king began to have second thoughts and to weigh up Parmenion's recommendation against his own strategy – all too late, for they had reached the stage where only victory would allow their army to retire without incurring disaster. [22] Hiding his concern, Alexander therefore ordered the mercenary cavalry from Paeonia to advance. [23] As was observed above, he had already drawn out the phalanx in two bodies, each of which received cavalry protection. Now the mist began to disperse and the brightening daylight revealed the enemy line. The Macedonians, eager for the fight or else tired of waiting, emitted a thundering war-cry; the Persians replied, and the woods and valleys round about rang with a terrifying noise. [24] Restraining the Macedonians from charging the enemy was no longer possible, but Alexander still thought it preferable to fortify his camp there on the hill, and ordered a rampart to be built. This task was quickly finished and he then withdrew into his tent, from which the whole enemy battle line could be seen.

. . .

> Editor's note: At this point Parmenion, supported by Polyperchon, urges a night attack on the Persians, which Alexander rejects. This is one of several such exchanges between Alexander and Parmenion that are intended to place Parmenion in a bad light. See Carney (2000b: 264–73).

13   [26] Alexander had the rampart levelled; then he ordered the troops to march out and drew up his line of battle. On the right wing was placed the cavalry unit called the *agema*, which was led by Cleitus. To him, Alexander also adjoined Philotas' cavalry squadrons, stationing on his flank the other cavalry commanders, [27] with Meleager's squadron standing last and the phalanx following it. Behind the phalanx were the *argyraspides*,[18] under the command of Parmenion's son Nicanor. [28] In reserve stood Coenus and his detachment, and behind him were placed the Orestae and Lyncestae, followed by Polyperchon and then the foreign troops. The latter, in the absence of their general Amyntas, were commanded by Philip, son of Balacrus;[19] only recently had they entered an alliance with the Macedonians. This was how the right wing appeared.

[29] On the left Craterus was in charge of the Peloponnesian cavalry – to which were added the squadrons of Achaeans, Locrians and Malians – and the rear was brought up by the Thessalian horse under Philip. The infantry

18   The "Silver Shields." Their mention here and in Diodorus 17.57.2 is an anachronism ascribable to the common source, probably Cleitarchus of Alexandria (see Introduction). Arrian correctly identifies them as hypaspists (see §VI.2g, above). At some point, probably in India, the hypaspists decorated their shields with silver and changed their name: see glossary s.v. *argyraspides*, with modern literature.
19   Amyntas son of Andromenes was on a recreciting mission in Macedonia, His unit comprised *pezhetairoi* from Upper Macedonia, not "foreign troops." Curtius' text is corrupt at this point, and even the words Philip son of Balacrus must be restored from the otherwise meaningless *philagrus* and *baracri*.

line was given protection by the cavalry. Such was the appearance of the left wing in front.

[30] To prevent an encircling movement by the numerically superior Persians, Alexander had enclosed his rear with a strong division, and he also strengthened his wings with reserves which he faced to the side, not the front, so that the wings would be ready for combat in event of the enemy trying to encircle them. [31] In this position were the Agrianes commanded by Attalus, along with the Cretan archers. The rearmost ranks he faced away from the front, so that the circular formation could give protection to the whole army, and here were placed the Illyrians plus the mercenary troops. Alexander had also stationed the Thracian light-armed troops in this position. [32] So flexible was the battle formation which he arranged that the troops standing at the rear to prevent an encircling movement could still wheel round and be transferred to the front. Consequently his flanks received as much protection as the front line, and the rear as much as the flanks.

[33] After making these troop dispositions Alexander gave instructions to the men. If the Persians shouted as they released their scythed chariots, they were to open ranks and receive the charge in silence – Alexander was sure that meeting no resistance the chariots would pass through the ranks without inflicting damage – but if the enemy did not shout they should strike panic into them with war-cries and stab their frightened horses in the belly from both sides. [34] The wing commanders were instructed to extend the wings so that they would not be surrounded by being too compressed, but not to weaken the rear in doing so. [35] Baggage and prisoners, including Darius' mother and children, who were kept under guard, he positioned close to the army on high ground, leaving a small force in charge of them. As on other occasions, Parmenion was given command of the left wing; Alexander himself took his position on the right.

[36] Before they were within javelin range a certain deserter, Bion, came galloping at full speed to Alexander with a report that Darius had dug iron spikes into the ground at the point at which he thought his enemy was going to unleash his cavalry, and he had clearly marked the spot to enable his own men to avoid the trap. [37] Alexander had a guard put on the deserter and assembled his generals. Revealing what had been reported, he warned them to avoid the designated area and to inform the horsemen of the danger.

. . .

Editor's note: At this point, Alexander encourages his troops, and Darius does likewise.

15   Alexander meanwhile gave the order for his line to advance at an angle; he wanted to circumvent the trap revealed to him by the deserter and also to meet Darius, who commanded a wing. [2] Darius, too, turned his line at the same angle, telling Bessus to order the Massagetan cavalry to charge Alexander's

left wing on the flank.[20] [3] Before him Darius kept his scythed charioteers which, on a signal, he released *en masse* against the enemy. The charioteers charged at full speed in order to increase the Macedonian casualties by taking them by surprise, [4] and accordingly some were killed by the spears that projected well beyond the chariot poles and others dismembered by the scythes set on either side. It was no gradual withdrawal that the Macedonians made but a disordered flight, breaking their ranks. [5] Mazaeus struck further panic into them in their consternation by ordering 1,000 cavalry to ride around and plunder the enemy's baggage, thinking the captives who were kept under guard with the baggage would break free when they saw their own people coming.

[6] Parmenion, on the left wing, had not missed this, and so he swiftly despatched Polydamas to advise the king of the danger and to ask for his orders. [7] After hearing Polydamas, Alexander said: "Go tell Parmenion that if we win this battle we shall not only recover our own baggage but also capture the enemy's. [8] So there is no reason for him to weaken the line in any way. Rather his actions should do credit to me and my father, Philip – let him ignore the loss of the baggage and fight courageously."

[9] Meanwhile the Persians had been pillaging the baggage. With most of the guards killed, the prisoners broke free, grabbed whatever they came upon that would serve as weapons and, joining forces with their countrymen's cavalry, attacked the Macedonians, who were now exposed to danger on two fronts.

[10] Sisigambis' attendants joyfully brought her the message that Darius had won, that the enemy had been routed with great loss of life, and that they had finally even been stripped of their baggage. For the attendants believed the fortunes of the battle to be the same everywhere, and that the victorious Persians had split up to plunder. [11] Though the other prisoners urged her to end her sorrow, Sisigambis retained her former demeanour: not a word left her lips and there was no change in her colour or expression. She sat motionless – afraid, I think, of aggravating fortune by expressing joy prematurely – so that people looking at her could not decide what she would prefer the outcome to be.

[12] In the meantime Alexander's cavalry commander, Menidas, had arrived with a few squadrons to bring help to the baggage (whether this was his own idea or done on Alexander's orders is unknown), but he was unable to hold out against an attack from the Cadusians and Scythians. With no real attempt at fighting he retreated to the king, less a champion of the baggage than a witness to its loss! [13] Indignation had already crushed Alexander's resolve, and he was afraid – not without justification – that concern with recovering the baggage might draw his men from the fight. Accordingly, he sent Aretes, the leader of the lancers called *sarissophoroi*, against the Scythians.

[14] Meanwhile, after causing havoc in Alexander's front lines, the chariots had now charged the phalanx, and the Macedonians received the charge with a firm resolve, permitting them to penetrate to the middle of the column. [15]

---

20   This is the Macedonian *left* as viewed from the Persian side of the battlefield. Bessus thus attacked the Macedonian *right*, near Alexander's own position.

Their formation resembled a rampart; after creating an unbroken line of spears, they stabbed the flanks of the horses from both sides as they charged recklessly ahead. Then they began to surround the chariots and to throw the fighters out of them. [16] Horses and charioteers fell in huge numbers, covering the battlefield. The charioteers could not control the terrified animals which, frequently tossing their necks, had not only thrown off their yokes but also overturned the chariots, and wounded horses were trying to drag along dead ones, unable to stay in one place in their panic and yet too weak to go forward. [17] Even so a few chariots escaped to the back line, inflicting a pitiful death on those they encountered. The ground was littered with the severed limbs of soldiers and, as there was no pain while the wounds were still warm, the men did not in fact drop their weapons, despite the mutilation and their weakness, until they dropped dead from loss of blood.

[18] In the meantime Aretes had killed the leader of the Scythians who were looting the baggage. When they panicked he put greater pressure on them, until on Darius' orders some Bactrians appeared to change the fortunes of the battle. Many Macedonians were crushed in the first onslaught, and more fled back to Alexander. [19] Then, raising a shout as victors do, the Persians made a ferocious rush at their enemy in the belief that they had been crushed in every quarter. Alexander reproached and encouraged his terrified men, singlehandedly reviving the flagging battle and then, their confidence finally restored, he ordered them to charge the enemy.

[20] The Persian line was thinner on the right wing, since it was from there that the Bactrians had withdrawn to attack the baggage; Alexander advanced on these weakened ranks, causing great loss of Persian life with his attack. [21] The Persians on the left wing, however, positioned themselves to his rear as he fought, hoping that he could be boxed in. He would have faced terrible danger, pinned in the middle as he was, had not the Agrianian cavalry come galloping to assault the Persians surrounding the king and forced them to turn towards them by cutting into their rear. There was confusion on both sides. Alexander had the Persians before and behind him, [22] and those putting pressure on his rear were themselves under attack from the Agrianian cavalry; the Bactrians on their return from looting the enemy baggage could not form up again; and at the same time several detachments broken off from the main body were fighting wherever chance had brought them into contact.

[23] With the main bodies almost together the two kings spurred on their men to battle. There were more Persian dead now, and the number of wounded on each side was about equal. Darius was riding in his chariot, Alexander on horseback, [24] and both had a guard of handpicked men who had no regard for their own lives – with their king lost they had neither the desire nor the opportunity to reach safety, and each man thought it a noble fate to meet his end before the eyes of his king. [25] But the men facing the greatest danger were, in fact, those given the best protection, since each soldier sought for himself the glory of killing the enemy king.

[26] Now whether their eyes were deceiving them or they really did sight it, Alexander's guards believed they saw an eagle gently hovering just above the

king's head, frightened neither by the clash of arms nor the groans of the dying, and for a long time it was observed around Alexander's horse, apparently hanging in the air rather than flying. [27] At all events the prophet Aristander, dressed in white and with a laurel-branch in his right hand, kept pointing out to the soldiers, who were preoccupied with the fight, the bird which he claimed was an infallible omen of victory. [28] The men who had been terrified moments before were now fired with tremendous enthusiasm and confidence for the fight, especially after Darius' charioteer, who drove the horses and was seated before the king, was run through by a spear. Persians and Macedonians alike were convinced that it was the king who had been killed, [29] and though the fortunes of battle were, in fact, still even, Darius' "kinsmen" and squires caused consternation almost throughout the battlefield with their mournful wailing and wild shouts and groans. The left wing was routed, abandoning the king's chariot which the close-formed ranks on the right received into the middle of their column.

[30] It was said that Darius drew his scimitar and considered avoiding ignominious flight by an honourable death but, highly visible as he was in his chariot, he felt ashamed to abandon his forces when they were not all committed to leaving the battle. [31] While he wavered between hope and despair, the Persians gradually began to give ground and broke ranks.

Alexander changed horses – he had exhausted several – and began to stab at the faces of the Persians still resisting and at the backs of those who ran. [32] It was no longer a battle but a massacre, and Darius also turned his chariot in flight. The victor kept hard on the heels of this fleeing enemy, but a dust-cloud rising into the air obstructed visibility; [33] the Macedonians wandered around like people in the dark, converging only when they recognized a voice or heard a signal. But they could hear the sound of reins time and time again lashing the chariot horses, the only trace they had of the fleeing king.

16 On the left wing, which (as stated above) was under Parmenion's command, the fortunes of the battle were very different for both sides. Mazaeus exerted pressure on the Macedonian cavalry squadrons by making a violent attack on them with all his horse [2] and, having superior numbers, he had already begun to encircle their infantry when Parmenion ordered some horsemen to report their critical position to Alexander and tell him that flight was inevitable unless help came quickly. [3] The king had already covered a great distance in his pursuit of the fleeing Persians when the bad news from Parmenion arrived. His mounted men were told to pull up their horses and the infantry column came to a halt. Alexander was furious that victory was being snatched out of his hands and that Darius was more successful in flight than he himself was in pursuit.

[4] Meanwhile news of the king's defeat had reached Mazaeus, and he, in his alarm at his side's reverse of fortune, began to relax his pressure on the dispirited Macedonians despite his superior strength. Although ignorant of why the attack had lost its impetus, Parmenion quickly seized the chance of victory. [5] He had the Thessalian cavalry summoned to him and said: "Do you see how

after making a furious attack on us a moment ago those men are retreating in sudden panic? It must be that our king's good fortune has brought victory for us, too. The battlefield is completely covered with Persian dead. [6] What are you waiting for? Aren't you a match even for soldiers in flight?"

His words rang true, and fresh hope revived their drooping spirits. At a gallop they charged their enemy, who started to give ground not just gradually but swiftly, and all that prevented this being termed a flight was the fact that the Persians had not yet turned their backs. However, since he was ignorant of how the king was faring on the right wing, Parmenion checked his men [7] and, given the opportunity to retreat, Mazaeus crossed the Tigris – not taking a direct route but a longer, circuitous one which accordingly offered greater safety – and entered Babylon with the remnants of the defeated army.

[8] With only a few accompanying him in his flight, Darius had sped to the river Lycus. After crossing he considered breaking down the bridge, since reports kept arriving that the enemy would soon be there, but he could see that destroying the bridge would make the thousands of men who had not yet reached the river an easy prey for his enemy. [9] We have it on good authority that, as he went off leaving the bridge intact, he declared that he would rather leave a road to those chasing him than take one away from the Persian fugitives. Darius himself, covering a huge distance in his flight, reached Arbela about midnight.

2(i)   Plutarch, Alexander 33.8–11

Darius could now see all the perils, and the forces that had been deployed ahead of him were being driven back towards him. It was no easy task to turn his chariot and drive through: the wheels were becoming entangled and stuck amidst all the corpses, and the horses, caught up †and hidden† in the mass of bodies, were rearing up and alarming the driver. The king then abandoned the chariot and his arms, mounting and taking to flight on a mare that (they say) had recently foaled. [9] It seems that even then he would not have made good his escape but for the arrival of a second set of horsemen from Parmenion calling on Alexander for assistance. A large section of the Persian force was still in formation in his quarter, said Parmenion, and the enemy were not giving ground.

[10] There is general criticism of a lacklustre and apathetic performance on Parmenion's part in that battle, either because age was by now to some extent sapping his courage or because, as Callisthenes has it, he was embittered and envious of the officious and self-important way in which Alexander was wielding his authority. [11] In any case, Alexander was annoyed by Parmenion's call for help, but did not tell his men the truth about it. Instead, he gave the signal to fall back on the ground that he was calling a halt to the slaughter and that night was coming on. He was riding to the supposedly dangerous quarter when he heard on the way that the enemy had been totally vanquished and was now in flight.

The Hydaspes River

In 326 Alexander had successfully brought under his sway the regions to the west of the Indus (see the accounts of Aornus, below). The marshals Hephaestion and Perdiccas had bridged that river and prepared the way for Alexander's alliance with the dynast, Taxiles, who ruled the territory between the Indus and the Hydaspes (Jhelum). With Taxiles' help, the Macedonians now prepared to confront the most powerful leader in the Punjab, a king whose physical stature matched the extent of his military power, Porus. But Porus occupied the eastern banks of the Hydaspes River, and he possessed numerous elephants which rendered suicidal any direct attack by Alexander across the river. It would not be possible to repeat the tactics of the Granicus, and the Hydaspes was at any rate a much more imposing obstacle. Hence Alexander was forced to split his forces and to attempt an encircling manoeuvre, which involved a crossing of the river some 17 kilometers upstream. The resulting battle was a bloody one and the Macedonian victory hard won; Porus became an indispensable ally in the East, though once Alexander returned to the West his subjection to the Macedonian empire was at best nominal. See Hamilton (1956) and Devine (1987). For the location of the crossing, see Stein (1932) and Wood (1997: 184–7).

2(j) Arrian 5.9–19

Alexander pitched camp on the bank of the Hydaspes, and Porus was to be seen on the other bank with his whole army and his force of elephants. Porus himself remained there and mounted guard on the crossing at the point where Alexander was encamped; but he established guard posts at the various other points where fording the river was comparatively easy, assigning officers to each post. His intention was to prevent the Macedonians from crossing the river.

[2] When Alexander observed this, he thought he should move his troops in all different directions so that Porus would be kept puzzled. He split his force into several sections, and personally led some of his men to various points in the countryside where he would lay waste enemy territory or scout out places where the river seemed to him more easily fordable; others he assigned to various commanders and sent these off in all directions, as well. [3] Also, grain was continually being brought to his camp from all over the country on his side of the Hydaspes. This made it clear to Porus that Alexander was determined to stick to the bank until the water level in the river fell during the winter, thus enabling him to cross at many points. His boats were also sailing up and down the river, there were hides stuffed with hay in view, and the bank could be seen teeming with horsemen and infantry.

All this would not allow Porus to rest easy, or permit him to select one particular spot to watch and on which to focus his preparations. [4] Moreover, at that particular time, all the Indian rivers were flowing with high and muddy waters, and with a swift current. It was the season of the year when the sun was turning after the summer solstice, and that is when torrential rain pours from the heavens on the land of India. It is also the time of the melting of the snows in the Caucasus[21] – where the sources of most of the rivers are to be found – which greatly swells the volume of the rivers. In winter, in fact, they contract again and become small and clear. They are then also fordable in places, though not the Indus and Ganges. But the Hydaspes, at least, becomes passable.

10   Alexander declared openly that he would await that season of the year if he were prevented from crossing at this particular time. But he neverthe-less waited there on the lookout for any possibility of a swift and unobserved crossing. He realized that he could not cross at the point where Porus was encamped on the bank of the Hydaspes – his elephants were too numerous, and he had a mighty army, already deployed and armed to the teeth, that would fall on the Macedonians as they emerged from the river. [2] He even thought it likely that the horses would refuse to set foot on the opposite bank: the elephants would immediately come bearing down on them and terrify them by their appearance and their trumpeting. In fact, it seemed to him that, even before reaching that point, the horses would not remain on the hides during the crossing; they would jump into the water in frenzy at the sight of the elephants on the far bank. [3] Alexander therefore made up his mind to make a furtive crossing, taking the following course of action. At night he would take most of his cavalry to various points along the river bank where he would create a clamour, raise the war cry and produce all other such noises as would come from men preparing to cross the river. Porus would actually parallel his movements on the other side, leading his elephants towards the shouting, and Alexander got him into the habit of making these corre-sponding movements. [4] This went on over a long period and it would turn out to be no more than shouting and yelling. Porus accordingly no longer reacted to the sorties of the cavalry: knowing his anxiety was groundless, he remained in place in his camp, though he did have lookouts posted at many points along the bank. When Alexander had eased Porus' fears with regard to the nocturnal operations, he devised the following scheme.

11   There was a headland that projected from the bank of the Hydaspes at a spot where there was a major bend in the river. The headland was thickly forested with trees of all kinds, and facing it was an island in the river that was wooded and, being deserted, trackless land. Alexander observed that the island faced the headland, and that both spots were wooded and suitable for concealing an attempt at crossing, and so he decided that this was where he would ferry his army over. [2] The headland and the island were some 150 stades away from the main encampment. Sentinels had been posted all along the bank by Alexander, and the distance between them was such that they

---

21   Generally and inaccurately used to describe the mountains to the north. The Alexan-der historians have earlier referred to the Hindu Kush as the Caucasus.

could see each other and easily hear orders, wherever they came from. Moreover, during the night, shouts were raised from every direction for several
nights running, and fires were kept alight.

[3] Once Alexander had made the decision to attempt the crossing, preparations for the passage were begun quite openly in the camp. Here, Craterus
was left in command, with his own cavalry squadron, the cavalry of the Arachosians and the Parapamisadae. He also had the Macedonian infantry battalions of Alcetas and Polyperchon, and the nomarchs of the Indians in this
area, together with the 5,000 men under their command. [4] Craterus was
instructed not to make the crossing before Porus had left his camp with his
troops to confront Alexander and his men, or before he knew that Porus was
in flight and the Macedonians victorious.

"If Porus comes against me at the head of some part of his force,"
Alexander said, "and another part is left behind in the camp along with
elephants, then you stay in position where you are. But if he leads his entire
pack of elephants against me, with part of his army left behind in camp, then
you must cross quickly. For the elephants alone stand in the way of the horses
disembarking; the rest of the army presents no problem."

12 Such were the orders issued to Craterus. Between the island and the
main camp, where Craterus had been left in command, Meleager, Attalus and
Gorgias were posted with the mercenary cavalry and infantry. Their instructions, too, were to cross the river – in sections, into which they were to divide
the force – whenever they saw the Indians already engaged in the battle.

[2] For his own force, Alexander selected the following: the *agema* of the
Companions; the cavalry squadrons of Hephaestion, Perdiccas and
Demetrius; the cavalry from Bactria, Sogdiana and Scythia; and the mounted
archers of the Dahae. In addition, from the phalanx, he chose: the hypaspists;
the battalions of Cleitus and Coenus;[22] the archers; and the Agrianes.

He took these stealthily along a route a considerable distance from the bank
so that he would not be seen making his way towards the island and the headland, the location where he had decided to make the crossing. [3] There, in
the course of the night, the hides – they had been brought here well in
advance – were filled with hay and meticulously sewn up. During the night
a violent downpour came from the heavens, and by this Alexander's preparations and attempt to cross were even better concealed – the noise from the
weapons and the hubbub of orders being passed along were drowned out by
the thunder and the rain. [4] Most of Alexander's boats had been brought to
the place in sections; they had been reassembled covertly and were now all
hidden in the wood, the triacontors included.

Just before dawn the wind and rain died down. Alexander's cavalry
embarked on the rafts made of the hides along with as many infantrymen as

---

22 Cleitus here is the taxiarch "White" Cleitus. The famous "Black" Cleitus was already
dead. Coenus' battalion is no longer under his personal command. As Arrian's account
shows, Coenus himself was leading a cavalry unit (hipparchy).

these floating platforms would hold, and they crossed in the direction of the island. This was to prevent their being sighted by the watchmen posted by Porus before they had passed the island and were only a short distance from the bank.

13   Alexander himself made the crossing on board a triaconter, accompanied by his Somatophylakes Ptolemy, Perdiccas and Lysimachus, as well as by Seleucus – one of the *hetairoi*, who subsequently became a king – and by half the hypaspists. Other triacontors ferried over the rest of the hypaspists. Once the force passed the island it could now be easily seen approaching the bank, and the watchmen, observing its swift approach, rode off to Porus with all the speed their horses could muster. [2] Meanwhile Alexander, who disembarked first, took with him the men from the other triacontors and drew the cavalry up in the order in which they kept disembarking (for the cavalry had been ordered by him to disembark first). He then took these and advanced in battle order.

He had, in fact, through ignorance of the terrain, unwittingly disembarked not on the mainland but on an island, one of large proportions (which was why he was unaware that it was an island), but cut off from the land by a narrow stream of river water. [3] At the same time, a fierce downpour that had kept up for most of the night had swollen the stream so that Alexander's cavalry failed to discern a place to wade across, and fear spread that the crossing required again all the effort already expended on the first one. But then the ford was found, and Alexander led the men over, though he had difficulty in doing so: where the water was at its deepest, it was above the chests of the infantrymen, while the horses had only their heads above the surface.

[4] But when this section of water was passed as well, the king led the *agema* of the cavalry to the left wing and selected the best of his other cavalry officers to go with them. He then lined up his mounted archers in front of the entire cavalry force. Immediately next to the cavalry he placed the royal hypaspists, who were under Seleucus' command, and next to them the *agema*, followed by the rest of the hypaspists,[23] ordered according to the precedence of commanders at that particular time. On the wings of the phalanx stood his bowmen, the Agrianes and the javelin-throwers.

14   After configuring his forces in this manner Alexander ordered the infantry to come up behind in battle order and at a quick march. They were little short of 6,000 in number. It seemed to him, however, that he enjoyed cavalry superiority, and so he personally took the cavalrymen apart from the rest and led them forward at a rapid pace. These numbered about 5,000. He instructed the commander of his archers, Tauron, to lead the bowmen, also

---

23   There is a problem here. Arrian mentions too many units of hypaspists. Various interpretations are possible, but it seems most likely that Seleucus' "royal hypaspists" and the *agema* are identical. See Heckel (1992a: 244–6); for other possibilities, see Bosworth (1995: 283–5).

at a rapid pace, along with the cavalry. [2] His reasoning was that, if Porus engaged him with his entire force, he would either have little difficulty in defeating him with cavalry charges, or else he would keep him at bay until the infantry came to join the action. Should the Indians be stunned by his singularly audacious crossing and take to their heels, he would not keep far behind them in their flight – the greater the bloodshed in the retreat, the less there would remain for him to do later.

[3] Aristobulus records that Porus' son arrived on the scene with some 60 chariots before Alexander's final crossing from the large island. He could have prevented Alexander from making a crossing that was difficult even when nobody was trying to stop him, he says; the Indians only had to jump down from their chariots and fall upon the men who were the first to land. Instead, the son passed by with his chariots and allowed Alexander to cross without risk, after which the king set his mounted archers upon the Indians and had no difficulty in driving them back, injuring a number.

[4] Others have it that there was actually a battle at the point of landing fought against Alexander and his cavalry by the Indians who arrived with Porus' son. These say, in fact, that Porus' son arrived with a larger force, that Alexander sustained wounds at his hands and that the king's much-loved horse, Bucephalas, was killed in the battle, his wounds also inflicted by the son of Porus. But Ptolemy son of Lagus, with whom I find myself in agreement, has a different version. [5] Ptolemy says that the son was indeed sent by Porus, but not at the head of a mere 60 chariots. (And, in fact, that Porus would have sent out his son with only 60 chariots, after being told by his scouts that Alexander had himself crossed the Hydaspes, or that some part of his army had crossed, is somewhat implausible. [6] If these chariots were on an intelligence-gathering mission, their number was large and lacking the flexibility needed for the withdrawal. If, on the other hand, their goal was to prevent the crossing of those of the enemy who had yet made it over, and to attack those who had already landed, they were insufficient for the operation.) Ptolemy actually says that Porus' son came on the scene with 2,000 cavalry and 120 chariots, but that Alexander stymied him, having already made his final crossing from the island.

15 Ptolemy, like other writers, adds that Alexander initially sent his mounted archers against these troops, while he himself led the cavalry. For, says Ptolemy, the king thought Porus was advancing on him in full force, with this cavalry as an advance detachment riding ahead of the rest of the army. [2] When he received precise information regarding the Indian numbers, however, he made a swift attack on them with the cavalry he had with him. The Indians then buckled when they caught sight of Alexander in person and the solid cavalry division around him, which was attacking not in line but by squadrons. The result, says Ptolemy, was that about 400 of their cavalry fell, and with them the son of Porus, after which the Indians' chariots were taken, horses and all. They were too heavy in the retreat, and in the action itself they had been rendered ineffectual by the mud.

[3] The Indian cavalry who made good their escape reported to Porus that Alexander had made the crossing with his army in full force and that his son had been killed in the battle. Porus was now in a dilemma, especially as the men left with Craterus in the main camp opposite him were evidently getting their crossing under way. [4] The decision he reached was to march against Alexander himself with his entire force; he would fight a decisive battle against the strongest part of the Macedonian army and its king. He still left behind in the camp a few elephants with a small detachment of men to deter Craterus' cavalry from the bank. He then took his entire cavalry – some 30,000 men – and all his 300 chariots, together with 200 elephants and the pick of his infantry (about 30,000 men), and set out to face Alexander.

[5] Porus reached a spot that seemed to him to be without mud, where the sandy soil provided a completely flat and firm surface that would enable his horses to charge and wheel around. Here he deployed his force. He set his elephants in front, with no more than a plethron between them. In this way the elephants formed a line before the entire infantry phalanx and provided a deterrent for the cavalry in Alexander's force. [6] Porus did not think that any of the enemy would have the nerve to plunge into the spaces between the elephants – not those with horses (because the horses would take fright), and even less the infantry. For these would be kept at bay by the heavy Indian infantry who would be attacking them head-on, and trampled under when the elephants turned on them.

[7] Next to the elephants were stationed Porus' infantry, who did not form the front line with the animals but were in a second row behind them, the disposition of companies virtually corresponding to the spaces between the beasts. He also had infantry positioned on the wings stretching beyond the elephants, and cavalry was deployed next to the infantry on both wings, with chariots before them.

16   Such was the deployment of Porus' line of battle. Alexander, however, saw the Indians forming up and halted his cavalry so that those of the infantry still advancing could catch up with them. When the phalanx, too, had come up to join him, advancing at speed, he did not immediately draw up the line and lead it forward – he wanted to avoid presenting a spirited barbarian force with an adversary who was exhausted and out of breath. Instead, he kept his cavalry performing circular manoeuvres and rested the infantry until he had revived them.

[2] When he looked at the Indian battle order, Alexander decided against heading for the centre where the elephants had been put out front and where the infantry formation was most dense. He felt apprehensive about those very aspects that were at the basis of Porus' calculations in making his deployment. Instead, feeling that he enjoyed cavalry superiority, he personally took most of the cavalry and rode towards the enemy left, where he planned to attack. [3] He sent Coenus towards the right at the head of his own cavalry squadron and that of Demetrius. When the barbarians should see the dense formation of the Macedonian cavalry facing them and bring up their own to

counter them, Coenus was under orders to attack them from the rear. Command of the infantry phalanx was assigned to Seleucus, Antigenes and Tauron, and these were not to engage until they saw the enemy infantry and cavalry phalanx thrown into disorder by the king's cavalry.

[4] Alexander was now coming into spear range, and he sent forward against the Indian left wing his mounted archers, who numbered about a thousand. The idea was to disrupt the enemy stationed at that point with showers of arrows and with charging horses. Taking the cavalry of the Companions, Alexander himself also rode swiftly against the barbarian left, eager to attack it while it was in chaos and still drawn up as a column, and before the enemy horse could be deployed.

17   Meanwhile, the Indians brought together their cavalry from every part of the field, and they rode parallel to Alexander to counter his moves. Coenus' troops then began to appear to their rear, as they had been instructed. When the Indians saw this, they were obliged to form up their cavalry so that it faced both ways; the largest and strongest section faced Alexander, and the rest turned towards Coenus and his troops. [2] And that had the immediate effect of breaking the Indians' formation, and their resolve. Alexander saw his chance when the Indian cavalry was turning to face both ways, and he charged at those who stood before him. The result was that the Indians did not even wait for the attack but fell back in disorder to the elephants, as though to a protective wall. [3] At that moment the drivers of the elephants drove their animals against the cavalry, and the Macedonian phalanx in its turn advanced on the elephants, throwing their javelins at the drivers and encircling the beasts, which they subjected to volleys of weapons from every side.

The engagement was now unlike any of the previous battles. The beasts were running into the infantry ranks and wherever they turned they caused heavy casualties in the Macedonian phalanx, dense though it was, while the Indian cavalry, seeing the infantry now engaged in the action, turned round once more and themselves attacked the Macedonian horse. [4] But Alexander and his men, with their clear superiority in strength and skill, got the better of them once more, and the Indians were again driven back to the elephants. At this juncture the whole of Alexander's cavalry had massed together into a single body, not under orders but simply brought into such a formation in the process of fighting, and wherever they charged the Indian ranks they disengaged only after inflicting massive slaughter.

[5] The elephants were now boxed in, and the damage inflicted by them fell on friend no less than foe, with men trampled under as the beasts twisted and turned. The Indian cavalry, because they were hemmed in around the elephants in a confined space, incurred heavy fatalities. Most of the drivers of the elephants, too, had been brought down by spears, and the elephants themselves no longer had their separate position in the battle, some of them wounded, and others fatigued and driverless. [6] Instead, virtually crazy with their distress, they were attacking friends and foes alike, butting and

trampling and massacring in every conceivable way. The Macedonians, however, had plenty of space and were attacking the animals when and as they liked. Retiring wherever they charged, they would nevertheless stay close to them, hurling their spears whenever the beasts turned back. It was the Indians, who had now withdrawn to a point amongst the elephants, who were actually incurring the greatest damage from them.

[7] Eventually the animals grew tired and their charges lost vigour. Now simply trumpeting, they proceeded to retreat, like ships backing water. Alexander then threw his cavalry in a circle around the entire force, and ordered the infantry to lock shields, to group tightly and to advance as a phalanx. And thus it was that, with few exceptions, the cavalry of the Indians went down in the engagement. Cut down, too, were their infantry, the Macedonians now pressing hard on them from every side. At this juncture an opening appeared in Alexander's cavalry, and the Indians all took to flight.

18   Craterus and the other officers of Alexander's army who had been left on the bank of the Hydaspes saw Alexander winning a glorious victory, and at this very moment they also proceeded to cross the river. And they were responsible for just as much slaughter as the Indians retreated, coming fresh to the pursuit as they were, and replacing Alexander's exhausted men.

[2] The Indian dead numbered slightly fewer than 20,000 infantry and some 3,000 cavalry, and all the chariots were destroyed. Two of Porus' sons were killed, as was Spitaces, governor of the Indians in that area, along with all the captains of the elephants and chariots and all the generals of Porus' army . . . Such elephants as had not been killed in the field were captured. [3] The dead in Alexander's force included some eighty foot, from a division totalling 6,000 at the first onset. In terms of cavalry, ten of the mounted archers – those who were the first into the action – were lost, and about twenty from the cavalry of the Companions, with other cavalry fatalities numbering about 200.

[4] Porus had performed magnificently in the engagement and not only as a commander, but as a valiant soldier. He now saw the massacre suffered by his cavalry and he saw that some of his elephants had fallen in the battle and that others were wandering about riderless and in pain; in addition, most of his infantry had perished. But he did not imitate Darius, the Great King, by leaving the field and leading his men in flight. [5] As long as there was some semblance of unity amongst the Indians in the battle he kept fighting on, and turned away only when he received a wound to the right shoulder. (In fact, this was the only spot on him that was unprotected in the engagement; his cuirass kept weapons from the rest of his body, for it was superior in terms of its strength and fit, as those who examined it later could see.) Only then did he leave the field, wheeling around his elephant.

[6] Alexander recognized the man's greatness and valour in the battle and wanted to keep him alive. He first of all sent to him the Indian Taxiles, who rode to what he considered a safe distance from the elephant carrying Porus and asked him to halt the animal. There was no possibility of further flight,

Taxiles told him, and he should listen to what Alexander had to say. [7] When Porus saw Taxiles, his enemy of old, he wheeled round and rode towards him, intending to strike him with his spear. In fact, he might well have killed him had not Taxiles anticipated him by galloping away. Alexander did not become indignant with Porus even over this; rather, he sent a succession of people to him, and in particular he sent the Indian Meroes, knowing as he did that Meroes was a long-standing friend of his. Porus listened to what Meroes had to say, and he was also overwhelmed by thirst; and so he halted his elephant and got down. Taking a drink and reviving himself, he told Meroes to take him promptly to Alexander.

19　Meroes did so, and when Alexander learned that Porus was coming he rode forward in front of the line with a few of his companions to meet him. Bringing his horse to a halt, he looked in amazement at Porus' size – for he was more than five cubits tall – and at his handsome features. He wondered, too, at the fact that he seemed not to be cowed but gave the impression of being one man of honour meeting another man of honour after putting up a fine battle for his realm.

[2] Alexander addressed Porus first, bidding him state what sort of treatment he wished to be given. The story goes that Porus answered: "Treat me like a king, Alexander." Alexander was pleased with the response. "Porus," he said, "you shall have that because it is my wish, but ask me now what you want for yourself," to which Porus replied that this request covered everything. [3] Alexander was even more pleased with this answer. He granted Porus sovereignty over the Indians of his realm and added further lands that were even greater than what he had previously held. And so it was that Alexander himself was acting like a king in his treatment of a noble warrior, and from that moment he enjoyed unfailing loyalty from him. Such was the ending of Alexander's battle against Porus and the Indians on the far bank of the Hydaspes. It took place when Hegemon was archon in Athens, in the month of Munychion.[24]

2(k)　Quintus Curtius Rufus 8.13.1–14.46

The next day ambassadors of Abisares came to the king. As they had been instructed, they made a total submission to Alexander and, after pledges had been exchanged, they were sent back to their king. [2] Believing that Porus could also be pressed into capitulation by the spreading fame of his name, Alexander sent Cleochares to him to instruct him to pay tribute and meet the king at the point of entry into his territory. One of these demands Porus agreed to meet: he would be present when Alexander entered his kingdom – but he would be under arms.

24　April/May 326. But this contradicts Arrian's earlier statement (5.9.4, above) that it was just after the summer solstice when Alexander moved against Porus.

[3] Alexander had now determined to cross the Hydaspes when Barzaentes, the ringleader of the Arachosian revolt, was brought to him in irons, together with thirty elephants which had been captured along with him. The latter were timely reinforcements against the Indians, for they put greater confidence and military strength in these beasts than in regular forces. [4] Samaxus was also brought to him in irons. He was the ruler of a small area of India who had allied himself with Barzaentes. [5] Alexander placed the deserter and the petty king under guard and delivered the elephants up to Taxiles. After this he came to the river Hydaspes, where Porus had taken up a position on the far bank, intending to bar his enemy from crossing.

[6] Against the Macedonians Porus had marshalled 85 enormously powerful elephants and, behind them, 300 chariots and some 30,000 infantry, including archers (who . . . were equipped with arrows too heavy to be shot effectively). [7] Porus himself rode an elephant which towered above the other beasts. His armour, with its gold and silver inlay, lent distinction to an unusually large physique. His physical strength was matched by his courage, and he possessed as much acumen as could exist among savages. [8] The Macedonians were alarmed not only by the appearance of their foes but also by the size of the river which had to be crossed: 4 stades wide and with a deep bed that nowhere revealed any shallow areas, this presented the appearance of a vast sea. [9] Nor was the current's force any the less in view of the wide expanse of water; in fact, it rushed ahead as a torrential cataract just as if it had been narrowly constricted by its banks, and waves rebounding at several points indicated the presence of unseen rocks.

[10] The bank supplied an even more terrifying scene, covered as it was with horses and men and, standing among them, those immense bodies with their huge bulk; deliberately goaded, these deafened the ears with their horrendous trumpeting. [11] The combination of the river and the enemy suddenly struck terror into hearts which were generally given to confidence and had often proved themselves in battle; for the Macedonians believed their unstable boats could neither be steered to the bank nor safely landed there.

[12] In mid-stream lay a thick cluster of islands. Indians and Macedonians both swam over to these, holding their weapons above their heads, and light skirmishes were in progress on them, with the two kings using these small-scale encounters to assess the outcome of the major one. [13] Now, in the Macedonian army, Hegesimachus and Nicanor had a reputation for daring and recklessness; they were young noblemen, encouraged by the continuing success of their countrymen to disregard any danger. [14] Led by these two and armed only with lances, the most intrepid of the young Macedonians swam to an island which was occupied by a large body of the enemy and, with nothing more than their enterprise for armour, cut down many of the Indians. [15] To retire with glory was possible – if recklessness when it meets with success could ever know moderation! But while they awaited the approaching enemy with disdainful arrogance, they were encircled by men who had swum over unobserved and fell beneath a shower of missiles hurled at long range. [16]

Those escaping the enemy were either swept away by the force of the current or sucked down into whirlpools. The engagement did much to bolster the confidence of Porus, who watched the whole thing from the bank.

[17] Perplexed, Alexander finally devised the following scheme to dupe his enemy. There was in the river an island larger than the others; it was, moreover, wooded and well suited for an ambush. There was also a very deep ravine close to the bank which he himself commanded, and this could conceal not only his infantry but even men on horseback. [18] To distract his enemy's attention from this promising spot, Alexander told Ptolemy to make cavalry manoeuvres with all his squadrons at a point far from the island and to strike fear into the Indians at regular intervals by shouting as if he were going to swim across the river. [19]Ptolemy did this for several days, and by this stratagem he also made Porus concentrate his forces in the area he was pretending to attack.

[20] By now the island was out of the enemy's view. Alexander ordered his tent to be pitched elsewhere on the river bank, the unit usually in attendance on him to stand guard before it, and all the sumptuous trappings of royalty to be deliberately flaunted before the enemy's eyes. [21] Attalus, who was Alexander's age and not dissimilar to him in face and build (especially when seen at a distance), he also dressed in royal robes to make it appear that the king himself was protecting that part of the bank and not planning to cross.

[22] The execution of this plan was first delayed, then assisted, by a storm, as fortune directed even disadvantages to a successful outcome. [23] Alexander was preparing to cross the river with the rest of his troops in the direction of the island mentioned above, the enemy's attention having now been diverted to the men occupying the bank downstream with Ptolemy. At this point a storm let loose a downpour scarcely tolerable even under cover and, overwhelmed by the rainstorm, the soldiers fled back to shore, abandoning their boats and rafts. However, the roaring winds rendered the noise of their confusion inaudible to the enemy. [24] Then, in an instant, the rain stopped, but the cloud-cover was so thick that it blocked out the daylight and even men in conversation could barely make out each other's features. [25] Another man would have been terrified by the darkness that shrouded the sky: they had to sail on a strange river, and the enemy was possibly occupying that very part of the bank to which they were directing their blind and reckless course. [26] But the king derived glory from perilous situations, and he saw as his opportunity the darkness which frightened all the others. He gave the signal for all to board the rafts in silence and ordered the boat in which he himself was sailing to be pushed off first. [27] The bank for which they were making was deserted by the enemy, for Porus' eyes were fixed entirely on Ptolemy. With the exception of one ship, stranded after a wave smashed it on to a rock, they all reached land and Alexander ordered his men to take up their arms and form ranks.

14 Alexander was advancing at the head of his army, now split into two wings, when news reached Porus that the banks were occupied by armed

troops and that a decisive moment was imminent. His initial reaction was to indulge in that natural weakness of mankind, wishful thinking: he believed that it was his ally Abisares who was approaching, as the two had arranged. [2] Presently the brightening daylight revealed the enemy battle line, and so Porus despatched 100 chariots and 4,000 cavalry against the advancing column.

These forces which he sent ahead were led by his brother Spitaces, and their main strength lay in the chariots, [3] each of which carried six men, two equipped with shields, two archers stationed on each side of the vehicle and finally the two charioteers who were, in fact, well-armed themselves; for when it came to fighting at close quarters they would drop the reins and fire spears upon the enemy. [4] On this particular day, however, the unit's effectiveness was virtually eliminated since, as mentioned above, there had been an unusually violent rainfall which had left the ground slippery and impossible to ride upon; and the heavy and almost immovable chariots became stuck in the mud and quagmires. [5] Alexander, on the other hand, made a brisk charge with his light-armed troops which could be easily manoeuvred. First to attack the Indians were the Scythians and the Dahae, after which Alexander sent Perdiccas and his cavalry against the enemy's right wing.

[6] When the battle was under way at all points, the charioteers began to drive into the thick of the fray at full speed, believing this to be the last resort for their side. [7] This inflicted damage on both sides for, while the Macedonian infantry were crushed under foot at the first charge, the chariots, being driven over slippery ground which it was impossible to negotiate, flung out their drivers. [8] Others found that their startled horses dragged the chariots not just into the quagmires and pools of water but even into the river, and a few of the animals, driven by the spears of the enemy, penetrated the ranks as far as Porus, who was vigorously urging on the fight.

[9] When Porus saw his chariots scattered and wandering driverless all over the field, he distributed his elephants to the friends closest to him, [10] and behind the elephants he stationed his infantry, his archers and the drummers. (The Indians used this instrument instead of the trumpet-call – the beat did not alarm the elephants, whose ears had long since become accustomed to the familiar noise.) [11] Before the infantry column was carried a statue of Hercules, which was a great stimulus to the warriors, and to desert its bearers was considered a disgrace for a soldier. [12] The Indians had even authorized the death penalty for failure to bring it back from battle, the fear they had once felt for that particular foe having been actually transformed into religious veneration.

The Macedonians were momentarily checked by the appearance not only of the elephants but also of the Indian king himself. [13] Set at intervals among the troops, the elephants looked like towers from a distance, while Porus himself was of almost superhuman size. The elephant which he was riding seemed to increase that size, for it stood above the other animals by as much as Porus towered over the other Indians.

[14] Alexander surveyed both the king and the army of the Indians. "At last," he declared, "I see a danger that is a match for my courage – I must take on beasts and fine warriors together." [15] Then he looked at Coenus and said: "Together with Ptolemy, Perdiccas and Hephaestion I am going to attack the enemy left wing. When you see me in the thick of the fight, set our right wing in motion and attack the enemy while they are in confusion. Antigenes, Leonnatus, Tauron: you three will attack the centre and put pressure on their front. [16] Our spears are long and sturdy; they can never serve us better than against these elephants and their drivers. Dislodge the riders and stab the beasts. They are a military force of dubious value, and their ferocity is greater towards their own side; for they are driven by command against the enemy, but by fear against their own men."

[17] So saying, Alexander was the first to spur on his horse. When he had attacked the enemy ranks according to plan, Coenus made a vigorous attack on the left wing. [18] The phalanx also succeeded in bursting through the Indian centre with a single charge. Porus meanwhile ordered elephants to be driven to the points at which he had observed the enemy cavalry attacking, but, being a ponderous, practically immobile animal, the elephant was no match for the swift Macedonian horses. The barbarians were even unable to use their arrows [19] because of their length and weight: it was awkward and difficult to fit them to the bow without first setting it on the ground, and in the second place the ground was slippery, causing them difficulty when they tried this, so that as they struggled to make a shot they were overtaken by their swift-moving enemy. [20] Thus they ignored the king's orders – as commonly happens when men are in confusion and fear usurps the leader's authority – and there were as many commanders-in-chief as there were groups of men wandering about. [21] One was giving orders to form a united line, another to split into companies; some called for making a stand, others for encircling the enemy rear. There was no common plan of action. [22] Porus, however, accompanied by a few whose sense of shame surpassed their fear, began to rally his scattered troops and to advance on his enemy, issuing instructions for the elephants to be driven before his line. [23] The beasts caused great panic. Their strange trumpeting unsettled not only the horses – animals always very easily startled – but also the men in the ranks.

[24] Victors moments before, the Macedonians were now casting around for a place to flee. Then Alexander sent the Agrianes and the Thracian light-armed against the elephants, for they were better at skirmishing than at fighting at close quarters. [25] These released a thick barrage of missiles on both elephants and drivers, and the phalanx also proceeded to exert relentless pressure on the frightened animals. [26] Some, however, pursued the elephants too energetically, provoking them to turn on them by the wounds they inflicted. Trampled underfoot, they served as a warning to the others to be more cautious in their pursuit. [27] A particularly terrifying sight was when elephants would snatch up men in armour in their trunks and pass them over their heads to the drivers. [28] So the fortunes of the battle kept shifting, with the

Macedonians alternately chasing and fleeing from the elephants, and the contest dragged on inconclusively till late in the day. Then the Macedonians began to use axes – they had equipped themselves with such implements in advance – to hack off the elephants' feet, [29] and they also chopped at the trunks of the animals with gently curving, sickle-like swords called *kopides*. In their fear not just of dying, but of suffering novel kinds of torment as they died, they left nothing untried.

[30] The elephants were finally exhausted by their wounds. They charged into their own men, mowing them down; their riders were flung to the ground and trampled to death. More terrified than menacing, the beasts were being driven like cattle from the battlefield [31] when, mounted on his elephant, Porus, who had been deserted by most of his men, began to shower on the enemy swarming around him large numbers of javelins which he had set aside in advance. He wounded many Macedonians at long range but he was himself the target of weapons from every direction. [32] He had already received nine wounds both to the back and to the chest, and had suffered severe loss of blood, so that the missiles he was throwing were slipping from his weakened hands rather than being hurled. [33] His elephant, roused to a frenzy and as yet unwounded, attacked the enemy ranks no less aggressively than before, until its driver caught sight of his king in a barely conscious state, arms dangling and weapons fallen. [34] At that he spurred the beast to flee. Alexander followed, but his horse was weak from taking many wounds and it toppled forwards, setting the king on the ground rather than throwing him [35] Changing horses thus slowed down his pursuit.

In the meantime the brother of Taxiles, the Indian king, had been sent ahead by Alexander, and he began to advise Porus not to persevere to the end but to surrender to the victor. [36] Although Porus' strength was spent and he had suffered considerable loss of blood, he started at the sound of this voice which he recognized. "I know you," he said, "brother of Taxiles, traitor to his empire and his throne", and he flung at him the one javelin which by chance had not fallen from his hands. It passed straight through his chest to emerge at the back. [37] After this final courageous act, Porus began to flee with greater urgency, but his elephant had received numerous wounds and it also began to falter, so he stopped running and threw his infantry in the path of the pursuing enemy.

[38]By now Alexander had caught up. He saw Porus' obstinacy and ordered that no mercy be shown to any who resisted. From every direction, missiles were showered on the Indian infantry and on Porus himself who, finally overwhelmed by them, began to slip from his elephant. [39] The Indian driving it thought he was dismounting, and ordered the animal to come to its knees in the usual way. When the elephant crouched down the others also sank to the ground as they had been trained to do, [40] and it was this that delivered Porus and the other Indians into the hands of the victors. Believing Porus dead, Alexander ordered his body to be stripped. Men quickly gathered to remove his cuirass and his clothing but then the elephant began protecting his master, attacking the men stripping him and lifting and setting Porus' body on his

back once more. So the beast was subjected to a volley of weapons from every direction and, when he was despatched, Porus was placed in a chariot.

[41] Then Alexander saw him lift his eyes. Moved by pity, not hatred, he said to him: "What folly forced you, knowing as you did the fame of my achievements, to try the fortunes of war, when Taxiles served as an example of my clemency towards those who surrender, an example so close to you?"

[42] "Since you ask," replied Porus, "I shall answer you with the frankness your inquiry has granted me. I did not think there was anyone stronger than I. Though I knew my own strength, I had not yet tested yours, and now the outcome of the war has shown you to be the stronger. Even so, being second to you brings me no little satisfaction."

[43] Alexander questioned him further, asking his opinion on what his victor should do with him. "What this day tells you to do," said Porus, "the day on which you have discovered how transitory good fortune is." [44] Porus' advice did him more good than pleas would have done. His greatness of spirit was not cowed or broken even in adversity, and Alexander felt obliged to treat him not only with mercy but with respect. [45] He tended to his wounds just as if Porus had fought on his side and, when he recovered contrary to everyone's expectations, Alexander made him one of his friends and, shortly afterwards, bestowed on him an empire larger than he had formerly held. [46] In fact, no trait of Alexander's was more firmly held or enduring than his admiration for genuine excellence and brilliant achievements, though he was fairer in his estimation of an enemy's praiseworthiness than a fellow citizen's, believing as he did that his own greatness could be eclipsed by his countrymen whereas it would be increased proportionately by the greatness of the peoples he defeated.

2(I)   Metz Epitome 53–62

Alexander accepted these and asked Mophis why he had mobilized an army.[25] Mophis replied that it was because he had intended doing whatever Alexander would have wished, at which Alexander further inquired of him whether any neighbour of his was causing him trouble. Mophis answered that two kings beyond the river were preparing to make war on him: Abisares, who lived in the mountains, and Porus, whose kingdom was in the plain adjacent to the river.

[54] Alexander thanked him for his generosity, declaring that he should succeed to his father's throne and ordering that his name be changed to Taxiles. Then, in company with Taxiles, he approached the river bank and saw that the enemy forces had taken up several positions in the plains alongside the river. He questioned Taxiles about the forces in the enemy camp and discovered that Porus had 85 elephants, 300 four-horse chariots, and more

---

25 Alexander has just met Mophis (Omphis-Sanskrit Ambhi), the ruler of Taxila, and accepted troops and gifts from him. The form "Mophis" is attested also in Diodorus 17.86.4–7.

than 30,000 infantry; he also learned that Porus himself was 5 cubits tall. [55]
Despite this intelligence from Taxiles, Alexander was nevertheless fired with
enthusiasm and he proceeded to consider where to cross the river.

Not many days after this, Abisares sent his own brother as an emissary
to Alexander to discuss terms of an alliance. Alexander sent back with him
Nicocles as his own emissary to Abisares, and to Porus he sent Cleochares;
these were to demand tribute and hostages from the two kings, and Alexander
also gave orders that Porus be told to present himself to him at the boundaries
of his kingdom. [56] Abisares did not want to dismiss the emissary, but when
Porus heard Alexander's message he became so angry that he had a savage
lashing inflicted on Cleochares. At the same time, he passed on a letter to
Alexander, the contents of which were as follows:

> Porus, King of India, has this to say to Alexander: No matter who you are – and
> I am told that you are a Macedonian – it is better for you to remain at a distance
> and to reflect upon your own misfortunes rather than envy another. Porus is
> declared undefeated up to this time, [57] and Darius causes me no alarm. So, imbe-
> cile, don't give me orders! Just set one foot in my territory with hostile intent
> and you shall learn that I am King of India, that none but Jupiter is my master.
> And Porus swears this oath by the great fire which rules the heavens: if I catch
> any of your men in my territory, I shall have his blood on my lance and I shall
> distribute your goods among my slaves – for I have an abundance of riches
> myself. I shall do only one thing that you demand – to be ready and waiting for
> you, in arms, at my borders.

[58] After reading this letter Alexander was furious. He rounded up a number
of infantry units and cavalry squadrons and told them to follow him at once;
he left a certain Macedonian, Attalus, with the army, a man who was not
unlike him in appearance, and instructed him to put on his cloak and the
other trappings of royalty and to make occasional forays with his retinue to
the river bank; [59] and he ordered Craterus to take the army across the river
when he saw him on the other side. Then he himself took his select body of
men and, on the first night, followed the river some 150 stades to encamp in
a solitary and wooded area. There he transported his force across the river, by
means of inflated skins with large quantities of wood placed over them, and
began to lead his light-armed towards the enemy. Craterus, who had been left
in charge of the camp, saw this happening and he too took the army across
the river on the boats – he had a large number at his disposal – and rafts. [60]
Porus, suddenly seeing two armies, decided to come to grips with Alexander,
but in the meantime Craterus had completed his landing and was attacking
from the other direction so that Porus, his troops under pressure on two
fronts, took to flight. Alexander instructed the so-called *hippotoxotai* to aim
their arrows at Porus and disregard the others. When Porus saw them coming
at him in droves, while he himself pressed ahead on his elephant . . . not to
postpone his surrender to the enemy, he held up both hands, begging for his
life.

[61] So, the matter finished, Porus delivered up to Alexander his elephants, his pack animals and his army; as for his own person he now began to beseech Alexander to consult his own feelings as a king. Alexander promised that he would do this, and he did, for he not only restored his kingdom to him but further added to his realm other areas of †neighbouring territories†. In that battle, 12,000 of Porus' men were killed and 80 elephants; Alexander lost 900 infantry and 300 cavalry, and there were many wounded. [62] There were also many horses killed, including Alexander's, Bucephalas by name, on whose back he had always been victorious in all his battles. Accordingly, Alexander founded a town in that place bearing the horse's name, which today is called Bucephala. Afterwards he ordered the customary burial of the dead, his own and the bravest of the enemy.

Sieges and Smaller Battles

The siege of Tyre (January–August 332)

Alexander's military genius and the efficiency of the Macedonian army can be seen in engagements that did not have the same immediate impact as the great victories at the Granicus, Issus, Gaugamela, and the Hydaspes. Perhaps one of the most impressive achievements was the siege and capture of the seemingly impregnable fortress of Tyre, which was situated on an island located some 0.8 kilometres off the Levantine coast. At the time, the Macedonians had not yet achieved mastery of the sea – and, indeed, it would have been virtually impossible to do so without possession of this strategically important city. Scholars have debated whether it was actually necessary (or practical) for Alexander to allow himself to be detained for seven months in order to capture Tyre. In retrospect, it is easy to answer in the affirmative; and it was more than a simple case of Alexander's wishing to prove that no enemy and no fortress, no matter how strong, could hold out against him. In the age of the Successors, when the city was already joined to the mainland by Alexander's causeway, it would take Antigonus the One-Eyed and his son Demetrius, the famous "Besieger," thirteen months to duplicate Alexander's feat. See Warry (1991: 41–52) and Romane (1987); for Alexander's strategy, see Bloedow (1998a, 1998b).

3(a)   Arrian 2.15.6–24.6

Alexander now moved from Marathus. He negotiated the surrender of Byblus and Sidon, the Sidonians having themselves invited him to come because of their hatred of Darius and the Persians. From there he advanced on Tyre, and was met en route by envoys of the Tyrians, sent by their state to report to him that the people of Tyre had decided to do his bidding. [7] Alexander complimented the city and its envoys – in fact, these were members of the Tyrian aristocracy and included, notably, the son of the king of Tyre, Azemilcus, who was himself at sea with Autophradates.[26] He instructed the envoys to go back

26 The Phoenicians served in – and, indeed, formed the nucleus of – the Persian navy: see Hauben (1970).

and tell the Tyrians that he wished to come to their city and sacrifice to Heracles . . .[27]

16 [7] When this information was brought to Tyre by the envoys, the citizens decided to follow all of Alexander's other instructions, but not to admit any Persian or Macedonian to their city. They believed that this was the most plausible tactic under the immediate circumstances, and that it was also the safest course when the outcome of the war was still unforeseeable. [8] When the response from Tyre was brought to Alexander, he flew into a temper and sent the envoys back. He then summoned his friends and the generals of his army, together with his regiment and company commanders, and addressed them in the following terms:

17 "Friends and allies, I can see that our march to Egypt would be unsafe while the Persians are masters of the sea. I see, too, that it would be unsafe to pursue Darius when we would be leaving to our rear this city of Tyre, which is still uncommitted, and when Egypt and Cyprus are under Persian control. This would be an unsafe course of action in general, [2] and particularly so as far as the Greek situation is concerned. The Persians could regain control of the coastal areas and, when we have gone in force towards Babylon and Darius, they might take a larger expedition and transfer hostilities to Greece. And there the Spartans are openly at war with us, while the city of Athens is kept in check by fear rather than feelings of good will towards us. [3] But if Tyre is destroyed, Phoenicia would be entirely ours and, in all probability, the largest and strongest component of the Persian navy, that is to say the Phoenicians, would defect to us. If their cities are occupied, the Phoenicians – oarsmen and marines alike – are not going to be happy to sail into danger for the sake of others. After that Cyprus will fall, either coming over to us voluntarily, or else easily taken with a naval invasion. [4] When we sail the seas with our ships from Macedonia and with the Phoenician ships as well, and when we also have Cyprus on our side – then our control of the sea would be secure, and our expedition to Egypt is likewise made easy. And once we have brought Egypt on side, Greece and our own country are no longer a cause for concern; and we shall undertake the journey to Babylon with security on the home front and with the greater glory. We shall have cut the Persians off entirely from the sea, and from the territory this side of the Euphrates, as well."

18 With these arguments Alexander had no difficulty in convincing his officers to mount an offensive against Tyre. Some incentive to action on his part also came from a divine sign. That night he had a dream that he was

27   That is, Melqart, whom the Greeks equated with Heracles (Hercules). A portion of the text (2.16.1–6), which discusses the myth of Heracles, has been omitted. Curtius (below) notes that there was a temple of Heracles at Palaetyrus ("Old Tyre") on the mainland, and that it was there that Alexander was told by the Tyrians to conduct his sacrifice. The Macedonian kings claimed descent from Heracles through Temenus, but it did not escape the Tyrians that the request was a transparent ploy to gain possession of the city. See Brundage (1958).

approaching the wall of Tyre, and that Heracles was welcoming him and escorting him into the city. Aristander interpreted this as meaning that while the city would be taken it would require an effort, inasmuch as the labours of Heracles had required an effort. And, in fact, it was perfectly clear that the siege of Tyre was a difficult undertaking. [2] The city of the Tyrians was an island, and it was fortified on every side with high walls. The naval advantage also seemed to lie with the Tyrians at that moment since the Persians controlled the sea and the Tyrians themselves still had a strong navy.

[3] But Alexander's arguments prevailed in any case, and he determined to construct a mole running from the mainland to the city just where there was a narrow stretch of shallow water used as a crossing point. On the mainland side there is a short section of shoals, but on the side of the city, where the deepest part of the channel is situated, the depth reaches about three fathoms. However, there was a plentiful supply of stones, and of wood, which they piled on top of the stones. Moreover, stakes could easily be driven into the mud, and the actual mud became a bonding material to stabilize the stones. [4] The Macedonians showed great enthusiasm for the undertaking, as did Alexander, who was there in person supervising its every particular, at times giving words of praise, and using gifts to reward those who did outstanding work.

While the mole was rising close to the mainland, the work proceeded without problems: it was being built in shallow water, and nobody was trying to stop it. [5] But as they approached the deeper water and came close to the actual city, the men suffered casualties since they became targets for projectiles from the towering walls. They were specifically equipped for working rather than fighting, and the Tyrians, still having control of the sea, would sail up to the mole at various points in their triremes, making the process of building up the mole impossible for the Macedonians in many places. [6] The Macedonians then placed two towers on the end of the mole, which had now advanced quite some way into the sea, and placed catapults on the towers. The towers also had coverings of leather and hides to counteract volleys of incendiary projectiles from the city wall, as well as to screen the workers from arrows. In addition, any of the Tyrians sailing up to inflict damage on the mole-builders would be subject to weapons hurled from the towers and thus in all likelihood be pushed back.

19　The Tyrians, however, devised the following means of combating this. They proceeded to fill a cavalry transport ship with dry brushwood and other flammable material, and they set two masts on its bows. Then they extended its bulwarks all round as far as they could to maximize its capacity for kindling material and pine-wood, and they also piled in pitch, sulphur and anything else with highly incendiary qualities. [2] To each of the two masts they added a double yard-arm, and from it suspended cauldrons of any substance that could boost the flames when poured or thrown on them. They next set ballast in the stern so as to raise the prow up high by throwing the weight to the rear of the vessel. [3] Then they waited for a wind that was blowing in the direction of the mole, fastened the vessel to some triremes and towed it out by the stern. As they approached the mole and the towers, the Tyrians ignited the materials, towed the ship with the triremes with as much force as they could and drove it onto the end of the mole. The men in the now-blazing ship had no difficulty swimming to safety.

[4] Meanwhile, a mighty conflagration engulfed the towers. The yard-arms crumpled, pouring onto the fire the material that had been provided to fuel the flames, and the men in the triremes, in a holding position near the mole, shot arrows at the towers, making access unsafe for those bringing anything to quench the blaze. [5] At that point, with the towers going up in flames, many people ran from the city, climbed aboard boats and ran them aground at various points along the mole. They then had no difficulty in demolishing the palisade erected to protect it, and in burning all the catapults that the fire from the transport had left untouched.

[6] Alexander now ordered his men to broaden the mole, right from its starting point on the mainland, so that it could accommodate more towers, and he instructed his engineers to build more catapults. And while these measures were being implemented, he personally took the hypaspists and Agrianes and set off for Sidon to concentrate there all the triremes he possessed. For it was evident that the siege was going to be particularly difficult while the Tyrians had control of the sea.

20 Meanwhile King Gerostratus of Aradus and King Enylus of Byblus learned that their cities were in Alexander's power. They left Autophradates and the ships he had with him and came to Alexander with their own fleet, and the Sidonian triremes came with them. The result was that Alexander received the support of some eighty Phoenician vessels. [2] During this same period triremes joined him from Rhodes – the so-called "Guardship",[28] and nine others with her – and there were also some from Soli and Mallus (three), and from Lycia (ten). In addition to these there was a pentecontor from Macedon, with Proteus son of Andronicus in command. [3] Not long after this the kings of Cyprus also landed at Sidon with about 120 ships, after they learned of Darius' defeat at Issus and became alarmed that the whole of Phoenicia was now in Alexander's hands. Alexander accorded them all a pardon for their past actions in the belief that it was from necessity that they had joined the Persian naval force, and not of their own volition.

[4] During the time that his siege engines were being assembled and his ships were being equipped for a naval assault and for battle at sea, Alexander took a number of cavalry squadrons along with the hypaspists, the Agrianes, and the archers, and marched to a mountain called Antilebanon in Arabia. [5] The country there he brought under his control either by armed force or by negotiation, and in ten days returned to Sidon to find that Cleander son of Polemocrates had come from the Peloponnese along with some 4,000 Greek mercenaries.

---

28   Otherwise unattested. This is perhaps an official state trireme.

[6] When Alexander's fleet dispositions were complete, he put on the decks of the ships as many hypaspists as he considered sufficient for the operation, on the assumption that the battle would involve hand-to-hand fighting more than naval manoeuvres. He then raised anchor and sailed from Sidon to Tyre with his vessels drawn up for action. Alexander personally took command of the right wing, which was on the side of the open sea, and with him were the kings of Cyprus and all the Phoenicians apart from Pnytagoras. Pnytagoras and Craterus were in charge of the left wing of the whole armada.

[7] The Tyrians had earlier decided on a naval battle, if Alexander advanced against them by sea. But then they caught sight of a fleet of unexpected proportions – for they had not yet received word that Alexander now had on side all the Cypriot and Phoenician ships – [8] and, in addition, this was an out-and-out naval attack. (In fact, shortly before the advance on the city, Alexander's flotilla had held back out at sea in the hope of drawing the Tyrians into battle, but then it surged noisily ahead in close order when they failed to come out to fight.) At the sight of this, the Tyrians refused to join battle. Instead, they tightly fenced off access to the city with as many triremes as the entrances to their harbours would accommodate, and kept a close eye on them to prevent the fleet of the enemy from coming to anchor there.

[9] When the Tyrians failed to come out against him, Alexander sailed on to the city. He decided against forcing his way into the harbour opposite Sidon because its mouth was narrow and because, in addition, access was blocked by large numbers of triremes with prows facing outwards. The Phoenicians, nevertheless, did go on the attack and, with a head-on charge, sank three of the triremes anchored outermost at the harbour mouth (the men in these ships had little difficulty in swimming to shore, which was in friendly hands). [10] Alexander and his men then moored along the shoreline where a spot sheltered from the wind came into view, not far from the completed section of the mole. The following day Alexander ordered the Cypriots to blockade the city with their fleet, under their admiral Andromachus, at the harbour facing in the direction of Sidon, and the Phoenicians to do so at a point on the other side of the mole (where Alexander's own camp was), facing Egypt.

21 By now large numbers of engineers had been brought together for Alexander from Cyprus and the whole of Phoenicia, and numerous siege engines had been assembled. Some of these were mounted on the mole, some on the cavalry transport ships that Alexander had brought with him from Sidon, and also on those of the slower triremes. [2] When all the preparations had been made, they brought up the engines along the completed part of the mole, for an attack that was to be made simultaneously from the ships, which were anchored at various points along the wall, probing its defences.

[3] The Tyrians set wooden towers on their battlements that looked towards the mole so they could fight from them, and they used projectiles to defend themselves at all other points at which the engines were brought up. They also shot flaming arrows directly at the ships, making the Macedonians afraid

to come close to the wall. [4] In addition, their walls on the side of the mole had a height of around 150 feet, and a breadth appropriate to that, and were put together with huge stones set in mortar. The cavalry transports and triremes of the Macedonians that were bringing the siege engines up to the wall also had no easy time advancing on the city, and for a particular reason: a large number of stones had been thrown down into the sea and these hindered a close approach. [5] Alexander made the decision to dredge the stones from the water, but getting the job done was difficult, since the work was proceeding from ships and not from solid ground. A particular problem was presented by the Tyrians. They equipped ships with armour and with these headed for the anchors of the triremes, cutting through the anchor ropes and so making it impossible for the enemy vessels to remain stationary. [6] Alexander fitted a large number of triacontors with the same kind of armour and placed them side-on before the anchors so as to check the advance of the enemy ships, but divers would still go down and sever the ropes. The Macedonians then sent down their anchors with chains attached to them instead of ropes, and that ended the divers' effectiveness. [7] The Macedonians were now able to fix loops of rope around the stones and drag them out of the sea from the mole, and then, hoisting them aloft with cranes, drop them into deep water where they were no longer likely to obstruct them and cause damage. At the points where they had cleared the obstacles from the wall the ships had no difficulty in positioning themselves close in to it.

[8] The Tyrians were now completely stymied, and they made the decision to attack the Cypriot ships that were blockading the harbour opposite Sidon. They used outstretched sails to screen a large section of the harbour mouth so that the triremes could be manned unobserved. They then waited till about midday, when the sailors had dispersed to go about their duties and just when Alexander was leaving the fleet on the other side of the city to go to his tent. At this time they manned three quinqueremes, [9] an equal number of quadriremes and seven triremes with their most skilful crews and with well-equipped soldiers who would fight from the decks, men who were also the most courageous fighters in engagements at sea. At first, rowing gently, they left the harbour in single file, passing the harbour bar without anyone calling the stroke. But when they turned to face the Cypriots and were almost in sight of them, they burst into loud shouts and cheers of encouragement to each other, charging forward with powerful strokes.

22   It so happened that, while Alexander did, indeed, go off to his tent that day, he did not spend the usual amount of time there but shortly afterwards returned to the ships. [2] The Tyrians now fell unexpectedly on the ships at their moorings. They found some of them completely empty; others were with difficulty being manned by people who happened to be at hand while the actual war-cry was going up and the attack was in progress. With their first onset, the Tyrians immediately sank the quinquereme of King Pnytagoras along with those of Androcles of Amathus and Pasicrates of Curium, and the other ships they wrecked by driving them ashore.

[3] When Alexander saw the Tyrian triremes sailing out, he ordered most of his flotilla, as soon as each ship was manned, to ride at anchor at the harbour mouth to prevent the further exit of Tyrian ships. Then, taking the quinqueremes at his disposal and about five triremes that had managed to get manned at greater speed than the others, he sailed around the city in pursuit of the Tyrian vessels that had sailed out for the attack. [4] Those on the walls could see the enemy sailing after them, and Alexander there in the flotilla in person, and they kept shouting to the men on their ships to head for home. But as the men were engaged in the action the shouting was inaudible, and so the Tyrians resorted to various kinds of signal to tell them to return. All too late did the sailors see Alexander's flotilla coming at them, at which point they turned and ran for the harbour. [5] A few Tyrian ships did, in fact, manage to escape in time, but Alexander's squadron rammed most of them, crippling some and capturing a quinquereme and a quadrireme right at the harbour mouth. There was not much bloodshed in the case of the crews, however; when they saw their vessels overtaken they quite easily swam into the harbour.

[6] For the Tyrians there was now no help to be had from their fleet, and the Macedonians were in the process of bringing the engines up to the wall. Those brought forward along the mole had no success of any note because of the strength of the wall at that point. Some of the men brought up a number of ships with these engines on board to that part of the city facing Sidon, [7] but no progress was made there, either. Alexander then concentrated instead on the section facing south, towards Egypt, probing the work at every point. And this was the first place at which some damage was done to the wall, and over a large stretch of it; here there was some cracking and disintegration. Alexander merely threw down some gangplanks where the wall had collapsed and made a cautious move a short distance along them. The Tyrians drove back the Macedonians without difficulty.

23 Alexander now waited for calm weather and, two days later, after encouraging his company commanders to action, he brought his engines up to the city on ships. First he pounded a large section of the wall. When the breach appeared sufficiently wide, he ordered the ships bearing the engines to move back and [2] brought up two others carrying gangplanks, which he intended throwing into the breach in the wall.

The hypaspists manned one of the ships, which was under the command of Admetus, and Coenus' battalion called the *asthetairoi*[29] manned the other. Alexander himself was going to climb in with the hypaspists wherever an opening appeared in the wall. [3] He ordered some of his triremes to sail to the two harbours in the hope that they could force their way in while the Tyrians were occupied with his own squadron. The vessels that had projectiles

---

29　A number of battalions of the Macedonian infantry (*pezhetairoi*) were so designated. See glossary s.v. *asthetairoi*. The strength of a phalanx battlion was about 1,500. Hence, there was no way it could be transported in a single ship.

still to be fired from their machines, or which had archers on their decks, he ordered to sail around the wall, landing wherever it was possible or else remaining at anchor while they were still in range and where disembarkation was impossible. The Tyrians would thus find themselves under pressure from all directions, at a loss what to do in their hour of peril.

[4] When Alexander's flotilla reached the city and the gangplanks were thrown down, the hypaspists advanced boldly along them up to the wall. Admetus acquitted himself with valour at that point, and Alexander went along with them, resolutely involving himself in the enterprise and also looking at the others to see who was responsible for any conspicuous act of gallantry. [5] In fact, it was just there, where Alexander had taken up his position, that the wall was first taken; for the Tyrians were beaten back without much difficulty once the Macedonians had a way in that was firm under foot and not precipitous on every side. Admetus was the first to get onto the wall, and there he died, hit by a javelin as he urged his men to follow him up. Alexander came up after him and held the wall with the *hetairoi*.[30] [6] When some towers had been taken, along with sections of the wall between them, the king made his way through the battlements in the direction of the royal apartments, as these seemed to afford an easier way down into the city.

24 Down at the ships, the Phoenicians who were moored off the harbour facing Egypt had succeeded in forcing their way in, smashing the booms, and they were shattering the vessels in the harbour by ramming some on the water and driving others onto the shore. The Cypriots were at the other harbour facing Sidon; this did not have a boom, and so they sailed in and immediately seized control of the city in that sector. [2] The mass of the Tyrians abandoned the wall when they saw it in enemy hands, but they regrouped at the so-called "Shrine of Agenor" and here turned to face the Macedonians. Alexander and the hypaspists advanced on them, killing some in battle, and pursuing those who fled. [3] And there was a lot of bloodshed, for those coming from the harbour were now in control of the city and Coenus' company had also succeeded in gaining entrance. The Macedonians' advance was everywhere marked with vindictive anger. They were exasperated by the length of the siege and, in addition, the Tyrians had earlier captured a number of their men who were sailing out of Sidon. They had taken these up onto the wall, so the act would be visible from the Macedonian camp, slit their throats and hurled them into the sea.

[4] The Tyrian dead numbered as many as 8,000. On the Macedonian side, Admetus died a hero's death, being the first on the wall in the initial attack, and twenty hypaspists died with him. In the entire siege Macedonian losses reached about 400.

---

30 It is not clear who these people are. Possibly, they are the dismounted members of the Companion Cavalry. More likely, the terminology is imprecise and Arrian refers to the "royal hypaspists," whose commander, Admetus, has just been killed.

[5] Some of the enemy sought refuge in the temple of Heracles; these included the most powerful of the actual Tyrian population along with King Azemilcus, and a number of Carthaginian envoys who had come to their mother-city to venerate Heracles in conformity with some old tradition. All these were pardoned by Alexander. The rest he reduced to slavery, and some 30,000 souls, Tyrians and such foreigners taken in the city, were sold off.

[6] Alexander offered sacrifice to Heracles, and staged a parade of his men in battle array. The fleet also took part in the ceremonies in Heracles' honour, and the king put on in addition an athletic contest and a torch race in the temple precinct. The engine responsible for the initial rupture in the wall he dedicated at the temple, and to Heracles he also dedicated the ship which the Tyrians held sacred to that god and which Alexander captured in the fighting at sea. (There was a dedicatory inscription on the vessel, composed by Alexander himself or someone else. It is not worthy of record, and so I decided against copying it.) Such was the capture of Tyre, which took place during the archonship of Nicetes in Athens, and in the month of Hecatombaeon.[31]

3(b)   Quintus Curtius Rufus 4.2.15–4.19

Since Alexander's navy was a long way off and he could see that a protracted siege would severely impede his other plans, he sent heralds to urge the Tyrians to accept peace terms; but the latter, violating international conventions, killed them and threw their bodies into the sea. Outraged by the disgraceful murder of his men, Alexander now resolved to lay siege to the city.

[16] First, however, a mole had to be constructed to join the city and the mainland, and the sight of the fathomless deep filled the soldiers with despair, for it could scarcely be filled even if they had divine aid. How could rocks big enough be found, or trees tall enough? To make a mound to fill such a void they would have to denude whole regions; the strait was perpetually stormy, and the more constricted the area of its movement between the island and the mainland, the more fierce it became. [17] But Alexander was not inexperienced in dealing with the soldier's temperament: he announced that he had seen in a dream a figure of Hercules extending his right hand to him, and himself entering Tyre as Hercules led him and opened the way. He included a reference to the murdered heralds, and the Tyrians' violation of international conventions, and added that this was the only city that had dared delay his victorious progress. [18] Then the generals were instructed to reprove their men, and when they were all sufficiently aroused he set to work.

Large quantities of rock were available, furnished by Old Tyre, while timber to construct rafts and siege towers was hauled from Mt Libanus. [19] The

---

31 July or August (probably the latter) 332; the MS reading is actually "Anicetus"; Diodorus (17.40.1) has Niceratus.

structure had reached some height from the sea-bed without yet breaking the surface of the water [20] when the Tyrians began to bring up small boats and to hurl insulting taunts at the men about "those famous warriors carrying loads on their backs like pack animals." They would ask, too, if Alexander "had more power than Neptune." Their jeers actually served to fuel the soldiers' enthusiasm. [21] Little by little the mole now began to rise above the surface and the mound's width increased as it approached the city. The Tyrians, who had hitherto failed to notice the mole's growth, now perceived its size. With their light skiffs they began to encircle the structure, which was not yet joined to the island, attacking with missiles the men standing by the work. [22] Many were wounded without a casualty on the part of the Tyrians, who could both withdraw and bring up their boats without hindrance; and so the Macedonians were diverted from their work to protecting themselves. Furthermore, as the mole proceeded further from the shore, the materials piled on it were increasingly sucked into the sea's depths. [23] Alexander, therefore, had hides and sheets of canvas stretched before the workmen to screen them from Tyrian missiles, and he erected two turrets on the top of the mole from which weapons could be directed at approaching boats. The Tyrians, in turn, landed their boats on the coast well out of sight of their enemy, put soldiers ashore, and cut down the Macedonians who were carrying the rocks. On Mt Libanus, too, Arab peasants made an attack on the Macedonians while they were scattered, killing some thirty of them and taking a smaller number prisoner.

3   The incident obliged Alexander to split his forces. Not to appear to be frittering away time in besieging a single city, he gave the operation to Perdiccas and Craterus while he himself made for Arabia with a detachment of light-armed troops. [2] Meanwhile the Tyrians took an enormous ship, loaded its stern with rocks and sand so that its prow stood high out of the water, and daubed it with bitumen and sulphur. Then they rowed out the ship which, after its sails caught a strong wind, quickly came up to the mole. [3] At this point the oarsmen fired the prow and then jumped into boats that had followed the ship expressly for this purpose. The vessel flared up and began to spread the blaze over a large area. Before help could be brought it engulfed the towers and other structures built on top of the mole.

[4] The men who had jumped into the small boats also tossed firebrands and anything else that would fuel the flames on to these buildings; the topmost sections of the turrets, as well as the lower ones, had now caught fire, while the Macedonians on them were either consumed in the conflagration or else threw aside their arms and hurled themselves into the sea. [5] Preferring to take them alive rather than kill them, the Tyrians would beat their hands with sticks and stones as they swam until they were disabled and could be safely taken on board. [6] Nor was it just a matter of the superstructure being burned down. The same day it so happened that an especially high wind whipped up the sea from its very depths and smashed it against the mole. The joints loosened under the repeated battering of the waves, and the

water running between the rocks caused the work to rupture in the centre. [7] As a result the whole structure crashed into the deep water, so that on his return from Arabia Alexander found scarcely a trace of his huge mole.

There followed what usually happens when things go wrong: they resorted to mutual recrimination when they might have complained with more justice about the violence of the sea. [8] The king set to work on a fresh mole, but now he aimed it directly into the headwind, instead of side-on to it, so that the front offered protection to the rest of the work which, as it were, sheltered behind it. Alexander also added breadth to the mound so that towers could be raised in the middle out of range of the enemy's missiles. [9] Moreover, the Macedonians threw into the sea entire trees complete with their huge branches on which they set a load of rocks. Then they added another mass of trees to the pile and heaped earth on them; and over this they built up another layer of rocks and trees, thus forming a structure virtually bonded together into a solid whole.

The Tyrians meanwhile applied themselves energetically to any device that might impede the mole. [10] Particularly helpful to their purpose were the swimmers who would submerge out of their enemies' sight and swim unobserved right up to the mole, where they would pull towards them with hooks the projecting branches of the trees. Often these came away, taking much of the building material into the deep water, and the swimmers then had little difficulty managing the logs and tree trunks, once the weight on them had been removed. After that the whole structure, which had been supported by the logs, followed into the deep when its base collapsed.

[11] Alexander was dejected, undecided whether to continue or leave. At this point the fleet arrived from Cyprus, and Cleander simultaneously came with the Greek soldiers who had recently sailed to Asia. Alexander split the 190 ships into two wings: the Cypriot king, Pnytagoras, and Craterus took command of the left, and Alexander himself sailed on the right in the royal quinquereme. [12] The Tyrians had a fleet, but they refused to risk a naval engagement, setting a mere three vessels in the Macedonians' path directly below the city walls. These Alexander rammed and sank.

[13] The next day he brought the fleet up to the city's fortifications. At all points his artillery, especially his battering rams, shook the walls. The Tyrians hurriedly repaired the damage by setting rocks in the breaches and also started an inner wall which would give them protection should the first wall give way. [14] But disaster was closing in on them at every point: the mole was within javelin range; Alexander's fleet was encircling their walls; they were facing disaster in a battle waged concurrently on land and sea. The Macedonians had lashed pairs of quadriremes together in such a way that the prows were locked together but the sterns were as far separated as could be managed. [15] The space between the sterns they filled with yardarms and stout beams bound together, with decking laid over these to form platforms for infantrymen. After equipping the quadriremes in this manner they moved them up to the city, and from there missiles could be safely discharged on the defenders because the infantrymen were protected by the prows.

[16] At midnight Alexander ordered the fleet, equipped as described above, to encircle the walls and, as the ships closed in on the city at all points, a numbing despair descended on the Tyrians. Then, suddenly, thick clouds shrouded the sky and a layer of fog extinguished such twilight as there was. [17] By degrees the sea began to roughen and swell; a stronger wind whipped it up into waves and the vessels started to collide with each other. The lashings keeping the quadriremes together began to snap and the platforms to shatter with a huge roar, dragging the soldiers with them into the deep. [18] Since the vessels were lashed together, manoeuvring them in the rough water was impossible: infantrymen obstructed oarsmen in the performance of their tasks and oarsmen infantrymen. And as usually happens in such circumstances, the skilled began to obey the unskilled, with helmsmen, who customarily gave orders, now following instructions out of fear for their lives. The sea, lashed by their oars with greater determination, finally surrendered the vessels to the sailors, their rescuers, who brought them to shore, most of them as wrecks.

[19] Thirty ambassadors from Carthage happened to arrive during this period, more to encourage the besieged than to help them: for the Carthaginians, they announced to the Tyrians, were handicapped by a war at home and were fighting not for power but simply for survival. [20] The Syracusans were even then putting the torch to the crops in Africa, and had made camp not far from the walls of Carthage. Though frustrated in their great expectations, the Tyrians did not lose heart; instead they handed over their wives and children for evacuation to Carthage, being ready to face whatever might happen with increased fortitude if they had the most precious part of their community removed from the common peril. [21] One of their fellow citizens had also made it known at an assembly that he had dreamed that Apollo, a deity especially revered by the Tyrians, was leaving the city and that the mole laid in the sea by the Macedonians turned into a woodland glade. Despite the unreliability of the speaker, [22] the Tyrians in their panic were ready to believe the worst; they bound the statue of Apollo with a golden chain which they attached to the altar of Hercules, the deity to whom they had consecrated their city, in the hope that he would hold Apollo back. The statue had been brought from Syracuse and erected in the land of their forefathers by the Carthaginians, who had not decorated Carthage itself more lavishly than Tyre with the many spoils taken from cities which they had captured. [23] Some also advocated the revival of a religious rite which had been discontinued for many generations and which I certainly would not have thought to be at all acceptable to the gods – namely the sacrifice of a free-born male child to Saturn. (Such sacrilege – to use a more appropriate word than sacrifice – the Carthaginians had inherited from their founders, and they are said to have continued the practice right down to the time of their city's destruction.) Had it not been vetoed by the elders, whose judgement carried weight in all matters, cruel superstition would have triumphed over civilized behaviour.

[24] However, the urgency of the situation (more efficacious than any art) provided some novel means of defence beyond the conventional ones. To hamper the ships that approached the walls the townspeople had lashed stout beams to ropes; moving the beams forward with an engine, they would suddenly slacken the ropes and drop them on the ships. [25] Hooks and blades hanging from the beams would also injure either the mariners or the actual vessels. Furthermore, they would heat bronze shields in a blazing fire, fill them with hot sand and boiling excrement and suddenly hurl them from the walls. None of their deterrents aroused greater fear than this. The hot sand would make its way between the breastplate and the body; there was no way to shake it out and it would burn through whatever it touched. The soldiers would throw away their weapons, tear off all their protective clothing and thus expose themselves to wounds without being able to retaliate. The "crows" and "iron hands" let down from the engines also eliminated a large number of them.[32]

4   At this point a weary Alexander had decided to raise the siege and head for Egypt. After sweeping through Asia at a headlong pace he was now detained before the walls of a single city, with so many magnificent opportunities lost. [2] Yet it was as disgraceful for him to leave a failure as to linger there; he thought, too, that his reputation would suffer – his reputation which had gained him more conquests than military action – if he left Tyre as witness that he could be beaten. To leave nothing untried, he ordered more ships to be brought up and manned with hand-picked infantrymen. [3] Now it also happened that a sea-creature of extraordinary size, its back protruding above the waves, came to rest its huge body on the mole which the Macedonians had laid. Both sides caught sight of it as it parted the water and raised itself up. Then it submerged once more at the head of the mole, [4] and alternately rearing most of its body above the waves and diving beneath the surface it finally went under not far from the city's fortifications. The sight of the creature cheered both sides. [5] According to the Macedonian interpretation, it had pointed out the path the mole should take. According to the Tyrians, Neptune, exacting vengeance for the occupation of the sea, had snatched the beast away, which meant the mole was sure to collapse shortly. Exhilarated by the omen, they turned to feasting and excessive drinking and at sunrise they unsteadily boarded their vessels which they had decorated with flowers and wreaths – so premature were they not only in seeing an omen of their victory but in actually celebrating it!

[6] Now it so happened that the king had ordered his fleet to be moved in the other direction, leaving thirty smaller vessels on the beach. The Tyrians captured two of these and struck sheer panic into the others until Alexander, hearing the shouts of his men, eventually brought the fleet to the beach from

---

32   Although the defenders made use of grappling hooks, these are not to be confused with the *corvus korax* (often translated as "crow" or "raven") employed for the first time by the Romans in the First Punic War (see Polybius 1.22.4ff.).

which the commotion had come. [7] The first of the Macedonian ships to appear was a quinquireme superior to the others in speed, and when the Tyrian vessels sighted it two of them charged against its sides from opposite directions. The quinquereme turned on one of these, to find itself rammed by the enemy's prow, but the Macedonian vessel in turn grappled this ship. [8] The other Tyrian ship, which was not caught up and had a free run, began a charge at the quinquereme's other side, at which point a trireme of Alexander's fleet, arriving very opportunely on the scene, charged into the ship bearing down on the quinquereme with such violence that the Tyrian helmsman was hurled into the sea from the stern. [9] More Macedonian ships then appeared and the king also came up. The Tyrians backed water, with difficulty retrieved their entangled ship, and all their vessels retreated to the harbour together. The king followed up swiftly, and though unable to enter the harbour because projectiles kept him away from the walls, he still managed to sink or capture nearly all the enemy ships.

[10] The men were then given two days' rest, after which they were ordered to bring up the fleet and siege engines simultaneously so that Alexander could press his advantage at all points against a demoralized enemy. The king himself climbed the highest siege tower. His courage was great, but the danger greater; [11] for, conspicuous in his royal insignia and flashing armour, he was the prime target of enemy missiles. And his actions in the engagement were certainly spectacular. He transfixed with his spear many of the defenders on the walls, and some he threw headlong after striking them in hand-to-hand combat with his sword or shield, for the tower from which he fought practically abutted the enemy walls. [12] By now the repeated battering of the rams had loosened the joints in the stones and the defensive walls had fallen; the fleet had entered the port; and some Macedonians had made their way on to the towers the enemy had abandoned. The Tyrians were crushed by so many simultaneous reverses. Some sought refuge in the temples as suppliants while others locked their doors and anticipated the enemy by a death of their own choosing. Others again charged into the enemy, determined that their deaths should count for something. But the majority took to the rooftops, showering stones [13] and whatever happened to be at hand on the approaching Macedonians.

Alexander ordered all but those who had fled to the temples to be put to death and the buildings to be set on fire. [14] Although these orders were made public by heralds, no Tyrian under arms deigned to seek protection from the gods. Young boys and girls had filled the temples, but the men all stood in the vestibules of their own homes ready to face the fury of their enemy. [15] Many, however, found safety with the Sidonians among the Macedonian troops. Although these had entered the city with the conquerors, they remained aware that they were related to the Tyrians (they believed Agenor had founded both cities) and so they secretly gave many of them protection and took them to their boats, on which they were hidden and transported to Sidon. [16] Fifteen thousand were rescued from a violent death by such subterfuge. The extent of the bloodshed can be judged from the fact that 6,000 fighting-men were slaughtered within the city's fortifications. [17] It was a sad spectacle that the furious king then provided for the victors: 2,000 Tyrians, who had survived the rage of the tiring Macedonians, now hung nailed to crosses all along the huge expanse of the beach. [18] The Carthaginian ambassadors Alexander spared, but he subjoined a formal declaration of war (a war which the pressures of the moment postponed).

[19] Tyre was captured six months after the start of the siege . . .

The Persian (or Susian) Gates (end of 331 BC)

The battle at the Persian Gates is of military, topographical and historiographical interest. Whether it was necessary to fight the battle at all is debatable. Alexander certainly thought so, for he was convinced that only a rapid approach to Persepolis could prevent the enemy from removing or destroying the treasures that were housed there. Parmenion had taken the heavy-armed, the sick and wounded, and the baggage train along the wagon road that led into Persia, while Alexander with a smaller and more mobile force followed the more direct route through the mountains in the hope of preempting the Persians. Ariobarzanes, with a substantial force of defenders, attempted to forestall him at the Persian Gates. The episode calls to mind, as it was no doubt intended to do, the defence of Thermopylae in 480, where a small force of Greeks threatened to bring Xerxes' massive army of invasion to a halt. But, like Xerxes, Alexander found herdsmen who knew the terrain and helped him circumvent the defenders' position. Further discussions can be found in Heckel (1980) and Speck (2002). For discussions of the location of the gates, all based on autopsy, see Stein (1938, 1940), Wood (1997: 103–8), MacDermot and Schippmann (1999), and Speck (2002). Hammond (1996: 24–7) discusses the Polyaenus passage, but the source criticism is flawed.

3(c)   Arrian 3.18.1–10

After this Alexander sent off the baggage, the Thessalian cavalry, the allies, the foreign mercenaries and any others in the army who were more heavily armed, all under the command of Parmenion, who was to take them by the high-road leading into Persia. [2] The king himself took the Macedonian infantry, the cavalry of the Companions, the mounted skirmishers, the Agrianes and the archers, and followed the route through the mountains at a rapid pace.

Arriving at the Persian Gates, Alexander found the Persian satrap Ariobarzanes already there, at the head of about 40,000 infantry and some 700 cavalry. He had built a defensive wall across the pass, and had pitched camp at the wall to prevent Alexander from getting through.

[3] Alexander bivouacked there for the time being, but the next day he drew up his forces and brought them forward to attack the wall. Capturing it, however, seemed impossible because of the difficulty of the terrain; and his

men were now taking a severe beating since they were targets for missiles hurled from higher ground and from catapults. For the moment Alexander retired to his camp. [4] Then his prisoners informed him they would take him around by another route that would enable him to get into the pass. Told that this route was rough and narrow, Alexander left Craterus behind at the camp in command of his own battalion and that of Meleager, a small number of archers and around 500 cavalry. [5] He instructed Craterus to make an assault on the wall when he knew that Alexander had completed the circuit and was already approaching the Persian camp – and that Craterus would easily know because the trumpets would give him the signal.

Alexander went off under cover of night and advanced about 100 stades. He then took the hypaspists, Perdiccas' battalion, his lightest-armed archers, the Agrianes and the *ile basilike* of the Companions (along with a single cavalry squadron) and, with these and guided by the prisoners, he made a turn towards the pass. [6] Amyntas, Philotas and Coenus he left with orders to take the rest of the army down to the plain, and to bridge the river that he had to cross to go into Persia. He himself proceeded along a difficult and rough track, leading the men along it for the most part at a rapid pace. He fell upon the first guard post of the barbarians before dawn. This he wiped out, and most of the second too, [7] but most of the men in the third escaped. These did not run to the camp of Ariobarzanes, however – in terror they ran to the hills from their position – and the result was that Alexander's attack on the enemy camp, which took place at dawn, was a complete surprise.

When Alexander attacked the ditch, the trumpets at the same time gave the signal to Craterus' men, and Craterus launched his assault on the defensive wall. [8] The enemy, under attack from all directions, began to flee before even engaging their foe; but they were hemmed in on every side, with Alexander bearing down on them in one quarter and Craterus' men running up in another. The result was that most of them were obliged to turn and run back to the walls for safety – but by now the walls, too, were in the hands of the Macedonians. [9] For Alexander had correctly surmised what had happened and had left Ptolemy in place with about 3,000 infantry. Most of the barbarians were cut down by these in hand-to-hand fighting, and the others perished after throwing themselves from the cliffs in what became a panic-stricken rout. Ariobarzanes himself took flight to the mountains with a few cavalrymen.

[10] Alexander continued his speedy advance as far as the river and, finding the bridge there already finished, had no difficulty crossing with his army. From there he drove on into Persepolis, again moving speedily, so that he arrived before the treasury was plundered by its guards. He also captured the moneys in the treasury of Cyrus the First at Pasargadae.

3(d)   *Quintus Curtius Rufus 5.3.16–4.34*

Alexander then added the conquered Uxians to the satrapy of Susiana. After this he split his forces between himself and Parmenion and ordered the latter to advance along the route through the plains, while he himself with some light-armed troops took the mountain chain that runs in an unbroken line into Persia. [17] Laying waste this whole area he entered Persia after two days, and after four the narrow pass they call the Susian[33] gates. This pass Ariobarzanes had occupied with 25,000 infantry. It comprises steep cliffs, precipitous on all sides, on top of which stood the Persians, out of weapon range, deliberately inactive and giving the impression of being fear-stricken, as they waited for the Macedonian force to enter the narrowest part of the defile. [18] When they saw the Macedonians advancing with no regard for their presence, they began to roll massive rocks down the mountain slopes, and these would frequently rebound from rocks lower down and fall with even greater velocity, crushing not only individuals but entire companies. [19] Stones, shot from slings, and arrows were also showered on them from every direction. But the greatest source of anguish for Alexander's courageous men was not this but their inability to strike back, their being caught and slaughtered like animals in a pit. [20] Anger turned to rage. They grasped at the jutting rocks and, one giving another a lift, kept trying to clamber up to their enemy, but with the hands of many simultaneously pulling at them the rocks would break loose and fall back on the men who had dislodged them. [21] Thus they could neither make a stand nor press ahead, nor even gain protection from a tortoise-formation of shields, because of the vast size of the objects hurled down by the barbarians. Alexander suffered agonies, as much of shame as despondency, at his foolhardiness in stranding his army in the gorge. [22] Till that day he had been unbeaten; none of his undertakings had failed. No harm had come to him entering the ravines of Cilicia, or when the sea had provided him with a new route into Pamphylia. But now his good fortune was arrested, stopped dead, [23] and the only remedy was to go back the way he had come. And so, signalling the retreat, he ordered the men to leave the pass in close formation with shields interlocked above their heads; and they drew back a distance of 30 stades.

4   Alexander then pitched camp in an area open on every side and, besides giving rational consideration to his next move, he was also prompted by his superstition to summon the soothsayers. [2] But in these circumstances what could even Aristander, his most trusted soothsayer, predict? So Alexander halted the sacrifices on the grounds that the time was unsuitable, and ordered men with a knowledge of the area to be brought to him. These told him of a way through Media that was safe and open, [3] but the king's conscience would not permit him to leave his men unburied, for by Macedonian

---

33 Curtius, like Diodorus 17.68.1 and Polyaenus 4.3.27, calls them Susian rather than Persian Gates, which suggests the use of a common source. The existence of two names need not be doubted: Atkinson (1994: 84), citing Herzfeld and Hansman, suggests that it may reflect the direction in which one travels. (I would note that in my own city, the road that used to link Calgary with Edmonton is called Edmonton Trail, but the same road, in Edmonton, is referred to as Calgary Trail.) The Alexander historians were, no doubt, all approaching the gates from the same direction, but the difference may be explained by the vantage point of the informants who identified the pass.

convention there is hardly any duty in military life as binding as the burial of one's dead. Accordingly, Alexander ordered the recently captured prisoners to be summoned to him. [4] Among them was one who spoke both Greek and Persian. He told Alexander that he was wasting his time trying to take an army into Persia over the mountain ridge: the paths through the woods barely afforded passage for one man at a time; everything was overgrown with brush and the intertwining tree-branches produced one continuous forest. [5] Persia, in fact, is enclosed on one side by unbroken mountain chains; the range runs from the Caucasus mountains to the Red Sea (and measures 1,600 stades in length and 170 in width), and where the mountains come to an end they are replaced by another barrier, the sea. [6] Beyond the foothills lies an extensive plain, a fertile stretch of land containing numerous villages and cities. [7] Through the fields the river Araxes brings down the water of a large number of torrents into the Medus, and the latter, making a southerly turn, goes on into the sea as a smaller river than its tributary. [8] No river encourages a greater growth of vegetation: it carpets with flowers whatever it flows past and its banks are covered with plane trees and poplars; seen from a distance these give the impression that the woods on the banks are a continuation of the mountains. For the well-shaded river glides along in a bed cut deep into the soil, and is overhung by hills bearing rich foliage themselves because of the moisture that seeps into their base. [9] No area in all Asia is believed to possess a healthier climate; its temperate weather is due to the unbroken mountain chain on one side, which affords a cover of shade and alleviates the heat, and to the sea's proximity on the other, which provides the land with moderate temperatures.

[10] After this description the prisoner was asked by Alexander whether his information derived from hearsay or personal observation. He replied that he had been a shepherd and had travelled over all the paths in question, and added that he had been twice captured, once by the Persians in Lycia and the second time by Alexander. [11] The king was put in mind of a prophetic statement made by an oracle whose reply to him during a consultation was that his guide on the road to Persia would be a citizen of Lycia. [12] So he heaped on the captive such promises as the exigencies of the situation and the man's fortune in life required, told him to arm himself like a Macedonian and, with a prayer for the success of the venture, instructed him to point the way without regard for its difficulty or steepness. For, said Alexander, he and a few men would win through, unless the prisoner believed that Alexander in his pursuit of glory and undying fame could not go where his own sheep had taken him! [13] At the captive's repeated insistence on the difficulty of the path, especially for men in armour, the king said: "You can take my word for it; none of the men following you will refuse to go anywhere you lead them."

[14] Alexander now left Craterus in charge of the camp with his regular troops plus the forces under Meleager's command and 1,000 mounted archers, and instructed him to keep up the routine appearance of the camp, deliberately increasing the number of fires so that the Persians would be led

to believe that Alexander himself was in the camp. [15] However, should Ariobarzanes discover that he was coming through by means of the winding mountain paths and attempt to block his passage with a detachment of his troops, then Craterus was to give him some cause for alarm to attract his attention, making him divert his troops to the more imminent danger. [16] But if Alexander stole a march on his enemy and gained possession of the woods, then when Craterus heard the confused uproar of the Persians chasing the king, he was to set out without hesitation on the road from which they had been driven the previous day, for with the enemy's attention focused on Alexander he would find it undefended.

[17] At the third watch Alexander himself set out for the mountain path which had been described to him, his troops silent and not even a trumpet-signal being sounded. The men were lightly armed and under orders to take three days' supplies. [18] But even apart from the impossible crags and precipitous rocks that time and again made them lose their footing, their progress was further impeded by snow-drifts, into which they fell as if into pits and, when their comrades tried to lift them, instead of coming out themselves they would pull in their helpers. [19] Night and the unfamiliar landscape also multiplied their fears, as did the guide, whose loyalty was not above suspicion – if he escaped from his captors, they themselves could be trapped like wild animals. The king's safety and their own depended on the loyalty or the life of a single prisoner. [20] At last they reached the top. The path to Ariobarzanes went off to the right, and at this point Alexander left Philotas, Coenus, Amyntas and Polyperchon with a troop of light-armed men. They were told to advance slowly because their force included horsemen among the infantry and the soil in the area was very rich and productive of fodder; and they were given some of the captives to act as guides.

[21] Alexander himself took his bodyguard and the squadron called the *agema* and advanced with considerable difficulty along a path which was steep but well-removed from the enemy outposts. [22] It was midday, they were tired and they needed sleep, since they had as much of a journey before them as behind them, though it was not so steep and difficult. [23] Alexander therefore refreshed his men with a meal and some sleep, resuming the march at the second watch. Nothing caused him great difficulty on the journey until the point at which the mountain range gradually sloped down to the more level land, where the road was broken by a huge chasm formed by merging mountain streams. [24] In addition, the tree-branches at this point intertwined and clung together to bar their way with a continuous hedge. At this, deep despair descended on them, so deep that they could hardly keep from weeping. [25] The darkness especially terrified them, any stars that were out being hidden from sight by the trees with their unbroken covering of foliage. They were not even left their sense of hearing because the woods were shaken by a wind that smashed the branches together and produced a noise greater than its force would warrant. [26] Finally the long-awaited daylight diminished the terrors exaggerated by the night. The ravine could be circumvented by a short

detour, and each man had begun to act as his own guide. [27] They emerged on a high peak from which they could see an enemy outpost. They quickly armed themselves and appeared at the rear of the Persians, who had no fear of such an attack. The few who risked a fight were cut down, [28] and the groans of the dying plus the dismayed expressions of the men who ran back to the main body also prompted the fresh troops to flee even before they tasted the danger themselves. [29] The noise penetrated to the camp commanded by Craterus, who now took out his men to seize the defile in which they had been brought to a halt the day before. [30] At the same time further panic was instilled in the Persians by Philotas, Polyperchon, Amyntas and Coenus, who had been told to take a different route. [31] The Persians were under attack from two directions and Macedonian arms were gleaming all around them, but they put up a memorable fight. To my mind, pressure of circumstances can turn even cowardice into courage, and desperation often provides the basis for hope. [32] Unarmed men grappled with men who were armed, dragging them to the ground by virtue of their bodily weight and stabbing many with their own weapons.

[33] With a force of some 40 cavalry and 5,000 infantry Ariobarzanes broke through the centre of the Macedonian line, causing great loss of Macedonian and Persian blood, as he hurried to occupy the regional capital, the city of Persepolis. [34] But he was shut out from there by the city garrison and vigorously pursued by the enemy. Renewing the battle, he fell with all those who had fled with him. Craterus also came on the scene, driving on his troops at a rapid pace.

3(e) *Polyaenus*, Stratagems 4.3.27

Alexander defeated Darius at Arbela. Darius' kinsman, Phrasaortes,[34] was holding the Gates of Susa – lofty mountains with narrow defiles – at the head of a large Persian force. When the Macedonians made their attack they were easily beaten back by the barbarians with a barrage of catapult projectiles, arrows and rocks, and so Alexander proceeded to construct a fortified camp 30 stades back.

There was an oracle of Apollo to the effect that a foreign wolf[35] would become the king's guide for the road into Persia, and Alexander was now approached by a man who tended cattle and wore an animal skin for clothing. The man acknowledged that he was a Lycian. He also said that there was a path encircling the mountains and hidden in the thickly shaded woods, but

---

34 An error for Ariobarzanes. Phrasaortes became satrap of Persia after its capture by Alexander. Cf. Arrian 3.18.12.

35 The Greek word for wolf is *lykos*; the word for Lycian is *Lykios*. Cf. also Plutarch, *Alexander* 38.1–2.

that it was known to him, and to him alone, because he pastured his cattle there. Alexander remembered the prophecy and put his trust in the cowherd.

He instructed the entire army to remain in camp and to light a large number of fires, thereby attracting the enemy's attention, and he secretly gave Philotas and Hephaestion the order to attack from below when they saw the Macedonians appear on the crest of the mountains. Alexander then took the hypaspists, one phalanx of hoplites, and such Scythian archers as he had, and made his way along the narrow path for 80 stades, bivouacking under the thick cover of the woods. In the middle of the night he went around, and took a position above the sleeping enemy.

At break of day the trumpets gave the signal from the crest of the mountains, and Hephaestion and Philotas led the Macedonians forward from the fortified camp. The Persians were now hemmed in, with enemies above and enemies below; some were killed, some threw themselves from the heights, and some were taken alive.

Campaigns in Sogdiana: The Scythians and Spitamenes

Bessus and the others who had killed Darius III fled to Bactria in order to regroup. Alexander had intended to pursue them via the Merv Oasis (Margiana) but was diverted from his goal by the defection of Satibarzanes, who ruled in the Helmand Valley region of Afghanistan (Aria and Drangiana). From there the Macedonian army continued to Bactra (Balkh), crossing the Hindu Kush. Although the rebels arrested Bessus and turned him over to Alexander, they continued to resist in the valleys of the Oxus (Amu-darya) and Iaxartes (Syr-darya) and the mountain fortresses between them. In 329 and 328 Spitamenes emerged as Alexander's most dangerous enemy, supported by the Scythian Massagetae. For more on Alexander in Bactria, see especially Holt (1988); for the battle at the Polytimetus river, see Hammond (1991c).

3(f)   Itinerary of Alexander 38

Now those Macedonians who were under siege in the citadel at Maracunda[36] had made a sally before help reached them, and scattered the enemy, putting them to flight. They pursued the fugitives too far into the land of the Sogdiani, however, and when they began to take thought for getting back (they were now near the Polytimetus river),[37] the Scythians in their turn gradually became the pursuers. The Macedonians came to a part of the river bed which they had not reconnoitred, and became utterly bogged down in mud. On seeing this the enemy, who were familiar with the district, cut them off; launching an attack on the Macedonians, who had no experience of such conditions and could not easily retreat, they got to close quarters and killed

36   Maracanda: modern Samarcand.
37   The Zeravshan.

them all apart from a few who had eluded them because they were capable of moving – and indeed of seeing their way. Not more than forty cavalry (with but half their gear) and three hundred infantry made their escape.

3(g)   Metz Epitome 8–12

Leaving a garrison there, Alexander continued his march towards his original objective, the Tanais,[38] and encamped beside the river. But, in the meantime, the ruler of the Scythians sent his brother Carthasis with a large contingent to prevent him from crossing.

[9] Word was then brought to Alexander that Spitamenes and Catanes had defected and had routed with heavy casualties the Greek company which he had left with a garrison in the royal citadel. The survivors, he was told, had formed up in a wedge and sought refuge in a well-protected spot in the province of Bactria, where they were now under attack from Spitamenes. On hearing this, Alexander was uncharacteristically incensed and spent a sleepless night reflecting upon the wrongs he had suffered. [10] The best idea seemed to be to press on to his original objective and so the next day he ordered rafts to be made ready on the river . . .

3(h)   Arrian 4.3.6–7

Spitamenes' forces were also reported to be blockading on the acropolis the men left behind in Maracanda, and [7] Alexander thereupon sent Andromachus, Menedemus and Caranus to combat Spitamenes' troops. These men had with them about 60 of the cavalry of the Companions and 800 mercenary cavalry, under the command of Caranus, and some 1,500 mercenary infantry. Alexander also assigned the interpreter Pharnuches to this force. Pharnuches was a Lycian by race who was familiar with the language of the barbarians in that quarter and who, in general, seemed to have a flair for dealing with them.

3(i)   Itinerary of Alexander 43

Alexander sent out detachments to guard the area with their presence while he himself made haste to Maracunda. Spitamenes, who had renounced his alliance and departed from there to join the Massagetae, was now reported to be taking the field and apparently fighting a regular campaign. When

---

38   The Alexander historians thought that the Iaxartes (Syr-darya) was the Tanais, which was thought to form the boundary between Europe and Asia.

Spitamenes forced his way into a fortified place to capture plunder in Sogdian territory, Pithon[39] and Aristonicus[40] (a lyre-player), who were both employed there as musicians, made a sally with eighty horsemen; with a good deal of determination and alacrity they fell upon the enemy as their booty was being taken off. Later, though, they were caught in an ambush by Spitamenes and most of them, Aristonicus included, were killed. Subsequently Spitamenes fled because of his guilty conscience and his force was cut down in the desert when Craterus went in pursuit. Spitamenes himself was arrested and found guilty by his own men of instigating the wrongdoing; he was then handed over to Alexander to be subjected to flogging and due process of execution.[41]

3(j)   Arrian 4.5.2–6.5

Meanwhile, the Macedonians blockaded on the acropolis in Maracanda faced a direct assault from Spitamenes and his men. They mounted a counter-attack, killing a number of the enemy and driving back the entire force, and then retreated to the acropolis without suffering any losses themselves.

[3] News was now reaching Spitamenes that the forces sent out by Alexander were already approaching the town, at which he abandoned the blockade of the citadel and retired to the northern sector of Sogdiana. Pharnuches and the officers with him were eager to drive him from the country altogether, and so they kept on his tail as he fell back to the boundaries of Sogdiana. There – something they had not counted upon – they came up against the Scythian nomads as well. [4] Spitamenes had by now also enlisted the support of some 600 Scythian cavalrymen, and he was sufficiently encouraged by their co-operation to face the oncoming Macedonians. He deployed his forces on a level piece of ground at the edge of the Scythian desert, but his intention was neither to withstand the enemy attack, nor yet to take the offensive against them himself. Encircling the Macedonian infantry phalanx with his cavalry, he proceeded to shower it with arrows, and [5] when Pharnuches' men responded with an attack he slipped away with ease. The barbarian horses were faster, and at that point fresher, for Andromachus' men had mounts that had suffered the effects of the unbroken ride and also of a shortage of fodder. But if they stopped or pulled back they faced a vigorous attack from the Scythians, [6] many falling victim to arrow wounds, and some

---

39   Not the famous Somatophylax, but the son of Sosicles (Arrian 4.16.6). He was, however, not a musician as far as we know.
40   The text has "Aristobolus," but see Arrian 4.16.6 (3k, below).
41   Something has gone wrong here. According to Arrian 4. 17. 7, Spitamenes was murdered by his Scythian allies (the Massagetae), who sent his head to the king; Curtius 8. 3 and the *Metz Epitome* 20–3 have a more sensational story of Spitamenes murdered by his own wife, who brought his head to Alexander's camp (see §VIII.5a–b).

being killed. The Macedonians then put their men into a square formation and started to retreat towards the River Polytimetus, where there was a wood. There it would no longer be easy for the barbarians to fire their arrows at them, and the Macedonians could make better use of their infantry.

[7] However, the cavalry commander, Caranus, attempted to cross the river – his intention was to get his horsemen to safety there – without sharing his plan with Andromachus. The infantry, who were not under orders to do so, simply followed him, and made a panic-stricken and chaotic descent down the precipitously steep banks into the river.

[8] The barbarians could see the mistake that the Macedonians had made, and they charged into the stream on both sides of their enemy. Some stuck to the heels of those who had already crossed and were making their getaway; others ranged themselves to face those who were actually crossing, and drove them back into the river. [9] Others again fired arrows at them from the flanks or bore down on those still in the process of entering the water. The result was that the Macedonians were in a hopeless situation, under pressure from every side, and they sought refuge on one of the smaller islands in the stream. The Scythians and the cavalry with Spitamenes encircled them and killed them all with their arrows. A few they took prisoner, but all these they put to death, as well . . .

6   Aristobulus, however, relates that most of the army was destroyed in an ambush; the Scythians hid in a park and made a surprise attack on the Macedonians when the action was in progress. This happened, according to Aristobulus, when Pharnuches was trying to renounce his leadership in favour of the Macedonians who were also on the expedition. He had no experience of military matters, he claimed; he had been sent on the mission by Alexander for the purpose of communicating with the barbarians rather than taking command in battle – and his fellow officers were Macedonians and the king's *hetairoi* as well. [2] Andromachus, Caranus and Menedemus, however, refused the command. This was, in part, so as not to appear to have taken any personal initiative that infringed Alexander's orders. In addition, in the crisis that was now upon them, they were reluctant to accept responsibility even for their individual role in any bungled operation, and much less for the misdirection of the entire enterprise. They were in this sort of muddle and confusion when the barbarians attacked them, says Aristobulus, causing wholesale carnage, to the extent that no more than 40 cavalry and about 300 infantry escaped with their lives.

[3] When he was brought the report of this, Alexander was distraught by what had befallen his men and decided on a swift march against Spitamenes and the barbarians under his command. He took half the cavalry of the Companions, all the hypaspists, the archers, the Agrianes and the most lightly armed troops in the phalanx, and with these marched to Maracanda. He had been told that Spitamenes had returned to the city and was again blockading the men on the acropolis. [4] Alexander covered 1,500 stades in the space of three days, and towards the dawn of the fourth he drew near the city. When

news of Alexander's approach reached them, Spitamenes and his men did not remain in place but left the city in flight, [5] with Alexander in close pursuit. On reaching the site of the battle, the king did as much as he could in the circumstances to see to the burial of his soldiers, and then followed the fleeing enemy as far as the desert.

3(k)   Arrian 4.16.4–17.7

. . . Spitamenes and a number of men who had fled with him from Sogdiana sought refuge in the land of those Scythians who are called the Massagetae. Gathering together here 600 Massagetic cavalrymen they went ahead to one of the fortresses in Bactria. [5] The garrison commander here was anticipating no movement from an enemy, and when the barbarians fell on him and his garrison they managed to kill the soldiers and capture the commander, whom they kept under guard. Heartened by the capture of the fortress they moved up to Zariaspa[42] a few days later. They decided against an assault on the town; instead, they surrounded it and made off with large quantities of plunder.

[6] In Zariaspa a small number of the cavalry of the Companions had been left behind for medical reasons, and with them were Pithon son of Sosicles – he had the post of supervisor of the royal attendants in Zariaspa – and the harpist Aristonicus. By now these two men had recovered from their malady, and were again bearing arms and mounting their steeds. When they came to learn of the Scythian incursion, they gathered together about 80 mercenary cavalry who had been left as a defensive force for Zariaspa, and a number of the royal pages, and with these mounted a counter-attack on the Massagetae. [7] Falling on the Scythians, who were taken completely by surprise, they robbed them of all their plunder with the very first charge, killing not inconsiderable numbers while they were in the process of removing the spoils. But the Macedonians withdrew in disarray since they had nobody in command, and were ambushed by Spitamenes and the Scythians, losing seven of the Companions and 60 mercenary cavalry. Aristonicus the harpist lost his life here, showing more courage than one might have expected from a harpist. Pithon was wounded and taken alive by the Scythians . . .

17 [3] In the meantime Alexander acceded to Artabazus' request that he be relieved of the satrapy of Bactria on grounds of advancing age, and he made Amyntas son of Nicolaus satrap in his stead.[43] Coenus he left in place with his own battalion and that of Meleager, some 400 of the cavalry of the Companions, all the *hippakontistai* and the Bactrian and Sogdianian troops that were attached to Amyntas. These were to be under Coenus' orders and were to winter there in Sogdiana, the aim of this being to give protection to

42   Bactra (Balkh). The variant probably came from Aristobulus (cf. Bosworth 1995: 19).
43   Curtius 8.1.19 says that Alexander planned to assign the satrapy to Cleitus before the fateful drinking-party in Maracanda.

the area and, if possible, catch Spitamenes in a trap should he be on the move during the winter.

[4] Spitamenes and his men could now see that everywhere was secured by Macedonian garrisons and that for themselves there was no chance of escape in any direction. They therefore turned on Coenus and his forces, believing that here their fighting capability would perhaps count for more. They reached Gabae, a stronghold of Sogdiana that was situated on the border of Sogdiana and the territory of the Massagetic Scythians, and here had little difficulty in convincing some 3,000 Scythian horsemen to join them in an attack on Sogdiana. [5] These particular Scythians live in abject poverty, and at the same time they have no cities and no fixed abodes to cause them to harbour fears for what might be very dear to them. As a result persuading them to take on war after war is not difficult.

When Coenus and his troops learned of the approach of Spitamenes and his cavalry, they went forth themselves to meet them. [6] There was a hard-fought battle, and the Macedonians were victorious, with more than 800 of the barbarian horsemen falling in the clash, and twenty-five cavalry and twelve infantry on Coenus' side. In the flight the Sogdian forces still with Spitamenes, and most of the Bactrians, deserted their leader and came to Coenus to surrender. The [7] Massagetic Scythians had been badly beaten in the fighting and they now pillaged the baggage of the Bactrians and Sogdians who had stood at their side, after which they proceeded to flee into the desert. But when the news reached them that Alexander was on his way and heading towards the desert, they decapitated Spitamenes and sent the head to Alexander, hoping this act would keep the king from pursuing them.

3(I)   Strabo, Geography 11.11.4 C518

They also say that Alexander captured, through treachery, two rocky outcrops that were extremely well defended, that of Sisimithres[44] in Bactriana, where Oxyartes kept his daughter Roxane, and that of Oxus in Sogdiana (though some call this one the Rock of Ariamazes.) According to accounts of it, the Rock of Sisimithres is fifteen stades in height, with a circumference of 80 stades, and its top is level and fertile enough to support 500 men. Here Alexander met with a warm welcome, and married Oxyartes' daughter Roxane. The outcrop in Sogdiana is said to be twice the height of the other.

It was in these regions, they say, that Alexander also destroyed the city of the Branchidae. These people Xerxes had settled there after they volunteered to march with him from their home. The Branchidae had handed over to Xerxes the money and treasures of the god that were located in Didyma, and Alexander destroyed their city from revulsion at their desecration of the temple and their treachery.

---

44   His "official" name was Chorienes (cf. Omphis–Taxiles).

Aornus

Aornus (the name appears to be an approximation of the Sanskrit or Old Persian word for "stronghold") was located by Stein (1929: 113ff.) at Pir-sar; see Wood (1997: 180) for a color photograph. Recently, some have argued for Mount Ilam, which is located south of Ude-gram (Ora): see Tucci (1977) and Badian (1987: 117 n.1). But Curtius' account (below) makes it clear that the Indus flows past the base of the rock, which suits Pir-sar but not Mount Ilam; see full discussion in Bosworth (1995: 179–80). Alexander's reasons for attacking were threefold: to crush the last remnants of the Assacenian resistance (their chief city of Massaga had recently surrendered: see §VIII.7a–b); to outdo Heracles, whose attack on the place had been thwarted by an earthquake (see §IX.1k–l); and to reaffirm his own invincibility.

3(m)　*Quintus Curtius Rufus 8.11.1–25*

From here Polyperchon was despatched with an army to the city of Ora, where he defeated the disorganized inhabitants in battle, drove them within their fortifications and, pressing his advantage, brought the city into subjection. [2] Many cities of little consequence fell to the king after being deserted by their inhabitants. The latter took up arms and occupied a rocky outcrop called Aornis.[45] According to popular tradition this had been unsuccessfully besieged by Hercules, who had been obliged to abandon the siege by an earthquake. [3] Alexander was baffled: the rock was precipitously sheer on every side. Then he was approached by an old man who knew the area. He came to him with his two sons and promised that he would show him a way up, for a price. [4] Alexander contracted to give him 80 talents and, keeping one of the young men behind as a hostage, sent the old man off to fulfil his commitment. [5] The king's secretary, Mullinus, was put at the head of a light-armed unit which, Alexander decided, was to make its way to the summit by a circuitous route to avoid detection by the enemy.

[6] Unlike most rocky prominences, this one does not reach its high elevation by gradual and gentle slopes. It rises very much like a cone, its lower section comparatively broad but the upper part tapering until it terminates in a sharp peak at the top. [7] Its base is lapped by the Indus river, which is extremely deep with steep banks on both sides. On the far side of the rock are sheer chasms and ravines, and the only way to take it by storm was by filling them in. [8] Alexander issued orders for a nearby wood to be felled and the logs thrown into the chasm stripped (since the branches and their foliage would have hindered the men carrying them). Alexander was himself the first to strip and throw in a tree, and the shout that followed from the troops revealed their enthusiasm, for none refused a job the king had undertaken

---

45　Aornus.

before him. [9] Within seven days they had filled in the caverns, and the king now ordered the archers and the Agrianes to scale the steep cliffs. From his own unit he selected thirty of the bravest young men, [10] and assigned to them as leaders Charus and Alexander (reminding the latter of the name they both shared). In view of such palpable danger, it was at first decided that the king should not take part in the hazardous undertaking himself; [11] but as soon as the trumpet-signal was given, this resolute man of action turned to his bodyguards, told them to follow him, and was the first to clamber up the rock. After that not one Macedonian held back. They left their posts and followed the king of their own accord. [12] Many were overtaken by a pitiful fate. Slipping from the sheer cliff-face, they were swallowed up by the river flowing past it. This was a painful spectacle even to those not in danger but, when another's death demonstrated to them what they had to fear themselves, their pity turned to terror and their lamentation was no longer for the dead but for themselves.

[13] By now they had reached the stage where returning was impossible without destroying themselves, unless they were victorious. As they climbed, the barbarians rolled huge boulders on to them, and those who were hit fell headlong from their unsure and slippery footholds. [14] Alexander and Charus, however, had scaled the cliff, and had already begun to engage the enemy in hand-to-hand fighting, though, since the barbarians were pouring weapons on them from higher ground, they received more wounds than they inflicted, [15] Alexander, bearing in mind both his name and his promise, fought with more vigour than caution and finally fell, pierced by weapons from every side. [16] Charus saw him on the ground. Everything but revenge left his mind and he began a charge at the enemy, many of whom he despatched with his lance, some with his sword. But he was alone and his antagonists many. He fell dead on his friend's body.[46] [17] Distressed, as one might expect, by the death of his best young fighters and others of his men, the king signalled a retreat. [18] What saved them was the fact that they withdrew gradually and confidently, while the barbarians were content with having driven back their enemy and refrained from pressing them as they retreated.

[19] Alexander had now decided to abandon the project – there was apparently no hope of gaining the rock – but he nonetheless made a show of persevering with the siege, ordering roads to be blocked, siege towers moved up, and exhausted troops replaced by others.

[20] The Indians saw his persistence but they spent two days and nights feasting and beating drums in their usual manner, ostentatiously demonstrating not only their confidence but their belief that they had won. [21] On the third night, however, drumbeats were no longer heard. Torches blazed all over the rocky hill, lit by the barbarians to make their flight safer when they would, in the darkness of night, be running over crags impossible to negotiate. [22]

---

46 The episode seems to be influenced by Virgil's story of Nisus and Euryalus (*Aeneid* 9.176–449).

Alexander sent Balacrus ahead to reconnoitre and learned that the barbarians had fled and abandoned the rock. Then, giving the signal for his men to raise a concerted shout, he struck terror into the Indians in their disordered flight. [23] Many thought the enemy were upon them and hurled themselves to their deaths down the slippery crags and impassable rocks. A larger number suffered mutilations to some part of their bodies and were abandoned by their uninjured comrades.

[24] Although his victory was over the terrain rather than the enemy, the king nonetheless fostered the belief that he had won a decisive victory by offering sacrifices and worship to the gods. Altars were set up on the rock in honour of Minerva Victoria. [25] The reward was duly paid to the guides for the path on which Alexander had ordered the light-armed to ascend, although they had accomplished less than they had contracted to do; and the rocky prominence and the adjoining land was put under Sisocostus' authority.

3(n)   Arrian 4.29.1–30.4

It was at that point that some of the local people came to the king. They offered their surrender and also told him they would guide him to the most easily assailable part of the rock, to a point from which, they said, he would have no difficulty in capturing the entire location. With these men Alexander sent his bodyguard, Ptolemy son of Lagus, at the head of the Agrianes, as well as the other light infantry (and, in particular, some elite hypaspists). He ordered Ptolemy to strengthen the position with a powerful defensive force as soon as he took it, and then signal to him that it was in his hands.

[2] Ptolemy made his way along a rough and difficult path, and took the spot without the barbarians' knowledge. He fortified it by encircling it with a palisade and a ditch and raised a beacon on the hill at a point where Alexander would see it. The flame was indeed spotted, and the next day Alexander led forward his army, but when he met barbarian resistance the offensive faltered on the difficult ground. [3] The barbarians realized that his assault was impracticable, and so turned to attack Ptolemy's men. There was some vigorous fighting between them and the Macedonians, the Indians doing all they could to break down the palisade, and Ptolemy doing his best to protect the position. The barbarians had less success than the Macedonians in the encounter, and they withdrew with the onset of night.

[4] Amongst the Indians who had deserted to him there was a man whom Alexander trusted and who, in particular, knew the area well. The king picked out this man and sent him at night to Ptolemy with a letter. In it Ptolemy was given orders not to content himself with holding his position but to charge down on the barbarians from the height when Alexander launched his own attack on the rock, so that the Indians would be caught in a pincer

movement, under assault from both directions. [5] At daybreak Alexander struck camp and led his forces to the path that Ptolemy had used to mount the rock unobserved. He reckoned that if he could force a passage this way and join up with Ptolemy's men the job would be easy for him.

And matters turned out as planned. [6] There was fierce fighting between the Indians and the Macedonians that lasted until midday, with the Macedonians attempting to force their way up the path and the Indians hurling their spears at them as they climbed. But the Macedonians did not relax their pressure, one group coming up hard on the heels of another, with those in front taking a break. Early in the afternoon, though only after much effort, they gained control of the path and linked up with Ptolemy's men. The now-united force then advanced to make a concerted attack on the rock itself. The attack at that point still proved unsuccessful, however, and with that the day ended.

[7] At dawn, Alexander gave orders for each of his men to cut a hundred stakes. When the stakes were cut, the king proceeded to raise a large embankment, starting from the peak of the hill where they were encamped, and rising in the direction of the rock. From this, he thought, his men's arrows and the projectiles fired from his catapults would reach the defenders. Every man took a hand in building the work, and Alexander personally attended, keeping an eye on the structure and giving praise where it proceeded with energy and chastisement where deficiencies could be immediately seen.

30 On the first day the army piled up the earth to about the length of a stade. On the following the slingers shot at the Indians from the already-completed section of the mound, and that, together with projectiles flying from the artillery, checked Indian sorties against the men involved with the construction. For three days in a row the embankment was continued in that area, and on the fourth some Macedonians – they were few in number – charged forward and took possession of a hill which was small, but on a level with the rock. Losing not a moment, Alexander pushed the embankment forward in that direction, wishing as he did to connect the mound with the hill that this small group of men was holding for him.

[2] The Indians were taken aback by the bold manner – words could not describe it – in which the Macedonians had charged the hill; and, as they now saw the embankment was joined to it, their resistance began to crumble. They sent messengers to Alexander to say they were prepared to surrender the rock if given peace terms. In fact, they had really decided to play for time and spin out the day negotiating the peace terms, and then to scatter to their homes at night. [3] But Alexander came by this information. He thereupon gave the Indians time to fall back and withdraw the guards stationed at all points around the hillside. He then waited until they began to withdraw, at which point he took some 700 bodyguards and hypaspists to that part of the rock which they had left. He was the first to climb up, and the Macedonians, pulling one another up at various points, scaled it after him. [4] A signal was given, and these men turned on the barbarians who were now falling back,

killing many as they fled, while others, in their panic to get away, flung themselves to their deaths from the cliffs. The rock was now in Alexander's hands, the rock that Heracles failed to take. Alexander sacrificed on it and set up a garrison there.

The Mallian campaign

After he had been forced to turn back at the Hyphasis (Beas) River, Alexander retraced his steps to the Hydaspes (Jhelum), where he had established the towns of Nicaea and Bucephala, and there provisioned a fleet which accompanied the army downstream. Beyond the confluence of the Hydaspes and the Acesines (Ravi), he came upon the warlike Sudracae (incorrectly referred to by some authors as Oxydracae) and the Mallians. In the attack on one of their towns, Alexander was briefly trapped within the walls, accompanied by only a handful of bodyguards. Some scholars have suggested that the army was reluctant to follow him after the Hyphasis "mutiny"; on the other hand, Alexander was habitually reckless and had escaped serious injury and death by sheer luck. On this occasion, however, he was seriously wounded.

3(o)   Quintus Curtius Rufus 9.4.26–6.2

After this the Macedonians came to the capital town of the Sudracae. Most of the enemy had sought refuge here, though their confidence in its walls was no greater than their confidence in their arms. [27] Alexander was already making his move towards the town when a seer began to issue warnings against the siege which, he said, the king should at least postpone since it was predicted that his life was in danger. [28] Alexander looked at Demophon (that was the seer's name). "If someone interrupted you like this," said the king, "when you were preoccupied with your craft and observing the entrails, I am sure you would consider him an exasperating nuisance." [29] After Demophon replied that such would certainly be the case, Alexander continued: "When I have my mind on weighty matters and not on animal intestines, do you think anything could be a greater hindrance to me than a superstitious seer?"

[30] Waiting only to give this reply, the king ordered the ladders to be taken forward and, as the others hesitated, scaled the wall. This had a narrow cornice and, on top, in place of the usual crenellated battlements, passage was blocked by a continuous parapet. [31] Thus the king was hanging, rather than standing, on the parapet, using his shield to parry the weapons falling all round him, [32] for he was the target of projectiles hurled at long range from all the towers about him. His men were unable to reach him because they were overpowered by the missiles showered on them from above, but finally shame prevailed over the magnitude of their danger, since they could see that by hanging back they were delivering their king to the enemy. Their

haste, however, actually retarded their aid: [33] while they all tried to scale the wall before their comrades, they overloaded the ladders, which then failed to support them so that they fell to the ground and robbed the king of his only hope. Now he stood in total isolation in the face of a huge army.

5   By now his left arm was weary from swinging around his shield to parry enemy missiles. His friends called to him to jump down to them and were standing ready to catch him. At this point Alexander made an incredible and phenomenal move which added far more to his reputation for recklessness than to his glorious record. [2] With a wild leap, he flung himself into a city full of his enemies – even though he could barely hope to die in combat without uselessly sacrificing his life, since he could have been overpowered and taken alive before he got up. [3] As it happened, his balance was such that he landed on his feet, and so he began to fight from a standing position – and fortune had seen to it that he would not be surrounded. [4] Not far from the wall stood an old tree whose thickly leaved branches gave the king some cover, as though its purpose had been to provide him with protection. Alexander pressed himself against its thick trunk so that he could not be encircled and then used his shield to parry the weapons being showered on him from in front. [5] For, though he stood alone, being attacked by so many at long range, no one dared move up on him, and more spears hit the branches than his shield.

[6] Supporting the king in the fight was, first of all, the widespread fame of his name; then there was his desperation, providing a keen incentive to gain an honourable death. [7] But the enemy kept pouring on to him and by now he had taken a large number of missiles on his shield, his helmet had been shattered by rocks and his knees had buckled under the severe and relentless pressure. [8] Accordingly, the Indians standing closest to him rushed at him without due regard or caution. Alexander disposed of two of them with his sword so that they fell dead at his feet. After that no one had the courage to come to close quarters with him: they kept their distance and fired spears and arrows at him. [9] Though exposed to all these enemy weapons, Alexander still had no difficulty in protecting himself, down on his knees as he was, until an Indian fired an arrow 2 cubits long (for the Indians had arrows of this size, as I explained above) which passed through his cuirass to lodge itself slightly above his right side. [10] When he received the wound, a thick jet of blood shot forth. He dropped his weapons and appeared to be dying. He was so weak that he did not even have the strength to pull out the arrow with his right hand. [11] The man who had inflicted the wound therefore ran up to strip the body, all eager and exultant. Alexander felt him put his hands on his body and I suppose the indignity of this final insult brought him round. Summoning back his failing spirit, he brought his sword beneath his enemy and plunged it into his unprotected side.

[12] Three bodies now lay around the king, and the other Indians kept their distance in bewilderment. Alexander tried to pull himself up on his shield, intending to go down fighting before his last breath left him. [13] He had not

the strength left for the effort, so he attempted to stand by grasping the over-hanging branches with his right hand. Even thus he could not control his movements. He sank back to his knees, with a gesture of his hand challenging any of the enemy to come and fight him.

[14] Finally, after dislodging the defenders in another sector of the city, Peucestes[47] appeared, following in the king's steps. [15] When he saw him, Alexander thought Peucestes' arrival meant consolation in death rather than hope of life, and he allowed his exhausted frame to drop on his shield. Immediately afterwards Timaeus[48] came up, and shortly after him Leonnatus, then Aristonus. [16] The Indians, neglecting everything else when they learned the king was within their walls, also converged swiftly on that spot and proceeded to attack Alexander's defenders. Of these Timaeus went down with many frontal wounds after a heroic fight. [17] Peucestes, too, had received three javelin wounds, but even so he was using his shield to protect his king, not himself. Leonnatus received a serious neck wound while trying to check a fierce barbarian charge, and fell half-dead at the king's feet. [18] By now Peucestes was also exhausted from his wounds and had let his shield drop. Alexander's last hope lay in Aristonus – but he, too, was seriously wounded and unable to withstand further the violent pressure of the enemy.

[19] Meanwhile a report reached the Macedonian main body that the king had fallen. What would have dismayed others stirred them to action. Regardless of risk, they smashed through the wall with pick-axes and, bursting into the city where they had made the breach, they cut down the Indians, more of whom took to flight than dared engage the enemy. [20] Old men, women, children – none was spared. Anyone the Macedonians encountered they believed responsible for their king's wounds. Mass slaughter of the enemy finally appeased their just rage. [21] According to Cleitarchus and Timagenes,[49] Ptolemy (who was subsequently a king) took part in this battle. Ptolemy himself, however, certainly from no desire to detract from his own reputation, records that he was not there, since he had been sent on an expedition. Such was the carelessness of the compilers of the older histories or, an equally reprehensible shortcoming, their gullibility.

[22] Alexander was brought back to his tent, where the doctors cut off the shaft of the arrow embedded in his body without moving the arrow-head. [23] They then stripped him naked and observed that the arrow was barbed and could only be removed without serious damage to Alexander if the wound

47   He was rewarded for his bravery by being appointed an exceptional eighth member of the *Somatophylakes* (Arrian 6.28.4). See §I.3g.

48   His name in the Greek texts is Limnaeus.

49   Both historians were from Alexandria: Cleitarchus was a contemporary of Alexander, though (apparently) not a participant in the events he described; Timagenes lived in the late first century BC. Curtius may not have read Timagenes: possibly he took over the reference from the work of Pompeius Trogus, who must have been familiar with Timagenes' work, *On Kings*.

were surgically enlarged. [24] They feared, however, that the operation would be impeded by profuse bleeding, since the arrow buried in his flesh was huge and had apparently penetrated his vital organs. [25] Critobulus was a doctor possessed of extraordinary skill,[50] but in such a critical situation he was terrified, fearing to undertake the operation in case an unsuccessful outcome resulted in serious repercussions for himself. [26] Alexander caught sight of him weeping and fearful, the anxiety almost draining him of colour. 'Why are you waiting?' he said to the doctor. 'What is the moment you are waiting for? If I have to die, why do you not at least free me from this agony as soon as possible? Or are you afraid of being held responsible for my having received an incurable wound?'

[27] Eventually, his fear passing or else hidden, Critobulus started urging Alexander to let himself be held down until he extracted the arrow-head, since even a slight movement of the body would have grave consequences.

[28] The king declared that he had no need of people to hold him and, following instructions, he submitted his body to the knife without flinching. So the wound was enlarged and the barbed head extracted. A stream of blood now began to gush forth. Alexander started to lose consciousness and, as darkness covered his eyes, he lay stretched out as though on the point of death. [29] In vain they tried to check the bleeding with medications, and shouting and wailing broke out simultaneously from his friends who believed their king was dead. Finally the bleeding stopped; Alexander gradually regained consciousness and began to recognize those at his bedside. [30] All through that day and the night that followed, the troops remained in arms crowded around the royal quarters, admitting that all their lives depended on his alone. They refused to leave until they were told that he was taking a short sleep, after which they returned to camp with more sanguine hopes for his recovery.

3(p)   Justin 12.9.1–13

From there Alexander proceeded to the River Acesines and sailed down it to the Ocean, [2] where he accepted the surrender of the Agensonae and the Sibi, whose founder was Hercules. [3] From here he sailed to the Mandri[51] and Sudracae, tribes which faced him with an armament of 80,000 infantry and 60,000 cavalry. [4] He defeated them in the field and then led his army to their city. [5] The first to scale its wall, he observed that the city was without defenders and so, without a single bodyguard, he leapt down to the ground within. [6] When the enemy saw him thus isolated, they raised a shout and rushed at him from all sides in the hope of terminating with the life of a single man a

---

50   He may have been the same doctor who treated Philip II when he was struck in the eye with an arrow (Pliny, *Natural History* 7.37). Arrian calls the doctor Critodemus, but this appears to be an error of transcription: see Heckel (1981c).
51   Malli.

worldwide war, and of avenging so many nations. [7] Nevertheless, Alexander resolutely defended himself and single-handedly engaged several thousand men. [8] Incredibly, he was not terrified by the enemy numbers, by their dense shower of missiles or the loud cries of his attackers; on his own he cut down or drove back many thousands. [9] When, however, he saw that he was being overwhelmed by their numbers, he pressed himself against the trunk of a tree which at that time stood close to the wall [10] and, using this to protect himself, long kept the horde at bay until, learning of his perilous situation, his friends leapt down to join him, many of them being killed by the enemy. [11] The battle long remained undecided until the wall was breached and the entire army could come to their comrades' aid. [12] In that engagement, Alexander was struck by an arrow beneath the breast. Weakened from loss of blood, he dropped to one knee and continued fighting until he killed the man who had wounded him. [13] The treatment was riskier than the wound.

3(q)   Itinerary of Alexander 52

There was a city in India where a great number of the enemy had taken refuge; it was all-too massive in size and of a strength that seemed beyond storming. Alexander attacked it with siege works, ordering tall ladders to be made, corresponding to the height of the wall. These were set in place but the enemy fought back, smashing them with huge rocks dropped from above. One ladder alone held out and on this the king, with two companions, fought his way to the top while he himself came under attack from countless enemies who sought, from above or from wherever any of them could get at him, to thrust him down off the ladder. Despite having seen all the other ladders of his men broken in pieces and knowing he would be endangering himself with no prospect of adequate assistance, he nevertheless charged ahead into the enemy in all their thousands, alone save for the two companions mentioned above (Peucestes, that is, and Ptolemy)[52] and thereby at once turned upon himself the attention of the entire host of that city. All day long then, with his two companions at his side, he continued to fight his whole army's battle and would have so continued, had he not been wounded in the side near his armpit at the day's end. The steel point penetrated quite deeply and his strength began to fail. The Macedonians who were in action outside the wall guessed what was happening or feared something worse (since the entire body of those inside was concerned only with the king and was no longer repelling from the top of the wall any attempt to rush in), and broke the bolts of the gate by force, to bring help and to rescue just in time the king who was by now beginning to despair of his own life. Finally, their indignation making them the more vindictive, they used their right hands with no

---

52 Ptolemy, by his own admission, was not present when this occurred (Arrian 6.5.6–7, 11.8; Curtius 9.5.21).

discrimination as to age or sex as they took their turn and cut down all the inhabitants in a general massacre.

3(r)   Arrian 6.11.3, 7–8

[3] In the first place, it is invariably recorded that this misfortune overtook Alexander among the Oxydracae. In fact, it happened amongst the Malli, an autonomous Indian tribe. The city was a Mallian one and it was the Mallians who discharged their weapons at Alexander; for these people had decided to join forces with the Oxydracae, but Alexander preempted them by marching on the Mallians through the desert before they could get any help from the Oxydracae or they themselves could be of any service to the oxydracae . . .

[7] With respect to the men who protected Alexander in his hour of peril, there is universal agreement that Peucestas was present, but then there is no agreement concerning Leonnatus and Abreas the *dimoirites*.[53] Some have it that Alexander was struck on the helmet with a club and that he fell in a daze, but that he then stood up again and was hit in the chest by a missile that pierced his cuirass.

[8] But in my opinion the most serious error of the Alexander historians is as follows. Some have written that Ptolemy son of Lagus climbed the ladder with Alexander, along with Peucestas. They say that Ptolemy held his shield over the king when he fell and was therefore given the name Ptolemy Soter.[54] However, Ptolemy himself has put it on record that he was not present at this episode – he was fighting in other engagements against other barbarians at the head of his own troops.

---

53 A soldier who receives double pay.
54 Soter means "Saviour." The epithet has its origins in Ptolemy's role in saving the Rhodians when they were blockaded by Demetrius the Besieger in 305/4.

VII Alexander and the Barbarians

Despite Aristotle's well-known view that Hellenes were vastly superior to barbarians, Alexander showed early signs of adopting a conciliatory policy. He kept Mithrenes, the Persian who surrendered Sardis, in his entourage and eventually entrusted him with the satrapy of Armenia; he allowed Ada, queen of Halicarnassus to adopt him; he showed great respect to the wife and mother of Darius III; and he retained Mazaeus and Aboulites as satraps. All this before he began to adopt Persian dress and court ceremonial. The political advantages of such policies are obvious enough to the enlightened modern historian, but to the Macedonians, who fought to defeat and, indeed, punish the Persians for alleged atrocities in the past, it was a betrayal and sign of instability on the king's part. The extent to which Alexander's orientalism formed a policy of fusion has been the subject of considerable debate. See especially Berve (1938), Bosworth (1980b), and Hamilton (1987).

Alexander Adopts Persian Dress and Practices

1(a)   Quintus Curtius Rufus 6.6.1–10

It was at this point that Alexander relinquished control of his appetites. His self-restraint and continence, supreme qualities at the height of good fortune, degenerated into arrogance and dissipation. [2] The traditional ways of his people, the healthy, sober discipline and unassuming demeanour of the Macedonian kings he considered beneath his eminent position and he began to ape the Persian royalty with its quasi-divine status. [3] Men who had conquered scores of nations he wished to lie prostrate on the ground to venerate him, and he sought gradually to inure them to servile duties and to bring them down to the level of captives. [4] Accordingly he wore on his head a purple headband interwoven with white, like the one Darius had once had, and he assumed Persian dress – without fearing the omen implicit in his moving from the victor's insignia to the garb of the conquered. [5] His claim was that he was wearing Persian spoils, but the fact was that with the clothes he had also adopted Persian habits, and a contemptuous demeanour accompanied the ostentatious dress. [6] Furthermore, he sealed letters sent to Europe with the stone of his old ring, but on those written to Asia was set the seal of Darius' ring – apparently one man's mind could not cope with the fortunes of two. [7] He had also forced Persian clothing on his friends and on the cavalry, the elite of the troops. They found it distasteful, but did not dare refuse to wear it. [8] The royal quarters had a complement of 365 concubines, the number Darius had possessed, and along with them were hordes of eunuchs practised in playing the woman's part.

[9] Towards all this, smacking as it did of extravagance and foreign habits, the veterans of Philip, a group inexperienced in sensuality, displayed open revulsion. Throughout the camp one sentiment and one view found expression, that they had lost more by victory than they had gained by war, [10] and that at that very moment they were experiencing defeat, surrendering to the ways of aliens and foreigners. How could they face people, they asked, returning home dressed like captives? They felt ashamed of themselves now, they said, and their king resembled one of the conquered rather than a conqueror – demoted from King of Macedon to satrap of Darius.

1(b)   Metz Epitome 1–2

Alexander the Great, King of Macedon, subsequently made clear his true aspirations. [2] He then appointed a large number of personal bodyguards and made Darius' brother Oxyathres ⟨. . .⟩;[1] he assumed a diadem, a white-flecked tunic, a staff, a Persian girdle and all the trappings of royalty which had belonged to Darius. He also ordered the mounted retinue which he maintained to attend him in Persian attire.

1(c)   Plutarch, Alexander 45.1–4

From Hyrcania Alexander moved the army into the land of Parthia, and it was during a period of inactivity here that he first assumed the dress of the barbarian. He may have wished to conform to the culture of the region inasmuch as shared conventions and ethnicity do much to conciliate people; or possibly it was Alexander surreptitiously experimenting with *proskynesis* on the Macedonians, habituating them by degrees to acceptance of a change of behaviour and manners on his part. [2] In fact, he did not adopt that infa-

---

1   He enrolled Oxyathres amongst his *Hetairoi* (cf. Quintus Curtius Rufus 6.2.11), the noble retinue of the Macedonian king, an honor extended to only a few barbarians. But Diodorus (17.77.4), whose details at this point are otherwise very similar, says that he was included in the bodyguard itself.

mous Persian style that is completely *outré* and bizarre, and he eschewed the trousers, the Medic shirt and the tiara. Instead, he aimed at something roughly between the Persian and Median styles that was less ornate than the one but more impressive than the other.

[3] He wore this, at first, when he was associating with the barbarians or with his comrades in his quarters; but presently he was to be seen in such dress in public when he went out riding or gave audiences. [4] The Macedonians found the sight offensive, but their admiration for his other superb qualities made them feel they should to some extent be indulgent with him where his whims and his image were concerned.

1(d)   Quintus Curtius Rufus 6.2.1–11

Alexander could better cope with warfare than peace and leisure. As soon as he was free of these worries that beset him, he yielded to dissipation, and the man whom the arms of Persia had failed to crush fell before its vices. [2] There were parties early in the day; drinking and mad revelry throughout the night; games; women by the score. It was a general decline into the ways of the foreigner. By affecting these, as though they were superior to those of his own country, Alexander so offended the sensibilities and eyes of his people that most of his friends began to regard him as an enemy. [3] For the Macedonians clung tenaciously to their own practices and were used to satisfying their natural requirements with a diet that was sparing and easily accessible; and these he had now driven into the depraved customs of foreigners and conquered nations. [4] This explains the increase in the plots against his life, the mutiny of his men and the more public displays of resentment and mutual recrimination among them; it explains why Alexander subsequently oscillated between anger and suspicion which arose from groundless fears, and it explains other similar problems which will be recounted later.

[5] Since he was spending his days as well as his nights on these protracted banquets, Alexander would use stage performances to relieve the tedium of feasting. But he was not content with the large number of performers he had requisitioned from Greece; instead, female captives would be ordered to sing in their native manner their artless songs which grated on the ears of non-natives. [6] The king himself noticed one of these women more downcast than the others and out of shyness resisting those trying to bring her forward. She was exceptionally beautiful, and her modesty lent further charm to her beauty. With eyes fixed on the ground and her face veiled as far as was allowed, she made the king suspect that she was too highly born to appear among such dinner-table displays. [7] So she was asked who she was, and answered that she was the granddaughter of Ochus, the former king of Persia, being the daughter of his son; and that she had been the wife of Hystaspes (who had been related to Darius and who had himself commanded a powerful army).

[8] There yet lingered in the king's heart slight traces of his former quali-ties. He felt respect for a woman of royal stock who had suffered a reversal of fortune and for so eminent a name as that of Ochus. [9] He not only ordered the captive released but he also had her possessions returned to her and a search instituted for her husband so that he could return his wife to him if he were found. The following day he instructed Hephaestion to have all the prisoners brought to the royal quarters and there he verified the lineage of each of them, separating from the common people those of noble birth. The latter numbered 1,000 and included Oxathres, brother of Darius, who was as distinguished for his nobility of character as for his brother's station in life. [11]2 Oxydates, a Persian nobleman kept in shackles because he had been condemned to execution by Darius, was freed and given the satrapy of Media by Alexander. The king also admitted Darius' brother to his circle of friends, allowing him to retain all the honour due his ancient and distinguished lineage. [10] Twenty-six thousand talents had accumulated in booty from the most recent engagement, 12,000 of which were disbursed as bonuses for the men while a similar sum was embezzled by the scandalous dishonesty of those in charge of it.

The Attempt to Introduce *Proskynesis*

What motivated Alexander's attempt to introduce the Persian practice of obeisance (*proskynesis*) is not entirely clear, though there has been no shortage of speculation. It would be wrong, however, to link the experiment with Alexander's desire to be accorded divine status during his lifetime. *Proskynesis* was an established practice in the Near East: it is attested on Assyrian and Median reliefs, and Herodotus explains the principle in his *Histories* 1.134. Although Greeks found the practice abhorrent, believing that such reverence should be shown only to the gods, it was generally understood – even by earlier Greek writers who depicted the king as 'god-like' – that the Persian king was not worshipped as a god. It appears, rather, that Alexander wished the Greeks and Macedonians to follow the example of the barbarians, who were already doing obeisance, in order to put his subjects on an equal footing. One may imagine that the Persians would have lost respect for a king who did not insist on such ceremonial (cf. Badian 1996: 22, though he thinks that "unifying court cer-emonial" was merely "a factor" and not the whole story). Bosworth (1995, II: 68–70) notes that the essential difficulty, as Alexander himself must have been aware, was that what the Persians regarded as a purely secular act of royal protocol was viewed by Greeks as an act of worship.[3] For Alexander's claims to divine status, see §IX.3a–h.

2   Several editors have reversed the order of sections 10 and 11.
3   For earlier accounts of *proskynesis* at the Persian court and Greek attitudes, see Herodotus 7.134–6; Cornelius Nepos, *Life of Conon* 3.3; Aelian, *Varia Historia* 1.21. The last example tells the story of a Theban named Ismenias who loosened the ring on his finger as he approached the Great King and then dropped it and bent down to pick it up. Thereby he satisfied the court requirements and kept his conscience clear by doing no more than retrieve the ring.

2(a)   Plutarch, Alexander 54.2–55.4

So Aristotle was apparently not far off the mark in stating that while Callisthenes was a capable and powerful speaker he had no judgement. [3] But Callisthenes' firm and philosophical rejection of *proskynesis*, when he alone listed openly the objections secretly harboured by all the best and oldest of the Macedonians, was rather different. By restraining Alexander from establishing the practice of *proskynesis*, he saved the Greeks from great disgrace, and Alexander even more so. However, he precipitated his own destruction because he appeared to have forced the king's hand rather than to have persuaded him.

[4] Chares of Mytilene claims that when Alexander was once at a symposium he took a drink and passed the cup to one of his friends. The friend took the cup and rose to face the household altar; then, after drinking, he first did *proskynesis* before Alexander, and after that kissed him and took his seat once more. [5] All present followed this procedure in turn. Callisthenes then took the cup, but at that point Alexander, who was in conversation with Hephaestion, was paying no attention. Callisthenes drank and went forward to kiss the king, [6] at which juncture Demetrius, who was surnamed Pheidon, said "Your majesty, do not kiss him. He is the only one not to have done *proskynesis* before you." Alexander turned away from the kiss, and Callisthenes declared in a loud voice: "So I shall leave short of a kiss!"

55   The first development while this rupture between the two was growing was Hephaestion's assertion that Callisthenes had promised to do *proskynesis* before the king but had then broken his word, and this was readily believed. [2] Next came the insistent claims of such people as Lysimachus and Hagnon that the sophist was going around very haughtily expressing ideas about overthrowing tyranny, and that the young were running to him and following him around – the only man amongst all those thousands who was truly free! [3] So it was that when Hermolaus and his friends conspired against Alexander and their plot was uncovered, the smears of Callisthenes' detractors seemed to have the ring of truth. They had said that when Hermolaus asked how he could become a very famous man, Callisthenes answered "By killing a very famous man." [4] And they added that, in spurring on Hermolaus to do the deed, he told him not to fear the golden couch but to remember that he would be dealing with a human being who fell sick and got wounded like any other.

2(b)   Quintus Curtius Rufus 8.5.5–6.1

With all the preparations made, Alexander now believed that the time was ripe for the depraved idea he had conceived some time before, and he began to consider how he could appropriate divine honours to himself. He wished to be believed, not just called, the son of Jupiter, as if it were possible for him to have as much control over men's minds as their tongues, [6] and he gave orders for the Macedonians to follow the Persian custom in doing homage to him by prostrating themselves on the ground. To feed this desire of his there was no lack of pernicious flattery – ever the curse of royalty, whose power is more often subverted by adulation than by an enemy. [7] Nor were the Macedonians to blame for this, for none of them could bear the slightest deviation from tradition; rather it was the Greeks, whose corrupt ways had also debased the profession of the liberal arts. [8] There was the Argive Agis who, after Choerilus,[4] composed the most execrable poems; Cleon of Sicily, whose penchant for flattery was a national as much as a personal defect; and the other dregs of their various cities. These were given preferential treatment by the king even over his relatives and the generals of his greatest armies, and these were the men who were then opening up the road to heaven for him, publicly declaring that Hercules, Father Liber and Castor and Pollux would make way before the new divinity!

[9] Accordingly, one festive day, Alexander had a sumptuous banquet organized so that he could invite not only his principal friends among the Macedonians and Greeks but also the enemy nobility. The king took his place with them but, after dining for only a short time, he withdrew from the banquet. [10] Following a prearranged plan, Cleon now launched into a speech of admiration for Alexander's fine achievements, and then he listed all that the king had done for them. The only way to thank him for this, said Cleon, was to acknowledge openly his divinity – of which fact they were well aware – and to be prepared to pay for such great benefactions with incense[5] that cost but little. [11] The Persian practice of worshiping their kings as gods was as much a matter of prudence as piety, he said, for it was the majesty of the empire that guaranteed their protection. Even Hercules and Father Liber were deified only after triumphing over the envy of their contemporaries, he continued, and what posterity believes about a man depends on the assurances they have of him from the present generation. [12] If the rest of them felt any hesitation, he would prostrate himself on the ground when the king entered the banquet, and the rest should do the same, especially those possessed of good sense, for it was they who should set the example of worshiping the king.

[13] These remarks were quite obviously aimed at Callisthenes, whose serious disposition and outspokenness had earned him the king's displeasure, as if he were the only obstacle to the Macedonians' readiness to adopt such obsequious behaviour. [14] Silence fell and all eyes were on Callisthenes. "Had the king been present when you spoke," he said, "then certainly no words of reply would be required, since he would himself be asking you not to force him to

---

4   Choerilus of Iasos was reputedly the most wretched of poets. He composed an epic in which Alexander appeared as Achilles. The king is said to have commented: "I would rather be Homer's Thersites than the Achilles of Choerilus."

5   The burning of incense was a general feature of worship in Greek and Roman culture.

lapse into the ways of foreigners and strangers, and not to stir up envy of his highly successful exploits by such adulation. [15] But in Alexander's absence I answer you for him in this way: a fruit cannot be both long-lived and early to ripen. You are not giving the king divine honours but depriving him of them. For a man to be believed a god takes time, and it is always posterity that gives thanks to great men in this fashion. [16] My own prayer for the king is that he achieve immortality late – so that his life be long and his majesty eternal. Divinity sometimes comes to a man after his life, but never attends him in it.

[17] "Just now you cited Hercules and Father Liber as instances of the granting of divine status. Do you believe they were deified after a decision made at a single banquet? No; the course of nature removed them from the eyes of men before fame took them up to heaven. [18] Of course, Cleon, you and I can create gods, and from us the king will gain complete assurance of his divinity! I should like to put your power to the test. If you can make a god, make someone a king. Is it easier to grant someone heaven than it is an empire? [19] I pray that in their mercy the gods have not taken offence at what they heard from Cleon, and that they allow matters to proceed as they have done until now. Let them grant that we be content with our own customs. I am not ashamed of my country, nor have I any wish to be told by peoples we have conquered how to pay my respects to my king. [20] In fact, I am prepared to recognize them as the victors if we accept from them rules by which to live."

Callisthenes was heard with approval as the champion of public freedom. He had extracted not only silent agreement from his audience but vocal support as well, especially from the older men who were offended by the substitution of foreign customs for their established traditions. [21] Nor was Alexander unaware of any of the comments made on either side, for he was standing behind a curtain which he had drawn as a screen around the couches. So he sent a message to Agis and Cleon instructing them to terminate the conversation and be content to have only the barbarians prostrate themselves in their usual manner when he entered the room. Shortly afterwards he returned to the banquet, as though he had been dealing with some particularly important business.

[22] The Persians now did homage before him and, when one of them touched the ground with his chin, Polyperchon, who was reclining above the king, began to ridicule him by telling him to beat it harder on the ground. This provoked an angry response from Alexander, who for some time now had been unable to keep his temper. [23] "Are you not going to do homage before me?" he said. "Is it only you who think we deserve ridicule?" Polyperchon answered that the king did not deserve ridicule, but no more did he himself deserve contempt. [24] Dragging him off the couch, Alexander threw him on the floor, and Polyperchon fell forward on his face. "You see," said Alexander, "you are doing just what you laughed at in another a moment ago." Then he ordered Polyperchon to be put under guard and terminated the banquet.

6 Although he punished him for a long time after this, Alexander did eventually pardon Polyperchon,[6] but in the case of Callisthenes, whom he had long suspected because of his outspokenness, his resentment was more persistent.

2(c)   Justin 12.7.1–3

Next came a piece of vanity characteristic of Persian royalty, the adoption of which Alexander had postponed for fear of provoking undue animosity by changing everything at once: he ordered people to do obeisance before him instead of saluting him. [2] The most outspoken of the objectors was Callisthenes, and this spelled death for him and many prominent Macedonians, who were all executed, ostensibly for treason. [3] Even so the Macedonians retained the conventional method of saluting their king and obeisance was rejected.

Mixed Marriages

Alexander experimented with mixed marriages – some ninety of the *hetairoi* (*philoi*) took prominent Persian brides – in 324, when he himself married Stateira and Parysatis, the daughters of Darius III and Artaxerxes III Ochus respectively, and thus attempted to legitimize his claims to the Achaemenid throne. (One thinks of the marriages of Darius I, when he ascended the throne in 522. See also Brosius (1996) ch.3, esp. pp. 76–8.) But the Greco-Macedonian writers were hostile to these marriages and accused Alexander of attempting to deflect criticism by extending the practice of mixed marriages to his *hetairoi*. These marriages are certainly historical, though many of the Macedonians repudiated them after the king's death; less credible is the assertion that Alexander conducted similar weddings in Sogdiana when he married Roxane (see §VII.3d–e, below).

Mass marriage at Susa

3(a)   Aelian, Varia Historia 8.7

After capturing Darius, Alexander celebrated his own wedding along with the weddings of his *philoi*. There were ninety bridegrooms, and the bridal chambers were also that number. The hall in which they were received and feasted held a hundred couches. Each couch had feet of silver, but Alexander's had

---

6 Arrian 4.12.2 tells a similar story about Leonnatus, "one of the *hetairoi*," almost certainly Leonnatus the Somatophylax. It appears that Curtius' story about Polyperchon is refuted by virtual certainty that he was absent from court when *proskynesis* was introduced: see Heckel (1992a: 190–1).

feet of gold, and they were all embellished with purple or multi-coloured drapes woven in a fashion much prized by barbarians. The king also took along with him to the drinking-party his personal friends from other countries and seated them opposite himself. The rest of the forces – infantry, navy and cavalry – dined in the courtyard, and ambassadors and Greek residents of the country were present at the banquet, as well.

The dinner proceeded with signals from a trumpet: the assembly-call when they had to go in to dine, and the retreat when Alexander gave the sign for them to leave. The king celebrated the weddings for five days in a row. There also came musicians and actors, comic and tragic, in large numbers, and from India there were superb jugglers, who were reputed to be superior to all others in the world.

3(b)   Arrian 7.4.4–8

Alexander also celebrated weddings for himself and the *hetairoi* in Susa. His own marriage was to Barsine,[7] eldest daughter of Darius, but according to Aristobulus he also took another wife in addition to her, Parysatis, the youngest daughter of Ochus. Roxane, daughter of the Bactrian Oxyartes, was already a wife of his.

[5] To Hephaestion Alexander gave Drypetis. She was another daughter of Darius and the sister of Alexander's own wife – he wanted the children of Hephaestion to be his own children's cousins.

To Craterus he gave Amastrine,[8] who was the daughter of Darius' brother, Oxyatres.[9]

To Perdiccas he gave the daughter of Atropates, satrap of Media.

[6] To Ptolemy the bodyguard and to Eumenes the king's secretary he gave the daughters of Artabazus, Artacama to Ptolemy and Artonis to Eumenes.[10]

To Nearchus he gave the daughter of Barsine and Mentor, and to Seleucus the daughter of Spitamenes the Bactrian.

He likewise gave the rest of the *hetairoi* the most high-born daughters of the Persians and Medes, some eighty of them. The marriages were conducted in the Persian manner. [7] Chairs were set out in a line for the grooms and, after a toast had been drunk, the brides arrived and took their seats beside their respective husbands, the grooms receiving them with a kiss. Alexander started off the process, for the weddings of all of them took place then and there, and this more than anything else seemed to demonstrate Alexander's cordiality and camaraderie.

---

7 Her name is given by other sources as Stateira. Barsine appears to be an error on the part of Aristobulus.
8 Amestris or Amastris. She was later married to Dionysius, tyrant of Heraclea Pontica.
9 Oxathres in many other sources, but possibly Oxyathres.
10 Cf. Plutarch, *Eumenes* 1.7, but Ptolemy's bride is named Apame.

[8] The grooms received their various brides and took them home, and Alexander gave all the women dowries. In addition, he ordered that all other Macedonians who had taken wives from amongst the Asian women should also have their names registered. These numbered more than 10,000, and they too were given wedding presents from Alexander.

3(c)   Justin 12.10.9–10

After this Alexander married Darius' daughter, Stateira; [10] at the same time he presented to the Macedonian noblemen unmarried girls selected from the best families amongst all the conquered peoples, so that any recrimination against the king might be lessened through their complicity in his action.

Earlier mixed marriages?

3(d)   Metz Epitome 29–31

Alexander took his cup, made a prayer to the gods and then proceeded to declare that many people often found that many things happen contrary to their expectations, that many kings had had sons by captives [30] or sent daughters to foreign nations to get married, using such a bond to ratify alliances. "So", he continued, "I do not consider the Macedonians your betters in terms of race and no more would I consider you unworthy of inter-marriage with us, even if you had sought alliance with us after a defeat. I am going to make such a match, and I shall ensure that the rest of the Macedonians follow my example." [31] After these words of exhortation from Alexander, each of his friends took away a girl as his bride, to the great delight of Oxyartes and the other barbarians.

3(e)   Diodorus Siculus, from the "Table of Contents" to Book 17[11]

How Alexander fell in love with Roxane, the daughter of Oxyartes, married her and persuaded many of his *philoi* to marry the daughters of eminent barbarians.

---

11   This episode was described in a section of Book 17 that is now lost.

The *Epigoni* and the Appointment of Orientals in the Army

4(a)   Plutarch, Alexander 47.5–6

Now, too, he began to adapt more and more to local customs in his way of life, and these customs he tried to accommodate to Macedonian culture. He thought amalgamation and synthesis preferable to force as a means of amicably consolidating the current state of affairs while he was far away. [6] Accordingly, making a selection of 30,000 boys, he issued orders for them to be taught Greek writing and given training in Macedonian weapons, and he appointed a large number of instructors for the purpose.

4(b)   Arrian 7.6.1

Satraps also came to Alexander from the newly founded cities and the rest of the territory that had been taken in war. They brought about 30,000 boys who were now coming to puberty and who were all the same age. They were equipped with Macedonian weapons and had been given training in the Macedonian fashion of warfare. Alexander called them "the Epigoni".

4(c)   Diodorus Siculus 17.108.1–3

At this time 30,000 Persians arrived in Susa. They were, in terms of age, very young, but they had been selected for their fine build and physical strength. [2] It was on an order given by the king that they had been brought together, and they had spent the requisite time under trainers and instructors of the military arts. They were all fully equipped with Macedonian armour, and they made their camp before the city, where they demonstrated to the king their military proficiency and skill and won high praise from him. [3] Now the Macedonians had balked at crossing the river Ganges; they had also shouted him down in their assemblies and ridiculed his claim to be the son of Ammon. It was for this reason that Alexander put together this corps from Persians of the same age, or close to it, one that was capable of being a counterweight to the Macedonian phalanx.

Barbarian troops serving with a Macedonian satrap

4(d)   Arrian 4.17.3

In the meantime Alexander acceded to Artabazus' request to relieve him of the satrapy of Bactria because of his advanced age, and in his place he appointed Amyntas, son of Nicolaus. He left Coenus in place there at the head of his own battalion and Meleager's, together with some 400 of the cavalry of the Companions, all the *hippakontistai* and such Bactrians and Sogdianians as there were in Amyntas' force.

Barbarian cavalry serving with Alexander at the Hydaspes

4(e)   Arrian 5.11.3

Craterus was left in command of the camp and he had with him his own cavalry squadron, the cavalry of the Arachotians and the Parapamisadae . . .

4(f)   Arrian 5.12.2

For his own force, Alexander selected the following: the *agema* of the Companions; the cavalry squadrons of Hephaestion, Perdiccas and Demetrius; the cavalry from Bactria, Sogdiana and Scythia; the *hippotoxotai* of the Dahae; and, from the phalanx, he chose: the hypaspists; the battalions of Cleitus and Coenus; the archers; and the Agrianes.

The Persian Seal

Alexander's signet ring is referred to in numerous passages (Curtius 3.6.7, 7.11; Arrian 6.23.4, 29.10; Plutarch, *Alexander* 39.8, *Moralia* 333) and it was this ring that the dying king was said to have handed to Perdiccas (see §XI.2b). Only once in the ancient sources is Alexander reported to have used a Persian signet ring (see below), and Hammond (1995b) dismisses this as a piece of Cleitarchean fiction, rejecting in the process the view of Baldus (1987) that the king had a personal ring, which was used for European subjects, and a new royal seal for Asiatics. Much of Baldus' work is highly speculative, but Alexander may well have experimented with a Persian seal in 330 – if it was, in fact, Darius' own seal then this may have been intended to counter the claims of the regicide and usurper, Bessus, to the kingship.

5(a)   Quintus Curtius Rufus 6.6.6

Furthermore, he sealed letters sent to Europe with the stone of his old ring, but on those written to Asia was set the seal of Darius' ring – apparently one man's mind could not cope with the fortunes of two.

The Tomb of Cyrus the Great

We have no reason to doubt that Alexander was an admirer of Cyrus the Great (thus Strabo, *Geography* 11.11.4 C518 = 60.6); probably he was familiar with Xenophon's *Cyropaedia* ("On the Education of Cyrus"), and Onesicritus, when he wrote his work on *How Alexander was Educated*, may have used Xenophon's work as an inspiration (thus Diogenes Laertius 6.84).[12] But Alexander, claiming to be the legitimate successor of the Achaemenid rulers, was required to protect the honor of his predecessors and the institution which they represented. His restoration of Cyrus' tomb and the punishment of those who desecrated it were thus acts of affected piety and political expediency.

6(a)   Plutarch, Alexander 69.3–4

Alexander found that Cyrus' tomb had been broken open, and he executed the guilty party, despite the fact that the offender was a man of not inconsiderable consequence from Pella by the name of Poulamachus. [4] After reading the epitaph, he ordered a version to be carved underneath it in Greek. It read as follows: "Sir, whoever you are and wherever you come from – for that you will come I am certain – I am Cyrus who won their empire for Persians. So do not begrudge me this small amount of earth that covers my body."

6(b)   Arrian 6.29.9–11

Alexander had always been anxious to visit the tomb of Cyrus once he had conquered the Persian capital, and he now found that everything there had been pillaged, apart from the sarcophagus and couch. The culprits had even defiled Cyrus' body after removing the sarcophagus lid, throwing out the corpse. The sarcophagus itself they had tried to make easier for them to handle and transport by breaking pieces off and crushing parts of it, but when their efforts proved fruitless they simply abandoned the sarcophagus and left. [10] Aristobulus records that he was personally instructed by Alexander to restore Cyrus' tomb to its original condition . . .

[11] Alexander arrested the Magi who stood guard over the tomb and put them on the rack to make them identify the culprits. Even on the rack, however, they incriminated neither themselves nor anyone else, and as there was no other evidence by which they could be proven guilty of involvement in the deed they were released by Alexander.

---

12 Cf. Brown (1949: 1, 13–23) and Pearson (1960: 89–90). Pearson believes that Strabo's description of Alexander as *philokyros* ("admirer of Cyrus") "suggests the hand of Onesicritus" (p. 94). For Alexander's own knowledge of the *Cyropaedia*, see Due (1993).

Macedonian Reaction to Alexander's Orientalism

The reaction of the Macedonian officers to Alexander's "orientalism" can be seen in various episodes: the alleged "conspiracy" of Hegelochus (Curtius 6.11.22–9, included in §X.3c), which was incited by Alexander's pretensions concerning Amun; the outspokenness of Cleitus in Maracanda in 328, which gave voice to Macedonian resentment of Alexander's increasingly autocratic nature (§X.4a–c); and the stubborn refusal of the *hetairoi* and Callisthenes to countenance the introduction of *proskynesis* (§VII.2a–c, above; cf. §X.5a–e). At Opis on the Tigris River in 324, the common soldiers mutinied (§X.9a–c) and revealed to their king hostilities that had long been festering, most of which had to do with Alexander's Eastern policies. In the passage that follows, Arrian sums up the nature and the cause of the Macedonian resentment: essentially it was a matter of wounded pride and xenophobia.

7(a)   Arrian 7.6.2–5

They say that the arrival of the Epigoni hurt the Macedonians; it was as though Alexander was doing all he could to make himself less reliant on his own people. Alexander's Median style of clothes also brought them no little anguish, it is said, and the Persian-style weddings were reportedly not to the liking of the majority, either – liked not even by some of the grooms, despite the great honour of being put on the same footing as the king. [3] There was also the case of Peucestas, the satrap of Persia, who adopted both Persian dress and language; that rankled because Alexander was pleased with his playing the barbarian. And then there was the matter of the cavalry of the Bactrians, Sogdianians and Arachotians being enrolled in the Companion cavalry. There were Zarangians, Areians and Parthyaeans, as well, and from the Persians the so-called Euacae – any that were clearly superior in rank, good looks or any other quality. [4] That hurt, too, as did the addition of a fifth hipparchy. This was not entirely composed of barbarians, but when the entire cavalry force was increased there was an enrollment of barbarian troops for it. Barbarian officers were also appointed to the *agema*: Cophes, son of Artabazus; Hydarnes and Artiboles, the sons of Mazaeus; Sisines and Phradasmenes, the sons of Phrataphernes, who was satrap of Parthyaea and Hyrcania; [5] Itanes, son of Oxyartes and brother of Roxane, the wife of Alexander; and Aegobares and his brother Mithrobaeus. The man appointed overall commander of these was the Bactrian Hystaspes, and they were issued Macedonian lances instead of the thonged javelins of the barbarians. All this was offensive to the Macedonians. It looked as if Alexander was developing a completely barbarian mentality, and placing Macedonian culture and the Macedonians themselves at a low level of esteem.

VIII Alexander and Women

Alexander and his "Mothers": Olympias, Ada, and Sisygambis

It is an oft-quoted comment of Tarn's (1948, II: 326) that Alexander "never cared for any woman except his terrible mother," and there is perhaps an element of truth in this. Certainly, she made an impression on him early in his life, and he retained his affection for her until his death; similarly, he seems to have been inclined to treat some other, older women as surrogate mothers, notably Ada of Halicarnassus and Sisygambis, the mother of Darius III.

Olympias

1(a) Plutarch, Alexander 9.5

But the malaise that reigned in the women's quarters because of Philip's marriages and love affairs in some way infected the realm, and the domestic upsets occasioned numerous reproaches and bitter antagonisms. (These were further exacerbated by the bad nature of Olympias, a jealous and resentful woman, who would spur Alexander to anger.)[1]

1(b) Plutarch, Alexander 39.13

On one occasion, however, after reading a long letter that Antipater had written criticizing Olympias, Alexander declared that Antipater did not realize that a single tear from a mother wiped out ten thousand letters.

---

1   This passage is quoted in full in §II.1c.

1(c)   Diodorus Siculus 17.32.1

In a letter to the king, Alexander's mother[2] gave him some generally useful advice, and in particular warned him to be on his guard against Alexander the Lyncestian.

Ada of Halicarnassus

1(d)   Arrian 1.23.7–8

Alexander appointed Ada, daughter of Hecatomnus and wife of Hidrieus, to the satrapy of all of Caria. Hidrieus was also Ada's brother, but had lived with her as her husband, as was customary in Caria. When he died he passed his power on to her, for a woman ruling over men had been accepted in Asia since the time of Semiramis. Pixodarus, however, ejected her from the throne and took power himself.

[8] When Pixodarus died, Orontobates, the brother-in-law of Pixodarus, was sent by the king to assume the rule of Caria. Ada now had only Alinda, which was the most powerful stronghold in Caria, and when Alexander invaded Caria she came to meet him. At this meeting she surrendered Alinda to the king and adopted him as her son. Alexander then placed Alinda under her command, and did not decline the title of "son". When he took Halicarnassus and gained control of the rest of Caria, he also conferred on her sovereignty over the whole country.

1(e)   Plutarch, Alexander 22.7–10

Alexander was also very abstemious in his diet. This he demonstrated in many ways and particularly in the words he addressed to Ada, whom he made his adoptive mother and ruler of Caria. [8] Ada pampered Alexander, sending him many cooked delicacies and cakes every day and finally sending men thought to be the most talented cooks and pastry-makers available. Alexander said he needed none of them. [9] He had finer cooks, he explained, who had been given to him by his pedagogue Leonidas: for breakfast a night's march, and

---

2   This is normally understood to be a reference to Olympias, but it has been suggested by Abramenko (1992) that the "mother" is actually Queen Ada. If this is so, then Diodorus was ignorant of the fact, since he does not mention Alexander's adoption. Nevertheless, the suggestion should not be dismissed out of hand, since a relative of Alexander the Lyncestian, namely Neoptolemus son of Arrhabaeus, had been fighting on the Persian side at Halicarnassus, and when Ada assumed control of the satrapy she may have learned details about the Lyncestian's negotiations with the Persian king. If Olympias wrote the letter, then her warning may have been intended in part to undermine the authority of Antipater, the Lyncestian's father-in-law.

for dinner a light meal. [10] "And that very same man," he added, "used to come and open the chests holding my bedding and clothes to make sure that my mother had not put in there for me some delicacy or unnecessary trifle."

Sisygambis (Sisigambis)

1(f)　Quintus Curtius Rufus 5.2.18

... Alexander showed Sisigambis every mark of respect and his regard for her was that of a son ...

1(g)　Quintus Curtius Rufus 10.5.18–25

Tidings of the great tragedy had spread to the neighbouring countryside and then to most of Asia this side of the Euphrates. [19] They quickly reached Darius' mother, too. She ripped off the clothes she wore and assumed the dress of mourning; she tore her hair and flung herself to the ground. [20] Next to her sat one of her two granddaughters who was in mourning after the recent loss of her husband, Hephaestion, and the general anguish reminded her of her personal grief. [21] But Sisigambis alone felt the woes that engulfed her entire family: she wept for her own plight and that of her granddaughters. The fresh pain had also reminded her of the past. One might have thought that Darius was recently lost and that at the same time the poor woman had to bury two sons. [22] She wept simultaneously for the living and the dead. Who would look after her girls, she wondered? Who would be another Alexander? This meant a second captivity, a second loss of royal status. On the death of Darius they had found a protector, but after Alexander they would certainly not find someone to guard their interests.

[23] Amid such reflections, Sisigambis was reminded of how her eighty brothers had all been butchered on the one day by the most barbarous of kings, Ochus,[3] and how the slaughter of so many sons was augmented by that of their father; of how only one child remained of the seven she had borne[4] and how even Darius' prosperity had been short-lived and served only to make his death more cruel. [24] Finally, she surrendered to her sorrow. She covered her head, turned away from her granddaughter and grandson, who fell at her knees to plead with her, and withdrew simultaneously from nourishment and the daylight. Five days after deciding on death, she expired. [25] Her end provides firm evidence for Alexander's gentle treatment of her and his fairness towards all the captives: though she could bear to live on after Darius, she was ashamed to survive Alexander.

3　Artaxerxes III. He succeeded his father Artaxerxes II in 359/8. See §IV.1a–e.
4　Oxathres (or possibly Oxyathres). See §§IV.2d, IV.3i, VI.2d, and VII.1d.

The Captive Persian Queens

Alexander visits Darius' family after his victory at Issus

2(a)   *Quintus Curtius Rufus 3.11.20–12.17; 3.12.21–6*

But the camp, filled with all manner of riches, had already been entered by the victors. Alexander's men had made off with a huge quantity of gold and silver (the trappings of luxury, not war) and, since they pillaged more than they could carry, the paths were littered everywhere with the meaner articles which they had greedily cast aside after comparing them with superior goods.

[21] Now they came to the women, and the more these prized their jewels, the more violently they were robbed of them. Not even their persons were spared the violence of lust. [22] They filled the camp with all manner of lamentation and screaming in reaction to their individual misfortunes, and villainy of every shape and form manifested itself as the cruelty and licence of the victor swept through the prisoners, irrespective of rank or age. [23] Then a true illustration of fortune's caprice was to be seen. The men who had formerly decorated Darius' tent and fitted it out with all kinds of extravagant and opulent furnishings were now keeping back the very same things for Alexander, as if for their old master. That tent, in fact, was the only thing the Macedonian soldiers had left untouched, it being their tradition to welcome the conqueror in the tent of the conquered king.

[24] However, it was Darius' mother and his wife, now prisoners, who had attracted to themselves everybody's gaze and attention. His mother commanded respect for her age as well as for her royal dignity, his wife for a beauty that even her current misfortune had not marred. The latter had taken to her bosom her young son, who had not yet turned six, a boy born into the expectation of the great fortune his father had just lost. [25] In the lap of their aged grandmother lay Darius' two grown-up but unmarried daughters, grieving for their grandmother as well as themselves. Around her stood a large number of high-born women, their hair torn, their clothes rent and their former gracefulness forgotten. They called upon their "queens" and "mistresses", titles formerly appropriate but no longer applicable. [26] They forgot their own plight and kept asking on which wing Darius had stood and how the battle had gone, claiming that they were not captives at all if the king still lived. But Darius' flight had taken him far away with frequent changes of horses.

[27] A hundred thousand Persian infantry and 10,000 cavalry were killed in the action. On Alexander's side about 504 were wounded, a total of 32 infantrymen were lost, and 150 cavalrymen died. At so small a cost was a huge victory secured.

12   The king was exhausted by his long pursuit of Darius and, as night was coming on and there was no hope of overtaking him, he came into the

camp which his men had captured a short time before. [2] He then had invitations issued to his most intimate friends – no mere graze on the thigh could keep him from attending a banquet. [3] Suddenly the diners were alarmed by the sound of lamentation, punctuated by typically barbarian shrieking and howling, coming from the next tent. The company on guard duty at the king's tent, fearing that this signalled the start of a more dangerous disturbance, had proceeded to arm themselves. [4] The reason for the sudden alarm was the lamentation of Darius' mother and wife and the other noble captives: believing Darius dead, they were raising a loud weeping and wailing in mourning for him. [5] One of the eunuch prisoners had happened to be standing in front of their tent when he recognized Darius' cloak in someone's hands (the man had found it and was now bringing it back) – the cloak which, as was mentioned a short while ago, Darius had cast off so that his identity would not be betrayed by his dress. The eunuch assumed it had been taken from Darius' dead body and so he had brought the false report of his death.

[6] When Alexander learned of the women's misunderstanding, they say he wept for Darius' reversal of fortune and their devotion to him. At first he ordered Mithrenes, the man who had surrendered Sardis, to go and console them, since he knew the Persian language, [7] but then he became concerned that a traitor might only rekindle the captives' anger and sorrow. So he sent Leonnatus, one of his courtiers, instead, instructing him to tell them that their lamentation was unwarranted since Darius still lived. Leonnatus came with a few guards to the tent that housed the captured women and ordered it to be announced that he had been sent by Alexander. [8] The people at the entrance, however, caught sight of their weapons and, thinking their mistresses were finished, ran into the tent shouting that their final hour had come, that men had been sent to kill the prisoners. [9] The women could not keep the soldiers out, nor did they dare admit them and so, making no reply, they silently awaited their victor's will. [10] Leonnatus waited for a long time for someone to let him in but, when no one dared escort him inside, he left his attendants in the entrance and entered the tent. That in itself produced consternation among the women: he had apparently burst in without an invitation. [11] So the mother and wife of Darius fell at his feet and began to beg him to allow them to give Darius' body a traditional burial before they were executed, adding that after paying their last respects to the king they would readily face death. [12] Leonnatus' answer was that Darius was still alive and that they would not only come to no harm but would also retain their royal status with all the dignity of their former positions. Only at that point did Darius' mother allow herself to be raised from the ground.

[13] The following day, Alexander diligently conducted the burial of the soldiers whose bodies he had found, and he also gave instructions for the same honour to be shown to the most noble of the Persians. Darius' mother he allowed to bury whomsoever she wished in traditional Persian fashion. [14] She ordered only a few close relatives to be buried, and those in a manner befit-

ting their present circumstances, thinking that the elaborate funerals with which Persians paid their last respects to their dead would cause ill-will in view of the simple cremation accorded the victors. [15] When the funeral services had been duly discharged, Alexander sent messengers to the female prisoners to announce his coming and then, leaving the crowd of his attendants outside, he went into their tent with Hephaestion. [16] Hephaestion was by far the dearest of all the king's friends; he had been brought up with Alexander and shared all his secrets. No other person was privileged to advise the king as candidly as he did, and yet he exercised that privilege in such a way that it seemed granted by Alexander rather than claimed by Hephaestion. While he was the king's age, in stature he was his superior, [17] and so the queens took him to be the king and did obeisance before him after their manner. Whereupon some of the captive eunuchs pointed out the real Alexander, and Sisigambis flung herself at his feet, apologizing for not recognizing him on the ground that she had never before seen him. Raising her with his hand, Alexander said, "My lady, you made no mistake. This man is Alexander too." ...

[21] ... The unmarried princesses, who were extremely beautiful, he treated with as much respect as if they were his own sisters. [22] As for Darius' wife, who was surpassed by none of her generation in beauty, Alexander was so far from offering her violence that he took the utmost care to prevent anyone from taking advantage of her while she was in captivity. [23] He gave orders for all their finery to be returned to the women, and as captives they lacked none of the magnificence of their former state – only their self-esteem.

[24] Accordingly, Sisigambis said to Alexander: "Sire, you deserve the same prayers as we made in the past for our king Darius. I can see, too, that you are worthy of them since you have excelled such a great king not only in good fortune but in fair-mindedness as well. [25] I know you call me "my lady" and "your majesty", but I confess that really I am your slave. I can cope with the high position I formerly enjoyed, but I can also endure the yoke of my present situation. As for the extent of your power over us, it is for you to decide whether you want that demonstrated by clemency rather than cruelty." [26] The king told them not to worry. He took Darius' son in his arms, and the child, not in the least frightened at the sight of Alexander (although this was the first time he had seen him), put his arms around his neck. Impressed by the boy's fearlessness, the king looked at Hephaestion and said: "How I could have wished that Darius had acquired something of this character." Then he left the tent.

2(b) Justin 11.9.11–16

In the Persian camp large quantities of gold and other treasures were found, [12] and among the prisoners taken in the camp were the mother of Darius, his wife (who was also his sister) and his two daughters. [13] Alexander came to pay them a visit and give them some encouragement, but at the sight of his armed escort the women embraced each other, believing their death imminent, and let out sorrowful cries. [14] Then, throwing themselves before Alexander's feet, they begged not for their lives but only for a stay of execution until they could bury Darius' body. [15] Moved by such loyalty on the women's part, Alexander informed them that Darius was still alive, dispelled their fear of execution and gave orders that they be treated and addressed as queens. [16] He also told the daughters to expect marriages not unbefitting their father's rank.

2(c)   Valerius Maximus 4.7 ext 2

After taking possession of Darius' camp, which contained all the king's relatives, Alexander came to address them, with his dear friend Hephaestion at his side. Darius' mother, encouraged by his visit, lifted her head from the ground where she had prostrated herself, and in the Persian fashion did obeisance to Hephaestion and saluted him as Alexander, since he was the superior of the two in height and good looks. Apprised of her mistake, she became extremely agitated and was searching for words of apology when Alexander said to her: "Your confusion over the name is unimportant, for this man is also Alexander."

2(d)   Diodorus Siculus 17.67.1

After that Alexander left behind in Susa Darius' mother, daughters and son, and he appointed people to teach them the Greek language.

The death of Stateira, wife of Darius III

The Alexander historians go to great lengths to demonstrate that, although Darius' wife was reputedly the most beautiful woman in Asia, Alexander did not abuse his position as her captor but rather treated her with the utmost respect. The popular tradition, based in all likelihood on the work of Cleitarchus of Alexandria (see Introduction, p. xxi), records her death, almost two years after her capture at Issus, in childbirth!

2(e)   Justin 11.12.6–7

While on the march, Darius was brought news that his wife had died after a miscarriage, that Alexander had shed tears over her death and given her a generous funeral, and that he had done this not from physical attraction for her but out of human compassion. [7] For, the report continued, Alexander had set eyes on her only once, whereas he frequently went to console Darius' mother and young daughters.

2(f)   Plutarch, Alexander 30.1

... when Darius' wife died in childbirth ... Alexander was clearly upset at having lost this great opportunity of demonstrating his generosity. Accordingly he spared no expense in burying the woman.

The Amazon Queen

The legend of Alexander's encounter with the Amazon queen began with the earliest Alexander historians. Certainly, we can trace the story to Cleitarchus, the common source of the popular tradition, and he may have taken the story from Onesicritus (see §VIII.3d, below). It is possible that the story had its origins in the story of Pharasmenes, king of the Chorasmians, who claimed to live on the borders of the Colchians and Amazons, and offered to guide Alexander in a campaign against the latter. Probably, the news of women who fought on horseback and the Macedonians' own experiences of Saca warrior women (cf. the well-known story of Queen Tomyris, who defeated Cyrus the Great) caused Greek writers to equate them with the Amazons. Furthermore, Alexander was offered, but rejected, a Scythian bride (Arrian 4.15.3). See Tyrrell (1984: 24), Baynham (2000), and for "warrior women" of the steppes, Davis-Kimball (2002).

3(a)   Diodorus Siculus 17.77.1–3

On his return to Hyrcania, the queen of the Amazons came to Alexander. Her name was Thallestris, and she ruled over the area between the Phasis and the Thermodon. She was possessed of exceptional beauty and physical strength, and was admired by her compatriots for her courage.

Leaving most of her army on the boundaries of Hyrcania, Thallestris appeared before Alexander with 300 Amazons equipped with their weapons. [2] The king expressed surprise at her arrival, which was totally unexpected, and at the dignified bearing of the women. He asked Thallestris the purpose of her visit, and she declared she had come to procreate a child. [3] She explained that Alexander was, thanks to his achievements, the greatest of all men, while she excelled all women in strength and courage – so it was reasonable to expect that what was born of these two finest of parents would have qualities surpassing those of everyone in the world. The king was delighted. He acceded to her request, spent thirteen days having sexual relations with her, and then sent her home after honouring her with impressive gifts.

3(b)   *Quintus Curtius Rufus 6.5.24–32*

On the border of Hyrcania . . . lived a tribe of Amazons. They inhabited the plains of Themiscyra in the area of the river Thermodon, [25] and their queen, Thalestris, held sway over all those between the Caucasus and the river Phasis. Passionately eager to meet Alexander, she journeyed from her realm and when she was not far off she sent messengers ahead to announce that a queen had come who was longing to see him and make his acquaintance. [26] Granted an immediate audience, she ordered her company to halt while she went forward attended by 300 women: as soon as she caught sight of the king she leaped unaided from her horse, carrying two spears in her right hand. [27] The dress of Amazons does not entirely cover the body: the left side is bare to the breast but clothed beyond that, while the skirt of the garment, which is gathered into a knot, stops short of the knee. [28] One breast is kept whole for feeding children of female sex and the right is cauterized to facilitate bending the bow and handling weapons.

[29] Thalestris looked at the king, no sign of fear on her face. Her eyes surveyed a physique that in no way matched his illustrious record – for all barbarians have respect for physical presence, believing that only those on whom nature has thought fit to confer extraordinary appearance are capable of great achievements. [30] When asked if she had a request to make she unhesitatingly declared that she had come in order to share children with the king, since she was a fitting person on whom to beget heirs for his empire. A child of female sex she would keep, she said, but a male she would give to his father. [31] Alexander asked if Thalestris wished to accompany him on his campaigns, but she declined on the grounds that she had left her kingdom unprotected, and she kept asking him not to let her leave disappointed in her hopes. [32] The woman's enthusiasm for sex was keener than Alexander's and she pressed him to stop there for a few days. Thirteen days were devoted to serving her passion, after which Thalestris headed for her kingdom and Alexander for Parthiene.

3(c)   *Justin 12.3.4–7*

Inspiring anew the hearts of his men with this speech, Alexander went on to subjugate Hyrcania and the Mardians. [5] It was here that he encountered Thalestris, or Minythyia, the queen of the Amazons. Accompanied by 300 women, she had travelled thirty-five days through thickly populated terrain in order to have a child by the king. [6] Her appearance and the purpose of her coming aroused general surprise: she was strangely dressed for a woman and she came seeking sexual intercourse. [7] The king paused for thirteen days for this purpose and Thalestris left when she thought she had conceived.

3(d)   Plutarch, Alexander 46.1–5

It was here that the Amazon queen came to Alexander according to most authorities, and these include Cleitarchus, Polycleitus, Onesicritus, Antigenes and Ister. [2] Aristobulus, however, as well as Chares the usher, Ptolemy, Anti-clides, Philo the Theban, Philip of Theangelia – and, in addition to these, Hecataeus the Eretrian, Philip the Chalcidian and Duris the Samian – claim this is pure fabrication; and it seems that support for these latter comes from Alexander. [3] The king gave a detailed account of the whole episode in a letter to Antipater, and while he declares that the Scythian king offered him his daughter in marriage he makes no mention of an Amazon. [4] It is said, too, that many years later, when Lysimachus had become king, Onesicritus was reading to him the fourth book of his history,[5] in which there is an account of the Amazon episode. Lysimachus is said to have smiled gently and said, "Where was I at that point?" [5] In fact, disbelieving the story would not make one admire Alexander the less, and accepting it would not make one admire him the more.

3(e)   Arrian 4.15.2–4

[Ambassadors] brought from the king of Scythia gifts for Alexander that are considered the greatest amongst the Scythians. They reported that their king wished to give his daughter in marriage to Alexander as confirmation of his pact of friendship with him. [3] If Alexander felt it beneath him to marry a princess of the Scythians, they added, the king was ready to give to his most trusted courtiers the daughters of the satraps of the land of Scythia and those of all the most powerful men in Scythian territory. If he were so ordered, he would come in person to hear from Alexander's own lips whatever commands he had to give.

[4] Meanwhile, Pharasmanes, king of the Chorasmians, also arrived at Alexander's camp, bringing with him 1,500 cavalry. Pharasmanes declared that where he lived made him a neighbour of the Colchian people and the female tribe, the Amazons. He offered to be the king's guide to the roads and furnish provisions for the campaign if Alexander wished to attack the Colchians and Amazons, and bring under his sway the peoples in the area as far as the Euxine Sea.

---

5   That is, no earlier than 306/5, but this should not be taken to mean (as some scholars have suggested) that Onesicritus' history was not written until this time.

Timocleia of Thebes

4(a)　Plutarch, Alexander 12.1–6

Amongst the numerous misfortunes and tribulations overtaking the city of Thebes was the episode of some Thracians breaking into the home of Timocleia, a distinguished and virtuous lady. The Thracians ransacked her belongings, but their leader forced himself on the woman and violated her, asking her then if she had gold or silver hidden anywhere.
[2] Timocleia acknowledged that she did, and she took him, on his own, into her garden. There she pointed to a well into which, she claimed, she had thrown her most valued possessions while the city was being taken. [3] As the man was bending over the well and examining the spot, she came up behind him, pushed him in and killed him by showering him with rocks.
[4] The woman was brought to Alexander in chains by the Thracians. It was immediately apparent from the way she looked and carried herself that she was a lady of rank and spirit, following the escort as she did without alarm or trepidation. [5] The king then asked her to identify herself, and she replied that she was the sister of Theagenes, a man who had fought against Philip for the liberty of the Greeks and who had fallen at Chaeronea where he was commander-in-chief. [6] Full of admiration at her reply and the action she had taken, Alexander gave orders that she should go free, along with her children.

4(b)　Polyaenus 8.40

Timocleia of Thebes was the sister of Theagenes, who fought against Philip at Chaeronea (it was Theagenes who, when a man shouted at him, "How far are you going to chase me?", answered, "All the way to Macedonia"). When Theagenes died his sister was still alive. Then Alexander demolished Thebes. Various people sacked various areas of the city, and a Thracian cavalry officer commandeered Timocleia's house.

After dinner, this Thracian not only summoned Timocleia to the bedroom, but also asked if she had gold and silver anywhere in the house and forced her to admit that she did. She said that she had a large quantity of decorative silver and gold in the form of necklaces, bracelets, cups and coins, but that when the city was being taken she had thrown it all into a well which contained no water. The Thracian believed her, and she took him into the garden of the house where the well was situated and told him to climb down into it. He climbed down, and was looking for the silver and gold when she, along with her maidservants, rolled down on him from above large numbers of stones and rocks, burying the barbarian under them.

The Macedonians arrested Timocleia and brought her to King Alexander. She admitted taking revenge on the Thracian, who was a criminal and a rapist, and Alexander in admiration set her free along with all her relatives.

The Wife of Spitamenes

The story of Alexander's encounter with the wife of Spitamenes is found only in Curtius and the *Metz Epitome*. In it Alexander is confronted with a moral dilemma: did the benefit that Alexander derived from the elimination of Spitamenes permit him to condone the actions of a woman who had treacherously murdered her husband? Like Spitamenes himself, Alexander ran the risk of being taken in by the woman's beauty. This version of the fate of Spitamenes – according to Arrian he was murdered by his Scythian allies, who sent his head to Alexander – may have inspired the story of Judith and Holophernes: see Burstein (1999).

5(a)   *Quintus Curtius Rufus 8.3.1–15*

Alexander had determined to march next on the Dahae, after learning that Spitamenes was among them. Fortune, which never tired of indulging him, also brought this expedition, like many of his other exploits, to a successful conclusion even in his absence. Spitamenes' ardent love for his wife exceeded the bounds of moderation, but she tired of their flight and repeated changes of place of exile as he dragged her with him into all his dangers. [2] Exhausted by the hardships, time and again she employed her female charms in an effort to induce him to stop running and to appease a man whose mercy in victory he had already tasted and whom he could not escape anyway. [3] She had had three children by Spitamenes who were now grown up, and these she brought into their father's arms, begging that he pity them at least – and to add weight to her entreaties, Alexander was not far off. [4] Spitamenes thought this was treachery on her part, not advice, and that her desire to surrender to Alexander at the first opportunity arose from her confidence in her beauty. He drew his scimitar and would have run his wife through if her brothers had not rushed up to stop him. [5] He ordered her from his sight, threatening her with death if she met his eyes again, and to ease his passion for her he began to spend his nights with concubines. [6] But his deep-seated love was actually inflamed by dissatisfaction with his bed-fellows of the moment. So, devoting himself exclusively to his wife once more, he incessantly begged her to eschew such advice as she had given and to acquiesce in whatever it was that fortune had in store for them, since he would find death less painful than surrender. [7] She excused herself by saying that she had given him what she thought was profitable advice, and that her recommendations, though characteristically feminine, nonetheless arose from loyal intentions. In future, she said, she would abide by her husband's will.

[8] Spitamenes was taken in by this show of devotion. He ordered a banquet arranged while it was still day, after which he was carried to his room, languid from excessive drinking and eating, and half-asleep. [9] As soon as his wife saw him in a deep, heavy sleep, she drew a sword which she had hidden under her clothes and cut off his head which, spattered with blood, she handed to a slave who had acted as her accomplice. [10] With the slave in attendance she came to the Macedonian camp, her clothes still drenched with blood, and had the message taken to Alexander that there was a matter of which he should hear from her own lips. [11] Alexander immediately had the barbarian shown in. Seeing her bespattered with blood, he assumed she had come to complain of an assault, and he told her to state what she wanted. [12] She asked that the slave, whom she had told to stand at the doorway, now be brought in. This slave had aroused suspicion because he had the head of Spitamenes concealed under his clothes; and when the guard searched him he showed them what he was hiding. [13] Pallor had disfigured the features of the bloodless face so that a firm identification was impossible. The king was now informed that the slave was bringing him a human head, so he went out of the tent, asked what was going on and learned the details from the statement made by the slave.

[14] Alexander was now prey to conflicting thoughts as he considered the various aspects of the matter. He believed it a great benefit to himself that a treacherous deserter had been assassinated, a man whose continued existence would have proved an obstacle to his great designs, but he was also repelled by the enormity of the crime – a woman treacherously murdering a man who had treated her well and who was the father of their children. [15] The savagery of the deed carried more weight with him than gratitude for the favour, however, and he had her ordered from the camp. He did not want her tainting the character and civilized temperament of the Greeks with this example of barbarian lawlessness.

5(b) Metz Epitome 20–3

At winter's end, Alexander led the army towards the Dahae. †Spitamenes had not fled from that place† because he had there a Bactrian wife of superlative beauty whom he adored and took with him on all his travels and exploits. When she heard of Alexander's approach, she refused to leave the town and later proceeded to make numerous entreaties to her husband to throw himself on Alexander's mercy. Spitamenes refused. [21] Unable to achieve her end, she pressed him to drink †a cup† at a banquet and when he became drowsy put him to bed. As soon as she felt that all was silent, she rose from the bed and withdrew the pillow from her husband's head. His throat thus extended, she cut his head from his body with a sword and, taking her leave with one slave, came to Alexander in his camp. [22] The king's guards brought her to him – elegant, despite the bloodstains, because of her dress and dignified appearance. The sudden sight of her put Alexander in a quandary – who was she and why had she come? Then she produced her husband's head. [23] "Ah, treacherous Spitamenes," exclaimed the king, "finally you have paid the penalty for your crimes!" After this he took the woman's hand and thanked her. He refrained, however, from according her any honours in case the motive for this be interpreted as lust for her beauty.

Alexander and Roxane

Alexander's decision to marry Roxane (Rhoshanak means "Little Star") in 328/7, whether from love or for political gain, brought peace and stability to the Upper Satrapies after almost three years of fighting. The move was, however, less popular with the Macedonians, who weighed the long-term prospect of a half-barbarian heir to the throne against the immediate benefits of peace in the region. Indeed, the first child of this union died in India (§VIII.6f) and, when Roxane was once again pregnant in 323, the uncertainty concerning the child's sex and chances of survival jeopardized the succession. Roxane herself took no chances, putting to death the rival princess Stateira (see §VII.3b–c) in the days that followed Alexander's death (Plutarch, *Alexander* 77.6 = §VIII.6g).

6(a)   Metz Epitome *28–31*

Alexander then devoted himself to pressing ahead with the journey he had begun towards Gazabes, during which he met a certain satrap named Chorienes with whom he formed an alliance. Chorienes entertained Alexander at his house and introduced as dancers at the banquet his own unmarried daughters along with the unmarried daughters of his friends. [29] Amongst them was the daughter of Oxyartes, Roxane, who was the most beautiful of all. Enchanted by the sight of her and fired with lust, Alexander asked who she was and who her father was, to discover that she was the daughter of Oxyartes, also a guest at the dinner. He took his cup, made a prayer to the gods and then proceeded to declare that many people often found that many things happen contrary to their expectations, that many kings had had sons by captives [30] or sent daughters to foreign nations to get married, using such a bond to ratify alliances. "So," he continued, "I do not consider the Macedonians your betters in terms of race and no more would I consider you unworthy of intermarriage with us, even if you had sought alliance with us after a defeat. I am going to make such a match, and I shall ensure that the rest of the Macedonians follow my example." [31] After these words of exhortation from Alexander, each of his friends took away a girl as his bride, to the great delight of Oxyartes and the other barbarians.

6(b) Quintus Curtius Rufus 8.4.21–6

After this Alexander entered the country governed by the illustrious satrap, Oxyartes.[6] Oxyartes placed himself under the king's authority and protection, whereupon Alexander restored his position to him and demanded only that two of Oxyartes' three sons join him on his campaigns. [22] In fact, the satrap also committed to him the son who was being left behind with himself.

Oxyartes had arranged a banquet of typical barbaric extravagance, at which he entertained the king. [23] While he conducted the festivities with warm geniality, Oxyartes had thirty young noblewomen brought in, one of whom was his own daughter Roxane, a woman of remarkable physical beauty with a dignified bearing rarely found in barbarians. [24] Though she was one of a number chosen for their beauty, she nonetheless attracted everybody's attention, especially that of the king, whose control over his appetites was weakening amid the indulgences of Fortune, against whom mankind is insufficiently armed. [25] So it was that the man who had looked with what were merely paternal feelings on the wife and two unmarried daughters of Darius – and with these none but Roxane could be compared in looks – now fell in love with a young girl, of humble pedigree in comparison with royalty, and did so with such abandon as to make a statement that intermarriage of Persians and Macedonians would serve to consolidate his empire, that only thus could the conquered lose their shame and the conquerors their pride. [26] Achilles, he said, from whom he traced his descent, had also shared his bed with a captive. Her people should not think they were being done any wrong – he was willing to enter into a lawful marriage with Roxane.

6(c) Plutarch, Alexander 47.7–8

And then there was the matter of Roxane. His actions[7] were motivated by passion – he had noted her beautiful and comely looks when he saw her participating in a dance during the after-dinner drinking – but the situation was not disadvantageous to what he had in prospect. [8] The barbarians were heartened by the partnership this marriage represented, and they were very fond of Alexander because he showed exceptional self-control and would not presume to touch the only woman who captured his heart unless the law permitted it.

6(d) Arrian 4.19.5

Oxyartes had a maiden daughter of marriageable age called Roxane. The men on campaign with Alexander claimed she was the best looking of the Asian

---

6 The text is corrupt at this point, and Alde restored the name Oxyartes, but in fact the MS reading *cohortandus* seems to suggest Chorienes, as in the *Metz Epitome* (§VIII.6a, above).
7 I.e., marrying her.

women after Darius' wife and that Alexander fell in love with her at first sight. Despite his desire for her he was unwilling to force himself on her, captive though she was – he did not consider marrying her beneath his dignity.

6(e)   *Lucian*, Herodotus sive Aëtion *4–6*

. . . they say the artist Aëtion painted *The Wedding of Alexander and Roxane* and took the picture to Olympia where he put it on display. The *Hellanodike*[8] Proxenidas was taken with his artistry and made Aëtion his son-in-law.

. . . The painting is in Italy, and I saw it, so I am able to describe it for you. There is a very beautiful chamber and a bridal bed. Roxane, represented as a beautiful maiden, is sitting there looking at the ground, bashful in the presence of Alexander. There are smiling Cupids. One of them stands behind Roxane, drawing the veil from her head and revealing her to the bridegroom. Another, much like a servant, removes the sandal from her foot as though she were already going to bed. A third (that is, another Cupid) has hold of Alexander's cloak and, with a forceful tug, is pulling him toward Roxane. As for the king himself, he holds out a garland to the girl, and Hephaestion is with them, holding a burning torch . . . and leaning on a very handsome boy – I think it is Hymenaeus, though the name is not inscribed. On the other side of the painting are other Cupids who are at play amongst Alexander's armour. Two carry his spear, looking like porters having difficulty carrying a beam. Two more are dragging along yet another Cupid, who is lying on the shield – this one is presumably their king – holding on to the shield by the handle. One has made his way into the corselet, which is lying chest up – he seems to be lying in ambush, to give a fright to the two when they reach him, pulling the third.

This is not just silliness or a meaningless waste of effort on Aëtion's part. He is also highlighting the fact that Alexander loved military affairs as well, and that, while he felt love for Roxane, he had not forgotten his armour.

6(f)   Metz Epitome *70*

There[9] he found the ships which Porus and Taxiles had built, 800 biremes and 300 store-ships, and he put on board crews and provisions. In the meantime Alexander's son by Roxane died.

---

8   One of the judges at Olympia.
9   At the Hydaspes (Jhelum), to which Alexander had returned after the Hyphasis mutiny. The *Metz Epitome* (69), like other writers of the popular tradition, speaks of the Acesines (Ravi), though these events clearly occurred at the Hydaspes.

6(g)　Plutarch, Alexander 77.6–7

Roxane was at that time pregnant, and for that reason enjoyed great respect amongst the Macedonians. She was, however, extremely jealous of Statira, whom she tricked into coming to her by means of a duplicitous letter. When she had Statira at her disposal, she murdered her along with her sister and threw the bodies into a well, which she then filled with earth. Perdiccas knew of Roxane's actions, and was her accomplice. [7] For it was Perdiccas who exercised the greatest authority immediately after Alexander's death, trailing around with him Arrhidaeus as a sort of puppet representative of the monarchy.

Alexander and Cleophis

Although there are several accounts of Alexander's meeting with the Assacenian queen, only Justin (Trogus), Curtius, and the *Metz Epitome* call her Cleophis. Gutschmid (1882: 553–4) suggested that the name may be a play on Cleopatra, and that her illegitimate son (who was named after his father) is meant to recall Caesarion. Furthermore, Justin refers to her as the "royal whore" (*scortum regium*), which perhaps suggests Cleopatra, whom Propertius (3.11.39) calls the "whore queen" (*regina meretrix*). If this is correct the source for the reworked account must be a writer of the late Republic or early Empire, possibly Timagenes of Alexandria. See also Yardley and Heckel (1997: 30, 241–2).

7(a)　Metz Epitome 39–45

Advancing from there, Alexander crossed the Cordiaean mountains and arrived at the satrapy of Assacana. From here he went on towards the town of Mazaga. This had been the kingdom of Assacenus, on whose death it was ruled by his mother Cleophis in conjunction with Assacenus' son. Here the king's brother, Amminais, had incited against Alexander and put under arms 9,000 mercenaries, whom he had brought into the state. [40] The town was encircled by a stone wall, 35 stades in circumference, and also protected by an enormous ditch. Alexander surrounded the town with a military cordon and prepared to make an assault but, while he was riding around the city's fortifications encouraging his men, he was suddenly hit in the left leg by an arrow shot from the wall. When the missile was extracted, a thick stream of blood followed it. That notwithstanding, Alexander would not quit the field; disregarding the wound and becoming increasingly incapacitated by it, he still exhorted his men to bring †tortoise formations† and siege towers up to the wall. [41] Then, because their king was wounded, the Macedonians exerted themselves all the more to set up scaling ladders and take the town. Some hurled at the defenders projectiles from slings on the towers; others brought siege engines up to the wall.

When Cleophis saw this – hordes of towers advancing on her city and huge quantities of missiles being shot from slings – she was filled with alarm by the extraordinary scene, for she thought that the rocks hurled by the thongs of the "scorpion"[10] and the catapult were actually flying! [42] Believing her enemy possessed a power of this order, she summoned †araplicem† and her other friends to a meeting, at which she urged them to surrender the town to Alexander. The mercenaries, however, objected and proceeded to become obstructive and mutinous. The next day, Cleophis sent a secret deputation to Alexander to discuss terms of surrender and to beg him to pardon them – they had been forced by the mercenaries to take the action they had taken. [43] The mercenaries, however, suspected that she had done this, and so they sent some of their number as a delegation to Alexander to beg his permission to leave the town and take their possessions with them. Alexander acceded to the requests of both parties. The mercenaries then came forth and took a position not far from the town.

The following day, Alexander began to lead some light-armed troops towards them and proclaimed that they were all to be put to death. [44] When the mercenaries surmised what was afoot, they brought their baggage together in one spot and positioned themselves around it under arms, ready to repel an assault or else go bravely to their deaths for their wives and children. At the same time, they began to cry out that Alexander was not standing by his agreement, to which Alexander replied that he had given them permission to go out of the town but not to leave the area. [45] And with that he attacked. The Macedonians outnumbered the mercenaries, who were killed to a man, though they long resisted and were with difficulty overcome only after a ferocious struggle. The Macedonians then returned to the town and there were met by Cleophis, who came with her most prominent citizens and her little grandson, all of them bearing before themselves, to mark their veneration of him, branches and harvest offerings covered with veils. Alexander was struck by the good looks of Cleophis; for her bearing and dignity were such that she was evidently of noble pedigree and well suited for royal power. Alexander then entered the town with a few men and remained there several days.

7(b)   Justin 12.7.9–13

From there Alexander headed for the Daedalian mountains and the realm of Queen Cleophis. She surrendered to him but subsequently regained her

10 An artillery device used for hurling stones, darts, and other missiles. It appears that Archimedes invented such weapons for the defense of Syracuse in the Second Punic War (Polybius 8.5.6). Even if scorpions were not Archimedes' own invention, the reference appears to be anachronistic and it is doubtful that Alexander possessed or used any in his campaigns.

throne which she ransomed by sleeping with him, attaining by sexual favours what she could not by force of arms. [10] The child fathered by the king she named Alexander, and he later rose to sovereignty over the Indians. [11] Because she had thus degraded herself Queen Cleophis was from that time called the "royal whore" by the Indians. [12] After traversing India Alexander now reached a rocky eminence which was extremely high and precipitous, on which many tribes had sought refuge, and he was told that Hercules had been prevented from capturing this by an earthquake. [13] So it was that, overcome by an urge to better Hercules' exploits, he braved extreme hardship and peril to take the height, finally accepting the surrender of all the local tribes.

IX   Gods and Heroes

Alexander may have had a natural desire to surpass the achievements of gods and heroes, and often his striving is presented as motivated by his *pothos* (on which see glossary, and Ehrenberg 1938: 52–61). Many of his actions were, however, carefully calculated for political gain. In general, see Edmunds (1971).

Imitation and Emulation of Achilles, Heracles, and Dionysus

Alexander's interest in Achilles, Heracles, and Dionysus has its origins in the fact that his parents traced their descent from two of these heroes; Olympias herself, in addition to her family's mythical genealogy that made her a descendant of Achilles, was a passionate devotee of Bacchic (i.e., Dionysiac) rites and similar rituals. The king may have had a boyhood interest in Achilles – after all, Aristotle (Plutarch, *Alexander* 8.2), or possibly Callisthenes (Strabo 13.1.27 C594), is said to have made a special edition (the "casket copy") of the *Iliad* for him, but Perrin (1895) has demonstrated that most of the stories that link Alexander with Achilles are literary fabrications after the king's death; for the most obvious parallel is the fact that Alexander, like Achilles, performed great deeds and died young. By contrast, Alexander's reverence for Heracles was genuine and methodical: he consciously emulated Heracles (the journey to Siwah; the capture of Aornus), he regularly sacrificed to him, and he minted Heracles-type coins. Undoubtedly, he was conscious of the traditions linking Dionysus with India, but Dionysus is also depicted as an enemy: the murder of Cleitus was portrayed by at least one writer as the result of the god's wrath against the man who destroyed Thebes.

Unlike Achilles and Heracles, whom Alexander claimed as ancestors, the links with Dionysus are more tenuous and may have been developed by the Alexander historians rather than actively exploited by Alexander himself. The revel in Carmania appears to be an exception: either this was a fabrication or, as seems more likely, Alexander used it as a means of providing much needed relief to the army that had just emerged from the devastating Gedrosian march. Olympias was, of course, a devotee of Dionysiac and similar practices, but it is doubtful that Alexander was particularly influenced by her activities.

1(a)   Strabo, Geography 15.1.8–9

It was on the basis of such stories that people designated certain individuals by the tribal name "Nysaeans", and also called a city amongst them "Nysa" (as being founded by Dionysus) and the mountain overlooking the city "Meron". They adduced as their reason the ivy growing in the region, along with the vine, which did not, in fact, reach the fruit-bearing stage (the grapes falling off before they darkened because of the excessive rainfall). They also identified the Sudracae as descendants of Dionysus because of the existence of the vine in their culture and the extravagance of their parades; their kings made military expeditions in bacchic fashion, and conducted their other official marches to the sound of drums and wearing flowery robes (a custom amongst the other Indians, as well).

Alexander took with his first assault a certain rocky outcrop called Aornus – the river Indus flows past its base, close to its sources – and the devotees of the king declared that Heracles had made three assaults on the rock, only to be repulsed three times. The Sibae, they said, were descended from the people who joined Heracles on this expedition, and these people retained the emblems of their ancestry, namely the Heraclean wearing of skins, the use of the cudgel, and the branding of cattle and mules with the figure of a club.

They further bolster this myth with the material relating to the Caucasus and Prometheus, transferring that to this area from Pontus on very tenuous grounds – they saw a cave in the territory of the Paropamisadae that was "holy". The cave they made out to be the prison of Prometheus, claiming that it was here that Heracles came to free Prometheus and that this was the Caucasus that the Greeks designated the prison of Prometheus.

9 This is a fiction of people who curried favour with Alexander. That is obvious in the first place from the lack of consensus amongst the historians, but it is clear, too, from the fact that some historians record it and others make no mention of it whatsoever. For lack of knowledge of something so spectacular and full of glamour is implausible, and so too is knowing about it but not considering it worth reporting – and we are talking about historians of the greatest credibility! After that there is the question of the people in between, those through whom the followers of Dionysus and Heracles would have had to pass to reach India, for they have no evidence to show for the passage of these personages through their own lands. In addition, the way in which Heracles is outfitted far post-dates any record of the Trojan war and is an invention of those who made up the epic of Heracles – be that Peisander or someone else. The ancient statues are not outfitted in this manner.

1(b)   Plutarch, Moralia 332a–b

In the circumstances you must forgive me, Diogenes, for imitating Heracles and emulating Heracles. Forgive me for following the footsteps of Dionysus, divine founder and forefather of my line,[1] and wishing to have Greeks dance in victory again in India and remind those mountain-men and savages beyond the Caucasus of the revels of Bacchus.

Achilles

1(c) Arrian 1.12.1–2

Some state that Alexander placed a wreath on Achilles' tomb (and they also say that Hephaestion placed a wreath on that of Patroclus). Indeed, Alexander declared Achilles a fortunate man, so it is said, because he chanced to have Homer to herald his praises to posterity. [2] And, to tell the truth, Alexander should have considered Achilles fortunate in this particular respect because in it he did not enjoy his usual good fortune. This was an area of deficiency in his career, and the deeds of Alexander did not receive the publicity that was their due; for no one gave them that either in prose or in verse. Alexander did not even have his praises sung in lyric verse, like Hieron, Gelon, Theron[2] and many others who are not on the same level as he, so that Alexander's career is much less known than the most trivial exploits of bygone times.[3]

1(d) Cicero, Pro Archia 24

How many were the writers Alexander the Great is said to have had with him to record his deeds! And, in fact, when he stood before the tomb of Achilles in Sigeum he declared, "O lucky young man – you found Homer as the herald of your prowess!"

1(e) Quintus Curtius Rufus 8.4.26

Achilles, he said, from whom he traced his descent, had also shared his bed with a captive.[4] Her people should not think they were being done any wrong – he was willing to enter into a lawful marriage with Roxane.

1   This is otherwise unattested. The speaker is Alexander himself.
2   All Sicilian tyrants commemorated in the odes of Pindar and Bacchylides. See also Bosworth (1980a: 105).
3   See also Plutarch, Alexander 15.7–9.
4   Briseis, Achilles' prize of war. It was Agamemnon's decision to take her for himself that constituted the slight, which led to Achilles' famous wrath in Homer's Iliad.

1(f)   Diodorus Siculus 17.97.1–3

Alexander once more boarded the ships with his *philoi* and made the journey downstream to the confluence of the above-mentioned rivers and the Indus. With these great waterways thundering together at this one point there are many dangerous whirlpools, and these engulfed the vessels and began to shatter them. The current was fast and furious, frustrating the skill of the helmsmen, and two warships went under with no small number of other vessels running aground. [2] The flagship became caught up in fierce rapids, and the king found himself in extreme peril. With death before his eyes, Alexander stripped off his clothes and, naked, clung to whatever could possibly help him. His *philoi* meanwhile swam beside the ship, anxious to grasp the king should the vessel capsize. [3] On board the ship there was complete turmoil. The men were trying to combat the force of the current, but the river thwarted all human skill and strength, and it was only by a hair that Alexander managed to make it to shore with the ships. Having gained safety against the odds, he offered sacrifice to the gods for his having managed to survive the greatest dangers and, like Achilles, fight a river.

Heracles (Hercules)

1(g)   Justin 11.4.5

Cleadas even appealed to the king's personal devotion to Hercules, who was born in their city and from whom the clan of the Aeacidae traced its descent, and to the fact that his father Philip had spent his boyhood in Thebes.

1(h)   Quintus Curtius Rufus 3.12.27

He consecrated three altars on the banks of the river Pinarus to Jupiter, Hercules and Minerva, and then made for Syria . . .

1(i)   Justin 11.10.2–3

It was now that he first started to hold sumptuous banquets and splendid dinners; now, too, that he began to fall in love with the prisoner Barsine because of her beauty [3] (by her he later had a son whom he named Hercules).

1(j)   Justin 11.10.10

The city of Tyre had sent Alexander a deputation with a heavy crown of gold in a show of congratulation. He accepted it with gratitude, then said he wished to go to Tyre to discharge his vows to Hercules.

1(k)   Quintus Curtius Rufus 8.11.2

According to popular tradition this place[5] had been unsuccessfully besieged by Hercules, who had been obliged to abandon the siege by an earthquake.

1(l)   Justin 12.7.12–13

After traversing India Alexander now reached a rocky eminence which was extremely high and precipitous, on which many tribes had sought refuge; and he was told that Hercules had been prevented from capturing this by an earthquake. [13] So it was that, overcome by an urge to better Hercules' exploits, he braved extreme hardship and peril to take the height, finally accepting the surrender of all the local tribes.

1(m)   Justin 12.9.1–2

From there Alexander proceeded to the River Acesines and sailed down it to the Ocean, [2] where he accepted the surrender of the Agensonae and the Sibi, whose founder was Hercules.

Dionysus

1(n)   Quintus Curtius Rufus 8.10.11–18

The people of Nysa claimed Father Liber as their founder, and this piece of genealogy is a fact. [12] The city is situated at the foot of a mountain which the local people call Meron, and it was because of this name that the Greeks presumed to invent their story of Father Liber being concealed in the thigh of Jupiter. [13] When the king learned from the local people how to reach the mountain he had supplies sent ahead and went up to its summit with his entire army. Ivy and vines grow in large quantities all over the mountain, and many year-round streams flow down it. [14] There are also various fruits whose juices have health-giving properties, the soil spontaneously producing a harvest from any seeds that happen to fall there. There are laurels and berry-bushes – a thick forest on the mountain's cliffs. [15] Personally I do not believe it was as a result of divine inspiration but simply to amuse themselves that the soldiers began to pick ivy and vine fronds here and there, and wandered

---

5   Aornus. For the full account see §VI.3m.

the length of the wood wearing leaf-garlands like bacchants. [16] The mountain-tops and hills echoed with the voices of many thousands worshipping the tutelary god of that wood for, as usually happens, though the fooling started with a few it suddenly spread to them all. [17] As if the world were at peace around them, they flung themselves down on the grass and on beds of leaves while the king, who did not object to this chance offer of merriment, provided an abundance of all things needed for a feast and had his army spend ten days in the worship of Father Liber. [18] Who would deny that even an illustrious reputation is a benefit conferred more often by fortune than merit? Not even when they were feasting and were drowsy with drink did the enemy venture to attack them – being just as terrified by their uproarious revelling and yelling as if what they had heard was the Macedonian battle-cry. The same good fortune protected the Macedonians while they were returning from the ocean and held a drunken revel before the eyes of their enemy.

1(o)   Quintus Curtius Rufus 9.10.24–9

So it was that Alexander, his pride soaring above the human plane, now proceeded, as mentioned above, to emulate not only the glory won from those peoples by Father Liber, but the Bacchic tradition as well: he decided to imitate the god's procession (whether that was, in fact, the original triumphal march that the god instituted or merely sport on the part of his bacchants). [25] He gave orders for villages along his route to be strewn with flowers and garlands, and for bowls full of wine and other vessels of extraordinary size to be set out on the thresholds of houses. Then he had wagons covered with planks (so that they would hold a greater number of soldiers) and rigged out like tents, some with white curtains, others with costly material.

[26] The friends and the royal company went in front, heads wreathed with various kinds of flowers woven into garlands, with the notes of the flute heard at one point, the tones of the lyre at another. The army joined the revels in wagons decorated as far as individual means allowed, and with their finest arms hung around them. The king and his drinking companions rode in a cart weighed down with golden bowls and huge goblets of the same metal. [27] In this way the army spent seven days on a drunken march, an easy prey if the vanquished races had only had the courage to challenge riotous drinkers – why, a mere 1,000 men, if sober, could have captured this group on its triumphal march, weighed down as it was from seven days of drinking. [28] But it is fortune that allots fame and a price to things, and she turned even this piece of disgraceful soldiering into a glorious achievement! People of those and later times marvelled that drunken men had made their way through countries as yet unsubdued, the barbarians mistaking for self-confidence what was in fact sheer recklessness. [29] This pageant was followed by the executioner, for orders were issued for the aforementioned Astaspes to be

put to death. It is true indeed: luxurious living and base cruelty are not mutually exclusive.

1(p)   Arrian 6.28.1–2

A number of authors have also given the following story, though I do not find their accounts credible. Alexander yoked together two war-chariots on which he reclined with his *hetairoi* and travelled through Carmania to the music of the pipe. The army followed him wearing garlands, and boisterously festive. Food and all the various luxurious accoutrements had been brought together and set out for the troops by the Carmanians. This event was staged by Alexander as a re-enactment of the Bacchic revel of Dionysus, [2] because there was a story told of Dionysus travelling in this manner over most of Asia after his subjugation of India. Indeed, it was said that Dionysus was himself called *Thriambos*, and that for this very reason processions celebrating military victory were called *thriamboi*.[6]

The Gordian Knot[7]

Spring 330. Gordium is on the Sangarius River and was thought by the Ionian geographers to mark the centre of the world. The oracle which foretold domination of all Asia must have referred to Asia Minor, not the entire Persian empire; Alexander's conquests may have occasioned a more generous interpretation of the prophecy after the fact. At the time, the propaganda value of the Gordian knot could scarcely be ignored, but only Alexander's ingenuity averted an unfavorable omen. See Fredricksmeyer (1961); cf. Atkinson (1980: 90–1) and Bosworth (1980a: 184–8). For the background, see Roller (1984) and Burke (2001).

2(a)   Plutarch, Alexander 18.1–4

Alexander then crushed all resistance amongst the Pisidians and conquered Phrygia. [2] After taking the city of Gordium, which was reputedly the capital of Midas of old, he saw the much-vaunted cart fastened with its bindings of cherry-wood bark, and was told by the barbarians a story attaching to it that had wide acceptance. The man who untied the knot, they said, was destined to become king of the world.

---

6   *Thriamboi* = "triumphs." This is a Roman practice and thus does not come from one of the lost contemporary Alexander historians.
7   Other ancient sources are Aelian, *Nat. Anim.* 13.1; Marsyas (of Philippi), *FGrH* 135/6 F4; Schol. Eur. *Hipp.* 671; Strabo 12.5.3 C568; Tzetzes, *Chil.* 6.72.690. (For these works and abbreviations see the *Oxford Classical Dictionary*.) Diodorus Siculus has nothing on the Gordian knot.

[3] Most people say that because the ends of the thongs were hidden and interlaced many times in twisted tangles Alexander had no idea how to untie them and so he cut through the knot with his sword, bringing to light with his slashing many of the ends. [4] Aristobulus, however, claims that untying the knot was easy for Alexander: he removed what they call the pole-pin, with which the yoke-knot was held together, and then drew back the yoke.

2(b)   Arrian 2.3

On arriving in Gordium, Alexander was overtaken by a desire to go up to the acropolis, the site of the palace of Gordius and his son Midas. He wished to see the wagon of Gordius and the knot binding the wagon's yoke. [2] There is a tale about that wagon that is widely told by the inhabitants of the region.

Gordius, the story goes, was one of the Phrygians of old who was a poor man and who worked, with his two oxen, the small piece of land that he possessed; one of these oxen was for ploughing and the other for pulling his wagon. [3] One day, as he was ploughing, an eagle settled on the yoke of the plough and remained there until the oxen were detached from it. Amazed at the sight, Gordius went off to the Telmissian seers to tell them about this sign from heaven; for the Telmissians have an aptitude for interpreting supernatural events, and possess – as do their wives and children – a hereditary gift of prophecy.

[4] As he was approaching one of the Telmissian villages, Gordius met a maiden who was fetching water, and he gave her an account of the episode with the eagle. The girl, too, had the hereditary talent for prophecy, and she instructed him to go back to the spot and sacrifice to Zeus the King. Gordius begged her to go along with him to conduct the sacrifice and direct the ritual. He then sacrificed in accordance with her prescriptions, married the girl and they had a son who was named Midas.

[5] Midas was now a fine man of noble bearing when the Phrygians found themselves in trouble with civil dissension; and they received an oracle stating that a wagon would bring them a king, and that this king would put an end to their civil discord. The people were still in the process of discussing the matter when Midas arrived with his father and mother, and came to a halt with the wagon right where they were meeting. [6] Proceeding to decipher the prophecy, the people decided that this was the man whom the god told them the wagon would bring. They appointed Midas their king, and he did put an end to their conflict. He then set the wagon of his father on the acropolis as a gift of thanks to Zeus the King for his sending of the eagle.

There was also this further story told of the wagon, that whosoever untied the knot that bound that wagon's yoke was fated to be the ruler of Asia. [7] The knot, however, was made up of the bark of cherry-wood, and there was no way of seeing where it began or ended. Alexander was at a loss to find a way of untying the knot, but was unwilling to leave it still tied for fear of creating a

measure of unrest amongst the masses. And so, according to some, he struck
and cut through the knot with his sword and declared it untied. Aristobulus,
however, says he removed the shaft-peg (a bolt passing right through the shaft
and holding the knot in place), and so separated the yoke from the shaft.

[8] I cannot make any categorical assertion about how Alexander dealt with
the knot, but when the Macedonians left the wagon they gave the impression that the oracle about the untying of the knot had been fulfilled. And
that night, in fact, there was thunder and lightning sending a sign from
heaven. In thanks for this, Alexander the following day offered sacrifice to
the gods for having revealed to him their divine signs, and shown him how
to untie the knot.

2(c)   Quintus Curtius Rufus 3.1.14–18

Alexander reduced the city,[8] and entered the temple of Jupiter. Here he saw
the carriage on which they said Midas' father, Gordius, used to ride. In appearance it was little different from quite inexpensive and ordinary carriages, [15]
its remarkable feature being a yoke, which was strapped down with several
knots all so tightly entangled that it was impossible to see how they were fastened. [16] Since the local people claimed that an oracle had foretold mastery
of Asia for the man who untied this impossible knot, the desire to fulfil the
prophecy came over Alexander. [17] The king was surrounded by a crowd of
Phrygians and Macedonians, the former all in suspense about his attempt at
untying it, the latter alarmed at the king's overconfidence – for, in fact, the
series of knots was pulled so tight that it was impossible to work out or see
where the tangled mass began or ended, and what particularly concerned
them about the king's attempt at untying it was that an unsuccessful effort
should be construed as an omen. [18] For some time Alexander wrestled unsuccessfully with the hidden knots. Then he said: "It makes no difference how
they're untied," and cut through all the thongs with his sword, thus evading
the oracle's prophecy – or, indeed, fulfilling it.

2(d)   Justin 11.7.3–16

Alexander then made for the city of Gordium, situated between Greater and
Lesser Phrygia. [4] He was seized by an urge to take this city, not so much for
its spoils as because he had heard that the yoke of Gordius was lodged there
in the temple of Jupiter, and that ancient oracles had foretold dominion over
all Asia for any man who succeeded in untying its knot.

[5] Why and how this came about is as follows. Gordius was ploughing in
these regions with hired oxen when birds of all kinds began to flutter around

8 Gordium.

him. [6] He went to consult the soothsayers in a neighbouring city and at the city gate he met a young woman of extraordinary beauty of whom he enquired which soothsayer he would be best advised to consult. [7] The woman knew the art of prophecy, which she had been taught by her parents; on hearing the reason for his consultation she replied that he was destined to hold royal power, and she offered to marry him and share his prospects. [8] Such a fine match struck him as being the start of the good fortune that should attend his rule. [9] After the wedding civil discord arose among the Phrygians, [10] and when they consulted the oracles about terminating the conflict, the reply they received was that to do this they needed a king. [11] When they questioned the oracle a second time on the identity of the king, they were instructed to return and accept as their king the first person they found coming in a wagon to the temple of Jupiter. [12] The person they met was Gordius, and they immediately hailed him as king. [13] Gordius lodged in the temple of Jupiter the wagon in which he had been riding when the throne was conferred on him, consecrating it to the majesty of kings. [14] He was succeeded by his son Midas who, after receiving religious initiation from Orpheus, filled Phrygia with religious cults, and this, throughout his life, protected him more effectively than could an armed guard.

[15] Alexander took the city and, entering the temple of Jupiter, asked where the wagon-yoke was to be found. [16] It was pointed out to him but he was unable to find the ends of the thongs, since they were hidden within the knots and so, interpreting the oracle in a somewhat cavalier manner, he slashed through the thongs with his sword, thus undoing the knots and finding the ends hidden within them.

Amun (Ammon) and Alexander's "Divinity"

The oracle of Amun at the oasis of Siwah in Libya was known to the Greeks long before Alexander's time. Greek and Roman writers called the god "Ammon" or "Hammon" and equated him with Zeus, but Alexander must have known that the legitimate Pharaohs of Egypt claimed to be sons of Amun, and the journey to Siwah was meant to appeal to Egyptian sensibilities.[9] Stories that Olympias had slept with Zeus, who thus became the true father of Alexander, arose after the king's visit to Siwah; indeed, the *Alexander Romance* went so far as to claim that the last Pharaoh of the Thirtieth Dynasty, Nectanebo, fled to Macedonia and there seduced and impregnated Olympias in the guise of Zeus–Amun. The Macedonian reaction to Alexander's apparent rejection of Philip II was more serious, and later the deification of Alexander in the Greek world established a precedent for the "divinity" of Hellenistic kings and Roman emperors. See Balsdon (1950), Habicht (1970), Badian (1981), and Cawkwell (1994); cf. Edmunds (1971).

9   But see Edmunds (1971: 378): "The detour to Siwah was non-strategic and had nothing to do with Alexander's pharaohship. It was a personal matter."

3(a)   Quintus Curtius Rufus 4.7.5–32

From Memphis Alexander sailed upstream and penetrated into the interior of Egypt where, after settling administrative matters without tampering with Egyptian traditions, he decided to visit the oracle of Jupiter Ammon. [6] The journey that had to be made could scarcely be managed even by a small band of soldiers lightly armed: land and sky lack moisture; the sands lie flat and barren, and when they are seared by the blazing sun the ground swelters and burns the feet and the heat is intolerable. [7] Apart from the high temperatures and dryness of the terrain one also has to contend with the tenacious quality of the sand which, because of its depth and the fact that it gives way to the tread, is difficult to negotiate on foot.

[8] The Egyptians, in fact, exaggerated these difficulties, but Alexander was nevertheless goaded by an overwhelming desire to visit the temple of Jupiter – dissatisfied with elevation on the mortal level, he either considered, or wanted others to believe, that Jupiter was his ancestor. [9] So he sailed downstream to Lake Mareotis with the men he had decided to take with him, and there ambassadors from Cyrene brought him gifts, asking for peace and requesting that he visit their cities. Alexander accepted the gifts, concluded treaties with them, and resumed his proposed journey. [10] The first and second day the difficulties seemed bearable, for they had yet to reach the vast stretches of naked desert, though even now the earth was barren and lifeless. [11] However, when plains covered with deep sand appeared, it was as if they were entering a vast sea and their eyes vainly looked for land – [12] no tree was to be seen, not a trace of cultivated soil. They had also run out of water, which had been carried in skins by camels, and in the arid soil and burning sand not a drop was to be found. [13] The sun had also parched everything, and their throats were dry and burned, when suddenly – whether it was a gift of the gods or pure chance – clouds shrouded the sky and hid the sun, providing enormous relief for them, exhausted as they were by the heat, even despite the absence of water. [14] In fact, though, high winds now showered down generous quantities of rain, of which each man collected his own supply, some of them, wild with thirst, attempting to catch it with gaping mouths.

[15] After four days in the desert wastes, they found themselves not far from the site of the oracle. Here a number of crows met the column, flying ahead of the front standards at a slow pace, occasionally settling on the ground, when the column's advance was relatively slow, and then again taking off as if they were going ahead to show the way. [16] At last the Macedonians reached the area consecrated to the god which, incredibly, located though it is among the desert wastes, is so well screened on all sides by encircling tree branches that the rays of the sun barely penetrate the shade, and its woods are sustained by a wealth of fresh-water springs. [17] The climate, too, is amazingly temperate, with the mildness of springtime, providing a healthy atmosphere through all the seasons of the year. [18] Next to the shrine to the east are the

nearest Ethiopian tribes; to the south they face Arab peoples called Tro-
godytes, whose territory extends right to the Red Sea; [19] to the west live other
Ethiopians called Simui; and to the north are the Nasamones, a tribe of the
Syrtes who make a living by looting ships (they haunt the shoreline and their
knowledge of the shallows enables them to seize vessels stranded by the tide).

[20] The people who inhabit the wooded area are called Hammonii; they live
in scattered huts, and regard the centre of the wood, which is encircled by
three walls, as a citadel. [21] The first rampart surrounded the old palace of
their kings; behind the second lived their wives, children and concubines,
and the oracle of the god is also in this area; the outermost fortifications were
the homes of the palace attendants and bodyguards. [22] There is also a second
wood of Ammon with a fountain called "The Water of the Sun' at its centre.
At sunrise it runs lukewarm, and yet at midday, despite the inordinate heat,
it is cold, warming up towards evening and growing boiling hot at midnight.
Then, as dawn approaches, it loses much of its nocturnal heat until at daybreak it drops back to its original lukewarm temperature. [23] The image worshipped as divine does not have the appearance commonly accorded deities
by artists; it most resembles a navel and is composed of an emerald and other
jewels. [24] When an oracular response is sought, priests carry this along in a
gilded boat from which a large number of silver cups hang on both sides, and
married and unmarried women follow singing in traditional fashion some
artless song by which they believe an infallible answer is elicited from Jupiter.

[25] On this occasion, as the king approached, he was addressed as "son" by
the oldest of the priests, who claimed that this title was bestowed on him by
his father Jupiter. Forgetting his mortal state, Alexander said he accepted and
acknowledged the title, [26] and he proceeded to ask whether he was fated to
rule over the entire world. The priest, who was as ready as anyone else to
flatter him, answered that he was going to rule over all the earth. [27] After
this Alexander went on to inquire whether his father's murderers had all
received their punishment. The priest's answer was that no harm could come
to his father from anybody's wrongdoing, but that as far as Philip was concerned all had paid the penalty; and he added that Alexander himself would
remain undefeated until he went to join the gods. [28] Alexander thereupon
offered sacrifice, presented gifts both to the priests and to the god, and also
allowed his friends to consult Jupiter on their own account. Their only question was whether the god authorized their according divine honours to their
king, and this, too, so the priest replied, would be agreeable to Jupiter.

[29] Someone making a sound and honest judgement of the oracle's reliability might well have found these responses disingenuous, but fortune generally makes those whom she has compelled to put their trust in her alone
more thirsty for glory than capable of coping with it. [30] So Alexander did not
just permit but actually ordered the title "Jupiter's son" to be accorded to
himself, and while he wanted such a title to add lustre to his achievements
he really detracted from them. [31] Furthermore, although it is true that the
Macedonians were accustomed to monarchy, they lived in the shadow of

uriant with the foliage of palm trees; and everywhere were flowing waters and the sound of rivulets. Those fountains, though, are far different in character from those seen in our lands: for they are scaldingly hot but grow gradually cooler from midnight until midday when they become as cold as snow; then growing warm again they increase in temperature until midnight. They also produce a salt which glitters as bright as rock-crystal and has a most pleasing taste as if it were skilfully spiced; the specimen is smooth and egg-shaped, a little larger than a goose's egg, longer than it is wide, and entirely transparent. Then finally it takes the place of incense, serving as salted grain for one performing sacrifice, and is more effective in producing the required odours.

　22　Confirmed by the oracle's assurance of his divine parentage, Alexander returned thence to Memphis . . .

3(d)　Valerius Maximus 9.5 ext 1

The valour and good fortune of King Alexander led to his excesses, his pride growing in three quite distinct phases. With disdain for Philip he claimed Jupiter Hammon as his father . . . with contempt for the human condition he aspired to that of the gods; and he was not ashamed to conceal the fact that he was the son of a man, the citizen of a state and a human being.

Alexander's deification

3(e)　Aelian, Varia Historia 2.19

After defeating Darius and making himself master of the Persian empire, Alexander was very pleased with himself, and because of the success that had attended him he felt like a god. He therefore sent an order to the Greeks to take a vote making him divine. It was an absurd order; he would not get what he did not have from nature by simply asking for it from human beings. Various states passed various decrees, but the Spartans' was worded as follows: "Since Alexander wants to be a god, let him be a god." It was a Laconic comment, quite typical of their country, which the Spartans used to expose Alexander's stupidity.

3(f)　Aelian, Varia Historia 5.12

I cannot help liking what the Athenians did. At a meeting of the assembly, the Athenian Demades came forward with a motion for Alexander to be regarded as the thirteenth god. The people could not tolerate such extreme impiety. They fined Demades a hundred talents for setting Alexander among the Olympians when he was just a mortal.

3(g)   Aelian, Varia Historia 9.37

When Alexander thought he was a god, Anaxarchus, who was nicknamed "Happy", laughed at him. Once, when Alexander was ill, his doctor prescribed that gruel be prepared for him. Anaxarchus laughed, saying: "So, our god's prognosis depends on a cup of gruel!"

3(h)   Plutarch, Moralia 219e
(= Sayings of the Spartans, Damis)

Faced with the communication concerning the resolution on Alexander's deification, Damis said: "Let us agree that Alexander be called a god, if that's what he wants."

X Alexander and the Macedonians: Disaffection, Conspiracy, and Mutiny

General Account of Alexander's Savagery

1(a)   Justin 12.6.1–17

. . . Alexander invited his friends to a banquet on a feast day. [2] Here, the topic of Philip's achievements arose in their drunken conversation and Alexander began to set himself above his father and to praise to the skies his own magnificent exploits, gaining the acquiescence of most of the guests. [3] One of the senior men, Cleitus, confident of his position in the first rank of the king's friends, began to defend Philip's memory and to praise his achievements, which so annoyed the king that he grabbed a spear from a guard and murdered Cleitus at the table. [4] Revelling in the bloodshed he proceeded to taunt the dead Cleitus with his vindication of Philip and his eulogy of the latter's military ability. [5] Then, sated with blood, his temper abated and anger gave way to reflection. He considered who it was he had killed and his motive for the killing, and now he began to regret his action, [6] sorry that praise of his father had roused him to a pitch of anger that outright personal abuse would not have merited and that he had killed an elderly and innocent friend in a setting of feasting and drinking. [7] As violently shaken by remorse as he was earlier by anger, he wished to die. [8] First, bursting into tears, he put his arms around the dead man, touched his wounds and, as if Cleitus could hear, admitted to him that he had been out of his mind. Then he seized a weapon, turned it on himself and would have carried out the deed but for the intervention of his friends. [9] His longing for death persisted even throughout the days that followed. [10] For his regret was intensified as he remembered his own nurse, who was Cleitus' sister; even in her absence it was she who aroused in him the deepest shame [11] as he reflected on how despicably she had been recompensed for nursing him – after spending his infancy in her arms he was now, a man and victorious, repaying her with death instead of kindness. [12] Then he considered how much idle rumour and animosity he had created in his own army as well as among the conquered nations, how much fear and resentment of himself amongst his other friends,[13] and into what a bitter tragedy he had turned his own dinner party – making himself as terrifying a figure at dinner as when he stood armed in battle. [14] His thoughts then turned to Parmenion and Philotas, to his cousin Amyntas, to his murdered stepmother and brothers, to Attalus, Eurylochus, Pausanias and the other Macedonian chieftains he had eliminated. [15] Thus it was that he went without food for four days, until he was won over by the entreaties of the troops who as one begged him not to let his grief for a single man's death destroy them all; [16] for, they said, after leading them to the last frontier of barbarian territory he would be abandoning them amongst hostile tribes embittered by conflict. [17] The entreaties of the philosopher Callisthenes proved especially effective; he was on intimate terms with Alexander because they had both been pupils of Aristotle, and he had also been invited by the king to be the author of the latter's chronicles.

Alexander the Lyncestian

Alexander son of Aëropus was the son-in-law of Antipater (the regent of Macedon) and brother of the convicted regicides, Heromenes and Arrhabaeus. Whether he favoured the plot against Philip, we do not know, but he avoided punishment by being the first to declare Alexander "King." Initially, he was assigned the generalship (*strategia*) of Thrace, but in 334 he accompanied Alexander in an unspecified capacity. After the battle of the Granicus River, he replaced Calas son of Harpalus as commander of the Thessalian cavalry, and soon afterwards he was suspected of plotting against the king's life. Since he was an adherent of a very powerful political faction, the king had to deal with him quickly and carefully (see Heckel 2003). The view that he was "framed" by Alexander the Great (Badian 2000b) will persuade only those who are predisposed to "conspiracy theory."

2(a)   Arrian 1.25.1–5, 9–10

Alexander was still engaged in the environs of Phaselis when a report was brought to him of a plot hatched by Alexander son of Aëropus, who was one of the king's companions and, most significantly, was at that time commander of the Thessalian cavalry. This Alexander was also the brother of Heromenes and Arrhabaeus, both of whom were party to Philip's murder. [2] In fact, for the moment, Alexander dismissed the charge against him, for he had been one of the first of the king's *hetairoi* to come to him after Philip's death, putting on his cuirass and accompanying him to the palace. Later Alexander kept him close in a position of honour, even despatching him to Thrace as commander-in-chief, and when the master of Thessalian cavalry, Calas, was sent abroad to take up a satrapy, the king gave Alexander the command of the Thessalian horse. The details of the plot were reported as follows.

[3] Amyntas deserted to Darius, bringing to him certain written communications from the Lyncestian Alexander, whereupon Darius sent to the coast Sisines, a Persian who was one of his confidants. The justification for the journey was a visit to Atizyes, satrap of Phrygia, but the truth of the matter was that he was going to meet the Lyncestian. He was going to provide him with guarantees that Darius would make him king of Macedon, and in addition give him a thousand talents of gold, if he killed King Alexander.

[4] Sisines was apprehended by Parmenion, to whom he divulged the aim of his mission. Parmenion then sent him under guard to King Alexander who was told the same story by the man. The king assembled his *hetairoi* and put before them the question of what decision should be made with regard to the Lyncestian. [5] His *hetairoi* felt that the king had made a mistake earlier in assigning to a man of questionable loyalty the strongest of their cavalry. He should now quickly get rid of him before he became too familiar with the Thessalians and fomented revolution with them ...[1]

[9] ... Alexander sent Amphoterus son of Alexander, a brother of Craterus, to Parmenion, and with him he sent some men from Perge to act as his guides. Amphoterus put on native clothing so that he would not be recognized on the journey, and he reached Parmenion without being detected. [10] He did not bring a despatch from the king – the decision was made not to write anything openly on a matter of this kind – but he did report verbally the instructions he had been given. The Lyncestian was accordingly arrested and put in chains.

2(b)   Justin 11.2.1–2

Alexander's primary concern was for his father's funeral, at which his first instruction was that all involved in the assassination be put to death at the tomb of his father. [2] The only person he spared was Alexander of Lyncestis, the brother ⟨of the assassins⟩,[2] for he wished to preserve in that man's person the good omen for his reign, since it was the Lyncestian who had first saluted him as king.

2(c)   Diodorus Siculus 17.32.1–2

In a letter to the king, Alexander's mother gave him some generally useful advice, and in particular warned him to be on his guard against Alexander

---

1 Sections 6–8 relate an omen at Halicarnassus that was thought to warn Alexander of danger from within.

2 Without the insertion of these words, the text would read "Alexander's brother."

the Lyncestian. This man was possessed of exceptional courage and was full of ambition; he accompanied the king and enjoyed his confidence as one of his *philoi*. [2] Since there were many other credible pieces of evidence combining to support the charge, the Lyncestian was arrested, clapped in irons and put under guard so that he could face trial.

2 (d)   Diodorus Siculus 17.80.2

In the same category as this[3] is the case of Alexander the Lyncestian. He stood accused of plotting against the king and had spent three years in prison, his judgement delayed because of his family ties to Antipater. On that occasion, however, he was brought to trial before the Macedonians and, at a loss for words for his own defence, was put to death.

2 (e)   Quintus Curtius Rufus 7.1.5–9

Then Atarrhias began to make what was no doubt a pre-arranged demand that Alexander the Lyncestian be brought before them (the man who, long before Philotas,[4] had planned to assassinate the king). [6] This Alexander had been denounced by two informers, as I stated above,[5] and was now in the third year of imprisonment. It was thought certain that he had also conspired with Pausanias to murder Philip, but the fact that he had been the first to salute Alexander as king had gained him a reprieve, though not an acquittal. [7] Moreover, the pleas of the Lyncestian's father-in-law, Antipater, also served to reduce the king's warranted anger. But the festering resentment against him broke out afresh, for anxiety over the current crisis began to revive memories of the former one. [8] Alexander was therefore brought from confinement and told to plead his case. Although he had had all of three years to rehearse his defence, he was faltering and nervous, deploying few of the arguments which he had stored up in his mind, until finally his very thought processes, not just his memory, failed him. [9] No one doubted that his discomposure betokened a guilty conscience rather than a defective memory. Accordingly some of the men standing next to him ran him through with their lances while he still grappled with his loss of memory.

---

3   The case of Philotas.

4   The trial of Alexander the Lyncestian followed the conviction of Philotas on charges of treason (330 BC).

5   Curtius appears to have discussed the arrest of Alexander the Lyncestian in the lost second book of his history.

The Elimination of Philotas and Parmenion

One of the most troublesome episodes in the history of Alexander is the execution of Philotas on charges of conspiracy and the subsequent death of his father,
Parmenion. That Philotas himself was actively conspiring against the king is unlikely,
and the evidence shows only that he was guilty of negligence, for failing to bring information concerning a conspiracy to the king's attention. For the events and the roles
of Alexander and his young commanders, see Badian (1960a, 2000b), Heckel (1977,
1992a, 2003), Rubinsohn (1977), and Goukowsky (1978: 38–41; 1981: 118–34).

3(a)   Arrian 3.26

It was at this point that Alexander also came to learn of the conspiracy of
Philotas, son of Parmenion. Ptolemy and Aristobulus both say that it had
already been reported to the king on an earlier occasion, in Egypt, but that
Alexander found it implausible because of his long-standing friendship with
the man, the honour he had shown Philotas' father Parmenion, and the trust
he had placed in Philotas himself.

[2] Ptolemy son of Lagus says that Philotas was hauled before the Macedonians, where Alexander roundly accused him and Philotas presented his
defence. But then the men who had laid the information about the plot came
forward and refuted his testimony, and that of his accomplices, with convincing evidence. In particular, they pointed out that, on his own admission,
Philotas had learned of some plot being hatched against Alexander but had, it
was shown, kept quiet about it to the king, despite visiting his tent twice a day.

[3] Philotas was speared to death by the Macedonians, as were all the others
implicated in the plot. In the case of Parmenion, however, one of the *hetairoi*,
Polydamas, was sent out to him, and he carried a letter from Alexander to
the generals in Media, Cleander, Sitalces and Menidas, for these had been
given positions in the force commanded by Parmenion. [4] It was by these that
Parmenion was killed. Possibly Alexander thought it unlikely that when
Philotas was hatching the plot Parmenion would not have had a hand in his
son's scheme; or possibly, if he had no part in it, it was simply dangerous for
Parmenion to remain alive when his son had been eliminated. For Parmenion
had enjoyed great esteem, both with Alexander personally and with the rest
of the army, and not only the Macedonian troops but with the foreign soldiers, as well . . .

3(b)   Plutarch, Alexander 48.1–49.13

Philotas, son of Parmenion, enjoyed great distinction amongst the
Macedonians, for he had a reputation for courage and endurance, and only

Alexander surpassed him in generosity and camaraderie. [2] There is, at any rate, a story that one of his intimates asked him for money, and Philotas issued instructions for it to be given to him; then, when his steward said the cash was not available, he retorted: "What do you mean? Don't you even have a cup or a piece of clothing?"

[3] But Philotas also had self-importance and great financial resources, and a personal fastidiousness and way of life that, found in an ordinary man, aroused resentment. At that particular time, too, his high-handed and swaggering manner was particularly tasteless; in fact, he had no charisma, and cut a rather gauche and affected figure. He thus provoked suspicion and antipathy, to the extent that even Parmenion once said to him: "Son, please tone yourself down."

[4] As it happened, incriminating remarks about Philotas had been passed along to Alexander for quite some time. When Darius had been defeated in Cilicia and his treasure was subsequently captured at Damascus, a large number of prisoners were taken to the Macedonian camp. Amongst these was found a woman called Antigone who came from Pydna and who was pleasing to the eye. She fell to Philotas. [5] He chattered on to her, making the usual opinionated and boastful comments a young man makes to his mistress, especially as the drink flows; and he declared that the greatest exploits belonged to himself and his father. Alexander he styled a mere youngster who enjoyed only nominal power, and that thanks to them. [6] These remarks the woman reported to one of her friends, and he, as usually happens, passed them on to another, until the story came to Craterus. Craterus then took hold of the woman and brought her secretly to Alexander. [7] The king heard her out and told her to continue her relationship with Philotas, and to come and report back to him whatever she learned from him.

49   And so Philotas was unaware that a trap was being laid for him. He continued his meetings with Antigone, during which he would let drop many impulsive and boastful comments and many remarks disrespectful of the king. [2] Much incriminating evidence against Philotas was now coming to Alexander, but he still suffered in silence and held back, either through confidence in Parmenion's good will towards him, or because he feared the reputation and power the two men commanded.

[3] Now at that time a Macedonian called Limnus,[6] from Chalaestra, was hatching a plot against Alexander, and he invited Nicomachus, one of the young boys – Limnus was infatuated with him – to join him in the enterprise. [4] Nicomachus did not accept the invitation, but he informed his brother Cebalinus of the proposed coup. Cebalinus then went to Philotas, telling him to bring the two of them before Alexander as they had urgent and important matters to communicate to him. [5] Philotas, however, for some

---

6   Thus the MSS. The *lambda* (λ) and *delta* (δ) are easily confused. Elsewhere the name is Dimnus or Dymnus.

reason – what it was is unknown – would not take them, claiming the king was involved in more important matters. And this he did on two occasions.

[6] The brothers now began to suspect Philotas and so they turned to somebody else, by whom they were taken to see Alexander. They began by recounting the Limnus affair, and then gradually revealed Philotas' failure to attend to them on the two occasions. [7] And this cut Alexander to the quick. A man was sent to fetch Limnus, but this man killed the conspirator when he tried to resist arrest. Alexander was even more unnerved by this because he thought the proof of the plot had slipped through his fingers. [8] He felt bitterly angry with Philotas, and he brought in those who had long held grudges against him. These now openly declared that the king had been too complacent in assuming that Limnus, a man from Chalaestra, had independently taken on such a daring act. [9] No, they said, he was just a pawn, an instrument employed by a greater authority, and the source of the plot was to be sought amongst those who had most to gain from it being concealed.

[10] The king was by this time giving his ear to such innuendo and insinuations, and these people then proceeded to pile accusation on accusation against Philotas. [11] He was apprehended and interrogated, the *hetairoi* being present at the torture session and Alexander listening from behind a curtain drawn between them. [12] They say that Philotas resorted to pathetic and abject wails of entreaty to Hephaestion, and Alexander said: "Did you attempt such a major coup, weakling and coward that you are?"

[13] Immediately after Philotas' execution Alexander also sent men into Media and had Parmenion killed. Parmenion was a man who had shared many of Philip's exploits and, amongst the older *philoi* of Alexander, he was the only, or at least the most vigorous, proponent of his crossing to Asia. Of his three sons he had seen two die on the campaign before this, and now he had been despatched along with the third.

3(c)　Quintus Curtius Rufus 6.7–11

Alexander was not merely undefeated by foreign assailants but secure from attack, when after eight days back in camp he became the object of an internal conspiracy. [2] Dymnus, a man of slight influence or favour with the king, had a passionate infatuation for a catamite called Nicomachus; he was totally devoted to the boy, whose favours he alone enjoyed. [3] Practically beside himself, as one could see from his face, Dymnus went with the young man into a temple, with no one else present, saying to him first that what he had to tell him were secrets that were not to be divulged. [4] Nicomachus was now on tenterhooks, and Dymnus begged him in the name of their mutual affection and the pledges each had made of their feelings to swear on oath to remain silent about his disclosures. [5] Nicomachus did not think that Dymnus would tell him anything he would be obliged to divulge even if it meant perjury on his part, so he took the oath by the gods of the place. [6] Then Dymnus revealed that a plot had been hatched against the king which was to be executed in two days' time, and that he was involved in the plan along with some courageous and distinguished men.

[7] On hearing this, the youth resolutely denied that he had sworn to be party to treason and asserted that he could not be constrained by any religious consideration to cover up a crime. [8] Demented with both passion and fear, Dymnus grasped the catamite's right hand. In tears, he first begged him to take part in planning and executing the plot [9] and then, if he could not bring himself to concur with that, at least not to give him away. He said that he had given Nicomachus ample proof of his devotion by his behaviour towards him in general, but now especially by entrusting his life to one of untested loyalty. [10] Finally, when Nicomachus persisted in expressing abhorrence of the crime, he resorted to threats of death to deter him, telling him that the conspirators' noble enterprise would start with Nicomachus' assassination. [11] Then, alternately calling him an effeminate coward and a traitor to his lover, and making him lavish promises (sometimes adding one of royal power), he kept working on a character that utterly recoiled from so heinous a crime. [12] Next, drawing his sword, he put it first to Nicomachus' throat, then to his own, both entreating him and threatening him, and finally he extracted from him a promise not just of silence but even of cooperation. [13] In fact, Nicomachus possessed the steadfast resolve appropriate to a clean-living man; he had not wavered from his earlier decision but pretended that out of love for Dymnus he could deny him nothing. [14] He now proceeded to inquire about the identity of the accomplices in this important enterprise, saying that the quality of the people involved in so significant an undertaking made all the difference. [15] Crazed as much by love as by guilt, Dymnus offered him both thanks and congratulations on unhesitatingly joining a brave group of young men, comprising the bodyguard Demetrius,[7] Peucolaus and Nicanor. To these Dymnus added the names of Aphobetus, Iolaus, Dioxenus, Archepolis and Amyntas.

[16] Following this conversation Nicomachus relayed what he had heard to his brother, whose name was Cebalinus. The two decided Nicomachus should remain in the tent in case, by entering the royal quarters, he made the conspirators aware that they had been betrayed, for he was not an intimate of the king's. [17] Cebalinus himself stood before the entrance to the royal tent, not being permitted to proceed further, and waited for someone of the first order of Alexander's friends who would take him in to the king. [18] As it happened, only Parmenion's son Philotas had remained in the royal quarters after the others had been dismissed; why he did so is not known. To him Cebalinus, noticeably in great agitation, disclosed in confused speech what

---

7 His role is corroborated by Arrian, who says that he was not arrested (and presumably executed) until they reached the land of Ariaspians (near Lake Seistan).

he had learned from his brother, and insisted that it be reported to the king without delay. [19] Philotas commended him and straightway went in to Alexander but, after engaging him in lengthy conversation on other matters, he reported none of the information he had received from Cebalinus. [20] Towards evening the young man caught Philotas at the entrance to the royal tent as he was on his way out, and asked if he had carried out his request. [21] Philotas claimed Alexander had had no time to talk to him and then went on his way. The next day Cebalinus was there when Philotas came to the royal quarters and, as he went in, he reminded him of the matter he had communicated to him the day before. Philotas replied that he was seeing to it – but even then he failed to disclose to the king what he had heard.

[22] Cebalinus had begun to suspect him. Thinking it inadvisable to accost him again, he gave the information of the villainous plot to a young nobleman called Metron who had charge of the armoury. [23] Metron hid Cebalinus in the armoury and immediately revealed the informer's allegations to the king, who happened to be taking a bath. [24] Alexander despatched guards to arrest Dymnus and went into the armoury. Cebalinus was transported with joy. "You are safe!" he said. "I see you delivered from the hands of criminals!" [25] Alexander then inquired into the pertinent details and, after he was given a coherent account, made a point of asking how many days it had been since Nicomachus brought him his information. [26] When Cebalinus admitted it had been two days, Alexander ordered him to be clapped in irons because he thought that the fact that he had taken so long to report what he had heard meant that his loyalty was questionable. [27] Cebalinus, however, began to cry out that he had run to Philotas the very moment he had heard of the plot, and that Philotas had learned the details from him. [28] The king asked again if he had approached Philotas, if he had insisted that they come to Alexander. When Cebalinus persistently reaffirmed his story, Alexander held his hands up to the sky and, bursting into tears, bemoaned the fact that he had been so repaid by one who had formerly been the dearest of his friends.

[29] Dymnus, meanwhile, well aware of the reason for his summons by the king, dealt himself a mortal wound with the sword he happened to be wearing, but guards rushed up to restrain him and he was carried into the royal quarters. [30] Alexander looked at him. "Dymnus," he said, "what is the vicious crime I have plotted against you to justify your decision that Philotas deserves royal power more than I myself?" But Dymnus had already lost the power of speech. He groaned, turned his face away from the king's eyes, and immediately collapsed and died.

[31] The king ordered Philotas to the royal quarters. "Cebalinus deserved the supreme penalty," he said, "if for two days he covered up a plot that had been hatched against my life. But he shifts the guilt for his crime to Philotas by his claim that he passed the information on to him immediately. [32] Because of your closer ties of friendship with me, such suppression of information on your part is all the more reprehensible, and it is my opinion that conduct such as this suits Cebalinus more than it does Philotas. You now have a judge

who is on your side – if there is any way of clearing yourself of what should not have happened."

[33] Philotas was not in the slightest alarmed, if his emotions could be judged by his expression. In reply he said that, yes, Cebalinus had indeed reported to him his conversation with the catamite, but Philotas had set no store by it since the source was so unreliable – he feared that reporting a quarrel between a male prostitute and his lover would make him a laughing stock. [34] However, Dymnus' suicide now revealed that the facts, whatever they were, should not have been suppressed. Philotas put his arms around the king and proceeded to entreat him to consider his past record rather than his present error – which, anyway, involved merely keeping silent, not committing an act. [35] It would be difficult to say whether the king believed him or kept his anger concealed deep in his heart. He offered Philotas his right hand as a sign of reconciliation, and said that in his opinion it was a case of information not being taken seriously rather than being deliberately suppressed.

8   Even so, Alexander called a meeting of his friends, without inviting Philotas, and ordered Nicomachus to be brought before it. [2] The latter repeated the whole story which he had brought to the king. Now Craterus, being an especially close friend of the king's, was consequently hostile to Philotas because of their jockeying for position, [3] and he was not unaware that Philotas' excessively boastful talk about his courage and his services had often grated on the ears of Alexander, who therefore entertained the notion that while he was no criminal he was certainly self-willed. [4] Believing there would be no better opportunity for crushing his opponent, Craterus masked his personal animosity with feigned loyalty to Alexander and declared: "I wish you had also discussed this matter with us in the beginning! [5] If you were set on pardoning Philotas, we would have urged you to keep him ignorant of how much he owed you. Rather that than that he now have cause to think more about his own danger – since he has been taken to the brink of death – than about your generosity. You see, he will always be able to plot against you, but you will not always be able to pardon Philotas. [6] And you have no reason to suppose that a man whose daring has been so great can be changed by a pardon: he knows that those who have exhausted someone's clemency can expect no more in future. [7] But even supposing penitence or your generosity induced him to take no further action, I for my part am sure that his father Parmenion will not be happy at being indebted to you for his son's life – he is the leader of a mighty army and, because of his long-standing influence with your men, holds a position of great authority not much inferior to yours. [8] Some acts of kindness we resent. A man is ashamed to admit that he has deserved execution; the alternative is to foster the impression that he has been dealt an injury rather than granted a reprieve. So you can be sure that you must fight for your life against the men in question. [9] The enemies we are about to pursue are still numerous enough. Protect yourself against enemies within our ranks. Eliminate those and I fear nothing from the foreigner."

Such were Craterus' words, [10] and the others were also in no doubt that Philotas would not have suppressed evidence of the conspiracy if he had not been the ringleader or an accomplice. For, they reasoned, any loyal and well-intentioned person, even if he were of the lowest order and not a friend of Alexander, would have run immediately to the king on hearing the charges that had been brought to Philotas. [11] But the son of Parmenion did not do that, commander of the cavalry and confidant of all the king's secrets though he was, not even when he had before him the example of Cebalinus who had reported to Philotas what he had learned from his brother. He had even pretended that the king had had no time to talk to him, intending thereby to prevent the informer from looking for a second go-between. [12] Nicomachus had rushed to unburden his conscience in spite of the sacred obligation of his oath; Philotas, who had spent almost the entire day on frivolous amusements, was reluctant to insert into his lengthy and possibly inconsequential conversation a word or two vital to the king's survival. [13] But, if he had felt no confidence in such a report from mere boys, why then would he have made the affair drag on for two days as if he believed their disclosures? He ought to have sent Cebalinus away if he rejected his charges. [14] Being brave is appropriate when it is a question of one's own risk, but when there is concern for the life of the king one should be credulous and pay attention even to men who bring false information.

[15] So the decision was unanimous that Philotas should be interrogated under torture to force him to name his accomplices in the crime. Then Alexander dismissed them, telling them to remain silent about their decision and, in order not to betray any hint of the course of action they had recently adopted, he had marching orders issued for the following day. [16] Philotas was even invited to a banquet, which was to be his last, and the king was able not merely to dine with the man he had condemned but even to engage him in friendly conversation. [17] Then, at the time of the second watch, when the lights were out, some of the king's friends, namely Hephaestion, Craterus, Coenus and Erigyius, met in the royal quarters with a few men, along with Perdiccas and Leonnatus from the bodyguard. Orders were issued by these for the men on guard at the king's tent to keep watch under arms. [18] Cavalrymen had already been posted at all the entrances to the camp with orders also to block the roads so that no one could slip off secretly to Parmenion, who at that time was governor of Media and in command of strong forces.

[19] Atarrhias had now entered the royal tent with 300 armed men. He was given ten attendants, each accompanied by ten armour-bearers [20] and, while these were sent in groups to arrest the other conspirators, Atarrhias and his 300 were despatched to Philotas. With 50 of his best young men around him he set about forcing the door, which was closed, having ordered the others to cordon off the house entirely so that Philotas could not slip away by a secret entrance. [21] Philotas was in a deep slumber, his relaxation the result of an easy conscience or else of exhaustion, and he was still half-asleep when Atarrhias grasped him. [22] Finally he shook off the drowsiness and, as the

shackles were placed on him, said: "Your Majesty, the bitter hatred of my enemies has triumphed over your kindness." This was all he said before they covered his head and took him into the royal quarters. [23] The next day the king gave orders for a general assembly in arms.

Some 6,000 soldiers had arrived and a crowd of camp followers and servants added to the total in the royal tent. [24] Philotas was hidden by a column of men-at-arms so that he could not be seen by the crowd until the king had addressed the men. [25] In capital cases it was a long-established Macedonian practice for the king to conduct the trial while the army (or the commons in peace-time) acted as jury, and the position of the king counted for nothing unless his influence had been substantial prior to the trial. [26] So now, at the start, the corpse of Dymnus was brought in, the majority of the crowd having no idea of his plot or of how he had died.

9 Alexander marched into the assembly. His expression betrayed the anguish he felt, and the gloominess of his friends had charged the affair with considerable anticipation. [2] The king stood for a long while with eyes fixed on the ground, looking dazed and nonplussed. Finally he pulled himself together and said: "Men! I was almost snatched from you by a criminal conspiracy: it is thanks to the gods' providence and mercy that I still live. And the awe-inspiring sight of your gathering has made me feel even more angry with the traitors because my first pleasure in life – no, my only pleasure – is that I am still able to repay all the brave men who have deserved well of me."

[3] Groans from the men interrupted him, and tears welled up in every eye. "I shall stir far deeper emotions in your hearts when I reveal to you the instigators of such villainy," the king continued. "I still shudder to mention them and I keep from naming them as though it were possible to save them. [4] But the memory of my former intimacy with them must be expunged; a conspiracy plotted by treacherous citizens of ours must be exposed. How could I remain silent about such an outrage? Parmenion, despite his age and obligations from all the benefits he received from me and from my father; although he is the oldest of all my friends – it was he who offered to head this monstrous crime. [5] His accomplice was Philotas, who suborned Peucolaus, Demetrius and Dymnus, whose body you see before you, and other equally insane individuals to assassinate me." [6] Roars of pained outrage broke forth throughout the gathering, as typically happens in a crowd, and especially in a crowd of soldiers, when it is fired with enthusiasm or anger. [7] Nicomachus, Metron and Cebalinus were now brought in. They repeated their various accounts, but the evidence of none of them marked Philotas as an accomplice in the crime and so, after the initial outburst of indignation from the crowd, the statements of the witnesses were received in silence.

[8] Then Alexander said: "So what do you think were the intentions of a man who suppressed the actual information he was given about this affair? That there was some substance to it is shown by Dymnus' death. [9] When the matter was still uncorroborated, Cebalinus reported it, undeterred by fear of torture, and Metron lost no time at all in unburdening himself of his infor-

mation – going as far as to break into my bathroom. [10] Only Philotas feared nothing and believed nothing. What a courageous fellow! Would a man like that be distressed at the thought of his king's peril? Would he alter his expression or feel anxiety as he listened to the bearer of such momentous news? [11] Obviously some criminal intention lurks in his silence: it was greedy anticipation of the throne that sent his thoughts speeding towards the vilest of crimes. His father governs Media and, because of my support, Philotas himself exercised great influence with many of the officers – so that his aspirations exceed his ability to fulfil them. [12] My childless state, the fact that I have no offspring, also arouses his contempt. But Philotas is wrong. In you I have children, parents, kinsmen, and while you are safe I cannot be childless."

[13] He then read out a letter which had been intercepted, written by Parmenion to his sons Nicanor and Philotas. But it did not really contain evidence of some dangerous plot. Its gist was as follows: [14] "First of all take care of yourselves and then of your people – that is how we shall accomplish our purpose." [15] The king added that the letter was worded in this way so that if it reached his sons it could be understood by those involved in the plot whereas, intercepted, its meaning would escape those who were ignorant of it.

[16] Alexander continued: "Dymnus, you will say, did not name Philotas despite designating the others involved in the crime. That is not evidence of Philotas' innocence but of his standing: he is so feared by the people who can betray him that, even when they confess their own guilt, they withhold his name. But Philotas' own record accuses him. [17] When my cousin Amyntas engineered a treacherous plot against me in Macedonia, it was Philotas who made himself his ally and his accomplice. It was Philotas who gave his sister in marriage to Attalus, the worst enemy I have ever had! [18] In view of our close association and friendship, I had written to him of the oracular response of Jupiter Ammon. It was Philotas who had the effrontery to reply that, while he congratulated me on being received among the gods, he nevertheless felt pity for people who would have to live under a man who was more than human. [19] These are all indications that he has long been alienated from me and become envious of my fame. I have kept them locked in my heart for as long as I could, men, thinking that to bring down in my own estimation men to whose careers I had made such great contributions was like ripping away part of myself. [20] But it is no longer mere words that call for punishment. Unbridled speech has led to the sword – which, if you believe me, Philotas has sharpened against me or which, if you believe him, he has permitted to be sharpened against me. [21] Where am I going to turn, men? To whom am I to entrust my life? I made Philotas sole commander of the cavalry, the pick of my troops, the best of our young noblemen. To his loyalty and his protection I have entrusted my life, my hopes, and my victory. [22] I have promoted his father to the same eminence in which you have placed me; I have set under his command and authority the richest of all countries, Media, along with many thousands of our citizens and allies. Where I looked for help

I found only danger. [23] How happy should I have been to die in battle, a prey to my enemy rather than a victim of a fellow citizen! As it is, I have been saved from the only perils I feared, only to face others which I should not have had to fear. [24] Men, you keep on asking me to look after myself, and now it is within your power to help me follow your advice. I take refuge in your hands and your weapons. To survive against your will I do not wish; but even in accordance with your will, survival is impossible unless you avenge me."

[25] Alexander then ordered Philotas to be brought in with his hands tied behind his back and his head covered with an old cloak. There was clearly an emotional reaction to the pitiful condition of a man who shortly before had been regarded with envy. [26] The men had seen him as cavalry commander on the previous day, and they knew he had attended the king's banquet. Suddenly they saw him not merely on trial but condemned – even in fetters. [27] They also began to reflect on the misfortunes of Parmenion: a great general and an illustrious citizen, he had recently lost two sons, Hector and Nicanor, and now in his absence he would be on trial with the only son his calamitous fate had left him. [28] Consequently, since the assembly was inclining towards pity, Amyntas, one of the king's generals, stirred it up again with a speech attacking Philotas. They had been betrayed to the barbarians, he said. None of them would have returned to his wife and his parents, but they would have been like a decapitated body devoid of life, without a name, an object of ridicule to the enemy in a foreign land. [29] Amyntas' words were not at all as pleasing to the king as he had hoped – reminding the men of their wives and country merely decreased their enthusiasm for tackling the jobs that remained.

[30] Coenus spoke next and, although he had married a sister of Philotas, he attacked him more fiercely than anyone, loudly proclaiming him a traitor to his king, country and army. [31] He then picked up a stone which happened to be lying before his feet to throw at Philotas – from a wish to save him from torture, many thought – but the king stayed his hand, declaring that the defendant must first be given an opportunity to make his defence and that he would not permit the case to proceed otherwise. [32] Philotas was then instructed to make his defence. Distracted and nonplussed, either from a guilty conscience or because of the magnitude of his peril, he did not dare to lift his eyes or open his mouth. [33] Then he burst into tears and fainted into the arms of the man holding him. He gradually recovered both his breath and his voice and, using his cloak to wipe his eyes, seemed to be about to speak. [34] Alexander fixed his gaze on him. "The Macedonians are going to judge your case," he said. "Please state whether you will use your native language before them."

[35] "Besides the Macedonians," replied Philotas, "there are many present who, I think, will find what I am going to say easier to understand if I use the language you yourself have been using, your purpose, I believe, being only to enable more people to understand you."

[36] Then the king said: "Do you see how offensive Philotas finds even his native language? He alone feels an aversion to learning it. But let him speak as he pleases – only remember that he is as contemptuous of our way of life as he is of our language." So saying, Alexander left the meeting.

10   Then Philotas spoke. "When a man is innocent, finding words is easy," he said, "but when he is in trouble, limiting them is difficult. [2] I am caught between a clear conscience and calamitous misfortune, not knowing how to find terms to match both my feelings and my circumstances. [3] The man who can best judge my case is not present, though why he should refuse to hear me himself I simply cannot fathom. After hearing both sides, he is as much at liberty to condemn as to acquit me whereas, if he does not hear both, I cannot be absolved by him in his absence – not after being declared guilty by him when he was present.

[4] "The defence of a man in fetters is not merely useless; it also engenders ill-feeling, because the defendant appears not to be giving his judge information but to be finding fault with him. Even so I shall not forfeit my case, however I am allowed to conduct my defence, nor shall I foster the impression that I have added my own vote to the conviction.

[5] "I do not understand, quite frankly, of what crime I stand accused. None of the conspirators names me; Nicomachus said nothing about me; and Cebalinus could have known no more than what he had been told. [6] And yet Alexander believes I headed the conspiracy. Then could Dymnus have omitted to mention the man whose lead he followed? Especially when my name *should* have been included, even falsely, at the time when Nicomachus was asking Dymnus about his confederates – should have been included to persuade Nicomachus when overtures were being made to him. [7] Now Dymnus' motive for omitting my name when the conspiracy was uncovered was not that he might be seen to be protecting a confederate. When he confessed to Nicomachus who, he believed, would keep secret his part in the affair, he identified all the others but still omitted my name and mine alone. [8] I ask you, my comrades: if Cebalinus had not come to me, if he had wanted me to know nothing about the conspirators, would I be on trial today – when no one names me? [9] Let us suppose that Dymnus were alive and also that he wished to protect me. What about the others? Of course they are going to confess their own guilt but omit me! Misfortune is spiteful. Generally speaking, a guilty person finds comfort in another's punishment when he feels the pain of his own. [10] Will so many conspirators fail to admit the truth, even when put on the rack? No, just as no one protects the condemned man so, I believe, the condemned man protects no one.

[11] "I must turn to the one real charge against me, which goes: 'Why did you remain silent about the matter that was reported to you? Why so little concern when you heard?' Alexander, wherever you are, I confessed to this misdemeanour, such as it is, and you pardoned me. I clasped your right hand, a gesture of our reconciliation, and I attended your banquet. [12] If you believed me, I was declared innocent; if you forgave me, I was given a reprieve. Just

abide by your decision. What was it that I did last night after leaving your table? What new crime has been reported to you to make you change your mind? [13] I was in a deep sleep when, as I rested unperturbed by misfortune, my enemies put the fetters on me and woke me. How does a murderer and a traitor achieve such deep, relaxed sleep? [14] Criminals cannot get to sleep because their consciences will not let them: they are hounded by the Furies not just after committing a crime but even after planning one. But I had gained a feeling of security, first from my innocence and then from your right hand, and I felt no apprehension that the cruelty of others would influence you more than your own merciful inclinations.

[15] "But (not to have you regret that you believed me) the matter was reported to me by a mere boy. He was unable to produce any witness or any corroboration for his charges and, if he had begun to be heard, he would have filled everybody with alarm. [16] Unfortunately for me, I thought that what was coming to my ears was a quarrel between lover and boyfriend, and my doubts about Nicomachus' reliability arose from the consideration that he did not bring the information in person but induced his brother to bring it. [17] I was afraid he would deny having given instructions to Cebalinus and I myself would then appear responsible for having put many of the king's friends in jeopardy. [18] Even as things are, when I have done nobody any harm, I have found someone who prefers to see me dead than safe – so what kind of hostility do you think I would have incurred by attacking innocent people?

[19] "But Dymnus committed suicide, you will say. Surely you do not think I could have foreseen that he would? Of course not. So the one thing supporting this charge – that thing could not possibly have had any effect on me when I was accosted by Cebalinus. [20] My god, suppose I had been Dymnus' accomplice in such a horrible crime. I ought not to have hidden for those two days the fact that we had been betrayed – and Cebalinus himself could have been eliminated without difficulty. [21] Then, after the information which I was going to suppress had been brought, I went into the king's bedroom alone, actually wearing a sword. Why did I postpone the deed? Was it that without Dymnus I didn't dare do it? [22] Then it was Dymnus who was the leader of the conspiracy! I was merely lurking in his shadow – I, Philotas, who have eyes on the throne of Macedon! Was any one of you suborned with bribes? To what general or what officer did I pay undue attention?

[23] "One charge made against me is that I disdain to communicate in my native language, that I have no respect for Macedonian customs (which means I have designs on an empire I despise)! That native language of ours has long been rendered obsolete through our dealings with other nations, and conquerors and conquered alike must learn a foreign tongue.

[24] "Indeed, that kind of charge is as little damaging to me as the charge that Perdiccas' son, Amyntas, plotted against the king. As for my friendship with him, I am not reluctant to defend myself on that score – unless it was wrong for us to feel affection for a brother of the king. [25] If, however,

someone of such elevated status also demanded respect, then tell me, please, am I on trial because I did not see into the future or is death also mandatory for the innocent friends of traitors? And if *that* is justice, why have I been left alive so long? If it is injustice, why then am I facing death at this very moment?

[26] "Another charge: I wrote that I felt sorry for people who had to live under anyone who believed himself to be Jupiter's son. Ah, loyalty in friendship! Ah, perilous candour in giving honest advice! It was you who let me down! It was you who urged me not to conceal what I felt. [27] I admit I wrote this *to* the king – but not *about* the king. I was not trying to generate animosity against him – I was afraid for him. It seemed to me more befitting Alexander's dignity that he acknowledge in silence his descent from Jupiter than bandy it about in public declarations. [28] But since the trustworthiness of the oracle is beyond question, let the god bear witness in my case: keep me in shackles while Ammon is consulted as to whether I embarked on some dark, sinister crime. After acknowledging our king as his son, he will not suffer any of those who have plotted against his progeny to escape detection. [29] If you think torture to be more reliable than oracles, I do not refuse even this method of exposing the truth.

[30] "Men on capital charges usually bring their relatives before you. In my case I have recently lost my two brothers while I cannot produce my father, nor dare I name him since he is also accused of this terrible crime. [31] Until recently the father of many children, he must now be content with one, and it is not enough for him to be deprived of that one, too – no, he is being placed upon my funeral pyre himself. [32] So, dearest father, you are going to die along with me as well as because of me. It is I who take away your life, I who terminate your advanced years. Why did you give me my wretched life when the gods were against it? Was it to reap from me the harvest that now awaits you? [33] I do not know which is more pitiful, my youth or your old age, for I die in the prime of my years while the executioner will take from you a life that nature was already calling in – were fortune only prepared to be patient.

[34] "The reference to my father reminds me of how necessary my timidity and hesitation really were in disclosing the information that Cebalinus had brought to me. After Parmenion heard of a plot to poison the king by the physician Philip, he wrote a letter because he wished to deter Alexander from drinking the potion which the doctor intended to give to him. My father wasn't believed, was he? His letter had no influence, did it? [35] In my own case, how often have I reported things I have heard only to be snubbed and laughed at for being over-credulous! If we face unpopularity when we report things and suspicion when we remain silent, what must we do?" [36] And when one of the crowd of onlookers exclaimed, "Don't hatch plots against your benefactors," Philotas said: "You're right, whoever you are. [37] So if I have hatched a plot, I do not ask to be excused punishment, and I conclude my speech since my last words were apparently offensive to your ears." Then he was led away by the men acting as his guards.

11   Among the officers was a certain Bolon, a good fighter but a man of no refinement or cultivation, an older soldier who had risen from the ranks to his present position. [2] The rest now fell silent but Bolon, with boorish impudence and in a brazen manner, began to remind them all of the time they had each been ejected from quarters they had taken over so that the scum of Philotas' slaves might have the places from which they had thrown out their colleagues. [3] Philotas' wagons, piled high with gold and silver, had been parked all through the streets, he said, while not one of their comrades had even been allowed close to his quarters; no, the servants he had guarding him while he slept moved them all far away so that fop would not be disturbed by the noise – no, *silence* is a better word – of hushed conversation. [4] Philotas had ridiculed men from the country, he continued, calling them Phrygians and Paphlagonians – this from a man who, Macedonian born, was not ashamed to use an interpreter to listen to men who spoke his own language. [5] Why did he now want Ammon consulted? It was Philotas who had accused Jupiter of lying when he acknowledged Alexander as his son; he was, of course, afraid that this gift of the gods would excite envy! [6] When he plotted against the life of his king and friend, he did not consult Jupiter; now he wanted to send to the oracle so as to give his father time to win over his subjects in Media and use the money placed in his care to hire desperate men to abet their crime. [7] Yes, he said, they would send a deputation to the oracle, not to ask Jupiter about what they had heard from Alexander but to give him thanks and to repay their vows for his protection of their fine king.

[8] At this the whole assembly really became aroused. It started with the bodyguards crying out that they should tear the traitor to pieces, a suggestion which Philotas in fact heard without undue anxiety, since he feared more dire punishment. [9] The king returned to the assembly and adjourned the hearing to the following day, either to subject Philotas to further torture in prison or to conduct a more thorough investigation of the entire episode and, though the day was drawing on towards evening, he nevertheless called a meeting of his friends. [10] The general feeling was that Philotas should be stoned to death according to Macedonian custom, but Hephaestion, Craterus and Coenus declared that torture should be employed to force the truth out of him, and those who had advocated other punishment went over to their view. [11] So, when the council was adjourned, Hephaestion, Craterus and Coenus got up together to conduct the interrogation of Philotas. [12] The king summoned Craterus and, after some conversation with him, the contents of which were not made public, withdrew to the inner section of his quarters. There, dismissing all who were present, he awaited the outcome of the investigation till late in the night.

[13] The torturers laid out before Philotas' eyes all the instruments used to inflict pain. [14] Philotas, on an impulse, asked: "Why hesitate to execute your king's enemy, a confessed assassin? What need is there for interrogation under torture? I planned the crime: I wanted it to succeed." Craterus insisted that

he also make his confession under torture. [15] Philotas was seized, blindfolded and his clothes stripped from him, while all the time he invoked the gods of his country and the laws of humanity – to no avail, for their ears were deaf. He was racked with the most cruel tortures: not only was he a condemned man but his torturers were personal enemies trying to please the king. [16] Though subjected both to fire and beatings – no longer to make him talk but as punishment – he managed at first to keep not only from screaming but even groaning. [17] But his body began to swell with weals and he could not bear the blows that cut to the bone. He promised to tell them what they wished to know if they put an end to the torture, [18] but he wanted them to swear on Alexander's life that the interrogation would be terminated and the torturers removed. On being granted both those terms Philotas said: "Craterus, say what you want me to say." [19] Craterus was annoyed that Philotas was mocking him and he recalled the torturers. But Philotas began to beg for time to get his breath back, after which he was prepared to tell all he knew.

[20] In the meantime word of the torture of Philotas had got around, and this spread panic among the cavalry, the men from the best families and especially those closely related to Parmenion. What they feared was the Macedonian law which provided the death penalty also for relatives of people who had plotted against the king. Some, therefore, committed suicide and others fled into remote mountains and desert wastes as sheer terror spread throughout the camp. Finally, the king learned of the consternation and proclaimed that he was suspending the law relating to the punishment of relatives of the guilty.

[21] Whether Philotas told the truth or whether he lied from a wish to deliver himself from torture is debatable, for the end in view of both those who confess the truth and those who lie is termination of the pain. [22] "You are aware of the close friendship my father had with Hegelochus," said Philotas. "I mean that Hegelochus who died in combat – he was the cause of all our problems. [23] When the king first commanded that he be addressed as the son of Jupiter, Hegelochus was indignant and said: "Well, do we recognize this man as our king? He disclaims Philip as his father. If we can stand that, we're done for. [24] A man who demands to be believed a god shows contempt not only for men but for the gods as well. We have lost Alexander, we have lost our king! We have come up against an arrogance that can be tolerated neither by the gods, to whom he considers himself an equal, nor by men, from whom he excludes himself. [25] Have we spilt our blood to make a god who despises us, who balks at attending a meeting of mere mortals? Listen to me: if we are true men, we also will be adopted by the gods! [26] Who avenged the murder of this man's ancestor Archelaus, of Alexander after that, and of Perdiccas? But this man granted a pardon to his father's murderers."

[27] "Such were Hegelochus' words over dinner. The next day at dawn I was sent for by my father. He was in low spirits and could see that I was also dejected; for what we had heard was enough to strike anxiety into our hearts.

[28] So, to see whether Hegelochus had poured out those ideas under the influence of drink or whether they were spawned of some deep conviction, we decided he should be summoned. He came and without prompting spoke again in the same terms, adding that if we dared take the lead he would stand right behind us, but if we lacked the heart for it he would keep silent about the plan. [29] With Darius still alive, Parmenion thought the plan premature, since killing Alexander would benefit the enemy, not themselves, whereas with Darius removed the reward of killing the king that would fall to his assassins would be Asia and all of the East. The plan was approved and pledges given and accepted on it. [30] As for Dymnus, I know nothing. I realize, though, that after this confession it does me no good that I am entirely unconnected with his crime."

[31] Once again they applied the instruments of torture, now themselves also using their spears to strike him in the face and eyes, and they extracted from him a confession to this crime as well. [32] Then they demanded the full programme of the crime they had contrived. Philotas replied that it appeared as though Alexander would be detained in Bactria for a long time and he had feared that his father might die in the meantime, since he was 70 years old. Parmenion was then leader of a great army and in charge of a large quantity of money; if he, Philotas, were deprived of such great resources, killing the king would serve no purpose. [33] Accordingly he had made haste to execute the plan while he still had the prize in his hands. If they did not believe his father took no part in it, he did not refuse further torture, even though he could no longer endure it.

[34] After conferring, his tormentors concluded that the interrogation had gone far enough. They went back to the king, who gave orders for Philotas' confession to be read out the next day and for Philotas himself to be carried to the assembly because he was unable to walk. [35] Since Philotas admitted everything, they brought in Demetrius, who was accused of complicity in the most recent conspiracy. With vigorous protestations and with the confidence which he felt showing in his expression, he denied any plot against the king, going so far as to demand torture for himself. [36] Then Philotas' eyes shifted round, falling eventually on one Calis who stood close by. Philotas told him to come closer and, when Calis showed agitation and refused to come over to him, he said, "Are you going to permit Demetrius to lie and me to be tortured again?" [37] Calis was left speechless and pale. The Macedonians began to suspect that Philotas wished to incriminate the innocent, for the young man had been named neither by Nicomachus nor by Philotas himself under torture but, when he saw the king's officers around him, Calis confessed that he and Demetrius had planned the crime. [38] Thereupon all those named by Nicomachus, when the signal was given, were stoned to death in the traditional Macedonian manner.

[39] Alexander had been saved from great danger, danger to his popularity as much as to his life. Parmenion and Philotas had been his principal friends

and their condemnation would have been impossible without causing personal indignation among the troops, unless they were demonstrably guilty. [40] So attitudes to the interrogation shifted. While Philotas denied the crime his torture was thought cruel, but after his confession he no longer won pity even from his friends.

Cleitus

The death of Cleitus in late summer 328 at Maracanda (Samarcand) is one of the tragic episodes in Alexander's life. It was no doubt the knowledge of Cleitus' murder that caused the primary historians to give special attention to the episode at the Granicus where he saved the king's life, and the observation that Cleitus' sister, Lanice (or Hellanice), had been Alexander's wet-nurse is further intended to magnify the crime. The stress of the campaign, aggravated by excessive drinking, was a contributing factor. But Cleitus' words betrayed a deep-rooted, festering hostility, a belief that Alexander had abandoned his conservative Macedonian roots, that he had lost touch with his people and been carried away by his success, his pretensions concerning his divine father, Amun, and the flattery of his courtiers.

4(a)   Plutarch, Alexander 50–1

The Cleitus affair followed not much later. Those who are told the simple facts of it may find it more brutal than the Philotas episode, [2] but when we consider its origin and context we find that it was not a premeditated affair but arose through an unfortunate set of circumstances. It was the king's anger and drunkenness that gave Cleitus' evil genius its chance. It happened as follows.

[3] Certain people came from the coast bringing the king some Greek fruit. Alexander was full of admiration for the freshness and beauty of the fruit, and he sent for Cleitus, wishing to show it to him and share it with him. [4] Cleitus happened to be offering sacrifice at that moment, but he abandoned that and went to the king; and three sacrificial sheep that had already been consecrated came following after him. [5] When the king was told this, he passed on the information to his seers, Aristander and Cleomenes the Spartan. The seers declared that it was a sinister omen, and Alexander issued orders that expiatory sacrifices be immediately offered on Cleitus' behalf. [6] For, two days earlier, the king himself had had a strange dream: Cleitus appeared to him in black clothes sitting with the sons of Parmenion, who were all dead. [7] But before the sacrifices ordered for Cleitus were concluded, Cleitus himself came to dine with the king, who had been sacrificing to the Dioscuri.

[8] Some lively drinking got under way, and poems were sung. These were the compositions of one Pranichus (or Pierion, according to some) on

generals who had recently suffered defeat at the hands of the barbarians,[8] subjecting these men to humiliation and ridicule. [9] Older diners were offended
and had harsh words for the poet and the singer, but Alexander and his group
were enjoying the performance and told the singer to carry on. By this time
Cleitus was drunk and, a man of truculent and wilful temperament, he flew
into a rage. It was not right, he said, in the presence of barbarians and
enemies, to insult Macedonians who were far better than the men mocking
them, even if they had fallen on bad luck. [10] Alexander then remarked that
in representing cowardice as bad luck Cleitus was pleading for himself, [11] at
which Cleitus sprang to his feet and declared: "Yes, it was this cowardice of
mine that saved the offspring of the gods when he was turning his back to
Spithridates' sword! And it is by the blood of Macedonians and by these
wounds that you have become so high and mighty as to disown Philip and
claim to be the son of Ammon."

51   Alexander was stung by the remark. "You bastard," he said, "do you
think you are going to get away with saying such things about me all the
time and causing friction amongst the Macedonians?"

[2] "We are not getting away with anything even now," replied Cleitus, "considering the rewards we receive for our efforts. We think those already dead
are the lucky ones for not living to see Macedonians flogged with Median
rods and pleading with Persians for a chance to see our king."

[3] Cleitus had spoken too freely. Alexander's companions stood up to face
him and proceeded to shower him with abuse, while the older men attempted
to calm the disturbance. [4] Turning then to Xenodochus of Cardia and
Artemius of Colophon, Alexander said: "Don't you think Greeks walking
amongst Macedonians are like demi-gods walking amongst wild animals?"

[5] Cleitus would not give up. He told Alexander to let him say what he
wanted or else not invite to dinner men who were free and spoke their minds
– he should live with barbarians and slaves who would prostrate themselves
before his Persian girdle and snow-white tunic.

No longer able to control his temper, Alexander threw one of the apples
within his reach at Cleitus and hit him, after which he looked round for his
sword. [6] But Aristophanes,[9] one of his bodyguards, got to it first and removed
it. The others surrounded the king and begged him to stop, but he jumped
to his feet and summoned his guards, loudly shouting in the Macedonian
tongue, which indicated that there was a serious crisis. He also ordered the
bugler to sound the alarm, and hit him with his fist when the man hesitated
and was unwilling to obey. [7] This man was subsequently held in high regard

---

8   Apparently a reference to the Macedonians who had been defeated by Spitamenes at
the Polytimetus River. However, Holt (1988: 78–9 n.118) makes the interesting suggestion
that this might have been a mock epic concerning Aristonicus the harpist, who fought gal-
lantly and was killed shortly before the Cleitus episode.

9   Probably a corruption of the name "Aristonus," one of Alexander's *Somatophylakes*; cf.
Ziegler (1936: 379–80).

as he was thought to be the one mostly responsible for the camp not having been thrown into turmoil.

[8] Cleitus still would not give up, however, and his friends with difficulty jostled him out of the dining room. But he re-entered by another door, reciting this iambic verse from Euripides with derisive bravado: "Alas! What a sad state of government there is in Greece!" [9] At this, Alexander grabbed a spear from one of the guards and, when Cleitus was drawing back the curtain before the door and came face to face with him, ran him through. [10] Cleitus fell with a groan that grew to a howl of pain, and Alexander's anger straightway left him. [11] Coming to his senses, and seeing his friends standing there speechless, he drew the spear from the body and made to stab himself in the throat. He was prevented from doing so, however, when his guards grabbed his hands and carried him under duress into his room.

4(b)   Arrian 4.8.1–9.4

It will not be inappropriate if I relate at this point (even though it took place slightly later) the misfortune that befell Cleitus son of Dropides and the distress it brought Alexander.

There was a day kept sacred to Dionysus by the Macedonians, and on that day Alexander would every year sacrifice to the god. [2] On this occasion, however, they say that Alexander passed over Dionysus[10] and sacrificed to the Dioscuri, something or other prompting him to sacrifice to the twin gods. The drinking had been going on for some time – in, fact, drinking practices that leaned towards the excesses of the barbarian were also one of Alexander's innovations – and during it talk arose of how credit for the birth of the Dioscuri had been filched from Tyndareus and assigned to Zeus.[11] [3] Some of those present – the sort who have always subverted, and will keep undermining, the functions of those in power at a given time – wished to flatter Alexander. They voiced the opinion that, with regard to Alexander and his attainments, Polydeuces and Castor were not in the same class. Some, as the carousing continued, did not even leave Heracles out of their conversation, saying that it was envy alone that stood in the way of humans receiving from their contemporaries the honours that were their due.

[4] It was clear that Cleitus had long been annoyed by Alexander's shift towards barbarian ways and by the things being said by those who flattered him. On that particular occasion his anger was further sharpened by drinking, and he could not stand these men's insolent irreverence towards heaven, or their showing Alexander kindness – which really was not kindness – by demeaning the achievements of the heroes of old. [5] Alexander's

---

10   Dionysus is associated with Thebes, the city that Alexander destroyed in 335.
11   Castor and Pollux (Polydeuces), named below, the sons of Leda. The name "Dioscuri" actually means "sons of Zeus" or "Zeus' boys."

accomplishments were not, in fact, as great and wonderful as their exaggerated talk made out, he said, and he certainly was not single-handedly responsible for them – for the most part they were the achievements of the Macedonian people.

[6] Cleitus' words stung Alexander. (And, in fact, I do not approve of what he said. In drunken company like that I think it is enough to remain silent and keep one's thoughts to oneself, simply avoiding the mistake of joining the others in their sycophantic comments.) Then some of them, also attempting to humour Alexander, proceeded, with no justification whatsoever, to advert to the deeds of Philip, claiming that these were neither great nor wonderful. Cleitus was now beside himself. He proceeded to rate Philip's achievements as the best and to denigrate Alexander and his. By now he was very drunk, and had nothing but insults for Alexander, noting in particular that it was by Cleitus himself that Alexander had been saved from death in the cavalry engagement against the Persians at the Granicus. [7] He even went so far as to raise his right hand in a disdainful manner and say: "This is the hand that saved you on that occasion, Alexander."

No longer able to tolerate Cleitus' drunken abuse, Alexander leaped angrily at him, but was held back by his drinking companions. And there was no let up in the insults from Cleitus. [8] Alexander cried out for his hypaspists, but no one obeyed, at which he declared that he had now reached the same point as Darius when he was seized and taken along by Bessus and his men – a king in name only!

His *hetairoi* could restrain him no longer and he sprang to his feet. [9] Then, some say, he grabbed a spear from one of his Somatophylakes, and struck and killed Cleitus with it, though others claim that it was a *sarissa* he took from one of the guards.

Aristobulus says nothing about how the drinking started, but attributes the blame exclusively to Cleitus. According to him, when Alexander flew into a temper and sprang at him with murder in mind, Cleitus was taken out through the doors, and over the wall and fosse of the citadel (where the incident took place) by Alexander's Bodyguard Ptolemy son of Lagus. But he could not control himself and came back. He bumped into Alexander just as he was calling out "Cleitus!", to which he replied, "Here I am, Alexander – it's me, Cleitus." And it was at that point that he received the blow with the *sarissa* and was killed.

9   For my part, I unequivocally blame Cleitus for his impudence towards his king. I feel pity for Alexander and the ordeal he went through, because in that incident he revealed himself overpowered by two vices which should never get the better of a decent man: anger and drunkenness. [2] But I applaud him for what happened after the event – his recognition that he had committed a heinous act was immediate. Indeed, some say that he held the *sarissa* against the wall and intended to fall on it himself, on the grounds that living after he had killed a friend in a bout of drunkenness was dishonourable. [3] Most of the sources, however, do not give this version, but claim that Alexan-

der went off to bed and lay there mourning, calling out Cleitus' name and that of Cleitus' sister. This was Lanice, daughter of Dropides, who had been Alexander's nurse. What a fine repayment for her nursing he had given her now that he had grown to manhood, he said; [4] she had seen her sons die fighting for him, and now he had killed her brother – and killed him with his own hand! He would not stop calling himself the murderer of his friends, and he remained without food or drink for three days and paid no attention to any other personal needs.

4(c)   *Quintus Curtius Rufus 8.1.19–2.10*

From here they returned to Maracanda. Alexander now accepted Artabazus' plea of advanced age and assigned his province to Cleitus. [20] It was Cleitus who had used his shield to protect the king when he was fighting bareheaded at the river Granicus, and who had lopped off Rhosaces' hand with his sword when he threatened Alexander's life. He was an old soldier of Philip's with a distinguished record in numerous campaigns, [21] and his sister Hellanice, who had brought Alexander up, was loved like a mother by the king. These were the reasons why he now committed to Cleitus' loyal protection the strongest section of his empire.

[22] Cleitus was ordered to prepare for a march the following day, and he was then invited to one of the usual early-starting banquets. At this, being tipsy with wine and no impartial judge of his own worth, the king began to eulogize his exploits to the point of annoying even those of his audience who accepted the truth of his statements. [23] However, the elder guests remained silent, until Alexander proceeded to disparage Philip's record and to boast that it was he himself who was responsible for Philip's famous victory at Chaeronea. The credit for that great achievement, he said, had been filched from him by his father's ill-will and jealousy. [24] A quarrel had arisen between the Macedonian forces and the Greek mercenaries, he explained, and Philip had been put out of action by a wound he had received in the mêlée. He lay on the ground, finding that to play dead was his safest course of action, and Alexander had protected him with his shield and killed with his own hand the men attacking his father. [25] His father, he said, could never bring himself to admit this: he was loath to owe his life to his own son. Then there was the campaign which he had conducted against the Illyrians without Philip. After his victory he had written to his father that the enemy were defeated and routed – and Philip had taken no part in the war. [26] The men who deserved credit, Alexander continued, were not those who attended the mystery ceremonies of Samothrace[12] at the time when Asia should have been burned and

---

12   The mysteries of the Cabeiri. This was where Philip met Alexander's mother, Olympias. This seems to echo a sentiment expressed by Alexander elsewhere, that a king ought to be engaged in conquest rather than wasting time on marriages and producing children.

pillaged; rather it was those whose magnificent achievements had surpassed belief.

[27] The younger men were elated to hear these and similar remarks, but the older ones found them offensive, mostly because of Philip, under whom they had lived most of their lives. [28] Then Cleitus, who was himself not wholly sober, turned to the men reclining below him and recited a passage from Euripides so that the king could catch the tone without fully hearing the words. [29] The gist of the passage was that the Greeks had established a bad practice in inscribing their trophies with only their kings' names, for the kings were thus appropriating to themselves glory that was won by the blood of others. Alexander suspected Cleitus' words were in a caustic vein and he proceeded to ask those next to him what they had heard him say. [30] These men maintained a resolute silence, and Cleitus, gradually raising his voice, now recounted Philip's exploits and the wars he had fought in Greece, ranking them all above their current campaigns, [31] and this led to an argument between the younger and older soldiers. As for Alexander, while he appeared unruffled as he heard Cleitus' disparaging remarks on his achievements, he had in fact become furiously angry. [32] It looked as if he would control his temper if Cleitus discontinued the insolent line of talk he had taken, but when the man showed no restraint whatever, Alexander's irritation increased.

[33] By this time Cleitus had the nerve to defend even Parmenion, and he favourably compared Philip's victory over the Athenians with the destruction of Thebes – for he was carried away not only by the drink but also by a perverse desire to pick a quarrel. [34] Finally he said: "If someone has to die for you, then Cleitus comes first. But when you come to judge the spoils of victory, the major share goes to those who pour the most insolent insults on your father's memory. [35] You assign to me the province of Sogdiana, which has often rebelled and, so far from being pacified, cannot even be reduced to subjection. I am being sent against wild animals with bloodthirsty natures. But my own circumstances I pass over. [36] You express contempt for Philip's men, but you are forgetting that, if old Atarrhias here had not brought the younger fellows back into line when they refused to fight, we should still be delayed around Halicarnassus. [37] How is it then that you have still conquered Asia with young men like that? The truth, I think, lies in what your uncle is generally believed to have said in Italy, that he had faced men in battle and you had faced women."

[38] Of all these ill-considered, impulsive comments none had provoked the king more than the reference to Parmenion, but he suppressed his resentment and was satisfied to order Cleitus from the banquet. [39] His only other comment was that, if he had gone on talking, Cleitus might possibly have cast in his teeth the claim that he had saved the king's life, an arrogant boast which, he said, he had often made. [40] Cleitus hesitated to get up, so those reclining next to him grabbed him, scolding and warning him as they tried to lead him off. [41] As he was dragged away, Cleitus' anger rose, augmenting his characteristic impetuosity. In the past, he exclaimed, his breast had given

protection to Alexander's back, but time had passed since he performed that valuable service and even the memory of it annoyed the king. [42] He also taunted Alexander with the murder of Attalus, and finally ridiculed the oracle of Jupiter and Alexander's claim that he was his father, saying that he, Cleitus, had been more truthful in his declarations to Alexander than his "father" had been.

[43] By now Alexander's temper was such that even sober he could hardly have controlled it; and since his senses had long since succumbed to the wine, he suddenly leapt from the couch. [44] His friends were startled. They rose in a body, throwing aside rather than setting down their cups, all agog to see how the affair he was starting so impulsively would resolve itself. [45] Alexander snatched a lance from the hands of a guard and, while Cleitus persisted with his frenzied outpouring of wild abuse, tried to run him through. He was stopped by Ptolemy and Perdiccas, [46] who grabbed him around the waist and held him back as he continued to struggle. Lysimachus and Leonnatus relieved him of the lance. [47] Alexander then appealed to the loyalty of the rank and file, crying out that he was being set upon by his closest friends as had recently happened to Darius, and he ordered a trumpet signal to be sounded for the men to come in armour to the royal quarters.

[48] At this, Ptolemy and Perdiccas fell to their knees and begged him not to persist with such hasty anger but to allow himself time to consider – he would settle the matter more equitably the next day. [49] But, deaf with anger, his ears took in nothing. He stormed into the vestibule of the royal quarters in uncontrollable fury. There he grabbed a spear from the guard on watch and stood at the doorway by which his dinner-guests had to exit. [50] The others had left, and Cleitus was the last to come out, without a lamp. The king challenged him, and the tone of his voice testified to the appalling nature of his criminal intent. [51] Cleitus thought now not of his own anger, but only of the king's. He replied that he was Cleitus and that he was leaving the banquet. [52] As he said this Alexander plunged the spear into his side and, bespattered with the dying man's blood, said to him: "Now go and join Philip, Parmenion and Attalus!"

2　The human character has been ill-served by nature: we tend to consider matters carefully after the fact, not before. When his anger had subsided and he had shaken off his intoxication, the king clearly perceived the enormity of his crime as he reflected upon it, but all too late. [2] He could see that he had murdered a fine soldier, even if he had taken liberties on that particular occasion, and a man who, if Alexander were not ashamed to admit it, had saved his life. Although he was king, he had assumed the abominable role of executioner: with a foul murder he had punished intemperate language that was attributable to wine. [3] The vestibule was completely soaked in the gore of a man who shortly before had been his guest. Shocked and looking dazed, the guards kept their distance from Alexander, and his isolation gave him even more opportunity for remorse. [4] He pulled the spear from the dead man's body and turned it on himself. He had already put it to his chest when the guards rushed up and, despite his resistance, wrested it from his hands, picked him up and carried him into his tent. [5] Alexander flung himself on the ground, and his entire quarters rang with the sound of his pitiful weeping and wailing. Then he tore at his face with his nails and begged the men standing around him not to let him survive such dishonour.

[6] His entire night was spent in entreaties such as this. He wondered whether it was divine anger that had driven him to this heinous crime, and it occurred to him that he had failed to offer the annual sacrifice to Father Liber at the appointed time. So it was that the god's anger had displayed itself against him – for the crime was committed amid drinking and feasting. [7] But what was more distressing was that he could see the alarm of all his friends. He felt that nobody would now hold a conversation with him; that he would be obliged to live a solitary existence like a wild beast which terrifies other animals and is in turn terrified by them.

[8] At dawn he ordered the corpse, still covered with gore, to be taken into his tent, and when it lay before him he said, with tears in his eyes: "This is how I have repaid my nurse, whose two sons fell at Miletus to win renown for me. This is her brother, her only source of comfort after her loss, and he has been murdered by me at the dinner table. [9] Where will the poor woman turn now? Of all her relatives only I survive – the one person she will be unable to look at without pain. I am the destroyer of my saviours. Shall I return home unable to hold out my right hand to my nurse without reminding her of her personal tragedy?" [10] And since his tearful lamentations continued without end, the corpse was removed on his friends' instructions.

Callisthenes and the Hermolaus Conspiracy

5(a)   Quintus Curtius Rufus 8.6.1–8.23

Although he punished him for a long time after this, Alexander did eventually pardon Polyperchon, but in the case of Callisthenes, whom he had long suspected because of his outspokenness, his resentment was more persistent. An opportunity to indulge this soon came his way. [2] As was observed above, it was customary for the Macedonian nobility to deliver their grown-up sons to their kings for the performance of duties which differed little from the tasks of slaves. [3] They would take turns spending the night on guard at the door of the king's bedchamber, and it was they who brought in his women by an entrance other than that watched by the armed guards. [4] They would also take his horses from the grooms and bring them for him to mount; they were his attendants both on the hunt and in battle, and were highly educated in all the liberal arts. [5] It was thought a special honour that they were allowed to sit and eat with the king. No one had the authority to flog them apart from the king himself. [6] This company served the Macedonians as a kind of seminary for their officers and generals, and from it subsequently came the kings whose descendants were many generations later stripped of power by the Romans.

[7] Now Hermolaus was a young nobleman who belonged to the group of royal attendants. He was flogged on Alexander's orders for having speared a boar before the king when the latter had ear-marked it for himself. Stung by this humiliation, he began to complain to Sostratus, [8] who also belonged to the group and was passionately in love with Hermolaus. Sostratus now saw the lacerations on the body he desperately loved, and it is possible that he bore the king some other grudge from the past. So, after the two had exchanged oaths of loyalty, Sostratus prevailed on the boy, who was already so inclined on his own account, to enter into a plot with him to assassinate the king. [9] Nor was it with the impulsiveness of youth that they put their plan into action, for they were discreet in selecting the people they would invite to join the conspiracy. They decided that Nicostratus,[13] Antipater, Asclepiodorus[14] and Philotas should be enlisted, and through these Anticles, Elaptonius and Epimenes were also brought in. [10] However, no easy method of executing the plan presented itself. It was imperative that all the conspirators be on guard duty the same night, so that there should be no problem with people not party to the plot, but it turned out that they were all on duty on different nights. [11] As a result, thirty-two days were taken up with altering the rota for guard duty and other preparations for executing the plot.

[12] It was now the night on which the conspirators were to be on duty. They were cheered by their unanimous commitment to the cause, demonstrated by the number of days that had gone by during which none had wavered through fear or hope – so strong was their common resentment towards Alexander or their loyalty to each other. [13] They now stood at the door of the room in which the king was dining, intending to escort him to his bedroom when he left the banquet. [14] But Alexander's good fortune, plus the conviviality of the banqueters, led the company to drink more than usual, and the dinner-party games also drew out the time, which made the conspirators alternately happy at the prospect of falling on a drowsy victim and anxious that he might prolong the party till daylight. [15] The problem was that others were due to relieve them at dawn, their turn of duty would not recur for seven days and they could not expect the discretion of all of them to last till that time.

[16] At the approach of dawn, however, the banquet broke up and the conspirators received the king, pleased that an opportunity for executing the crime had arrived. Then a woman appeared who, it was thought, was out of her senses and who used to frequent the royal quarters (for she appeared inspired and able to foretell the future). She not only met the king as he took

---

13　Nicostratus is otherwise unknown and it is likely that this is a scribal error for Sostratus (Heckel 1992a: 295).

14　Not Antipater *and* Asclepiodorus, but rather Antipater son of Asclepiodorus (Heckel 1992a: 289).

his leave but actually threw herself in his path. Her facial expression and her eyes indicating some inner agitation, she warned him to return to the banquet. [17] By way of a joke Alexander answered that the gods gave good advice. He once more summoned his friends and prolonged the banquet until almost the second hour of the day.

[18] By now other members of the group of attendants had succeeded to their positions and were ready to stand guard before Alexander's bedroom door, but the conspirators kept standing around even though their turn on duty was completed; so long-lived is hope once the human mind has seized upon it. [19] Addressing them more warmly than usual, the king told them to go and rest since they had been on their feet all night. They were given 50 sesterces each and commended for remaining on duty even when the turn of others had come. [20] Their great hope frustrated, they went home. They now began to wait for their next night on duty, all except Epimenes who experienced a sudden change of heart, either because of the friendly manner in which the king had greeted him and the other conspirators or because he believed that the gods opposed their scheme. So he revealed what was afoot to his brother Eurylochus, whom he had previously wished to remain ignorant of the plot.

[21] The spectre of Philotas' punishment was hanging before everybody's eyes. Eurylochus accordingly seized his brother immediately and came with him into the royal quarters. He alerted the bodyguards and declared that the information he brought related to the king's security. [22] The time of their coming and the expressions on their faces, revealing obviously troubled minds, plus the dejection of one of them – all this alarmed Ptolemy and Leonnatus, who were standing guard at the bedroom door. They opened the door, took in a lamp and woke Alexander, who now lay in a deep, drunken sleep. Gradually coming to his senses, he asked what news they brought. [23] Without a moment's hesitation Eurylochus asserted that the gods could not have entirely abandoned his family because his brother, although he had embarked on an impious crime, now regretted his actions and wished no one but himself to bring information about the plot to Alexander. The coup, he said, had been planned for that very night which was now passing, and those responsible for the heinous plot were men the king would least suspect.

[24] Epimenes then gave a detailed and systematic account, including the names of the conspirators. Callisthenes was certainly not named as one involved in the plot, but it did come out that he was in the habit of giving a ready ear to the talk of the pages when they were criticizing and finding fault with the king. [25] Some people also assert that, when Hermolaus complained before Callisthenes of having been flogged by Alexander, Callisthenes commented that they ought to remember that they were men; but they add that it is unclear whether this remark was meant to comfort Hermolaus after his beating or to provoke resentment in the young men.

[26] Shaking the drowsiness from mind and body, Alexander saw before his eyes the great danger he had escaped. He immediately gave Eurylochus 50

talents, plus the ample property of a certain Tyridates, and he restored his brother to him even before Eurylochus could beg for his life. [27] The culprits – and Callisthenes was included – he ordered to be kept in chains. They were brought to the royal quarters, but Alexander was tired from the drink and lack of sleep, and so he slept throughout the day and the next night. [28] The day after that, however, he convened a general assembly. This was attended by the fathers and relatives of the accused, not free of concern for their own safety in view of the Macedonian custom which required their death, since all blood relations of the guilty party were liable to execution. [29] Alexander had all the conspirators apart from Callisthenes brought in, and without hesitation they confessed their plan. [30] There was a general outcry against them, and the king himself asked what he had done to merit their hatching such a wicked plot against him.

7 They were dumbfounded, all except Hermolaus. "You ask as if you did not know," he said. "We plotted to kill you because you have begun to act not as a king with his free-born subjects but as a master with his slaves." [2] Of the whole assembly the first to react was Hermolaus' father, Sopolis. He rose to his feet shouting that Hermolaus was also the murderer of his own father and, putting his hand over his son's mouth, stated he should be heard no further because he was crazed by his guilt and his misfortune. [3] Alexander restrained the father and told Hermolaus to state what he had learned from his teacher, Callisthenes.

"I avail myself of your kindness," replied Hermolaus, "and state what I have learned from our misfortunes. [4] How few are the Macedonians who have actually survived your ruthlessness! How few, indeed, apart from those of meanest birth! Attalus ... Philotas ... Parmenion ... Alexander the Lyncestian ... Cleitus ... As far as the enemy is concerned, these are still alive today, are still standing in the battle line, protecting you with their shields, receiving wounds for your glory and your victory. [5] A fine thanks you gave them! One has spilled his blood on your table; another was not even granted a simple death; leaders of your armies have been put on the rack to provide a spectacle for the Persians they had conquered. Parmenion was butchered without trial – the man whose services you had used to kill Attalus. [6] Yes, you first use the hands of unfortunates to effect your assassinations, then you suddenly order others to butcher the men who shortly before served as your assassins."

[7] At this, cries of protest against Hermolaus came from the entire assembly. His father had drawn his sword to kill him and would certainly have run him through had he not been restrained by the king, who told Hermolaus to continue and asked the men to listen patiently as he added to the reasons for his own punishment. [8] The meeting was brought to order with difficulty and Hermolaus continued: "How kind of you to give the floor to boys inexperienced in speaking! But Callisthenes' voice is shut away in a prison – because he alone is able to speak. [9] Otherwise why is he not brought out, when even those who have confessed are being heard? Because, of course, you are

frightened to hear an innocent man speak freely; you cannot even look him in the face. [10] Yet I say he is not guilty. Here are the men who planned the noble deed with me. No one can say that Callisthenes was in league with us; although he has long been marked out for execution by a very just and tolerant king! [11] Such are the rewards Macedonians can expect from you for the blood which you squander as if it were overabundant and cheap. For you, 30,000 mules are transporting captured gold – yet your soldiers will take home nothing but scars for which there is no compensation.

"Even so, we could have tolerated all this, until you delivered us to the barbarians and (a novel twist!) sent the victors under the yoke!¹⁵ [12] But you revel in Persian clothes and Persian etiquette; you abhor the customs of your own country. Thus it was a king of the Persians, not of the Macedonians, we wanted to kill and, in accordance with the conventions of war, we pursue you as a deserter. [13] You wanted Macedonians to kneel before you and worship you as a god. You repudiate your father Philip and, if any of the gods were thought superior to Jupiter, you would despise Jupiter, too. [14] We are free men – are you surprised if we cannot bear your vanity? What can we hope for from you if even innocent men must either face death or – a fate worse than death – a life of slavery? [15] Actually, you are much indebted to me, if you can change your ways; for it was from me that you first came to learn what free-born men cannot endure. For the rest, have mercy: do not heap punishments on old men now deprived of their children. Have us taken to our execution that we may win from our own deaths what we had sought from yours." Such were the words of Hermolaus.

8   The king replied: "The falseness of these charges (which that fellow has picked up from his teacher) is obvious from my patience. [2] Although he admitted to the most heinous crime, I not only gave him a hearing myself but made you hear him, too; for I was aware that, when I gave this assassin permission to speak, he would exhibit the madness which drove him to decide to kill me – me, whom he should have respected as a father! [3] Recently he behaved rather impudently on a hunt. I resorted to our traditional custom, followed by kings of Macedon from the earliest times, and ordered him to be flogged. Such discipline is necessary. Pupils accept it from their teachers, wives from their husbands; we even allow our slaves to beat boys of this age. [4] Such is my 'savagery' against him, which he wanted to avenge with a treacherous murder. As for the other pages, they all allow me to follow my inclinations, and you know how mild I am in my treatment of them – reminding you of that is unnecessary.

[5] "That the execution of traitors does not earn Hermolaus' approval causes me very little surprise, for he has himself earned that penalty. In fact, he praises Parmenion and Philotas to further his own cause. [6] Now as for

---

15 *Sub iugum.* This is purely Roman terminology referring to the practice of humiliating the defeated enemy by sending them "beneath the yoke" (two upright spears with a third laid across them), symbolizing subjugation.

Alexander the Lyncestian, he twice plotted against my life and despite the testimony of two informers I still let him go free. When he was found guilty once again, I nevertheless delayed the matter for three years until you demanded that he finally pay the due penalty for his crime. [7] Attalus, you remember, posed a threat to my life before my accession. And Cleitus – I wish he had not forced me to lose my temper with him! But I tolerated his scurrilous comments, his insults to you and to me, longer than he would have tolerated the same coming from me. [8] The clemency of kings and leaders depends not just on their own character but on the character of their subjects, too. Authority is rendered less harsh by obedience; but when respect leaves men's minds and we mix the highest and lowest together without distinction – then we need force to repel force.

[9] "But why should I be surprised at that fellow's accusing me of cruelty when he has had the audacity to charge me with avarice? I do not wish to cite individual cases among you: I might come to resent my own generosity if I offend your self-respect. Look at the army as a whole. The soldier who had nothing but his weapons a short time ago now reclines on silver couches! The men pile their tables with gold, lead along troops of slaves and cannot carry all the spoils taken from the enemy!

[10] "But, says Hermolaus, the Persians whom we have defeated are held in high regard by me! Now that is actually the clearest proof of my restraint – my rule is not tyrannical even in the case of conquered peoples. I did not come into Asia to wipe out its races entirely or to transform half the world into a desert. Rather it was to make the people I conquered in warfare feel no regret at my victory. [11] As a consequence, you have men fighting along with you and shedding blood for your empire who would have rebelled had they been treated disdainfully. Possession achieved by the sword is not of long duration, but gratitude for kindness shown is everlasting. [12] If we wish to hold Asia and not merely pass through it we must impart our clemency to these people – it is their loyalty which will make our empire stable and enduring. And, to tell the truth, we have more possessions than we can use, and it is insatiable greed to keep on filling up something that is already overflowing. [13] But, he claims, I am foisting Persian habits on to the Macedonians. True, for I see in many races things we should not blush to imitate, and the only way this great empire can be satisfactorily governed is by our transmitting some things to the natives and learning others from them ourselves.

[14] "Then there was Hermolaus' insistence that I repudiate Jupiter who recognized me as a son by his oracle – that almost called for laughter. [15] Does he think I have power over the gods' oracular responses? Jupiter held out to me the title of son; accepting it has not been disadvantageous to the operations in which we are engaged. I only wish the Indians would also believe me a god! For reputation determines military success, and often even a false belief has accomplished as much as the truth. [16] Do you think I emblazoned your arms with gold and silver to indulge an extravagant taste? No! For the Indians nothing is a more common sight than these metals, and I wished to show

them that the Macedonians, unsurpassed in all else, cannot be outclassed even in respect to gold. [17] So I shall bedazzle them from the start: they are expecting a completely humble and sordid force, and I shall show them that we come not lusting after gold and silver but to subjugate the whole world. You, traitor, wished to abort this glorious enterprise and to deliver up the Macedonians to the races they had conquered by eliminating their king.

[18] "You suggest now that I pardon your relatives! Really, you should be kept ignorant of my decision concerning them, so that your deaths may be the more distressing, that is if you have any thought or concern for your kin. But in fact I long ago suspended that notorious custom of executing innocent kinsmen and relatives along with the guilty, and I publicly declare that they all shall retain their former rank. [19] As for your Callisthenes, the only person to think you a man (because you are an assassin), I know why you want him brought forward. It is so that the insults which you sometimes uttered against me and sometimes heard from him can be repeated by his lips before this gathering. Were he a Macedonian I would have introduced him here along with you – a teacher truly worthy of his pupil. As it is, he is an Olynthian and does not enjoy the same rights."

[20] With that Alexander closed the meeting and had the condemned men transferred to members of their own unit. The latter tortured them to death so that they would gain the king's approval by their cruelty. [21] Callisthenes also died under torture. He was innocent of any plot to kill the king, but the sycophantic character of court life ill-suited his nature. [22] As a result no other person's execution engendered greater resentment against Alexander among the Greeks. Callisthenes was a man of the finest character and accomplishments who had restored Alexander to life when he was determined to die after the murder of Cleitus. Alexander had not merely executed him but had tortured him as well – and without trial. [23] This barbarous act was, all too late, followed by feelings of remorse.

5(b)   Arrian 4.12.7–14.3

[7] In my opinion, Alexander's animosity towards Callisthenes was not unreasonable in view of the man's untimely outspokenness and his insufferable stupidity. I surmise that it was because of this that Callisthenes' accusers had no difficulty in gaining credence for their charge that he was implicated in the conspiracy of the pages against Alexander, some of them even claiming that it was he who urged them to hatch the plot. The conspiracy came about as follows.

13   From Philip's time it was customary for the sons of high-ranking Macedonians, when they were reaching puberty, to be enlisted for service to the king. These were entrusted with seeing to the king's personal needs in general and in particular with guarding him while he slept. And whenever he went riding they would receive the horses from his grooms and bring them

to him. They would then help him mount in the Persian manner and join the king in the competition of the hunt.

[2] One of these boys was Hermolaus son of Sopolis, known as a student of philosophy and for that reason a follower of Callisthenes. There is a story concerning Hermolaus. On the hunt a boar came charging at Alexander, and Hermolaus hurled a weapon at the animal before the king could throw. The boar fell when it received the blow, and Alexander, having missed his chance, flew into a temper with Hermolaus. In his anger, he gave orders for the boy to be flogged while the other pages looked on, and he confiscated his horse.

[3] Hermolaus was reportedly very hurt by the indignity, and he told Sostratus son of Amyntas (a boy of his age who was his lover) that life was not worth living for him unless he had his revenge on Alexander for the outrage. Since Sostratus was in love with him, Hermolaus easily persuaded him to join the undertaking and [4] others were induced to participate by these two: Antipater, son of the former satrap of Syria, Asclepiodorus, Epimenes son of Arsaeus, Anticles son of Theocritus, and Philotas, son of the Thracian Carsis. When the nightly sentry duty came round for Antipater, they made a pact that night to attack and kill Alexander as he slept.

[5] Some authors claim that, for no particular reason, Alexander simply happened to continue drinking till daybreak, but Aristobulus recorded the incident as follows. There was a Syrian woman who was divinely inspired and who would follow Alexander around. At first she was an object of ridicule for Alexander and his comrades, but when it became apparent that what she said when she was possessed came true she was no longer treated with disdain by the king. In fact, she was granted access to him night and day, and on many occasions she was at his bedside as he slept.

[6] Now, on that particular occasion Alexander was slipping away from the drinking-party when the woman, who was then inspired by the god, met him and begged him to go back and keep drinking all night. Alexander thought this was a sign from heaven. He went back and kept drinking, thus causing the plot to fail.

[7] The next day, one of the conspirators, Epimenes son of Arsaeus, told Charicles son of Menander about the attempted coup (Charicles had become his lover), and Charicles then told Eurylochus, the brother of Epimenes. Eurylochus went to Alexander's tent where he recounted the whole affair in detail to the king's bodyguard, Ptolemy son of Lagus, and Ptolemy told Alexander. Alexander thereupon ordered the arrest of all the people whom Eurylochus had named. These were subjected to the rack, and they admitted their own involvement in the plot and named some other people, as well.

14 Aristobulus claims that the boys said that it was Callisthenes who urged them to bring off the coup, and such is Ptolemy's version, too. But most authors do not follow this line, arguing that Alexander found it easy to believe the worst of Callisthenes because of the animosity he had already developed towards him and because of Hermolaus' very close relationship with the man.

[2] Some have also included the following details in their accounts. When he

was hauled before the Macedonians, Hermolaus confessed to the plot, saying that a free man could no longer put up with Alexander's overbearing behaviour. He then went on to tell all: the unconscionable killing of Philotas and the even more monstrous killings of Parmenion and the others who died at the time; the murder of Cleitus in his cups; the Median clothing; the obeisance that Alexander wanted and still had not abandoned as an idea; and the king's excesses in drinking and sleeping. This was what he could not tolerate, he said, and he had wanted to free himself and the rest of the Macedonians from it. [3] Hermolaus and those who had been rounded up with him were then stoned to death by all present.

The fate of Callisthenes

That the details concerning the death of such an important figure as Callisthenes, a kinsman of Aristotle and Alexander's "official" historian, could not have been known with certainty defies credulity. One assumes that there was an attempt, already in the king's lifetime, to exculpate Alexander. Aristobulus and Chares we know to have been apologists, and it may be that Ptolemy's account of torture and execution is correct. Crucifixion (or impalement) was the Persian punishment for traitors (and those who offended against the royal authority). It is thus significant that Callisthenes was not executed by the Macedonian method of stoning (see §I.3k–m). The story that he died while incarcerated (and awaiting formal trial) was almost certainly invented later.

5(c)　Arrian 4.14.3

According to Aristobulus, Callisthenes was clapped in irons and taken around with the army, and subsequently he died from an illness. Ptolemy son of Lagus, however, says that he was put on the rack and then crucified. So it is that even authors who are reliable sources and who were present with Alexander do not agree in their accounts of events which were generally known and not outside their experience.

5(d)　Plutarch, Alexander 55.9

There is disagreement about Callisthenes' death. Some say he was hanged by Alexander, others that he was put in irons and died of a disease. Chares says that after his arrest Callisthenes was kept imprisoned for seven months so that he could be tried before the council in the presence of Aristotle, but that he died, grossly overweight and louse-ridden, about the time that Alexander received his wound in India.

5(e)   Justin 15.3.3–5

The following episode illustrates Lysimachus' character. Alexander the Great was furious with the philosopher Callisthenes' opposition to the use of the Persian method of salutation and had falsely alleged that Callisthenes was party to a conspiracy that was afoot against him. [4] Brutally mutilating all his limbs and cutting off his ears, nose and lips, Alexander reduced him to a hideous and pitiful spectacle, [5] and he even had him carried around shut up in a cage with a dog to intimidate the others. Lysimachus, who had been a student of Callisthenes and used to ask his advice on moral issues, felt pity for this great man who was being punished not for a crime but for speaking his mind, and gave him poison to relieve his sufferings.

Coenus Opposes Alexander at the Hyphasis (Beas) River

Modern scholars have generally taken Alexander's claim that he wished to march across India and attack the Gangetic kingdom of the Nanda dynasty at face value (but see Spann 1999 for a dissenting voice). If this was really his intention, it would have marked a departure from all his previous encounters with the barbarians of Asia, in which he was content to secure the old boundaries of the Persian empire. In the passage that follows, Coenus, a courageous fighter and a loyal officer, espouses the cause of the common soldier and draws Alexander's attention to their sufferings. The soldiers' actions at the Hyphasis (Beas) constituted a strike (*secessio*) rather than a mutiny. It would be wrong to see anything sinister in Coenus' "opportune" death soon afterwards; thus Badian (1961: 22) *contra* Holt (2000); cf. Heckel (1992a: 64). See also Holt (1982) and Carney (1996b).

6(a)   Quintus Curtius Rufus 9.2.1–3.20

Alexander spent two days with Phegeus and by the third had made up his mind to cross the river. This presented difficulties not only because of its width but also because its channel was obstructed with rocks. [2] He therefore asked Phegeus for all the pertinent information and was told that beyond the river lay a twelve-day journey through barren wastes, [3] after which came the Ganges, the largest river in all India. On the far bank of the Ganges, he was told, lived two tribes, the Gangaridae and the Prasii, and their ruler was Aggrammes who was now blockading the roads with a force of 20,000 cavalry and 200,000 infantry. [4] In addition to this he had behind him 2,000 chariots and (his most frightening armament) elephants, which according to Phegeus totalled 3,000.

[5] This all seemed incredible to Alexander; he therefore asked Porus, who was with him, whether Phegeus' information was correct. [6] Porus declared that, as far as the strength of the tribe and its kingdom were concerned, there was no exaggeration, but he added that their ruler was not merely a commoner but a man from the lowest class. His father had been a barber whose regular employment barely kept starvation at bay, but by his good looks he won the heart of the queen. [7] By her he had been brought into a comparatively close friendship with the king of the time, whom he then treacherously murdered, seizing the throne ostensibly as protector of the king's children. He then killed the children and sired this present ruler, who had earned the hatred and contempt of the people by behaviour more in keeping with his father's station in life than his own.

[8] Porus' corroboration had generated many worries in the king's mind. For his enemy and the elephants he felt only contempt, but the terrain and the violence of the rivers alarmed him. [9] To track down and ferret out peoples removed almost to the limits of human habitation seemed a difficult undertaking, and yet his craving for renown and his insatiable lust for reputation permitted him to think nothing inaccessible or remote. [10] He also occasionally harboured doubts about the Macedonians. After covering so many huge expanses of land and after growing old in battle and military service, would they now follow him over the rivers that blocked their path, over all the natural obstacles confronting them? He thought that, laden as they were with a wealth of booty, they would prefer to enjoy what they had won rather than exhaust themselves acquiring more. [11] He and his soldiers saw things differently: while his thoughts encompassed worldwide empire and his programme was still in its initial stages, the men were exhausted by the hardships of the campaign and wished only to enjoy what profits from it lay closest to hand, now that the danger was finally past.

[12] Alexander's ambition prevailed over reason. He called the men to an assembly and addressed them . . .[16]

3   Not even this could force a response from any of the men, who were waiting for their generals and officers to report to the king that they were exhausted from their wounds and the relentless hardship of the campaign, that they were not evading their responsibilities but unable to fulfil them. The generals, however, were overwhelmed by fear and kept their eyes fixed on the ground. [2] So at first a spontaneous murmuring broke out among the men, followed by groans. Little by little their feelings of sadness began to gain freer expression and tears started to flow, so much so that the king's anger turned to pity and he was, despite himself, unable to keep the tears from his own eyes.

16   At this point Alexander gives a speech, meant to inspire the troops, but they were in no mood to be "inspired" by him; because it served only to bring the dangers more vividly before their eyes, it was met with rejection.

[3] Finally, when the entire assembly was weeping profusely, Coenus ventured to approach the tribunal, while the others all hung back, and he indicated his desire to speak. [4] Seeing him take his helmet from his head (the conventional procedure when addressing the king), the men started urging him to plead the army's case.

[5] "May the gods keep disloyal thoughts from us," Coenus declared, "and indeed they do so. Your men are as willing as ever to go wherever you command, to fight, to face danger, to shed our blood in order to transmit your name to posterity. So, if you are going on, we shall follow or go before you wherever you wish, even though we be unarmed, naked and exhausted. [6] But if you are prepared to hear the sincere words of your soldiers, wrung out of them by dire necessity, then please lend a sympathetic ear to men who have unfailingly followed your orders and your leadership and will continue to do so wherever you go.

[7] "By your magnificent achievements, Your Majesty, you have triumphed not over your enemies alone but over your own soldiers, too. Whatever mortals were capable of, we have achieved. We have crossed lands and seas, all of them now better known to us than to their inhabitants. [8] We stand almost at the end of the earth; you are preparing to enter another world and you seek an India even the Indians do not know. You wish to flush out from their coverts and lairs men who live among wild animals and serpents, so that you may traverse in victory more land than the sun looks upon! [9] That is a programme appropriate to your spirit, but beyond ours. For your valour will ever be on the increase, but our energy is already running out. [10] Look at our bodies – debilitated, pierced with all those wounds, decaying with all their scars! Our weapons are already blunt; our armour is wearing out. We put on Persian dress because our own cannot be brought out to us – we have stooped to wearing the clothes of foreigners! [11] How many of us have a cuirass? Who owns a horse? Have an inquiry made into how many are attended by their slaves and what anyone has left of his booty. Conquerors of all, we lack everything! And our problems result not from extravagance; no, on war have we expended the equipment of war. [12] Will you expose this fine army naked to wild beasts? Although the barbarians deliberately exaggerate how many they have of these, even from false reports I realize the quantity is large.

[13] "If you remain determined to push further into India, the area to the south is not so vast. Subdue that and you can proceed quickly to that sea which nature has decided should be the limit of human existence. [14] Why strive for glory by a circuitous route when it sits close at hand? Here, too, you face the Ocean. Unless you prefer aimless wandering, we have reached the point to which your fortune has been leading you. [15] I preferred to say these things to you rather than to the men behind your back, not in order to win the approval of the army standing around us but so that you should hear men speaking their minds rather than making disgruntled murmurings."

[16] When Coenus concluded his speech,[17] shouting and weeping arose all round him, the mingled cries of the men declaring Alexander their "king", their "father", their "lord". [17] By now, the same entreaties were also coming from other officers, especially those with some seniority, whose age gave them greater authority and made their plea to be excused less discreditable. [18] Alexander could not upbraid them for obstinacy, nor yet could his anger be appeased. At a loss for what to do, he jumped down from the dais and ordered his royal quarters to be closed, granting entrance to no one but his customary attendants. [19] Two days were devoted to his anger and on the third he emerged from his tent to issue instructions for twelve altars of square-cut stone to be erected to commemorate his expedition. He further ordered the camp fortifications to be extended and couches, on a larger scale than the human frame required, to be left behind, intending thereby to make everything appear greater than it was, for he was preparing to leave to posterity a fraudulent wonder.

[20] Retracing his steps from here, Alexander pitched camp at the river Acesines where it so happened that Coenus fell ill and died. Alexander grieved for his death but nonetheless added the comment that it was merely for the sake of a few days that Coenus had made his long speech, as if he were the only one who would see Macedonia again.

Rivalry between Craterus and Hephaestion

7(a)   Plutarch, Alexander 47.9–12

Alexander could see that, amongst his greatest friends, Hephaestion accepted his changes and was prepared to go along with them himself, whereas Craterus remained true to his own traditions. He therefore employed Hephaestion for his dealings with the barbarians, and Craterus for those with the Greeks and Macedonians. And, in general, he showed great affection to the former, and great respect to the latter, for he believed – and always said – that Hephaestion loved Alexander, but Craterus loved the king.[18]

As a result, there was a veiled animosity between these two which often led to clashes. Once, on the Indian campaign, they even drew their swords and came to blows; and when their respective friends came to their aid, Alexander rode up. He gave Hephaestion a dressing down in public and called him a senseless idiot for not realizing that he was nothing without Alexander. He also had sharp words for Craterus, in private. He then brought the two together and settled their dispute, and he swore by Ammon and all the other gods that they were the men he loved most of all. But, he added, if he found them quarelling again, he would kill the two of them, or at least the

---

17   Similar sentiments are expressed by Coenus in Arrian 5.27.1–29.1.
18   *Philalexandros* and *philobasileus*.

one who started it. And so, they say, after that they neither said nor did anything against each other, even in joke.

Harpalus, Alexander's Imperial Treasurer

Harpalus son of Machatas was one of the most colorful characters in Alexander's entourage (for his career, see Heckel 1992a: 213–21). Unfit for military service, he was appointed imperial treasurer, and, although he fled from his post before the battle of Issus, he was forgiven by the king and reinstated. During Alexander's absence in India, Harpalus, now residing in Babylon, descended into a life of crime and debauchery. Upon learning of Alexander's impending return, he fled to Tarsus and thence to Athens, taking with him considerable sums of the king's money. For his fate, see §V.4g–h, l; for Harpalus' first flight, see Badian (1960b), Carney (1982), Worthington (1984), and Kingsley (1986); for the satyr-play *Agen*, which lampooned Harpalus, see Snell (1964: 99–138). Cf. also Flower (1997: 258–62).

8(a)   Arrian 3.6.4–7

. . . Alexander assigned the stewardship of the moneys with him to Harpalus son of Machatas, who had recently returned from exile. [5] Harpalus was the first to go into exile while Philip was still king because he was a confidant of Alexander, and Ptolemy son of Lagus, Nearchus son of Androtimus, Erigyius son of Larichus, and Erigyius' brother, Laomedon, were also exiled for the same reason. This was because there had been mistrust between Alexander and Philip ever since Philip married Eurydice and brought shame on Olympias, the mother of Alexander.

[6] When Philip died, the men who had gone into exile because of Alexander now returned. Alexander then appointed Ptolemy as his bodyguard, and put Harpalus in charge of the moneys because he was physically unfit for military service. Erigyius he made cavalry commander of the allies, and his brother Laomedon, because he was bilingual and able to read the barbarian writing, he put in charge of the barbarian prisoners of war. Nearchus he made satrap of Lycia and the territory adjacent to Lycia as far as the Taurus range.

[7] Shortly before the battle that took place at Issus Harpalus was lured by Tauriscus, a vile character, into running off with him. Tauriscus journeyed to the camp of Alexander of Epirus, in Italy, where he died, but Harpalus sought asylum in the Megarid. However, Alexander persuaded him to return by giving him guarantees that no harm would come to him for his flight. And, in fact, it did not, and Harpalus was actually put in charge of the money once more.

8(b)   Athenaeus 13.586c–d

. . . Hyperides also says the following about Glycera in his speech *Against Mantitheus, on a Charge of Assault*: "Taking Glycera daughter of Thalassis with his chariot." It is not clear if this is the Glycera who lived with Harpalus. Talking of her in his books *On the Chian Letter* Theopompus reports that Harpalus sent for Glycera from Athens after the death of Pythionice. When she came, he says, she lived in the palace at Tarsus and was greeted by the common people there with obeisance and had the title of queen.[19] He further says that all were forbidden to honour Harpalus with a crown unless they also paid the same honour to Glycera, and that he had the effrontery to set up a bronze effigy of her in Rhossus beside his own statue. Cleitarchus gave the same story in his *Histories of Alexander*. But the man who wrote the short satyric play *Agen* (whether the author was Python of Catana or King Alexander himself) says the following:

(Speaker B) And yet I am told that Harpalus has sent over tens of thousands of measures of grain, no fewer than those sent by Agen, and thus has become a citizen.
(Speaker A) It was Glycera's, this grain you talk of. That perhaps is going to mean death for them, and will not be simply a deposit for a whore.[20]

8(c)   Athenaeus 13.594d–596b

The Macedonian Harpalus embezzled a lot of Alexander's funds [594e] and sought refuge in Athens. Here he became enamoured of Pythionice, on whom he spent large sums of money, though she was just a *hetaira*, and when she died he built her a monument costing many talents. "When he carried her out for burial," says Posidonius in the twenty-second book of his *Histories*, "he escorted the body with a great chorus of professional musicians, and all manner of instruments and sweet melodies."

In his books *The Descent into the Cave of Trophonius* Dicaearchus observes: [594f] "One would have the same experience arriving at the city of Athens by the so-called Sacred Road from Eleusis. For if a man stands at the point where the temple of Athena and the acropolis first come into view, he will see, built right beside the road, a monument like no other and which no other approaches in size. At first, one would, and with reason, say that this indubitably belonged to Miltiades, or Pericles, or Cimon, or one of the town's worthies. [595a] Certainly one would say it was built by the city and at public expense or, if not, that state authorization had been given for its construction. However, when a close examination shows it to belong to the *hetaira* Pythionice, what is one supposed to expect after that?"

In his *Letter to Alexander* Theopompus criticizes Harpalus' dissipation and says: "Consider and listen attentively to the reports from Babylon of how he

---

19 *Basilissa*.
20 That is, apparently, Harpalus' payment (or "security deposit") for Glycera.

buried Pythionice on her death. Pythionice was the slave of the flute-player Bacchis, and Bacchis had been the slave of Sinope the Thracian, who transferred her trade as a whore from Aegina to Athens. [595b] So Pythionice was not only three times a slave but three times a whore, as well. Now, for more than 200 talents, Harpalus erected two monuments to her. But what surprised everyone was this. Neither Harpalus nor any other of his generals has to this day honoured with a funerary monument the men who died in Cilicia fighting for your realm, whereas monuments to the *hetaira* Pythionice have clearly been completed for some time, one in Athens and one in Babylon. [595c] This woman had been generally available at the going rate to all who wanted her, and to her this man who professes to be your friend had the effrontery to dedicate a shrine and a sacred precinct, and to apply the name Aphrodite Pythionice to the temple and its altar. In doing this he was revealing his scorn for divine retribution and also trying to belittle your honours."

Philemon also mentions these people in his play *The Babylonian*:

Queen of Babylon will you be, if it so transpires;
You know Pythionice and Harpalus.

[595d] Alexis also mentions her in his *Lyciscus*.

After the death of Pythionice, Harpalus sent for Glycera, who was also a *hetaira*. Theopompus[21] documents this, and says that Harpalus refused to let anyone honour him with a crown unless he so honoured the whore as well. "He set up a bronze effigy of Glycera at Rhossus in Syria, where he is also going to set up a statue of you and himself. He also permitted her to live in the palace at Tarsus and allows her to receive *proskynesis* from the people and be addressed as a queen, and to be honoured with such gifts as were more appropriate for your mother and consort."

[595e] The person who wrote the minor satyric play "Agen" also corroborates this, whether the author was Python – of Catana or Byzantium – or even the king himself (the author produced the play when a Dionysiac Festival was held at the River Hydaspes). The play was put on stage when Harpalus had already run away to the coast and defected. It refers to Pythionice as already dead and to Glycera as being with Harpalus and accusing the Athenians of accepting bribes from him. It says:

"The fortress Aornus stands where this reed grows. Here, on the left, there is the whore's famous temple. This Pallides built, afterwards condemning himself to exile because of the affair. There some barbarian wise men saw him in a very sorry state, and persuaded him that they would bring back up the soul of Pythionice."

[596a] Here the playwright called Harpalus "Pallides", but in the following lines he gives him his true name and says:

---

21   Athenaeus 13.586c (above).

(Speaker B) Living so far from there as I do, I earnestly desire to learn from you the fortunes of the land of Attica, and how its people are doing.

(Speaker A) At the time that they were saying that they had been subjected to a life of slavery they dined sufficiently well. Nowadays they are eating only pulse and fennel, and absolutely no wheat.

(B) And yet I am told that Harpalus has sent over tens of thousands of measures of grain, no fewer than those sent by Agen, and thus has become a citizen.

(A) It was Glycera's, this grain you talk of. That perhaps is going to mean death for them, and will not be simply a deposit for a whore.

8(d) Diodorus Siculus 17.108.4–6

Harpalus had been entrusted with looking after the treasure in Babylon and the public revenues, but as soon as the king commenced his Indian campaign he felt he would never return and surrendered himself to a life of dissipation.

Appointed to authority over a vast territory, Harpalus' first "authoritative acts" were the violation of women and illicit affairs with native girls, and he spent much of the treasure on the most intemperate pleasures. He earned a very bad name for himself by importing large quantities of fish all the way from the Red Sea and launching into a very extravagant mode of life. [5] After this he had the most famous courtesan alive – her name was Pythonice[22] – brought to him from Athens. He honoured her with gifts fit for royalty while she lived, and when she died he gave her a lavish funeral and erected for her a very expensive grave in the Attic style.

[6] He next had another courtesan, Glycera by name, brought from Athens, and set her up in immoderate luxury with a very costly life-style. Recognizing fortune's vicissitudes, however, he sought to provide himself with a refuge by showering largesse upon the people of Athens.[23]

The "Opis Mutiny"

At Opis on the Tigris River, Alexander prepared to dismiss a large number of his Macedonian veterans, bringing into the camp at the same time new recruits from the Iranian satrapies known as the *Epigoni*. This, although it was not the only cause of discontent, triggered an angry reaction within the camp, one which Alexander suppressed by arresting and executing the most outspoken of the mutineers, as well as by offering words of conciliation. The appeal for "concord" (*homonoia*) gave rise to the idea that Alexander was trying to promote a "Brotherhood of Mankind", an idea which has been thoroughly discredited and is discussed today merely as a footnote to Alexander scholarship. Here we are confronted not with dreams of unity but with the reality of opposition within Alexander's army.

---

22 Thus Diodorus, but elsewhere "Pythionice."

23 For the rest of the account (§§6–8), see §V.4g, this volume.

9(a)　Diodorus Siculus 17.109.1–3

The king himself selected the most senior of the Macedonian citizens and released them from service – some 10,000 men. [2] Told that many of these were crippled with debt, he paid off what they owed in a single day, and this amounted to slightly less than 10,000 talents.

The Macedonians remaining behind, however, were becoming mutinous and were shouting him down in the assembly. Exasperated, Alexander boldly reviled their conduct. Frightening the whole gathering, he dared to jump down from the dais and, with his own hands, to deliver to his attendants for punishment the ringleaders of the mutiny.

[3] The disaffection greatly increased over this, and the king appointed certain hand-picked Persians as officers and promoted them to the highest ranks. The Macedonians then had a change of heart and showered Alexander with many tearful entreaties, but it was only with difficulty that they persuaded him to become reconciled with them.

9(b)　Quintus Curtius Rufus 10.2.8–14

Sending his older soldiers home, Alexander ordered a force of 13,000 infantry and 2,000 cavalry to be selected for him to keep back in Asia. He believed he could hold Asia with an army of modest proportions because he had deployed garrisons in a number of places and populated the recently established cities with colonists who wanted only to make a fresh start. [9] However, before choosing the men he would keep back, he ordered all the troops to declare their debts; for he had discovered that many were deeply in debt, and he had decided to discharge their obligations himself even though these derived from their own extravagance. [10] The men thought they were being put to a test to make it easier for Alexander to tell the extravagant from the thrifty, and so they let time slip by without doing anything. Alexander was well aware that it was embarrassment rather than insubordination that stopped them acknowledging their debts, so he had tables set at points throughout the camp and 10,000 talents put out on them. [11] With that an honest disclosure was finally made by the men and, from all that money, what remained was a mere 130 talents! Yes, that army which had defeated so many rich nations took from Asia more prestige than booty.

[12] Now when it was discovered that some were being sent home and others detained, the men assumed that Alexander was going to fix the royal seat permanently in Asia. Beside themselves and oblivious of military discipline, they filled the camp with mutinous comments and attacked the king with more abuse than ever before. Then they all proceeded to demand demobilization, at the same time displaying their scarred faces and grey heads. [13] Neither reprimands from their officers nor their own respect for the king restrained them. Alexander wished to address them, but they prevented him with their

mutinous shouting and soldierly truculence, as they publicly declared their refusal to take a step in any direction save homewards. [14] At last silence fell, more because they thought Alexander had experienced a change of heart than because they could do so themselves, and they awaited his reaction.

9(c)   Arrian 7.8–11

When he reached Opis, Alexander brought the Macedonians together and proclaimed that he was releasing from active service and sending home the men whom old age or physical impairment rendered unfit for fighting. On those who remained, he said, he would confer so much that it would make them the envy of people at home, and fire the rest of the Macedonians with a wish to share with them those very hardships and dangers that they were experiencing. [2] It was certainly with the intention of humouring the Macedonians that Alexander said this, but these felt they were already despised by him and were in his eyes totally unfit for fighting, and so they were indignant at the speech he made – and not without reason. It came on top of the numerous other things that had hurt them throughout the entire length of the campaign. Many were the occasions on which they had already been stung by his Persian dress (a deliberate insult), by the barbarian *Epigoni* being equipped in Macedonian manner, and the inclusion of foreign cavalry in the ranks of the Companions.

[3] As a result, they did not suffer this indignity in silence. They told him to release them all from service – he should continue the campaign with his father (a snide reference to Ammon). Alexander was, in the circumstances, more sensitive than usual, anyway, and after receiving all the attentions from the barbarians he was no longer as understanding with the Macedonians as he had been in the past. On hearing these comments, he leaped down from the dais with the officers who were around him and ordered the arrest of the most prominent of the rabble-rousers, personally indicating to the hypaspists with his finger the men who should be arrested. They numbered about thirteen. These he ordered to be hauled away for execution, and when the others fell into a stunned silence he mounted the dais once more and spoke as follows:

9   "Men of Macedon: This speech that I shall be delivering is not intended to check your desire to go home, for as far as I am concerned you can go wherever you wish. No, it is to make you realize, as you leave, the sort of person I am and the sort of people you have been in your dealings with me.

[2] "I shall open my address, as is only fair, with my father Philip. When Philip took you on, you were a pack of indigent drifters. Most of you were dressed in skins and grazed on the hills a few sheep, for which you fought – and fought badly – against Illyrians, Triballians and the Thracians on your borders. Philip gave you cloaks to wear in place of the skins, and he brought you down from the hills to the plains. He made you a match in war for the

barbarians on your frontiers; your security no longer depended on the strength of your position but on your own military prowess. He made you city-dwellers, and conferred on you the benefits of a civilized life of law and custom. [3] From being slaves and vassals he made you lords over those very barbarians for whom you and your possessions were earlier simply prey and plunder, and he made most of Thrace subject to Macedonia. He seized the most opportune spots on the coast and promoted the country's trade, while he also gave security to its mining operations. [4] He made you masters of the Thessalians, of whom you were scared to death in days of old, and he brought low the Phocians, thereby making the road into Greece wide and easy instead of narrow and difficult. The Athenians and Thebans were ever waiting to pounce on Macedonia. These he humbled to such an extent – and at the time I was actually working alongside him – that, instead of our paying taxes to the Athenians and being subject to Thebes, *their* security was in turn actually provided by us. [5] Entering the Peloponnese he settled matters there, as well, and, by being appointed commander-in-chief of the whole of Greece for the campaign against Persia, he did not bring more glory on himself than he did on the Macedonian people as a whole.

[6] "So much for the services rendered to you by my father. Considered on their own, they are great; but they are small compared with mine. My inheritance from my father consisted of a few gold and silver drinking-cups and less than 60 talents in the treasury. There were also about 500 talents' worth of debt contracted by Philip. I myself borrowed another 800 in addition to this, and then, launching forth from a country that was failing to sustain you properly, I immediately opened up a way through the Hellespont for you, despite Persian supremacy at sea at the time . . .

10   "Perhaps you will reply that I made all these gains through your exertions and hardships, while my leadership involved no such exertion and no such hardship. But is any of you aware of having endured more for me than I for him? Come now, any one of you with wounds – let him strip off and show them, and I shall show mine in turn. [2] In my case, there is no part of my body – not at the front, in any case – that has been left without a wound, and there is no kind of weapon, be it for hand-to-hand fighting or throwing, whose scars I do not have on myself. I have sword gashes from hand-to-hand fighting, arrow wounds, injuries from artillery projectiles; and I have been struck in many places by stones and clubs. All this for you and your glory and your riches, as I take you triumphant through every land and sea, over all the rivers, mountains and plains. [3] I have made the same marriage as you, and the children of many of you will be related to my own.

"In the case of someone being in debt I was not over-curious about how that occurred when you had so much pay and had so much plunder whenever there was looting after a siege – I simply settled the debts. Most of you have crowns of gold as everlasting memorials of your courage, and of the honour you were shown by me. [4] And as for any who lost his life, his passing was a glorious one, his burial splendid. Most have bronze statues standing at home, and their parents live in honour, exempt from all duties and taxes. For under my leadership not one of your number died in flight.

[5] "And at this point I was going to dismiss only those of you unfit for battle, men who would be envied by those at home. But since you all wish to leave, go, all of you, and when you return home report . . .[24] [7] [and tell them that] when you came back to Susa, you went off and left Alexander, transferring your protection of him to the barbarians he had conquered. Such a report will perhaps win you honour among men, and will certainly have the approval of heaven! Go!"

11   With these words he leaped swiftly from the dais and proceeded to the palace where he remained, oblivious to his personal needs, and was not seen by any of the *hetairoi*. In fact, he was not seen the next day, either. On the third day he called in his select group of Persians and allocated amongst them command of the army battalions. He designated some as his kinsmen, and to these he restricted the right to kiss him.

[2] In the immediate aftermath of the speech the Macedonians simply stood there by the dais, stunned to silence by his words, and none followed the king as he took his leave, save for the *hetairoi* who were in attendance on him and the Somatophylakes. The mass of the soldiers had nothing to do or say as they loitered there, but they did not want to leave, either. [3] Then the facts about the Persians and Medes were reported to them, the granting of commands to Persians and barbarian troops being enlisted in the Macedonian companies. They heard about the Macedonian names being used. They heard about a Persian *agema*, so-called, and Persian *pezetairoi*; they heard of others called *astheteroi*, of a Persian contingent of argyraspids and of a Persian Companions' cavalry, which now had *another* royal *agema*. At this point they were no longer in control of themselves. [4] They ran in a body to the palace and there threw down their weapons before the doors as a gesture of supplication to the king, and standing before the doors themselves they called out to him begging for admission. They said they were willing to surrender those responsible for the disorder, and that they would certainly not leave the doors, day or night, unless Alexander showed some compassion for them.

[5] When this was reported to the king, he quickly came forth. He saw their dejection and heard most of them weeping and wailing, at which he also shed tears. He went forward as if to say something, and they remained where they were, pleading with him. [6] Then one of their number, a man called Callines, who enjoyed some distinction because of his age and his position as officer in the Companion cavalry, said something like: "Your Majesty: What hurts the Macedonians is the fact that you have now made some of the Persians your kinsmen, that Persians are called 'Alexander's kinsmen' and these kiss you, while no Macedonian has yet enjoyed that honour."

[7] "But I regard all of you as my kinsmen," said Alexander in reply, "and from now on I shall call you that." When he said that, Callines went up to

---

24 Here Alexander tells them to report their various exploits in the East.

him and kissed him, followed by all others who wished to kiss him. And with that they shouldered their weapons and went off to the camp shouting and singing a song of victory.

[8] Alexander celebrated the occasion with a sacrifice made to his usual gods, and hosted a public feast. Here he was seated in the midst of all the guests, the Macedonians beside him, the Persians next to them and after these members of the other races, ranked according to their station or some other distinction. Alexander and those next to him drew from the same mixing-bowl and made the same libations, with the Greek soothsayers and the Magi initiating the proceedings. [9] Foremost among the blessings for which Alexander prayed was that the empire of Macedonians and Persians enjoy harmony and accord. It is said that participants in the feast numbered 9,000, and that these all poured one and the same libation, singing a victory song immediately afterwards.

XI Alexander's Final Days, Final Plans, and the Division of Power after his Death

Death of Alexander

The accounts of Alexander's death that follow attribute it to natural causes and derive, in part, from the *Ephemerides* or *Royal Journals* or *Royal Diaries* of the king. (Their author was supposed to be Eumenes of Cardia or Diodotus of Erythrae [or both]. If they were fabricated in order to disguise the true cause of Alexander's death, the name of Eumenes may have been used to lend credence to their claims.) The nature and authenticity of this work have been called into question, and it is also likely that some of the more sensational works, like those of Ephippus of Olynthus and Nicoboule, which attribute Alexander's death to heavy drinking, are attempts to deflect the charge that he was poisoned. The possible causes of his death are discussed as follows: for alcoholism, O'Brien (1980, 1992); for malaria, Engels (1978b); for typhoid, Borza and Reames-Zimmerman (2000). Even in death Alexander was able to influence the history of his successors: see Errington (1976: 138–45) and Erskine (2002).

1(a)   Plutarch, Alexander 73–7

As Alexander was heading for Babylon, Nearchus came back from his second sea voyage, having made his way through the ocean to the Euphrates. He told the king that he had met a number of Chaldeans whose advice was that Alexander keep away from Babylon. [2] The king ignored this and continued his journey. Then, when he stood at the city walls, he observed a large number of crows squabbling and pecking at each other, some of them falling dead before him. [3] After that he was brought incriminating information about his governor of Babylon, Apollodorus, to the effect that he had conducted a sacrifice to learn about the king's future. Alexander thereupon summoned the seer Pythagoras, [4] and when the latter did not deny what had gone on he asked him how the victims had turned out. Pythagoras stated that the livers had the lobe missing. "Oh God", replied Alexander, "that is a serious omen", [5] and yet he did not maltreat Pythagoras in any way. He did, however, regret not having listened to Nearchus, and now spent most of his time – under canvas or sailing on the Euphrates – outside the confines of Babylon.

[6] Alexander was disturbed by several omens. For example, a lion, which was the largest and finest of his animals reared in captivity, was attacked by a domesticated ass, which killed it with a kick. [7] Another time he had undressed for oiling down and was playing ball, and when he had to dress again the young men playing with him saw a man sitting in silence on his throne and wearing the king's diadem and royal robe. [8] Asked who he was, the man for a long while remained silent; then, pulling himself together with difficulty, he said his name was Dionysius and he was a native of Messene. He had been taken from the sea to Babylon on some criminal charge, he said, and spent a long time in prison; [9] but recently Serapis had appeared to him, removed his irons and brought him to that place. The god had then ordered him to put on the robe and diadem, and to sit on the throne and say nothing.

74　On hearing this, Alexander followed the priests' instructions and had the man done away with, but melancholy took hold of him, and he lost confidence in divine support and became suspicious of his friends. [2] His fears centred mostly on Antipater and his sons. One of these, Iolas,[1] was his chief wine steward. The other was Cassander, who, recently arrived in Babylon, had seen some barbarians performing *proskynesis* and, being brought up in traditional Greek fashion and never having beheld such sight before, burst into uncontrollable laughter. [3] Alexander was furious. With both hands he grasped him violently by the hair and beat his head against the wall. [4] On another occasion Cassander wanted to counter charges made by some accusers of Antipater, but Alexander cut him short. "What?" he asked, "Do you mean to say that men would come all this way when they have suffered no wrongdoing, just to make false accusations?" [5] Cassander's reply was that the very fact of their coming a long way from what could disprove their claims was itself an indication that the accusations were false. Alexander laughed and said: "Yes, such are the sophisms of Aristotle's students that serve both sides of the debate, but you will regret it if it becomes clear that you have done the slightest harm to these men." [6] They say that fear of the king became so intense and deeply rooted in Cassander's heart that he still felt it even many years later when he was now on the throne of Macedon and master of Greece. He was ambling around Delphi and looking at the statues when the sculpted figure of Alexander came into view. He was gripped with sudden terror, which made his body tremble and shake. The sight made his head swim, and only with difficulty did he pull himself together.

75　Alexander, then, lapsed into religiosity at that time, his thoughts troubled and full of dread, and there was no strange or unusual phenomenon, no matter how insignificant, that he did not interpret as a portent or as a sign from heaven. His palace was full of people making sacrifices, conducting purification ceremonies and seeking omens. [2] True it is that disbelief in the

---

1　Also "Iolaus" or "Iollas."

divine and disrespect for it is a terrible thing, but terrible, too, is superstition that, like water . . . †always runs to a lower level . . .†. [3] However, oracles from the god relating to Hephaestion were brought to him, and after that he put an end to his grieving and went back to his sacrificing and drinking. [4] He gave a magnificent banquet for Nearchus, and afterwards took a bath, as he usually did when about to go to bed, but then, pressed by Medius, he went to continue the party in Medius' tent. [5] There he spent the whole night and the next day drinking, during which he began to develop a fever. He did not drink the "cup of Heracles" nor did he suddenly feel a severe pain in the back as if he had been struck by a spear, though some authors think they should add these details as a way of fashioning a tragic and highly emotional finale to a great drama. [6] Aristobulus simply states that Alexander developed a high fever and that his raging thirst made him drink wine, after which delirium set in and he died on the 30th of the month of Daesius.

76   The following account of the illness is given in the *Ephemerides*. On the 18th of Daesius he slept in the bathhouse because of his fever. [2] The next day he took a bath and went back to his bedroom, where he spent the day playing dice with Medius. Then, late in the day, he bathed again and sacrificed to the gods, after which he took a bite and spent the night in a fever. [3] On the 20th he bathed once more, and made his usual sacrifice. He then made his bed in the bathhouse and spent his time with Nearchus and his officers, listening to an account of their sea voyage and the ocean. [4] The 21st he passed in the same manner, but his temperature was higher. He had a bad night and the following day his fever was extremely high. [5] Removed from the bathhouse he then lay by the large swimming pool, conversing here with his generals on the subject of assessing personnel with a view to filling the vacant posts in the army command.

[6] On the 24th his fever was again extremely high, and he was carried outside to perform the sacrifice. He gave orders for his highest-ranking officers to remain in the court, and for the taxiarchs and pentacosiarchs to spend the night outside. [7] He was then transported on the 25th to the palace on the other river bank and here he slept a little, but the fever did not subside. When his generals came to his side he was unable to speak, and that remained the case on the 26th. As a result the Macedonian rank and file thought he was dead. [8] They came to the doors shouting and uttering threats to the *hetairoi* until they had to give in to them. The doors were flung open for them, and they filed past his bed, one by one, wearing only their tunics. [9] That day, Python and Seleucus were sent to the temple of Sarapis to ask if they should bring Alexander there, but the god's reply was that they should leave him where he was. On the 28th, towards evening, he died [10/11 June, 323: ed.].

77   Most of the above account follows the *Ephemerides* word for word. [2] There was no suspicion of poisoning in the immediate aftermath,[2] but they

2   Or possibly the meaning is that "no one, i.e., no particular person, *incurred* suspicion of having poisoned Alexander" (Hamilton 1968: 213).

say that five years later Olympias was given information which led to her putting many to death and scattering the remains of Iolas, now dead, alleging that he had poured the poison for Alexander. [3] Those who maintain that Aristotle advised Antipater on the deed, and that it was he who was entirely responsible for providing the poison, say that their account comes from one Hagnothemis who purportedly heard it from King Antigonus. [4] According to them the poison was a chilly water, cold as ice, that came from a certain cliff situated in Nonacris. This they gathered as a fine dew and set in an ass's hoof since no other receptacle could hold it (any other it would shatter with its coldness and pungent strength). [5] Most authors, however, believe the story to be a complete fiction, and there is a piece of evidence favouring them which is not insignificant. During the quarrels between Alexander's generals, which lasted several days, the corpse lay unattended in hot and stifling conditions and yet showed no sign of the deterioration such a death would cause, but remained clean and fresh.

1(b)   Arrian 7.24–26, 28

But the end was now drawing near for Alexander himself, and according to Aristobulus there was some further portent of what was coming. It happened as follows.

Alexander, says Aristobulus, was in the process of distributing amongst the Macedonian contingents the forces that had arrived from Persia with Peucestes, and from the coast with Philoxenus and Menander. Feeling thirsty, he moved from his seat, leaving empty the royal throne, [2] which was flanked on both sides by couches with silver feet, on which his *hetairoi* would sit to attend on him. Some man,³ one of the people to whom nobody was paying attention – he was one of those under open arrest, some say – saw the throne and the couches unoccupied, with only eunuchs standing around the throne (for the *hetairoi* had got up with the king when he left). He made his way through the eunuchs, went up to the throne and sat himself down on it.

[3] Aristobulus says that the eunuchs, following some Persian custom, did not make him leave the throne; instead they tore their own clothes and beat their breasts and faces, as if reacting to some terrible calamity. When this was reported to Alexander, he issued orders for the man who had taken the seat to be put on the rack, for he wanted to know if his act was part of a treacherous scheme. But the man would say only that doing it was something that simply came into his head; and the seers' prediction that it boded no good for Alexander was strengthened by this.

[4] Not many days had elapsed after the incident and Alexander was holding a dinner with his friends, at which he drank well into the night (this followed the traditional sacrifices he made to ensure good fortune, and some conducted

3 Dionysius of Messene, otherwise unknown.

as a direct result of the prophecy). It is said that the king also distributed sac-rificial meat and wine to the individual companies and detachments. After the drinking, some have recorded, Alexander wished to leave to go to bed, but Medius, the most trusted of his *hetairoi* at the time, met him and pressed him to join his party – it would be a pleasant drinking session, he said.

25   The *Royal Diaries* report the matter as follows. Following the after-dinner drinking, Alexander drank on in Medius' quarters, then got up, took a bath and went to sleep. He then had dinner once more with Medius, and again drank far into the night. Leaving the drinking session, he took a bath and, after the bath, ate a little and slept where he was, because he was already suffering from a fever. [2] He was, however, carried out on a litter to perform the usual sacrifices for the day, and after discharging them he lay down in the officers' mess until dusk. At that point he gave his officers their instruc-tions *vis-à-vis* their forthcoming march or sea voyage, ordering those going on foot to be ready in three days, and those who were sailing to be ready for the voyage in four.

[3] From the mess he was taken on his litter to the river where he boarded a boat and crossed the river to the garden. Here he again bathed and took a rest, and the following day he bathed once more and performed the cus-tomary sacrifices. He then went to his bed where he lay down, chatting to Medius, and gave orders to his officers to come to him at dawn. [4] After this, he ate little at dinner and was once more taken back to his bed where he remained in the grip of the fever all night long.

The next day he took another bath and performed the appointed sacrifices, and from the point of his discharging his religious duties the fever never let up. Even so, he called his officers to his side and instructed them to have everything prepared for the sea voyage. In the evening he took his bath, after which he was now in a sorry state. [5] The next day he was moved to the build-ing by the swimming pool, and he performed the appointed sacrifices. He was suffering badly, but he none the less called to him his highest-ranking offi-cers and issued further instructions about the voyage.

It was only with difficulty that he could be carried out to offer the sacri-fices the following day, but he still gave his orders to the officers with regard to the voyage. [6] The day after that he again offered the prescribed sacrifices, despite his poor state of health, but he gave orders for the officers to remain in the court, and the chiliarchs and pentacosiarchs were to remain before the doors. By now he was in a very bad way, and was taken from the garden to the palace. His officers came to see him, and though he recognized them he no longer spoke to them – he had lost the power of speech. He remained in a high fever throughout the night and the following day, as well as the next night and the day that followed.

26   Such is the account in the *Royal Diaries*, where another detail is added, namely that the soldiers wished to see him. Some simply wanted to see him alive, but as there were already reports of his passing I imagine that others speculated that his death was being concealed by his bodyguards. But most

were prompted to force their way in to see Alexander simply by feelings of grief and regret at losing the king. They say that he had no ability to speak as the army filed past, but that he welcomed them individually by raising his head and giving a sign of recognition with his eyes.

[2] The *Royal Diaries* add that Pithon, Attalus, Demophon and Peucestas, along with Cleomenes, Menidas and Seleucus, slept in the shrine of Serapis. They asked the deity if Alexander would be better off being carried into the god's temple where he could supplicate the god and be tended by him, but a reply came back to the effect that he should not be carried to the shrine, that it would be better for him to remain where he was. [3] The *hetairoi* reported this and shortly afterwards Alexander expired, revealing this now to be the "better" thing.

There are no particulars other than these recorded by either Aristobulus or Ptolemy. Some, however, have recounted that the *hetairoi* asked the king to whom he was leaving his throne, and that his reply was, "To the strongest." Others say that he added to these words that he saw there would be "great funerary games in his honour."

. . .

28　Alexander died in the 114th Olympiad, when Hegesias was archon at Athens. He lived, according to Aristobulus, 32 years and was 8 months into his 33rd, and his reign lasted 12 years and 8 months.[4]

1(c)　*Quintus Curtius Rufus 10.5.1–6*

Tears welled up as they looked at him, and they appeared not as an army visiting its king but one attending his funeral. [2] The grief was especially intense among those at his bedside. Alexander looked at them and said: "After my death will you find a king who deserves such men?"

[3] Incredibly, he maintained the same posture which he had adopted before admitting the men until he had received the last salute from the whole army. He then dismissed the rank and file and, as though released from all life's obligations, collapsed in exhaustion. [4] He bade his friends draw near since, by now, even his voice had started to fail, and then he took his ring from his finger and handed it to Perdiccas. He also gave instructions that they should have his body transported to Hammon. [5] When they asked him to whom he bequeathed his kingdom, he answered, "To the best man," but added that he could already foresee great funeral games for himself provided by that issue. [6] When Perdiccas further asked when he wished divine honours paid to him, he said he wanted them when they themselves were happy. These were Alexander's last words; he died moments later.

4　By this calculation, Alexander's accession would date to October 336. See Hammond (1992c: 359–60).

1(d)   Justin 12.13.3–16.1

Then one of his Magi forewarned him against entering the city of Babylon, declaring the place was destined to be fatal for him. [4] He therefore passed by Babylon and withdrew across the Euphrates to the long-deserted city of Borsipa. [5] There he was prevailed upon by the philosopher Anaxarchus to disregard the predictions of the Magi as false and unreliable: what was subject to fate was beyond the knowledge of mortals, and what was due to nature could not be changed. [6] He therefore turned back towards Babylon where he gave the army several days' rest; and during this time he resumed his old practice, now long discontinued, of the ceremonial banquet. [7] Abandoning himself completely to revelry, he spent a day and a night without sleep. As he was leaving the dinner, the Thessalian Medius decided to renew the festivities and invited Alexander and his companions to join him. [8] Alexander took a cup, but had not yet drunk more than half of it when he uttered a groan as if he had been pierced by a spear [9] and was carried semi-conscious from the banquet. He was racked with such agony that he asked for a sword to put an end to it, and the pain of men's touch was like that of a wound. [10] His friends put it about that the cause of his illness was excessive drinking, but in fact it was a conspiracy, though the scandal was suppressed by the power of the successors.

14   The instigator of the conspiracy was Antipater. He could see that his closest friends had been put to death by Alexander, that his son-in-law, Alexander the Lyncestian, had been killed by him, [2] that his own great achievements in Greece had earned him the king's envy rather than appreciation [3] and that he had also been the object of various accusations made by Alexander's mother Olympias. [4] Then there were the cruel executions, a few days before, of the governors of the conquered nations. [5] On the basis of all this he thought he had been summoned from Macedonia not to join the campaign but to face punishment. [6] So, to anticipate the king's move, he suborned his own son, Cassander, who, along with his brothers Philip and Iollas, used to wait upon the king. He gave Cassander a poison, [7] the virulence of which was such that it could not be contained by bronze, iron or earthenware; it could be transported only in a horse's hoof. He forewarned his son to trust no one but his brothers and the Thessalian. [8] This was why the drinking-party was arranged and restarted in the Thessalian's quarters. [9] Philip and Iollas, who used to taste and add the water to the king's drinks, put the poison in cold water and added this to his cup after they had performed the tasting.

15   After three days Alexander felt that his death was certain and he declared that he could recognize the fate that had overtaken the house of his forefathers, for most of the Aeacids were dead by their thirtieth year. [2] Then the soldiers became restless, suspecting that their king was dying because of treachery, but Alexander himself placated them. He had himself carried to the

highest spot in the city where he let them all come to see him and, as they wept, held out his hand for them to kiss. [3] They were all in tears, but Alexander, so far from weeping, gave not the slightest indication of being in low spirits – he actually comforted some who could not control their grief and gave others messages for their parents. [4] He was as undaunted in the face of death as he had been in the face of the enemy.

[5] When the men were dismissed he asked his friends at his bedside if they thought they would find a king like him again. [6] All were silent; then Alexander himself added that, while he did not know the answer to that question, he did know something else, which he could predict and almost see with his own eyes, namely how much blood Macedonia would shed in this struggle, how much slaughter and gore she would sacrifice to his ghost. [7] Finally he gave instructions that his body be buried in the temple of Hammon. [8] When his friends saw that he was sinking they asked him whom he appointed as heir to his throne, to which he replied, "the most deserving man." [9] Such was his greatness of spirit that although he was leaving a son, Hercules, a brother, Arridaeus, and a wife, Roxane, who was pregnant, he gave no thought to family ties and named as his heir the most deserving man. [10] He implied it was wrong for a brave man to be replaced by anyone but a brave man, or for the power of a great kingdom to be left to any but those of proven worth. [11] It was as if by these words he had given the signal for war amongst his friends, or thrown amongst them the apple of Strife. They all rose to compete with each other, and canvassing the mob sought in secret the favour of the troops. [12] On the sixth day Alexander's voice failed. He removed his ring and handed it to Perdiccas, a gesture which quelled the growing dissension amongst his friends. [13] For even if Perdiccas had not been verbally designated heir by Alexander, it seemed that he was the chosen one in the king's judgment.

16   Alexander died in the month of June at the age of 33.

1(e)   Diodorus Siculus 17.117.1–5

The seers instructed Alexander to make lavish sacrifices to the gods, and meanwhile he received an extremely importunate invitation to a drinking-party in the quarters of one of his friends, the Thessalian Medius. There he consumed large quantities of neat wine, eventually filling, and draining, the great "cup of Heracles." [2] All of a sudden he let out a loud cry of pain, as if he had been struck a severe blow, at which his friends took him by the hand and escorted him out. His personal attendants took charge of him, immediately putting him to bed and keeping a careful watch over him, [3] but his distress worsened and the doctors were summoned. None of them could help him, and he was continually wracked with multiple pains and excruciating suffering.

Losing all hope of surviving, Alexander removed his ring and gave it to Perdiccas. [4] His friends asked: "To whom do you leave the throne?", and he answered "To the strongest," adding to this what were to be his final words, that the foremost of his friends would all organize a great funerary contest in his honour.

[5] So Alexander died, in the manner described above, after a rule of twelve years and seven months, and after accomplishing the greatest of feats, greater than those not only of the rulers that preceded him, but of those who were to come after him, right down to our day.

Rumors of Poisoning

Rumours that the king was the victim of foul play arose almost immediately after his death: Onesicritus is said to have withheld the names of the poisoners for fear of reprisals and, according to the pseudo-Plutarchean *Lives of the Ten Orators*, Hyperides was said to have proposed honors for Iolaus, the son of Antipater, for poisoning the king. In 317 Olympias overturned the grave of Iolaus claiming that he had murdered her son (Diodorus 19.11.8; see also §XI.1a). At some point, perhaps as early as 318/17 or as late as 308 BC, someone (possibly Holcias) authored a pamphlet on *The Last Days and Testament of Alexander the Great*, which purported to tell the whole story of the king's death and to give the terms of his will. See, in particular, Heckel (1988) and Bosworth (2000); cf. also Baynham (2000).

2 (a) *Quintus Curtius Rufus 10.10.5–20*

Some have believed that the distribution of the provinces was prescribed by Alexander's will, but I have ascertained that this report, though transmitted by our sources, is without foundation. [6] In fact, after the division of the empire, it seems they would have all individually established their own dominions – if a boundary could ever stand in the way of unbridled ambition. [7] For men who recently had been subjects of the king had individually seized control of huge kingdoms, ostensibly as administrators of an empire belonging to another, and any pretext for conflict was removed since they all belonged to the same race and were geographically separated from each other by the boundaries of their several jurisdictions. [8] But it was difficult to remain satisfied with what the opportunity of the moment had brought them: initial possessions are disdained when there is hope of greater things. So they all thought that expanding their kingdoms was an easier matter than taking possession of them had been in the first place.

[9] The king's body had been lying in the coffin for six days while everybody's attention had been diverted from the obsequies to forming a government. [10] Nowhere are more searing temperatures to be found than in the area of Mesopotamia, where they are such as to cause the deaths of many animals caught on open ground – so intense is the heat of the sun and the atmosphere, which bakes everything like a fire. [11] Springs are infrequent and are craftily concealed by the natives who keep them for their own use, while strangers are kept ignorant of them. What I report now is the traditional

account rather than what I believe myself: [12] when Alexander's friends eventually found time to attend to his corpse, the men who had entered the tent saw that no decay had set into it and that there was not even the slightest discoloration. The vital look that comes from the breath of life had not yet vanished from his face. [13] So it was that, after being instructed to see to the body in their traditional fashion, the Egyptians and Chaldeans did not dare touch him at first since he seemed to be alive. Then, praying that it be lawful in the eyes of god and man for humans to touch a god, they cleaned out his body. A golden sarcophagus was filled with perfumes, and on Alexander's head were placed the insignia of his rank.

[14] Many believed his death was due to poison, administered to him by a son of Antipater called Iollas, one of Alexander's attendants. It is true that Alexander had often been heard to remark that Antipater had regal aspirations, that his powers exceeded those of a general, that he was conceited after his famous Spartan victory and that he claimed as his due all the things that Alexander had granted him. [15] There is also a belief current that Craterus had been sent with a group of veterans to murder Antipater. [16] Now it is well known that the posion produced in Macedonia has the power to consume even iron, and that only an ass's hoof is resistant to the fluid. [17] (They give the name "Styx"[5] to the source from which this deadly venom comes.) This, it was believed, was brought by Cassander, passed on to his brother Iollas, and by him slipped into the king's final drink. [18] Whatever credence such stories gained, they were soon scotched by the power of the people defamed by the gossip. For Antipater usurped the throne of Macedon and of Greece as well, [19] and he was succeeded by his son, after the murder of all who were even distantly related to Alexander.

[20] Alexander's body was taken to Memphis by Ptolemy, into whose power Egypt had fallen, and transferred from there a few years later to Alexandria, where every mark of respect continues to be paid to his memory and his name.

2 (b)   Liber de Morte Testamentumque Alexandri Magni
(The Book on the Death and the Testament of Alexander the Great)

What follows is a translation of the complete text of the *Liber de Morte*, which was appended to the *Metz Epitome* but is not, in fact, part of the same work. Parallel texts in Greek can be found in the *Alexander Romance* (Pseudo-Callisthenes).

[87] ⟨. . .⟩ Alexander was brought a letter from his mother Olympias containing a detailed account of the wrongs she had suffered at the hands of Antipater, who had been left behind as his governor in Macedonia. If Alexander did not

5   This was, of course, also the name of a river in the Underworld, but in this case it was a stream located in Arcadia.

remove him, said Olympias, she would seek refuge in Epirus. Alexander was annoyed, and to reduce their feuding he wished to summon Antipater and replace him with Craterus. [88] Antipater suspected that his name had been blackened and, since he had heard that Alexander's successes had increased his arrogance and ruthlessness, he was anxious about his own safety. Accordingly, he formed a plan to assassinate Alexander, preparing for him some poison †which he set in an iron box. This he then enclosed in a mule's hoof bound with iron in order to contain the virulence of the poison†.

[89] Antipater passed the box to his son Cassander, to whom he unfolded the plot, at the same time giving him gifts to take to the king in Babylon and instructing him to confer on his arrival with his younger brother, Iollas, an attendant of Alexander's, and conclude the business in partnership with him.

[90] Meanwhile, after spending several days in Babylon, Alexander was taking a siesta in his bedroom when a peasant woman came into the palace bringing with her in a blanket a freak to which she had given birth. This had the following shape: the upper part, down to the loins, was that of a boy; the lower was encircled by the fore-parts of wild animals – those of a lion, then a wolf, third a panther, fourth a dog and, fifth, a wild boar – so that the entire figure looked very much as ⟨Scylla⟩ does in paintings.[6] [91] The animals, ⟨however⟩, were alive while the body of the boy was completely dead and livid.[7]

When the king's chamber-servants gathered around the woman, she asked them to report to him that she wished to bring him information about a miracle. The message was brought to Alexander and the woman was summoned to him. On entering, she asked him to tell ⟨all who were present⟩ to leave the room, and, when they were gone, she showed the king the monster, telling him that she was its mother. [92] The sight of it terrified Alexander, who had the magi and his Chaldaean acquaintances summoned to him. Four appeared, but Philip,[8] who was older than the others and on very good terms with the king, was less prompt than they †in coming to the meeting†. Alexander then revealed the monstrosity to those who had come and threatened them with execution unless they gave him a complete account of what this creature portended. They replied that it was a very favourable omen, that, just as the human body grew above the wild animals, so he was to have under his sway the wild and barbarous tribes of the whole world. After saying this they left.

[93] Not long afterwards the ⟨Philip⟩ whom I have mentioned above arrived. At the sight of the freak he cried out at the top of his voice, at the same time ripping his clothes and tearing out his hair with both hands in lamentation at the sight of so great a king and a man of such qualities at the very end of

6 For such paintings see Pollitt (1990: 157, 167).
7 For the possible significance of these beasts, see Baynham (2000).
8 The MS appears to have read *phippus*, but Philippus is not a plausible name for a Chaldaean. It is tempting to see a reference to either Apollodorus or, more likely, his brother Peithagoras, a seer from Amphipolis (*phippus* would thus be a corruption of the place of origin) who predicted the deaths of Hephaestion and Alexander.

his days. The sight of this made Alexander take notice and disturbed him. But still he urged Philip to be resolute and tell him what he saw. He was a man, he added, and he could not alter what was fated to come to pass. [94] Philip sighed deeply. "Ah, your Majesty," he said, "one cannot count you among the living – your body has practically left the mortal plane." Asked the reason for this remark, he replied: "Oh greatest of mortals, mark my words. This human portion which you see, that is you; the things you see which look like wild animals are †the savage and barbarous peoples under your rule†. Now, if the human part were alive, you would have power over them; ⟨but . . .⟩ just as these animals are the enemies of mankind, so the people you have around you are ⟨your⟩ foes, and in a short while your death will bring about a change in the power structure of the world." [95] So speaking he went outside and took the freak with him for burning. Then Alexander declared, "Oh Zeus,[9] I wish you had permitted me to complete my undertakings, but since you have made this decision accept me as your third mortal in heaven." Apparently he meant by this that he counted Dionysus[10] as the first to have been immortalized and Heracles second and, in placing himself third, that his achievements, not inferior to theirs, entitled him to sit at the tables of the gods. And so, despairing of his life after that, he awaited what was to come with resignation.

[96] Meanwhile, Antipater's son, Cassander, reached Babylon and gave the king the gifts he had brought. Then he summoned and had a meeting with his brother Iollas, to whom he revealed their father's instructions, the animosity of Olympias, Alexander's arrogance and pride, and the peril which threatened their whole family. He passed on the poison and urged him not to let slip any opportunity ⟨. . .⟩ [97] †Then Alexander†[11] ⟨. . . Medius⟩ said he would see to it for Iollas; that he would ask him while he was observing the holiday whether he wished to have a gathering of his friends ⟨. . .⟩.

It seems pertinent now to reveal the names of those whom Onesicritus, in his desire to avoid controversy, was reluctant to mention. There was Perdiccas, Medius, Leonnatus, †erat teon†, Meleager, †theoclus†, Asander, Philip, Nearchus, Stasanor, Heracleides the Thracian, †polydorus†, Holcias, Menander . . . ⟨Python,[12] Peucestas, Ptolemy, Lysimachus, . . . Europius, Ariston of Pharsalus, Philip the engineer, Philotas⟩.[13]

[98] No one was unaware of what was afoot, with the exception of Eumenes, Perdiccas, Ptolemy, Lysimachus, Asander and Holcias. The others were all Iollas' accomplices; they were eager for revolution and frightened of where Alexander's power would finally take him. Even before this they had talked among themselves about killing him.

---

9 The Latin text has Jupiter.
10 Father Liber.
11 The text is corrupt at this point and no sense can be made of it.
12 Peithon. †erat teon† may be a corruption of his patronymic, Crateua. Eumenes is missing from both the Greek and Latin versions, but he does appear in the Armenian text.
13 These names have been added by the editors of this volume from Pseudo-Callisthenes 3.31.8.

[99] As Alexander reclined at the banquet, Iollas handed him the poisoned cup. The king drank it and, after some brief conversation, he was suddenly seized with pain, crying out as if he had been struck by an arrow. Then, holding his stomach, he went to his room. The conspirators immediately retired, guiltily and fearful of how matters would turn out. In the meantime Alexander was in a sorry state. He wanted to vomit and so asked for a feather; Iolaus[14] gave the king a feather smeared with poison. When he put this down his throat, because ⟨. . .⟩, he was continuously racked with renewed and ever more excruciating pains. In this condition he passed the night.

[100] The next day he became aware that his tongue was beginning to swell, and he therefore ordered everybody to leave his bedroom so that he could decide on his own what to do.

Now, after the king had been given the poison, Cassander had set out by night for Cilicia where he began his wait for ⟨Iollas⟩; for it had been agreed that on Alexander's death he would immediately flee and join him. Cassander himself sent ahead one of his men to his father in Macedonia, describing their achievement in ambiguous language.

[101] When night fell, Alexander ordered his wife Roxane and all his friends to leave his bedroom so that he could get to sleep more easily, and the moment that he felt all was silent he got up, as best he could, and put out the lamp. Then, on all fours, he opened a door which afforded access to the river Euphrates – the river flowed through the centre of the city – and went out, looking behind him as he did so. Seeing his wife, Roxane, running towards him, he crouched down, hoping that he might, by chance, escape her notice.

[102] Roxane came to the bed, where she failed to find Alexander, and saw the door open. Then she caught the sound of groaning from the weeping Alexander and made her way towards him. Suddenly she saw him on the ground, so she put her arms around him and, in tears, lifted him up. Alexander slumped into her embrace and barely got out the words: "Ah, Roxane, in granting yourself a brief enjoyment of my company, you have robbed me of immortality. But see to it that nobody hears this from you." So, supported by Roxane, he returned to his bedroom.[15]

[103] When dawn came, Alexander had Perdiccas, Holcias, Lysimachus and Ptolemy summoned to him and ordered them not to grant anyone entrance to him until he had completed what he wanted to do.[16] These then left, but

---

14   Iolaus is the reading of the MS. Iollas is used elsewhere.
15   Cf. Arrian 7.27.2–3.
16   At this point we have another interpolation in Pseudo-Callisthenes 3.32.9–10: Perdiccas suspects that Alexander has left control of affairs to Ptolemy, since, according to rumor, Ptolemy was Philip's son. He takes him aside and swears that, if Alexander leaves him with supreme command, he will share it with Ptolemy; but Ptolemy, meanwhile, assumes that Perdiccas will inherit the kingdom and makes the same vow. The story discredits Perdiccas, who, in his dishonesty, outwits himself.

he kept with him two young boys, Hermogenes and Combaphes, the one to write down his testament and the other to see to the lamp. Thus he spent a day and a night writing his testament.

[104] Meanwhile, a rebellious clamour arose among the troops, who threatened to kill Alexander's entourage unless his body were brought before them. For they thought that his death was being concealed from them. So they converged rowdily and in large numbers on the palace, and, Alexander hearing the noise, asked what it was. Perdiccas then told him of the soldiers' suspicion and their rush to the palace, whereupon Alexander issued orders that he be taken from the bedroom and set in an elevated place so that they could be admitted despite their numbers and sent out by another door. [105] The men now visited him company by company, admitted wearing only a single tunic. After saluting him tearfully they then went out by the other door. Since he was already in the very throes of death and unable to speak, Alexander returned the salute in silence to all of them with a movement of the hand or a nod.

Amongst the men was a certain Peucolaus, who was of ⟨humble⟩ origins. He stood beside the king in tears and said: "Alexander, your father was the best king of Macedonia, who ⟨. . .⟩ you have raised to such a level of renown that you rival the glory of the gods. Now you are leaving us, and that means the name of our country, along with all the Macedonians, has also perished. So we should all die along with you."

[106] When he said this, Alexander wept with him, and, taking the Macedonian's hand, he squeezed it to indicate that he should take courage.

After all the men filed past and he was taken back to the bedroom, he had Perdiccas and the others called in. He handed Holcias his testament to read aloud to him, [but first he ordered that a letter which he had written to the Rhodians be read out clearly. The letter went as follows:

[107] "King Alexander to the senate and people of Rhodes: Greetings! We, beyond the pillars of our ancestral god, Heracles ⟨. . .⟩† from the territory, leaving our enemies† we have divided our realm and our wealth. We have considered you to be the most suitable executors and guardians of this; for we have experienced your exceptional reliability and integrity, and that is why we have always held your city in the highest esteem. We have accordingly sent written instructions to †Cebes† to remove the garrison from your town, and I have taken care that you should see from my will – a copy of which I have sent to you – that I am also sensitive to all your other interests.

[108] "Basing our assessment on individual merit and rank, we have made an allotment of territorial jurisdictions and we have directed all these governors to see that each be given from the royal treasury a sum which we decreed to be given. This includes 300 talents of gold coin for you to beautify your city, 40,000 bushels of wheat per year and 40 warships.[18] We have also given instructions that our body be transported to Egypt and the priests there look after the burial. In view of your integrity and authority you have a moral duty to make a special effort to see that this is done and to be painstaking in attending to my instructions. Farewell."

[109] When this had been written in the letter, Alexander ordered his will to be read out close to his ear. Setting numerous seals on this he handed it to Holcias, instructing him to find someone loyal to take the letter to Rhodes as soon as possible together with a copy of the will. Holcias brought in a certain Theban named Ismenias, handed him the letter and showed him the manner in which the king had dealt with the Thebans in the will. Delighted at the benefits conferred upon his fatherland, Ismenias was all the more diligent and speedy in bringing the letter to Rhodes.][17]

[110] A poultice set on Alexander's stomach by his wife, Roxane, brought him some relief from the pain and had now extended his life by five days when, wanting ⟨a drink of water, he was once more⟩ given a poisoned cup by Iollas. After he drank it, the pangs recommenced and made him cry aloud; then, controlling himself and emitting a sigh, he said to his friends: "I have written into my will what I would like done after my death. Perdiccas, you and Antipater look after things in the meantime and see to it that the terms of my will are carried out."

[111] At this point, Holcias took his hat from his head, set it before his streaming eyes and went out. Then Alexander called Lysimachus to him and said, "Leave for Thrace," at which Lysimachus left the room in tears. Alexander also said to Ptolemy: "You leave, too, for Egypt, and see you make sure that my body is well looked after." His other instructions he whispered in his ear. When Ptolemy heard them he could not hold back his tears; covering his face he left the company.

[112] By now the virulence of the poison was beginning to paralyze Alexander's tongue and darkness started to cover his eyes. With an effort he barely managed to groan the words: "Take me, Divine Heracles and Athena; and you, my friends, farewell!", after which he took his ring from his finger and handed it to Perdiccas. Roxane uttered a piercing shriek, tearing at her hair, and tried to throw herself at Perdiccas' feet, but Holcias[18] caught her and brought her to Alexander. The king, gnashing his teeth at the realization that he was breathing his last, took her in his arms and began to kiss her. Holding her right hand, he put it into Perdiccas' right hand and nodded his approval. Then death overtook him. Roxane closed his eyes and drew out his soul with her lips.

[113] So Alexander the Great left this life at the age of thirty-three and after a reign of thirteen years. Then, although the army was still unaware of their

---

17 Most, if not all, of the details within the square brackets are interpolated. The Letter to the Rhodians summarizes many of the provisions of the testament that follows and added terms favorable to Rhodes. This does not prove, however, that the positive treatment of Rhodes and Thebes was not to be found in the original pamphlet (i.e., within the actual testament).

Pseudo-Callisthenes 3.33.9 includes, in the letter to the Rhodians, references to Craterus' rule in Macedonia, Ptolemy's status as satrap of Egypt, and the shared rule of Perdiccas and Anti⟨pater⟩ in Asia.

18 Earlier, Holcias leaves the room. We must assume (what the author forgot to record) that he soon returned.

king's death, terror and panic suddenly broke out, for no reason. The men all rushed noisily to arms, yet none really knew what the problem was. Meanwhile, Perdiccas and those in the palace set the dead king in a coffin, dressed him in a tunic and purple cloak and put a crown on his head. They added many perfumes mixed with honey and covered the coffin with a purple mantle over which they set a Babylonian tapestry.

[114] Then, heads covered and with eyes fixed on the ground, they made their way to the dais to meet the troops. Here, after silence had been called by a herald, Perdiccas addressed a large gathering. "Macedonians," he said, "know that your king, Alexander, has joined the gods. You should, therefore, use words of good omen amongst yourselves and avoid unpropitious language." Then, after silence had once more been called by the herald, he told Holcias to read aloud the will, which ran as follows:

[115] "The testament made by King Alexander, son of Ammon and Olympias. If my child by my wife, Roxane, is a son, he before all others is to be King of Macedonia, and in the interim Arrhidaeus, son of Philip, should lead the Macedonians. If I should have a daughter by my wife, Roxane, let the Macedonians see that she is brought up and married in a manner befitting their loyalty to me and my rank, and let them elect as their king the man they think fit. The man so elected ⟨should be⟩ King of Macedonia . . .

[116] "To my mother, Olympias, I grant the right to live in Rhodes or anywhere else she wishes and the king of Macedonia is to see that she is every year given all the things she was given during my lifetime. ⟨Until the Macedonians decide to appoint a king, King Alexander, son of Ammon and Olympias, designates Craterus as overseer of his entire kingdom of Macedonia, and (gives) him as his wife Cynnane the daughter of Philip, the former King of Macedonia. Lysimachus he places in charge of Thrace and (gives) as his wife Thessalonice, daughter of Philip, the former King of Macedonia.⟩[19] To Leonnatus I give the satrapy of the Hellespont and the hand of Holcias' sister, Cleonice,[20] in marriage. I appoint Eumenes, who was my secretary, ruler of Cappadocia and Paphlagonia. I declare the islands free: let them retain their former possessions and be autonomous.

[117] "I appoint Antigonos governor of Pamphylia, Lycia and Greater Phrygia, and I assign authority over Caria to Asander.[21] †and the territory which lies beyond† the river called the Halys; over this land I appoint Antipater governor. I make Nicanor governor of Cilicia, and Peithon governor of Syria as far as the so-called Mesopotamian line. Babylon and Babylonian territory adjoining to it I put under the command of Seleucus who was my squire.[22] Phoenicia and Coele-Syria I assign to Meleager. The kingdom of

---

19   Added by the editors of this volume from Pseudo-Callisthenes 3.33.13.
20   Although the person is unknown, the name is attested in Macedonia. See *SEG* 31 (1981), no. 636.
21   Virtually all texts that mention the appointment of the satrap of Caria give his name incorrectly as "Cassander"; here, too, the name has been corrected.
22   Armiger or *hoplophoros*. Seleucus commanded the *agema* of the hypaspists.

Egypt I leave to Ptolemy,[23] along with the hand in marriage of my sister, Cleopatra.

[118] "As for the areas lying between the boundaries of Babylonia and Bactria, the satraps should retain what they variously govern, and as commander-in-chief over them all I appoint Perdiccas, on whom I also bestow as a wife, Roxane, who was my wife, the Bactrian daughter of Oxyartes.[24] The people of Rhodes are to be granted 300 talents of gold coin from the royal treasury for the beautification of their city; they are also to be given 40 triremes and a free annual subsidy of 20,⟨000⟩ medimni[25] of Egyptian grain and, also free and on an annual basis, 20,⟨000⟩ medimni of wheat from the regions of Asia adjacent to Rhodes. I also command the removal from the town of the garrison which I left there.

[119] "The priests in Egypt are to be granted 2,000 talents in gold coin from the public purse, and Ptolemy is to take care of the transportation ⟨to Egypt⟩ of my body, which the priests of Egypt are to tend to as they think best. The sarcophagus in which the body is to be laid is to be made from 200 talents of gold.

[120] "To the Thebans of Boeotia I grant 300 talents of coined gold to rebuild their city, and to the exiles who were refugees from there ⟨because⟩ of the war I restore all the property of which I had deprived them. I consider that they have been sufficiently punished for their foolhardy opposition to me. The Athenians are to be given a golden throne for the temple of Athena and also a robe of gold. My arms and insignia plus 1,000 talents of silver are to go to the temple of Hera at Argos, while Apollo at Delphi is to be given all the elephant tusks and †two† snake skins plus 100 golden libation bowls. The Milesians are to be given 150 talents of silver and the Cnidians are also to be given 150.

[121] "Taxiles is to be governor of those parts of India bordering the Indus river, Porus of those parts between the river Hydaspes and the Indus.[26] I appoint the Bactrian Oxyartes, father of my wife, Roxane, governor of Paropanisadae, and Sibyrtius is to rule the Arachosians and Cedrosians. I give command over the Areians and Drangians to Stasanor of Soli.

"Philip is to rule the Bactrians. Parthyaea and what adjoins Hyrcania I give to Phrataphernes, Carmania to Tlepolemus. Peucestas is to hold sway over all the Persians. From all †these† governorships Oxydates is to be relieved and Craterus[27] is to rule the Medes in his place. Argaeus is also to be removed from Susiana, and Coenus is to govern in his stead.

23   Pseudo-Callisthenes 3.33.15: "I give Egypt [to Perdiccas] and Libya to Ptolemy."
24   Pseudo-Callisthenes 3.33.15: the Upper Satrapies are given to Phanocrates, who also marries Roxane. This MS corruption is contradicted by §112, where Alexander clearly gives Roxane to Perdiccas.
25   A *medimnos* (Latin *medimnus*) = about 11.5 imperial gallons.
26   The territories of Porus and Taxiles are reversed.
27   An error for Peithon, son of Crateuas.

[122] "Over all the Illyrians[28] I appoint Holcias as governor and I award him a detachment of 500 requisitioned horses and 3,000 talents of silver coin, which he is to use for the making of statues of Alexander, Ammon, Athena, Heracles, Olympias and my father, Philip.[29] These he is to set up in the shrine at Olympia. The men to whom I have given supreme commands are to set up gilded statues of Alexander in Delphi, Athens, †hiolce†.[30] Ptolemy is to set up in Egypt gilded statues of Alexander, Ammon, Athena, Heracles, Olympias and my father, Philip.

[123] "Witnesses to all this be Olympian Zeus, Heracles, our national god, Athena, Ares, Ammon the Sun,[31] and King Alexander's Fortune.

"Should any of these named act in contravention of my testament, I beseech Zeus and the Olympian gods to see that he not go unpunished for doing so, and that he be held guilty of perjury before gods and men."

2(c)　Diodorus Siculus 17.117.5–118.2

Since a number of authors have given a different version of this king's death, claiming that his end was brought on by a deadly poison, I feel constrained not to omit their version of events.

118　Antipater had been left by Alexander as his governor of Europe, and these authors state that he had been at odds with the king's mother, Olympias. They claim that Antipater at first ignored her because Alexander paid no attention to the slurs she made against him, but that later, as the bad blood between the two kept on growing, the king wanted to gratify his mother in every regard to show his respect for the gods. Antipater then supposedly gave numerous hints of his estrangement from Alexander. In addition, the killing of Parmenion and Philotas filled Alexander's friends with dread, and Antipater at that point used the services of his own son, who was Alexander's wine steward, to give the king a deadly poison to drink. [2] After the death, according to this account, Antipater had supreme power in Europe, and later his son succeeded him on the throne, so that most writers did not dare include the poisoning in their works. But, the account goes on, Cassander was clearly shown by his own conduct to have been opposed to the cause of Alexander: he murdered Olympias and cast out her body unburied, and was strongly committed to rebuilding Thebes, which had been destroyed by Alexander.

28　Illyria was not part of Alexander's empire.
29　A contradiction: earlier Alexander has claimed Ammon as his father (§115; Pseudo-Callisthenes 3.33.13); Philip is, by contrast, "the former king of Macedonia" (Pseudo-Callisthenes 3.33.13).
30　Either a reference to Olympia or further instructions applying to Holcias (?).
31　Amun-Re.

2(d)   Valerius Maximus 1.7 ext 2

It was well, indeed, that King Alexander of Macedon had been forewarned by a dream to be more attentive with regard to his personal security – if only fortune had been willing to provide him with measures for taking precautions against the danger! He learned from the dream, before he was taught by the event, that the hand of Cassander would bring him death; he believed he would be killed by Cassander even though he had never set eyes on him. Some time later Cassander came into his presence, and before Alexander's eyes was the picture that was the cause of his nocturnal forebodings. But when he learned that he was Antipater's son, Alexander quoted a line of Greek poetry which belittled the credibility of dreams, and dismissed from his thoughts all suspicion he had of poison, though this had already been prepared for him and by it he is believed to have died at Cassander's hand.

The Hypomnemata and the Final Plans of Alexander

Upon Alexander's death, the king's notebooks (*Hypomnemata*) were found to contain the details of grandiose schemes for the construction of monuments – including a memorial to Hephaestion – and further conquest. It proved to be neither desirable nor feasible to carry these out. Perdiccas, however, had used the cancellation of the king's last wishes as a means of negating the political power of at least one of his enemies, Craterus. See Tarn (1921b) and Badian (1967b); cf. McKechnie (1995).

3(a)   Diodorus Siculus 18.4.1–6

Craterus had written instructions which the king had given him to carry out, but after Alexander's death the Successors decided against putting these plans into effect. [2] For in the *Hypomnemata* of the king, Perdiccas found orders for the completion of Hephaestion's pyre, which called for heavy expenditure, and for all his other designs, which, numerous and grandiose, required an inordinate outlay of money. He therefore decided it was expedient to leave them unfulfilled. [3] But not to appear to have diminished Alexander's prestige on his own authority, he brought the proposal concerning these matters before the common council of the Macedonians.

[4] The greatest and most significant projects in the *Hypomnemata* were the following. There was the construction of a thousand warships, larger than triremes, in Phoenicia, Syria, Cilicia and Cyprus. These were for a campaign against the Carthaginians and the other peoples living along the coast of Libya and Iberia and the area next to these along the coast as far as Sicily. There was the laying of a road along the coast of Libya as far as the Pillars of

Hercules and the provision, at strategic points, of ports and dockyards sufficient for an expedition of such proportions.[32] Next there was the building of six very expensive temples, each costing 1,500 talents. As well as this there was to be the establishment of cities and a transfer of populations from Asia to Europe, and in reverse from Europe to Asia, with the aim of bringing the largest continents into harmonious and familial unity through intermarriage and family ties.

[5] The aforementioned temples were to be built at Delos, Delphi and Dodona. There were also to be temples in Macedonia: to Zeus at Dium, to Artemis Tauropolus at Amphipolis, and to Athena in Cyrnus. At Ilium, too, a temple of the last-mentioned goddess was to be constructed, one that could not take second place to another. Alexander's father Philip was to have a tomb as great as the largest of the pyramids in Egypt, which some people count among the greatest works in the world.

[6] When these *Hypomnemata* were read out, the Macedonians, although they reacted favourably to the mention of Alexander, realized nevertheless that the projects were excessive and impractical, and decided against bringing the aforementioned ones to fruition.

Alexander's Will and the Division of Power after his Death

It became immediately clear that any "king" whom the marshals in Babylon selected as Alexander's successor – whether Roxane's unborn child, the illegitimate Heracles, or the mentally deficient Arrhidaeus – would not be able to function without a guardian. It was, no doubt, the price that some demanded of Perdiccas that, in exchange for their support of his claims to the guardianship, they be given portions of the empire to administer; similarly, Perdiccas will have found it advantageous to rid himself of potential rivals by sending them to the various satrapies of the empire. In the propaganda wars that ensued, the political pamphlet on the *Last Days and Testament of Alexander* (see §XI.2b, above) maintained that such a division of power had been prescribed by Alexander himself: see Heckel (1988) and Bosworth (2000). The following passage from Diodorus reflects the mistaken belief that such a testament existed and that it was deposited with the Rhodians. See Hornblower (1981: 56).

4(a) Diodorus Siculus 20.81.3

Alexander, the most powerful man in history, honoured Rhodes above all cities and deposited there his will which pertained to his entire empire.

---

32 Diodorus has not yet mentioned the expedition.

4(b)   *Quintus Curtius Rufus 10.10.1–4*

Perdiccas led the army into the city and convened a meeting of the leading Macedonians. It was there decided that the empire should be apportioned as follows. The king would hold supreme power, with Ptolemy becoming satrap of Egypt and of the African peoples subject to Macedon. [2] Laomedon was given Syria and Phoenicia; Philotas was assigned Cilicia; Antigonus was instructed to take charge of Lycia, Pamphylia and Greater Phrygia; Cassander[33] was sent to Caria and Menander to Lydia. Lesser Phrygia, which is adjacent to the Hellespont, they designated as the province of Leonnatus. [3] Cappadocia and Paphlagonia fell to Eumenes, who was charged with defending that region as far as Trapezus and with conducting hostilities against Ariarathes, the only chieftain refusing allegiance to Macedon. [4] Pithon was ordered to take command of Media, Lysimachus of Thrace and the Pontic tribes adjoining it. It was decided that the governors of India, of the Bactrians and Sogdians and the other peoples living by the Ocean or the Red Sea should all retain command of their respective territories. Perdiccas was to remain with the king and command the troops following him.

4(c)   *Justin 13.4*

After presenting these arguments with his unique eloquence, Perdiccas so impressed the infantry that his advice was accepted and he was unanimously elected their leader. [2] Then a reconciliation was effected with the cavalry, who agreed on the choice of Arrhidaeus as king, [3] with a part of the empire held in reserve for a son of Alexander, should one be born. [4] These arrangements they made with the body of Alexander set in their midst so that its majesty would witness their decisions.

[5] With the matter of the succession settled, next Antipater was made governor of Macedonia and Greece, Craterus was given charge of the royal treasury, and Meleager and Perdiccas were to look after the camp, the army and its affairs. [6] King Arrhidaeus[34] was instructed to escort Alexander's body to the temple of Hammon. [7] After this Perdiccas, furious at those responsible for the mutiny, announced suddenly, and without consulting his colleague, that because of the King's death there would be a ceremonial purification of the camp the following day. [8] He drew up the troops under arms upon an open plain and, to the general approval of the men, called out from individual companies, as he passed along the lines, those involved in the mutiny, secretly relaying orders for their execution. [9] On his return, he distributed provinces among the officers with the twofold aim of disposing of rivals and

---

33   Asander. See also n. 21 above.
34   This Arrhidaeus later became satrap of Hellespontine Phrygia. He is mistakenly identified as Alexander's half-brother, Philip III.

also making such awards of power seem like personal favours on his part. [10] First of all, Egypt and part of Africa and Arabia were allotted to Ptolemy, whom Alexander had promoted from the ranks for his personal qualities; [11] to administer the province Ptolemy was also assigned Cleomenes, the man who had built Alexandria, as his adjutant. [12] The province adjacent to this, Syria, was given to Laomedon of Mitylene, and Cilicia to Philotas. [13] Pithon the Illyrian was made governor of Greater Media and Perdiccas' father-in-law, Atropatos, of Lesser Media. [14] The people of Susiana were assigned to Coenus, Greater Phrygia to Antigonus, son of Philip. [15] Nearchus was allotted Lycia and Pamphylia, Cassander Caria and Menander Lydia. [16] Lesser Phrygia[35] fell to Leonnatus, Lysimachus was given Thrace and the coastline of Pontus, and Eumenes Cappadocia and Paphlagonia. [17] To Seleucus son of Antiochus fell supreme command of the camp,[36] [18] and Cassander son of Antipater was put in charge of the royal entourage and guards. [19] In the remoteness of Bactriana and the various parts of India the former governors were retained, [20] and Taxiles took control of the Seres between the Hydaspes and Indus rivers. [21] Pithon, son of Agenor, was sent out to the colonies established in India; Oxyartes was granted the Parapameni in the furthest part of the Caucasus; [22] Sibyrtius was given the Arachosians and Cedrosians, Stasanor the Drancae and Arei. [23] Amyntas was allotted the Bactrians, †Soleus Staganor† the Sogdiani, Philip the Parthians, Phrataphernes the Hyrcanians, Tleptolemus the Carmanians, Peucestes the Persians, Archon of Pella the Babylonians, and Arcesilaus Mesopotamia. [24] For each general the allocation was virtually a gift from heaven, but for a large number of them it also provided an excellent opportunity to expand their domains; [25] for shortly afterwards, as though they had been apportioning kingdoms rather than provinces, they became kings instead of governors, not simply acquiring great power for themselves but even bequeathing it to their descendants.

35 Hellespontine Phrygia, with its capital at Dascyleum.
36 That is, he became chiliarch.

XII Alexander and the Romans

A Roman View of Alexander's Conquests

Livy 9.19.10, in his account of the activities of Alexander I of Epirus, Alexander the Great's uncle and brother-in-law (see also Justin 9.5.8–7.14), in Italy, includes a disparaging remark about the Macedonian king's achievements. It is doubtful that Cleitus, who in Curtius' version repeats the remark, ever heard these words reported; for they were, most likely, invented by Livy himself. Even if they had been uttered by the Epirote king and had come to Cleitus' attention, it is doubtful that he repeated them, since by doing so he would have disparaged his own contributions as well.

1(a)   Quintus Curtius Rufus 8.1.37

[Cleitus, speaking to Alexander] ". . . your uncle is generally believed to have said in Italy, that he had faced men in battle and you had faced women."

Did the Romans Send an Embassy to Alexander?

It is a matter of some debate amongst modern scholars, as indeed it was in antiquity, whether the Romans sent an embassy to Alexander in Babylon. Pro-Roman accounts, especially Arrian and Trogus (Justin), salvaged Roman pride by mentioning Italians, but not the Romans specifically. On the other hand, Cleitarchus, the earliest historian to mention the Roman embassy, had no reason for inventing the story, since Rome's greatness lay in the future. At Cleitarchus' time of writing they had not yet encountered Pyrrhus, nor had they completed the conquest of Italy. See the full discussion in Bosworth (1988b: 83–93).

2(a)   Pliny, Natural History *3.57*
(Cleitarchus, FGrH 137 F 31)

Theopompus, earlier than whom nobody made any reference to Rome, said only that the city was captured by the Gauls, and Cleitarchus, who followed Theopompus, merely mentioned an embassy sent to Alexander . . .

2(b)   Arrian 7.15.5–6

Of the writers of histories of Alexander Aristus and Asclepiades claim that the Romans, too, sent emissaries to him. They say that Alexander met the deputation and made a prediction about subsequent Roman power from looking at the men's well-ordered appearance, their energy and their free spirit, as well as from inquiring into their system of government.

[6] I have set this down as being neither necessarily correct nor completely beyond belief. However, none of the Romans has mentioned this embassy sent to Alexander and neither of the Alexander historians with whom I am inclined to agree – Ptolemy son of Lagus and Aristobulus – mention it either. Nor was it reasonable for the Roman state to be sending embassies to a foreign king at a time when it was at the freest point of its history, and especially to a destination so far distant from home. And that when there was no fear to compel them to do this and no hope of profit, and they were a people more filled than any others with loathing of tyranny and its very name.

2(c)   Justin 12.13.1–2

While he was on his way back to Babylonia from the remote shores of the Ocean, Alexander was brought word that his arrival in Babylonia was awaited by embassies from Carthage and the other African states, and also by embassies from Spain, Sicily, Gaul and Sardinia, as well as a few from Italy.[1] [2] So far had the terror of his name pervaded the whole world that all nations were ready to fawn upon him as though he were destined to be their king.

---

1 Justin does not name the Romans specifically, and it may be that Trogus himself had changed what he found in his original from "Romans" to "Italians," thus obscuring the fact that some Alexander historians alleged that the Romans sent an embassy. Diodorus 17.113.2 also speaks of "the majority of those living around the Adriatic" and does not name the Romans themselves.

Could Alexander have Conquered the Romans?

The question of whether Alexander could have conquered Rome was one that had exercised many Roman minds, not only because it was a natural question for the historian to ask but because it was a frequent topic of debate in the rhetorical schools. The Romans, by Livy's time, had become the undisputed masters of the Mediterranean world. But, in the middle of the Republican era, they had been severely tested by the Carthaginians and their general Hannibal Barca. Earlier, a small army under Pyrrhus of Epirus, a kinsman of Alexander the Great on his mother's side, had defeated Roman armies with relative ease. Livy here presents arguments in favor of Rome's ability to withstand Alexander, but many of them can be turned on their heads and exposed as weaknesses instead of strengths.

3(a)   Livy 9.17.5–18.19

Let me begin with a comparison of the commanders, and at the outset I do not deny that Alexander was an outstanding leader. His reputation, however, was boosted by the fact that he was acting alone, and also that he died in his youth as his career was taking flight and when he had experienced no reversal of fortune. [6] I say nothing of the other famous rulers and generals and turn to Cyrus,[2] for whom the Greeks reserve the highest praise. What was it that exposed him to changing fortunes if not the fact that he lived so long – as in the recent case of Pompey the Great?[3]

[7] Let me review the Roman generals – not all of them throughout history, but just the ones that Alexander would have had to contend with as consuls or dictators. [8] I refer to Marcus Valerius Corvinus, Gaius Marcius Rutulus, Gaius Sulpicius, Titus Manlius Torquatus, Quintus Publilius Philo, Lucius Papirius Cursor, Quintus Fabius Maximus, the two Decii, Lucius Volumnius and Manius Curius. [9] (These were succeeded by some very great men, as Alexander would have discovered had he turned his attention to war with Carthage before war with Rome, and then crossed to Italy as an older man.) [10] The same innate qualities of courage and inventiveness were to be found in these as in Alexander, and by then the military discipline that had been a tradition since the city's inception had developed into a science organized on established principles. [11] It was with these principles that the kings had fought their wars, and with them too the men who drove out the kings, the Junii and Valerii. The same applied, after them, to the Fabii, the Quinctii and

---

2   Cyrus the Great of Persia (550–530). He was killed fighting the Scythian queen Tomyris in the northeastern corner of the empire.
3   Pompey was defeated by Caesar in the Civil War at Pharsalus in 48 BC. He was subsequently killed by the supporters of young Ptolemy XIII, who hoped thereby to win Caesar's goodwill.

the Cornelii, and to Furius Camillus, whose later years had been witnessed by the young men with whom Alexander would have had to fight.

[12] As far as taking on a soldier's duties in the field is concerned (for that enhanced Alexander's reputation as much as anything else) we certainly cannot believe that Manlius Torquatus or Valerius Corvus would have been inferior to him had they faced him in battle. Not when these men had gained fame as soldiers before they did as generals! [13] Nor would the Decii have been inferior – the men who rushed at the foe after pledging their lives to the underworld! Nor Papirius Cursor, a man of such physical strength and such strength of spirit!

The Senate would surely not have been outwitted by the strategies of this one young man – [14] the Senate which, not to name individuals, was said to be made up of kings by the one person[4] who had an accurate picture of the Roman governing body! [15] Nor, of course, was there any danger of his selecting a spot for his encampment with greater skill than any of the men I have named! Or of more skilfully arranging his lines of supply, taking precautions against ambush, selecting the time for battle, deploying his battle line, and using his supporting troops to advantage! [16] He was not now dealing with a Darius, Alexander would have said. The Persian dragged along with him a troop of women and eunuchs, and amid all the purple and gold was encumbered with the trappings of his status. He was plunder rather than an enemy, and all it took for a bloodless victory was having the enterprise to pay no attention to what did not matter. [17] Italy would have seemed to Alexander very different in nature from India, through which he made his way partying with his drunken army.[5] He would have looked on the passes of Apulia and the mountains of Lucania, seeing the traces of the disaster that recently struck his own family when his uncle, King Alexander of Epirus, fell in battle.

18   And we are talking about the Alexander who was not yet up to his neck in success, to which nobody had less resistance than he. [2] But consider how matters were after the change in his fortunes and, one might say, after the change of personality to the one that he took on after victory. [3] He would then have come to Italy more of a Darius than an Alexander, and brought an army that had forgotten Macedon and was already lapsing into Persian ways. [4] In the case of so great a king, I am reluctant to mention the conceited style of dress that he adopted, and his wish to receive grovelling obeisance, which would have been unacceptable even had the Macedonians been defeated, and was much more so when they were victorious. I hesitate, too, to mention the appalling punishments he inflicted, his killing of friends over drinking and the dinner table, and his fatuous lies about his parentage.[6]

---

4   Cineas, the adviser of Pyrrhus. See Plutarch, *Pyrrhus* 19.6.
5   See §IX.1o for the revel in Nysa. More famous, however, was the story of the drunken revel in Carmania (§IX.1p).
6   These are rhetorical plurals. Livy is referring to Alexander's murder of Cleitus and the king's claims to be descended from Amun rather than Philip II.

[5] What if his fondness for drink had become progressively more acute? Or his vicious and violent temper? And I am not talking of anything that is a matter of dispute amongst historians. Do we consider none of these things detrimental to his standing as a general? [6] And, I am sure, there is no danger of there being any truth in that idea always being brought up by those most simple-minded of the Greeks who set the reputation of even the Parthians above that of Rome![7] These men claim that the Roman people would not have been able to stand up to even the eminence of Alexander's name – though I do not think Alexander was even known to them from hearsay! Of all the leading men of Rome none would have dared utter a true word against him, these men say – [7] when, as we know from the speeches on record, people dared openly to produce public orations against him in Athens, a state shattered by Macedonian arms! And they did this at the very moment when they were looking upon the smoking ruins of Thebes close by.

[8] Whatever the man's greatness is conceived as being it is still the greatness of a single individual, and derived from successes accumulated over little more than ten years. [9] Some people extol Alexander on the grounds that the Romans, while never defeated in a war, were in fact defeated in numerous battles, whereas he never experienced a reverse in combat. But they do not realize that they are comparing the exploits of a man, and a young man at that, with those of a people that had already been engaged in warfare for 400 years. [10] When there are more generations to be counted on the one side than there are years on the other, should we be surprised that there were more fluctuating fortunes in such a long period of time than there were in a space of thirteen years? [11] Should one not compare one man's fortunes with another's, and one leader's with another's? [12] How many are the Roman commanders I could cite who never had an unsuccessful battle! In the annals and magistrate lists one can run one's eye over pages and pages of consuls and dictators, none of whom gave the Roman People cause to be dissatisfied with their courage and fortunes on any day.

[13] And there is reason to consider these men more worthy of admiration than Alexander, or any other monarch. Some held a dictatorship for ten or twenty days, and none held a consulship for more than a year. [14] Their troop levies were hampered by plebeian tribunes. They came to military campaigns late, and were recalled early to preside over elections. The year would expire when they were in the very process of conducting an operation, [15] and a colleague's foolhardiness, or perhaps his perversity, could stand in their way or cause them failure. They took over situations another had handled badly, or assumed leadership of an army of untried recruits or one that was poorly disciplined. [16] But monarchs are in a very different situation. They are not only free of all restraints but are the masters of situations and their timing; rather than following circumstances, they make circumstances conform to their strategy.

---

7 Thought to be a reference to historians like Timagenes of Alexandria (*FGrH* 88 T9).

[17] And so an undefeated Alexander would have been in combat with undefeated commanders, giving the same pledges to fortune as they. [18] In fact, he would have faced even greater danger than these would have because the Macedonians had only Alexander, a man who was not merely exposed to numerous hazards but actually threw himself in their way. [19] There would have been many Romans who were Alexander's equals in military renown and greatness of achievement, however, and each of these could have survived or died as his own fate dictated, without putting the state in jeopardy.

Roman Imitation and Emulation of Alexander

Despite Livy's bold assertion that Alexander could not have conquered the Romans, numerous generals and emperors were attracted to the mystique of the Macedonian conqueror and either consciously imitated him or encouraged favorable comparisons.

4(a)   Livy 26.19.6–8

. . . in some it generated the belief in the story – perhaps deliberately put about, perhaps spontaneous – that Scipio was a man of divine origin. [7] It also brought back the rumour that earlier spread about Alexander the Great, a rumour that was as fatuous as it was presumptuous. It was said that his conception was the result of sexual union with a snake, that this miraculous creature was often seen in his mother's bedroom, and that it slithered away and vanished from sight when people came in. [8] Scipio himself never ridiculed people's belief in these supernatural tales. In fact, he promoted it by developing a sort of talent for not rejecting that kind of thing, and not openly vouching for it either.

4(b)   Livy 35.14.5–11

[5] Claudius, who is following the Greek account by Acilius,[8] records that Publius Africanus was on that delegation, and that he conversed with Hannibal at Ephesus. Claudius gives an account of one of the topics of these conversations. [6] Africanus asked who Hannibal thought had been the greatest general, and Hannibal replied that it was King Alexander of Macedon, [7] because with a small force he had defeated armies of immense proportions and penetrated to the ends of the earth, which human beings had never

---

8   Claudius Quadrigarius was one of the Roman Annalists. He wrote in the first century (ca. 70) BC; Gaius Acilius was a Roman senator of the second century BC who wrote a history of Rome in the Greek language.

expected to visit. [8] When Scipio then asked whom Hannibal would put second, his answer was that it was Pyrrhus:[9] it was he who first taught the technique of laying out a camp and, [9] in addition, no one had selected his terrain and deployed his troops with more finesse. He also had a way of gaining men's support, so that the peoples of Italy preferred to be ruled by a foreign king than by the Roman people, despite the latter's long hegemony in the land. [10] Scipio went on to ask whom he considered third, and Hannibal replied that it was obviously Hannibal himself. [11] Scipio burst into laughter, and retorted: "What would your answer be if you had defeated me?" "In that case", Hannibal replied, "I should put myself ahead of both Alexander and Pyrrhus, and all the other generals in the world."

4(c)   Plutarch, Pompey 2.2–5

Pompey's hair was slightly swept back, and his features around the eyes had a softness that gave his face a resemblance (which was more often talked about than actually observed) to the artistic representations of King Alexander. In fact, many people applied this name to him early in his life, and Pompey did not shy away from it, so that some people actually called him "Alexander" to ridicule him. Also, when Lucius Philippus, a man of consular rank, was supporting him in court, he said it should occasion no surprise if, since he was a Philip, he was very fond of Alexander.

4(d)   Plutarch, Pompey 46.1–2

As for Pompey's age at that point, he was younger than 34, according to those who use every detail of his life to compare and liken him with Alexander; but in fact he was approaching 40. [2] He would have been better off had his life ended at this point, while he still enjoyed the good fortune that had attended Alexander. For the time that followed brought him only successes that exposed him to envy and reverses that were utterly calamitous.

4(e)   Plutarch, Caesar 11.5–6

In a similar vein is the story of when he (Caesar) had some free time in Spain and was reading part of the history of Alexander. He was for a long time absorbed in his own thoughts, and then he burst into tears. [6] His surprised companions asked the reason for this, and he said: "Do you not think it a crying matter when Alexander at my age ruled over so many peoples and I do not yet have a single spectacular achievement to my credit?"

---

9   King of Epirus and a kinsman of Alexander's mother, Olympias (see Stemma 2).

4(f)   Suetonius, Gaius 52

Caligula also appeared dressed as Venus. Even before his expedition he made a habit of wearing triumphal attire, sometimes even putting on the breastplate of Alexander the Great that he had taken from the king's sepulchre.

4(g)   Suetonius, Nero 19.2

Nero was also preparing an expedition to the Caspian Gates.[10] For this he raised a new legion made up of fresh recruits who were all 6 feet tall. He called it his "Alexander the Great Phalanx".

4(h)   Cassius Dio 68.29.1

From there Trajan came to the actual ocean. Noting its characteristics and seeing a ship bound for India, he remarked: "I would have crossed over to the Indians, as well, were I still a young man." For he was thinking about the Indians and making a close study of their affairs, and he considered Alexander to have been fortunate. Even so, he used to say that he had gone further than the king, and he would make that claim in letters to the senate, too, though he was unable to preserve the lands he had conquered.

4(i)   SHA, Caracalla 2.2

Caracalla was always talking about Alexander the Great and his achievements.

4(j)   Cassius Dio 78.7.1–4

So passionate was Caracalla's[11] enthusiasm for Alexander that he made use of certain weapons and goblets that were purportedly his and, in addition, erected numerous statues of the king both in the military bases and in Rome itself. He put together a phalanx, some 16,000 strong, manned exclusively by Macedonians, calling it the Phalanx of Alexander and furnishing it with military equipment used in Alexander's time. [2] This equipment comprised an

---

10 The Caspian Gates, through which Alexander passed, has been identified as Sar-i-Darreh. Nero's expedition moved through the Daryal Gorge. See Warmington (1969: 98–9).

11 Marcus Aurelius Antoninus Caracallus, better known as Caracalla, was emperor from AD 198 to 217.

ox-hide helmet, a three-layered linen cuirass, a bronze shield, a long lance, a short spear, high boots and a sword ... Even that was not enough for him, however; he would also call the man "the Eastern Augustus", and once wrote to the Senate to say that Alexander had entered the body of the Augustus so he could have further life through him, having earlier lived but a short time. [3] Moreover, he harboured an intense dislike of the so-called "Aristotelian Philosophers", to the point of even wanting to burn their books; and, in particular, he removed the common-rooms they had in Alexandria and the other benefits they enjoyed. The charge he made against them was that Aristotle appeared to have been implicated in the death of Alexander.

[4] Such then were Antoninus' actions. And (if you can believe it!) he would even take a large number of elephants around with him so as to appear to be imitating Alexander – or Dionysus, rather – in this, as well.

XIII   Cities Founded by Alexander

The cities founded by Alexander – their number, nature, locations, and indeed their historicity – have been the topic of much discussion. J. G. Droysen, in his *Geschichte des Hellenismus*, collected the evidence (see Droysen 1980: 23–7) which forms the basis of Berve's list (Berve 1926, I: 291–301). Much useful information can be found in Tarn (1948, II: 232–59), but the standard work is now Fraser (1996). Certainly not all the cities attributed to Alexander were founded by him – some not even in his era – and the sources do not always carefully distinguish between cities (*poleis*) and military settlements (*katoikiai*). Some foundations were established where nothing existed previously, while others involved rebuilding old cities (such as Ilium, Priene, Tyre, Gaza) or simply constructing defensive walls (e.g., Bazeira).

1(a)   *Plutarch,* On the Fortune or the Virtue of Alexander *1.5 = Moralia 328e*

Alexander founded more than 70 cities amongst the tribes of barbarians, and scattered Greek authority throughout Asia, thereby repressing the barbaric and savage mode of life found there.

1(b)   *Stephanus of Byzantium s.v. "Alexandrias"*

There are eighteen cities of Alexandria. The first is the Egyptian, or "Libyan" as most people call it, built by Alexander, son of Philip. Jason, composer of *The Life of Hellas*, says in his fourth book that the location of the city was foretold in a dream as follows:

> Then there is an island in the stormy sea, before Egypt, and they call it Pharos.

Alexander ordered the architects to mark out its contours. Not having chalk, they marked them out with barley, but birds flew down and suddenly seized the barley. Alexander was disturbed by this, but the prophets told him to cheer up since the city was going to feed everybody. This version is given by Arrian as well. The city was also called Rhacotis, Pharos and Leontopolis (because the stomach of Olympias was marked with the figure of a lion). Because of its prominence it was said to be "the city" and the people "citizens," just as Athens is "the town" and Athenians are "townspeople" or "men of the town" (and as in the Roman context there is the "urbs" [city]). Amongst the Romans it was called Augusta (Sebaste), Julia, Claudia, Domitiana and Alexenteria. The settlement is 34 stades long and 8 wide, and its total perimeter measures 110 stades.

The second Alexandria is a city on the Troad. This is the birthplace of the epic poet Hegemon, who wrote "The Battle at Leuctra between the Thebans and Spartans." Demosthenes[1] writes about the city in the fourth book of his *Bithyniaca*.

The third is in Thrace, close to Macedonia, and Alexander founded it when he was 17 years old, before he founded the great Alexandria.

The fourth is a city of the Oritae, a tribe of the Fish-eaters, and this was founded during the circumnavigation of India.[2]

The fifth is in Opiana,[3] close to the region of India.

The sixth is also in the Indian region.

The seventh is amongst the Arii, a tribe of the Parthyaei, close to the Indian region.

The eighth is in Cilicia.

The ninth is in Cyprus.

The tenth is near Mt Latmus in Caria, and in this city was a shrine of Adonis that housed an Aphrodite by Praxiteles.

The eleventh is in Bactra.[4]

The twelfth is in the land of the Arachotians.[5]

The thirteenth is in Macarene, past which flows the River Maxates.

The fourteenth is in the land of the Soriani, an Indian tribe.[6]

The fifteenth is in the land of the Arachotians and is on the Indian border.

The sixteenth is in the "Black Gulf."[7]

1 Not the famous orator, but an epic poet from Bithynia.
2 Not a circumnavigation of the subcontinent but when Nearchus' fleet sailed from the mouth of the Indus to the Persian Gulf.
3 Possibly Alexandria-in-the-Caucasus (Alexandria in Parapamisadae). Stephanus would not have known that Alexandria in Opiana was identical with the city in Parapamisadae; hence the duplication in Alexandria no. 17. See the discussion in Fraser (1996: 148–50).
4 In the opinion of Tarn (1948, II: 236) this was Alexander's refounding of Bactra (modern Balkh).
5 Or "Arachosians."
6 The settlement and the Soriani are both unknown.
7 Known only from Stephanus' list. Although this city is sandwiched between foundations in what is roughly the area of modern Afghanistan, the only "Black Gulf" that suggests itself is near the Thracian Chersonese. See Fraser (1996: 26–7; cf. 166 n.116).

The seventeenth is in Sogdiana close to the land of the Parapamisadae.

The eighteenth is a city that was personally founded by Alexander on the Tanais, as Ptolemy declares in his third book.

There is also a place on Trojan Ida called Alexandria where they say Paris passed his judgement on the goddesses (according to Timosthenes).

1(c)   Alexander Romance A-text 3.35

[Here the author of the *Alexander Romance* gives the following list of "Alexandrias"][8]

The Alexandria founded in honour of his horse Bucephalas.

The Alexandria that lies towards Persia.

The Alexandria by Porus.[9]

The Alexandria in Scythia.

The Alexandria on the Tigris.

The Alexandria in the vicinity of Babylon.

The Alexandria on the Troad.

The Alexandria near Susa.

The Alexandria in Egypt.

1(d)   Justin 12.5.12–13

To leave his name in these lands he founded the city of Alexandria on the river Tanais, completing its wall, which measured six miles, in seventeen days, and transferring to it the populations of three towns which Cyrus had founded. [13] He also founded twelve cities in Bactria and Sogdiana, dispersing amongst them those members of his army whom he regarded as malcontents.

1(e)   Plutarch, On the Fortune or the Virtue of Alexander 1.5 = Moralia 328f

[Without Alexander's conquests] Egypt would have no Alexandria, Mesopotamia no Seleuceia, Sogdiana no Prophthasia,[10] India no Bucephalia and the Caucasus no Greek city close by. For the foundation of these

---

8   Here we follow the text supplied by Fraser (1996: 203).

9   This is presumably Nicaea on the Hydaspes, "in the territory of Porus."

10   There is no Prophthasia ("Anticipation") in Sogdiana. Alexander renamed the town of Phrada (modern Farah) Prophthasia because it was here that Philotas' conspiracy was anticipated. Thus Stephanus of Byzantium s.v. "Phrada."

cities led to the eradication of barbarism, and the worst elements of those cultures changed under the influence of better ones, to which they became habituated.

1(f)   Strabo 11.11.4

They say that Alexander founded eight cities in Bactriana and Sogdiana, but that he also destroyed a number. These latter included Cariatae in Bactriana, where Callisthenes was arrested and put under guard, and Maracanda and Cyra in Sogdiana. Cyra was a foundation of Cyrus, and it lay on the River Iaxartes, which represented the boundary of the Persian empire. In spite of his affection for Cyrus, they say that Alexander utterly destroyed the city he had founded because of its frequent insurrections.

Alexandria in Egypt

2(a)   Quintus Curtius Rufus 4.8.1–6

[1] Returning from the shrine of Ammon, Alexander came to Lake Mareotis, not far from the island of Pharos. After an examination of the area's natural features he had at first decided to locate a new city on the island itself, [2] but it then became apparent that it had not the capacity for a large settlement, and so he chose for his city the present site of Alexandria (which draws its name from its founder). Taking in all the land between the lake and the sea he marked out an 80-stade circuit for the walls, and left men to supervise construction of the city. He then set out for Memphis . . .

[5] Apollonius was put in charge of the part of Africa adjoining Egypt, and Cleomenes was to exact taxes from that part of Africa and from Egypt. By ordering people to migrate from neighbouring cities to Alexandria, Alexander provided the new city with a large population. [6] There is a report that, after the king had completed the Macedonian custom of marking out the circular boundary for the future city walls with barley-meal, flocks of birds flew down and fed on the barley. Many regarded this as an unfavourable omen, but the verdict of the seers was that the city would have a large immigrant population and would provide the means of livelihood to many countries.

2(b)   Valerius Maximus 1.4 ext 1

When King Alexander wished to found a city in Egypt, the architect Dinocrates, having no chalk, traced the outlines of the future city with barley-meal, whereupon a large flock of birds rose from a nearby lake and came to eat the barley-meal. This was interpreted by the priests of the Egyptians as meaning that the city would be capable of feeding a large number of immigrants.

2(c) Itinerary of Alexander 20

On the seventh day after leaving Gaza Alexander reached Pelusium and the rich parts of Egypt, having already sent the fleet ahead; Mazaces the satrap of that district dared not offer any resistance. Alexander, therefore, ordered the ships to be taken up the Nile to Memphis, intending himself to make a rendezvous with them there after going on foot by way of Heliopolis; and there he sacrificed to the deities of Egypt and held sacred games, and at once went down from Memphis to Canopus with the army now on board the ships. He was delighted with the look of the surrounding terrain and was seized by a desire to found a city there, being well aware that for mere humans the nearest approach to divine immortality is by way of the perpetuation, in some illustrious work, of the doer's name. So, when the time came for the marking out of the site, we are told that the practitioners of that skill – architects, they call them – were short of the powdered chalk they use for marking out the boundaries on the ground; so the soldiers were ordered – and they immediately obeyed – to pile up whatever barley-meal any of them might be carrying for preparing food or drink, to be used for making visible markings on the soil. Soon, however, the king was occupied in the other arrangements, and birds flew down to gobble, and thus erase, the edible markings. This portent was taken as unfavourable by those who made conjectures about it, but the tradition is that Alexander made a pronouncement that this city was destined to provide nourishment for many tribes round about, as well as those near at hand. As he was engaged in this great work, all those who had previously given allegiance to the Persians deserted the satraps and came over to Alexander, and were publicly praised by him according to their merits or to the good will they showed.

Alexandria in the Hindu Kush (Parapamisus)

3(a) Arrian 3.28.4

Alexander meanwhile led his army to the Caucasus range. There he founded a city and named it Alexandria.

3(b) Arrian 4.22.4

Alexander crossed the Caucasus in ten days and reached Alexandria, a city that he had founded in the land of the Parapamisadae when he was making his first foray into Bactra. The governor who had been put in charge of the city by him on that occasion he now relieved of his command as he seemed not to have ruled well. The king also moved into Alexandria other people living around the city along with those of his soldiers unfit for service, and he instructed Nicanor, one of the *hetairoi*, to assume the governorship of the city itself.

3(c) Itinerary of Alexander 33

Alexander himself made for the Caucasus range,[11] out of a wish to triumph over the difficulty of crossing it; and there also he founded for himself a city, Alexandria, as a lasting witness to his laborious achievement, and to his name.

Alexandria-Eschate (Alexandria on the Iaxartes)

4(a) *Quintus Curtius Rufus 7.6.25–7*

Meanwhile, Alexander returned to the river Tanais and built a wall around the entire area of his camp. The wall thus formed, 60 stades long, constituted the wall of a city, which the king also ordered should be called Alexandria. [26] The work was so swiftly completed that the city buildings were finished on the seventeenth day after the fortifications were erected; fierce competition had arisen among the soldiers over who would be the first to display his completed project (for there had been a division of labour). [27] Inhabitants for this new city were provided in the form of captives whom Alexander liberated by paying their value to their masters. Even today, after such a lengthy lapse of time, the descendants of these people have still retained their identity among the population because of the memory of Alexander.

4(b) Itinerary of Alexander 38

... Alexander himself by the twentieth day built up the actual structure of the new city of whose foundation he had previously accomplished the preliminaries only. He made use of the forced labour of captives, as a form of punishment to hasten forward the work which, at such a critical time, was absolutely essential. He then assigned as inhabitants of the city those whose advancing age or disabling wounds gave grounds for discharge; also those who had no more stomach for soldiering or were incapable of doing so and were suitable for settling there because they had the skills required for necessary tasks.

11 I.e., the Hindu Kush.

Bucephala and Nicaea on the Hydaspes (Jhelum)

5(a) Quintus Curtius Rufus 9.3.23

He also founded two cities, naming one Nicaea[12] and the other Bucephala, thereby dedicating the latter to the memory and name of the horse which he had lost.

5(b) Diodorus Siculus 17.95.5

The naval preparations were finished and 200 open galleys were now ready along with 800 tender-ships. At this point Alexander accorded names to the cities he had founded along the river, calling one Nicaea, after his victory in the war, and the other Bucephala, after the horse that died in the battle against Porus.[13]

Alexandria in Carmania

6(a) Pliny, Natural History 6.107, 110

[107] The region is called Amysia; the towns of Carmania are Zetis and Alexandria . . .

[110] Beyond the promontory are the Harmozaei, who border on the Carmanians, though some place the Arbii between the two . . . Here on the promontory are the Harbour of the Macedonians and the Altars of Alexander.

Alexandria in Susiana

7(a) Pliny, Natural History 6.138

Charax is a town deep in the Persian Gulf (from which the Arabia Felix juts out), standing on a man-made hill at the confluence of the Tigris and the Eulaeus . . . It was originally founded by Alexander the Great who brought there settlers from the royal city of Durine, which was destroyed in that epoch, and who also left there soldiers unfit for military service. Alexander had ordered that it be called Alexandria, with the district that he had constructed specifically for the Macedonians being called the Pellaean district, after his native town.

---

12 The name is derived from the Greek nike ("victory") and thus commemorates the victory at the Hydaspes.
13 Cf. Diodorus 17.89.6. See also §III.8f–i.

Foundations Amongst the Cossaeans

8(a)   Arrian, Indica 40.7–8

Alexander meanwhile vanquished all these peoples,[14] attacking them during the winter season when they believed their land was inaccessible. [8] He also founded cities there to end their nomadic way of life and make them plough-men and tillers of the soil. Thus they would have possessions, and fear of losing them would end their mutual aggression.

---

14   I.e., the Cossaeans (Cassites).

Glossary

agēma: The elite unit of the infantry guard. It had a cavalry equivalent, at least in the later stages of Alexander's campaign. See Heckel (1986, 1992a: 245–50).

Agrianes: Sometimes "Agrianians." Thracian javelin-men. They were one of Alexander's favorite units, along with the king's hypaspists. At the beginning of the campaign they may have numbered only 500, but an equal number joined Alexander at Gordium in the spring of 333.

akontistai: Light-infantrymen (primarily Thracian) armed with the javelin (*akontion*). They were particularly effective in rough terrain and for neutralizing the scythed chariots of the Persians. For their deployment, see especially the accounts of Gaugamela (§VI.2g–h).

Ammon: The ram-headed Egyptian sun god, Amun, whom the Greeks equated with Zeus. Alexander visited his shrine at Siwah in Libya and was recognized as Amun's son, and thus as the legitimate Pharaoh of Egypt.

archihypaspistēs: Commander of the regular hypaspists. The office was held by Parmenion's son, Nicanor, until his death in 330, and then by Neoptolemus, apparently a kinsman of Alexander's mother, Olympias.

argyraspides: The so-called "Silver Shields." These were apparently the former hypaspists of Alexander the Great. The unit may have been created in India, when it assumed new armor. For modern views on their origins, see Lock (1977b), Anson (1981), and Heckel (1992a: 307–19). In the age of the Successors, the argyraspides were commanded by Antigenes (and Teutamus) and were best known, though perhaps unfairly, for the betrayal of Eumenes of Cardia.

asthetairoi: Four battalions (*taxeis*) of Macedonian infantry (*pezhetairoi*) from Upper Macedonia (i.e., those of Coenus, Polyperchon, Perdiccas, and Amyntas son of Andromenes). By this name these battalions were distinguished from the others, perhaps (as Griffith in Hammond and Griffith 1979: 719 suggests) by their military record (if *asth-* is an abbreviation of *aristoi*, "best"). Bosworth supposes that the term means "closest kinsmen" and marks out troops with common regional backgrounds; Hammond (1989a: 148–51) believes that they were recruited from the towns and that the term is a combination of *astoi* and *hetairoi*. Although this looks attractive philologically, it is historically implausible.

chiliarch, chiliarchēs, chiliarchos: Commander of a chiliarchy (see next).

chiliarchy: A military unit of 1,000, under the command of a chiliarch (*chiliarchos* or *chiliarchēs*). Chiliarchies (subdivided into two pentacosiarchies) were standard units for the hypaspists (after 331, if not earlier) and certain light- armed troops. The system was later applied to the cavalry units (hipparchies) as well. See *Hephaestion's Chiliarchy*, below.

Companion Cavalry: The Macedonian cavalry, about 1,800 strong and supported by some 900 "scouts" (*prodromoi*) and Paeonians. The cavalry was divided into squadrons called *ilai* (sing. *ile*). The king's personal guard was the Royal Squadron, commanded by Cleitus "the Black"; see *ile basilikē*, below.

Hephaestion's Chiliarchy: A cavalry unit, sometimes referred to as the "first hipparchy," of the Companion Cavalry, created as a result of military reforms in India (or, perhaps, after the death of Cleitus in 328). The chiliarchy appears to have been an honor intended to offset the fact that Hephaestion ceased to command one-half of the Companions, a task for which he seems to have been unfit. After Hephaestion's death the unit may have continued to bear his name, at least until the death of Alexander himself. See Heckel (1992a: 366–70).

hetaira: (pl. *hetairai*). Literally, female companion/friend. She was a prostitute or courtesan.

hetairoi: Literally, the "Friends" (they are also called *philoi*) or "Companions" of the Macedonian king. They formed the king's retinue and attended his councils, and were the high-ranking aristocrats of Macedon. The term came to be applied, in various forms (see *asthetairoi, pezhetairoi*), to certain types of Macedonian troops.

hippakontistai: Mounted javelin-men, the *hippakontistai* appear to have been formed during the course of the campaign. They are first attested in Arrian in the account of the year 330. They were presumably Balkan, rather than Macedonian, horsemen.

hippokomoi: Those who tended to the Macedonian horses, i.e., grooms.

hippotoxotai: Mounted archers. These were barbarians enrolled in Alexander's cavalry after the death of Darius III. They first appear fighting on the Macedonian side in the Indian Campaign.

hypaspists: Literally, "shield-bearers." These constituted the infantry guard, which was attached, in the infantry line, to the *pezhetairoi*. They seem to have been more lightly armed and it has been suggested that they carried the hoplite shield and spear: see Markle (1977: 329–30) and Warry (1991: 14). The "royal hypaspists" appear to have been separate from the regular hypaspists, the former recruited from the aristocracy, the latter selected on the basis of physical qualities. In Philip's time – before the term was applied to the regional Macedonian infantry – the regular hypaspists may have been called *pezhetairoi*. See Anson (1985), Ellis (1975), Heckel (1992a: 299–306), and Milns (1967, 1971).

Hypomnemata: The "Notebooks" of the king. These contained the final plans of Alexander for the building of monuments, ships, and roads, and for future campaigns. Because of their extravagant nature, and because some pertained to the political functions of his enemies, Perdiccas persuaded the army to cancel the plans in a general vote. See §XI.3a.

ile basilikē: The royal cavalry squadron commanded by Cleitus "the Black." Its strength was probably 250 horsemen.

kopis: A curved slashing sword used by both the Macedonians and the Persians (see §VI,2a).

League of Corinth: A political union of the Greek states under the military leadership (*hegemonia*) of Philip II and, later, Alexander the Great. Created in 338/7, after Philip's victory over the Greeks at Chaeronea, it was renewed in 336/5 by Alexander.

melophoroi: Literally, "apple-bearers." These were Persian guardsmen – 1,000 in number and of noble Persian birth – who were distinguished by the golden apples on their spear-butts (thus Athenaeus 12.514c = Heracleides of Cyme, *FGrH* 689 F1); see also Briant (1996: 272–3).

paides basilikoi: The "royal pages." Young men of the aristocracy (probably between the ages of 13 and 18) who were raised at the Macedonian court. Here they served the king in the hunt and as bodyguards. See Heckel (1986, 1992a: 237ff.), Hammond (1989b: 56–7; 1990) and Griffith (Hammond and Griffith 1979: 401ff.). See §I.3c–f.

Peltasts: Light-armed infantrymen – first employed in Thrace – named for the *pelte*, the crescent-shaped shield they carried along wih a sword and javelin. They became a common feature of Greek warfare in the fourth century BC.

pentacosiarchs: Commanders of 500 men.

pezhetairoi: The Macedonian infantry, organized into six (later seven) battalions (*taxeis*). The nominal strength of each *taxis* was 1,500 and each was commanded by a *taxiarchos*. Hence, there were 9,000 *pezhetairoi* at the beginning of the Asiatic expedition, and these were supported by 3,000 (three "chiliarchies") of hypaspists. The *pezhetairoi* employed the *sarissa* as their primary weapon.

Philoi: "Friends." This term was used in the Hellenistic period as a substitute for *hetairoi* (see above).

pothos: Alexander's famous urge or desire to do great things or to emulate heroes. It is a feature of the Gordian knot story, and of Alexander's journey to the oasis of Siwah (Amun).

prodromoi: The mounted "scouts" in Alexander's army. Four squadrons (*ilai*) of roughly 200 riders, they are identical with the *sarissophoroi* ("sarissa-bearers"). See *sarissa*, below.

proskynesis: The Persian practice of obeisance, performed by all subjects before the Great King. The extent of the abasement was determined by the status of the subject. The Greeks considered it inappropriate to perform such obeisance to a mortal, although they knew – or, at least, many of them knew – that it did not imply the divinity of the Persian king.

sarissa: Also *sarisa* (for consistency we use *sarissa* throughout). The Macedonian lance, made of hard (usually cornel [cherry]) wood and tipped with an iron point and butt-spike. The infantry *sarissa* ranged from 15–18 feet (longer *sarissai* are attested in the Hellenistic period) and weighed between 12 and 14.5 lbs; that is, about seven times the weight of a hoplite spear. Cavalrymen (*sarissophoroi*) could wield one that was up to 14 feet in length. See Markle (1977, 1978, 1982), Manti (1983), and Hammond (1980b).

satrap: From the Median term *khshathrapavan* ("protector of the realm"). Governor of a Persian province (satrapy); Alexander retained and modified slightly the Persian administrative system.

satrapy: A Persian (and, later, Macedonian) province, ruled by a satrap (above).

Somatophylax: (pl. *Somatophylakes*). A member of the elite, seven-man bodyguard of the Macedonian king. The number appears to have been fixed (we are told of the creation of an exceptional, and temporary, eighth member: Peucestas) and its membership may have been determined by family or geographical background.

stade: The Greek *stadion*. A stade measured about 600 feet; hence there are roughly 9 (8.8) stades to an English mile.

taxiarchēs (taxiarchos): Commander of a *taxis* (see below).

taxis: A brigade or battalion. Although the numbers of a *taxis* of *pezhetairoi* are closer to those of the modern brigade, the majority of Alexander scholars have tended to translate *taxis* as battalion.

trireme: Greek warship with three banks of oars. The ship was usually about 130 feet long and had 200 men, of whom 170 were rowers.

Bibliography

Abramenko, A. 1992. "Die Verschwörung des Alexander Lyncestes und die *'meter tou basileos'*. Zu Diodor XVII 32, 1," *Tyche* 7: 1–8.

Adcock, F. E. 1957. *The Greek and Macedonian Art of War.* Berkeley: University of California Press.

Anderson, J. K. 1930. "Bucephalas and his Legend," *AJPh* 51: 1–21.

Anderson, J. K. 1961. *Ancient Greek Horsemanship.* Berkeley: University of California Press.

Anson, E. M. 1981. "Alexander's Hypaspists and the Origins of the Argyraspids," *Historia* 30: 117–20.

Anson, E. M. 1984. "The Meaning of the term *Makedones*," *AncW* 10: 67–8.

Anson, E. M. 1985. "The Hypaspists, Macedonia's Professional Citizen–Soldiers," *Historia* 34: 246–8.

Anson, E. M. 1991. "The Evolution of the Macedonian Army Assembly (330–315 BC)," *Historia* 40: 230–47.

Ashton, N. 1983. "The Lamian War – A False Start," *Antichthon* 17: 47–63.

Atkinson, J. E. 1980. *A Commentary on Q. Curtius Rufus' Historiae Alexandri Magni. Books 3 and 4.* Amsterdam: J. C. Gieben.

Atkinson, J. E. 1994. *A Commentary on Q. Curtius Rufus' Historiae Alexandri Magni. Books 5 to 7.2.* Amsterdam: Hakkert.

Atkinson, J. E. 1998. "Q. Curtius Rufus' 'Historiae Alexandri Magni,'" *ANRW* II, 34.4: 3447–83.

Austin, M. M. 1981. *The Hellenistic World from Alexander to the Roman Conquest: A Selection of Ancient Sources in Translation.* Cambridge: Cambridge University Press.

Austin, M. M. 1986. "Hellenistic Kings, War and the Economy," *CQ* 36: 450–66.

Badian, E. 1960a. "The Death of Parmenio," *TAPhA* 91: 324–38.

Badian, E. 1960b. "The First Flight of Harpalus," *Historia* 9: 245–6.

Badian, E. 1961. "Harpalus," *JHS* 81: 16–43.

Badian, E. 1963. "The Death of Philip II," *Phoenix* 17: 244–50.

Badian, E. 1967a. "Agis III," *Hermes* 95: 170–92.

Badian, E. 1967b. "A King's Notebooks," *HSCPh* 72: 183–204.

Badian, E. 1971. "Alexander the Great 1948–67," *CW* 65: 37–83.

Badian, E. 1981. "The Deification of Alexander the Great," in H. J. Dell (ed.), *Ancient Macedonian Studies in Honor of Charles F. Edson*, Thessaloniki: Institute for Balkan Studies, 27–71.

Badian, E. 1982. "Greeks and Macedonians," in *Macedonia and Greece in Late Classical and Early Hellenistic Times*. Studies in the History of Art, no. 10. Washington, DC: 33–51.

Badian, E. 1987. "Alexander at Peucelaotis," *CQ* 37: 117–28.

Badian, E. 1994. "Agis III: Revisions and Reflections," in I. Worthington (ed.), *Ventures into Greek History*. Oxford: Clarendon Press, 258–92.

Badian, E. 1996. "Alexander the Great between Two Thrones and Heaven: Variations on an Old Theme," in A. Small (ed.), *Subject and Ruler: The Cult of the Ruling Power in Classical Antiquity. Papers presented at a conference held in the University of Alberta on April 13–15, 1994, to celebrate the 65th anniversary of Duncan Fishwick. Journal of Roman Archaeology*, Supplement 17: 11–26.

Badian, E. 2000a. "Darius III," *HSCPh* 100: 241–68.

Badian, E. 2000b. "Conspiracies," in A. B. Bosworth and E. Baynham (eds.), *Alexander the Great in Fact and Fiction*. Oxford: Clarendon Press, 50–95.

Bagnall, R. S. and P. Derow. 1981. *Greek Historical Documents: The Hellenistic Period*. Chico, CA: Scholars Press.

Balcer, J. M. 1978. "Alexander's Burning of Persepolis," *IA* 13: 119–33.

Baldus, H. R. 1987. "Die Siegel Alexanders des Grossen. Versuch einer Rekonstruktion auf literarischer und numismatischer Grundlage," *Chiron* 17: 395–449.

Balsdon, J. P. V. D. 1950. "The Divinity of Alexander the Great," *Historia* 1: 363–88.

Bauer, G. 1914. "Die Heidelberger Epitome. Eine Quelle zur Diadochengeschichte," Dissertation, University of Leipzig.

Baynham, E. J. 1995a. "An Introduction to the *Metz Epitome*: Its Traditions and Value," *Antichthon* 29: 60–77.

Baynham, E. J. 1995b. "Who put the Romance in the Alexander Romance? The Alexander Romance within Alexander Historiography," *AHB* 9: 1–13.

Baynham, E. J. 2000. "A Baleful Birth in Babylon: The Significance of the Prodigy in the *Liber de Morte* – An Investigation of Genre," in A. B. Bosworth and E. J. Baynham (eds.), *Alexander the Great in Fact and Fiction*. Oxford: Clarendon Press, 242–62.

Baynham, E. J. 2001. "Alexander and the Amazons," *CQ* 51: 115–26.

Bellinger, A. R. 1963. *Essays on the Coinage of Alexander the Great*. Numismatic Studies, No. 11. New York: American Numismatic Society.

Berve, H. 1926. *Das Alexanderreich auf prosopographischer Grundlage*, 2 vols. Munich.

Berve, H. 1938. "Die Verschmelzungspolitik Alexanders des Grossen," *Klio* 31: 135–68.

Blackwell, Christopher W. 1999. *In the Absence of Alexander: Harpalus and the Failure of Macedonian Authority*. New York: Peter Lang.

Bloedow, E. F. 1998a. "The Siege of Tyre in 332 BC: Alexander at the Crossroads in his Career," *La Parola del Passato* 301: 255–93.

Bloedow, E. F. 1998b. "The Significance of the Greek Athletes and Artists at Memphis in Alexander's Strategy after the Battle of Issus," *Quaderni Urbinati* 88 [n.s. 59]: 129–42.

Bloedow, E. F. and H. Loube. 1997. "Alexander the Great 'under fire' at Persepolis," *Klio* 79: 341–53.

Borza, E. N. 1971. "The End of Agis' Revolt," *CPh* 66: 230–5.

Borza, E. N. 1972. "Fire from Heaven: Alexander at Persepolis," *CPh* 67: 233–45.

Borza, E. N. 1990. *In the Shadow of Olympus: The Emergence of Macedon*. Princeton, NJ: Princeton University Press.

Borza, E. N. 1992. "Ethnicity and Cultural Policy in Alexander's Court," *AncW* 23: 21–5.

Borza, E. N. 1999. *Before Alexander: Constructing Early Macedonia.* Publications of the Association of Ancient Historians 6. Claremont, CA: Regina Books.

Borza, E. N. and J. Reames-Zimmerman. 2000. "Some New Thoughts on the Death of Alexander the Great," *AncW* 31: 22–30.

Bosworth, A. B. 1971a. "Philip II and Upper Macedonia," *CQ* 21: 93–105.

Bosworth, A. B. 1971b. "The Death of Alexander the Great: Rumour and Propaganda," *CQ* 21: 112–36.

Bosworth, A. B. 1980a. *A Historical Commentary on Arrian's History of Alexander, Books i–iii.* Oxford: Clarendon Press.

Bosworth, A. B. 1980b. "Alexander and the Iranians," *JHS* 100: 1–21.

Bosworth, A. B. 1986. "Alexander the Great and the Decline of Macedon," *JHS* 106: 1–12.

Bosworth, A. B. 1988a. *Conquest and Empire: The Reign of Alexander the Great.* Cambridge: Cambridge University Press.

Bosworth, A. B. 1988b. *From Arrian to Alexander.* Oxford: Clarendon Press.

Bosworth, A. B. 1995. *A Historical Commentary on Arrian's History of Alexander,* vol. 2. Oxford: Clarendon Press.

Bosworth, A. B. 1996a. *Alexander and the East: The Tragedy of Triumph.* Oxford: Clarendon Press.

Bosworth, A. B. 1996b. "The Tumult and the Shouting: Two Interpretations of the Cleitus Episode," *AHB* 10: 19–30.

Bosworth, A. B. 2000. "Ptolemy and the Will of Alexander," in A. B. Bosworth and E. J. Baynham (eds.), *Alexander the Great in Fact and Fiction.* Oxford: Clarendon Press, 207–41.

Bosworth, A. B. 2002. *The Legacy of Alexander: Politics, Warfare and Propaganda under the Successors.* Oxford: Clarendon Press.

Briant, P. 1996. *Histoire de l'empire Perse de Cyrus à Alexandre.* Paris: Fayard.

Brosius, M. 1996. *Women in Ancient Persia (559–331 BC).* Oxford: Clarendon Press.

Brown, T. S. 1949. *Onesicritus: A Study in Hellenistic Historiography.* Berkeley: University of California Press.

Brown, T. S. 1950. "Clitarchus," *AJPh* 71: 134–55.

Brown, T. S. 1967. "Alexander's Book Order," *Historia* 16: 359–68.

Brown, T. S. 1977. "Alexander and Greek Athletics, in Fact and Fiction," in K. Kinzl (ed.), *Greece and the Eastern Mediterranean in Ancient History and Prehistory: Studies Presented to Fritz Schachermeyr on the Occasion of his Eightieth Birthday.* Berlin: DeGruyter, 76–88.

Brundage, B. C. 1958. "Herakles the Levantine: A Comprehensive View," *JNES* 17: 225–36.

Brunt, P. A. 1975. "Alexander, Barsine and Heracles," *RFIC* 103: 22–34.

Brunt, P. A. 1976. *Arrian,* Loeb Classical Library, vol. 1. Cambridge, MA: Harvard University Press.

Brunt, P. A. 1983. *Arrian,* Loeb Classical Library, vol. 2. Cambridge, MA: Harvard University Press.

Buck, R. J. 1994. *Boiotia and the Boiotian League, 423–371 BC.* Edmonton: University of Alberta Press.

Buckler, J. 1980. *The Theban Hegemony, 371–362 BC.* Cambridge, MA: Harvard University Press.

Burke, B. 2001. "Anatolian Origins of the Gordian Knot Legend," *GRBS* 42: 255–61.

Burn, A. R. 1984. *Persia and the Greeks*, 2nd edn., with a postscript by D. M. Lewis. Palo Alto, CA: Stanford University Press.

Burstein, S. M. 1999. "Cleitarchus in Jerusalem: A Note on the *Book of Judith*," in F. B. Titchener and R. F. Moorton, Jr. (eds.), *The Eye Expanded: Life and the Arts in Graeco-Roman Antiquity*. Berkeley: University of California Press: 105–12.

Cahill, N. 1985. "The Treasury at Persepolis: Gift-Giving at the City of Persians," *AJA* 89: 373–89.

Capomacchia, A. M. G. 1986. *Semiramis una femminilità ribaltata*. Rome: L'Erma di Bretschneider.

Carney, E. D. 1980. "Alexander the Lyncestian: The Disloyal Opposition," *GRBS* 21: 23–33.

Carney, E. D. 1980–1. "The Conspiracy of Hermolaus," *CJ* 76: 223–31.

Carney, E. D. 1981. "The Death of Clitus," *GRBS* 22: 149–60.

Carney, E. D. 1982. "The First Flight of Harpalus Again," *CJ* 77: 9–11.

Carney, E. D. 1987. "Olympias," *Anc. Soc.* 18: 35–62.

Carney, E. D. 1988. "The Sisters of Alexander the Great: Royal Relicts," *Historia* 37: 385–404.

Carney, E. D. 1992. "The Politics of Polygamy: Olympias, Alexander and the Murder of Philip," *Historia* 41: 169–89.

Carney, E. D. 1993. "Olympias and the Image of the Virago," *Phoenix* 47: 29–55.

Carney, E. D. 1996a. "Alexander and the Persian Women," *AJPh* 117: 563–83.

Carney, E. D. 1996b. "Macedonians and Mutiny: Discipline and Indiscipline in the Macedonian Army," *CPh* 91: 19–44.

Carney, E. D. 2000a. *Women and Monarchy in Macedonia*. Norman: University of Oklahoma Press.

Carney, E. D. 2000b. "Artifice and Alexander History," in A. B. Bosworth and E. J. Baynham (eds.), *Alexander the Great in Fact and Fiction*. Oxford: Clarendon Press, 263–85.

Casson, S. 1926. *Macedonia, Thrace and Illyria*. Oxford.

Cawkwell, G. L. 1969. "The Crowning of Demosthenes," *CQ* 19: 163–80.

Cawkwell, G. L. 1978. *Philip of Macedon*. London: Faber and Faber.

Cawkwell, G. L. 1994. "The Deification of Alexander the Great: A Note," in I. Worthington (ed.), *Ventures into Greek History*. Oxford: Clarendon Press, 293–306.

Chroust, A. H. 1964. "Was Aristotle Actually the Preceptor of Alexander the Great?" *Classical Folia* 18: 26–33.

Classen, D. J. 1959. "The Libyan God Ammon in Greece before 331 BC," *Historia* 8: 349–55.

Colledge, M. A. R. 1967. *The Parthians*. London.

Collins, A. W. 2001. "The Office of Chiliarch under Alexander and the Successors," *Phoenix* 55: 259–83.

Cook, J. M. 1983. *The Persian Empire*. New York: Schocken Books.

Danforth, L. M. 1995. *The Macedonian Conflict: Ethnic Nationalism in a Transnational World*. Princeton, NJ: Princeton University Press.

Daskalakis, A. 1965. *The Hellenism of the Ancient Macedonians*. Thessaloniki.

Davidson, J. 2001. "Bonkers about Boys," *London Review of Books*. 1 November: 7–10.

Davies, Iolo. 1998. "*Alexander's Itinerary*: An English Translation," *AHB* 12: 29–54.

Davis-Kimball, J. 2002. *Warrior Women: An Archaeologist's Search for History's Hidden Heroines*. New York: Warner Books.

Develin, R. 1981. "The Murder of Philip II," *Antichthon* 15: 86–99.

Devine, A. M. 1975. "Grand Tactics at Gaugamela," *Phoenix* 29: 374–85.

Devine, A. M. 1980. "The Location of the Battle of Issus," *LCM* 5: 3–10.

Devine, A. M. 1984. "The Location of Castabulum and Alexander's Route from Mallus to Myriandrus," *AC* 27: 127–9.

Devine, A. M. 1985a. "The Strategies of Alexander the Great and Darius III in the Issus Campaign (333 BC)," *AncW* 12: 25–38.

Devine, A. M. 1985b. "Grand Tactics at the Battle of Issus," *AncW* 12: 39–59.

Devine, A. M. 1986a. "Demythologizing the Battle of the Granicus," *Phoenix* 40: 265–78.

Devine, A. M. 1986b. "The Battle of Gaugamela: A Tactical and Source-Critical Study," *AncW* 13: 87–116.

Devine, A. M. 1987. "The Battle of the Hydaspes: A Tactical and Source-Critical Study," *AncW* 16: 91–113.

Devine, A. M. 1988. "The Pawn-Sacrifice at the Battle of the Granicus: The Origins of a Favorite Stratagem of Alexander the Great," *AncW* 18: 3–20.

Devine, A. M. 1989. "The Macedonian Army at Gaugamela: Its Strength and the Length of Its Battle-Line," *AncW* 19: 77–80.

Droysen, J. G. 1980. *Geschichte des Hellenismus*, 3 vols., ed. E. Bayer. Reprint of the 1952–3 edn. Darmstadt: Wissenschaftliche Buchgesellschaft.

Due, B. 1993. "Alexander's Inspiration and Ideas," in J. Carlsen et al. (eds.), *Alexander the Great: Reality and Myth*. Rome: 53–60.

Edmunds, L. 1971. "The Religiosity of Alexander," *GRBS* 12: 363–91.

Ehrenberg, V. 1938. *Alexander and the Greeks*. Oxford: Blackwell.

Ellis, J. R. 1970. "The Security of the Macedonian Throne under Philip II," *AM* 1: 68–75.

Ellis, J. R. 1971. "Amyntas Perdikka, Philip II and Alexander the Great: A Study in Conspiracy," *JHS* 91: 15–24.

Ellis, J. R. 1973. "The Step-Brothers of Philip II," *Historia* 22: 350–4.

Ellis, J. R. 1975. "Alexander's Hypaspists Again," *Historia* 24: 617–18.

Ellis, J. R. 1976. *Philip II and Macedonian Imperialism*. London: Thames and Hudson.

Ellis, J. R. 1981. "The Assassination of Philip II," in H. J. Dell (ed.), *Ancient Macedonian Studies in Honor of Charles F. Edson*. Thessaloniki: Institute for Balkan Studies, 99–137.

Engels, D. W. 1978a. *Alexander the Great and the Logistics of the Macedonian Army*. Berkeley: University of California Pess.

Engels, D. W. 1978b. "A Note on Alexander's Death," *CPh* 73: 224–8.

Errington, R. M. 1969. "Bias in Ptolemy's History of Alexander," *CQ* 19: 233–42.

Errington, R. M. 1970. "From Babylon to Triparadeisos: 323–320 BC," *JHS* 90: 49–77.

Errington, R. M. 1975. "Arybbas the Molossian," *GRBS* 16: 41–50.

Errington, R. M. 1976. "Alexander in the Hellenistic World," in E. Badian (ed.), *Alexandre le grand: image et réalité*. Fondation Hardt. Entretiens 22. Geneva: 137–79.

Errington, R. M. 1978. "The Nature of the Macedonian State under the Monarchy," *Chiron* 8: 77–133.

Errington, R. M. 1990. *A History of Macedonia*, trans. C. Errington. Berkeley: University of California Press.

Erskine, A. 1989. "The Pezetairoi of Philip II and Alexander III," *Historia* 38: 385–94.

Erskine, A. 2002. "Life after Death: Alexandria and the Body of Alexander," *G & R* 49: 163–79.

Fears, J. R. 1975. "Pausanias, the Assassin of Philip II," *Athenaeum* 53: 111–35.

Flower, M. A. 1997. *Theopompus of Chios: History and Rhetoric in the Fourth Century* BC. Oxford: Clarendon Press.

Flower, M. A. 2000. "Alexander the Great and Panhellenism," in A. B. Bosworth and E. J. Baynham (eds.), *Alexander the Great in Fact and Fiction*. Oxford: Clarendon Press, 96–135.

Fontenrose, J. 1978. *The Delphic Oracle: Its Responses and Operations with a Catalogue of Responses*. Berkeley: University of California Press.

Foss, C. 1977. "The Battle of the Granicus: A New Look," *AM* 2: 495–502.

Fraser, P. M. 1996. *Cities of Alexander the Great*. Oxford: Clarendon Press.

Fredricksmeyer, E. A. 1961. "Alexander, Midas, and the Oracle at Gordium," *CPh* 56: 160–8.

Fredricksmeyer, E. A. 1990. "Alexander and Philip: Emulation and Resentment," *CJ* 85: 300–15.

Fuller, J. F. C. 1958. *The Generalship of Alexander the Great*. London.

Golan, D. 1988. "The Fate of a Court Historian: Callisthenes," *Athenaeum* 66: 99–120.

Goukowsky, P. 1978. *Essai sur les origines du mythe d'Alexandre*, vol. 1. Nancy: Publications de l'Université de Nancy.

Goukowsky, P. 1981. *Essai sur les origins du mythe d'Alexandre*, vol. 2. Nancy: Publications de l'Université de Nancy.

Granier, F. 1931. *Die makedonische Heeresversammlung. Ein Beitrag zum antiken Staatsrecht*. Munich.

Green, P. 1991. *Alexander of Macedon*. Berkeley: University of California Press.

Green, P. 1982. "The Royal Tombs at Vergina: A Historical Analysis," in W. L. Adams and E. N. Borza (eds.), *Philip II, Alexander and the Macedonian Heritage*. Washington, DC: 129–51.

Greenwalt, W. 1985. "The Introduction of Caranus into the Argead King List," *GRBS* 26: 43–9.

Greenwalt, W. 1988. "Amyntas III and the Political Stability of Argead Macedonia," *AncW* 18: 35–44.

Greenwalt, W. 1989. "Polygamy and Succession in Argead Macedonia," *Arethusa* 22: 19–43.

Griffith, G. T. 1947. "Alexander's Generalship at Gaugamela," *JHS* 67: 77–89.

Griffith, G. T. 1956–7. "*Makedonika*: Notes on the Macedonians of Philip and Alexander," *PCPhA* 4: 3–10.

Griffith, G. T. 1963. "A Note on the Hipparchies of Alexander," *JHS* 83: 68–74.

Guthrie, W. K. C. 1981. *A History of Greek Philosophy, Vol. 6: Aristotle: An Encounter*. Cambridge: Cambridge University Press.

Gutschmid, A. von. 1882. "Trogus und Timagenes," *RhM* 37: 548–55.

Habicht, C. 1970. *Gottmenschentum und griechische Städte*, 2nd edn. Munich.

Habicht, C. 1985. *Pausanias' Guide to Ancient Greece*. Sather Classical Lectures, Vol. 50. Berkeley: University of California Press.

Hamilton, J. R. 1953. "Alexander and his so-called Father," *CQ* 3: 151–7.

Hamilton, J. R. 1956. "The Cavalry Battle at the Hydaspes," *JHS* 76: 26–31.

Hamilton, J. R. 1961. "Cleitarchus and Aristobulus," *Historia* 10: 448–58.

Hamilton, J. R. 1965. "Alexander's Early Life," *G & R* 12: 116–25.

Hamilton, J. R. 1969. *Plutarch, Alexander: A Commentary*. Oxford: Clarendon Press.

Hamilton, J. R. 1973. *Alexander the Great*. London: Hutchinson.

Hamilton, J. R. 1977. "Cleitarchus and Diodorus 17," in K. Kinzl (ed.), *Greece and the Ancient Mediterranean in History and Prehistory: Studies Presented to Fritz Schachermeyr on the Occasion of his Eightieth Birthday.* Berlin: DeGruyter, 126–46.

Hamilton, J. R. 1984. "The Origins of Ruler-Cult," *Prudentia* 16: 3–16.

Hamilton, J. R. 1987. "Alexander's Iranian Policy," in W. Will (ed.), *Zu Alexander dem Grossen*, vol. 1. Amsterdam: Hakkert, 467–86.

Hamilton, J. R. 1999. *Plutarch, Alexander: A Commentary*, 2nd edn., with foreword and bibliography by P. A. Stadter. Bristol: Bristol Classical Press.

Hammond, N. G. L. 1972. *A History of Macedonia*, vol. 1. Oxford: Clarendon Press.

Hammond, N. G. L. 1980a. "The Battle of the Granicus River," *JHS* 100: 73–88.

Hammond, N. G. L. 1980b. "Training in the Use of the Sarissa and its Effect in Battle 359–333," *Antichthon* 14: 53–63.

Hammond, N. G. L. 1981. *Alexander the Great: King, Commander and Statesman.* London: Chatto and Windus.

Hammond, N. G. L. 1983. *Three Historians of Alexander the Great.* Cambridge: Cambridge University Press.

Hammond, N. G. L. 1989a. *The Macedonian State: Origins, Institutions and History.* Oxford: Clarendon Press.

Hammond, N. G. L. 1989b. "Casualties and Reinforcements of Citizen Soldiers in Greece and Macedonia," *JHS* 109: 56–68.

Hammond, N. G. L. 1990. "Royal Pages, Personal Pages and Boys Trained in the Macedonian Manner during the Period of the Temenid Monarchy," *Historia* 39: 261–90.

Hammond, N. G. L. 1991a. "The Various Guards of Philip II and Alexander III," *Historia* 40: 396–418.

Hammond, N. G. L. 1991b. "The Sources of Justin on Macedonia to the Death of Philip," *CQ* 41: 496–508.

Hammond, N. G. L. 1991c. "The Macedonian Defeat near Samarcand," *AncW* 22: 41–7.

Hammond, N. G. L. 1992a. "Alexander's Charge at the Battle of Issus in 333 BC," *Historia* 41: 395–406.

Hammond, N. G. L. 1992b. "The Archaeological and Literary Evidence for the Burning of the Persepolis Palace," *CQ* 42: 358–64.

Hammond, N. G. L. 1992c. "The Regnal Years of Philip and Alexander," *GRBS* 33: 355–78.

Hammond, N. G. L. 1993. *Sources for Alexander the Great: An Analysis of Plutarch's Life and Arrian's Anabasis Alexandrou.* Cambridge: Cambridge University Press.

Hammond, N. G. L. 1994a. *Philip of Macedon.* Baltimore, MD: Johns Hopkins University Press.

Hammond, N. G. L. 1994b. "Literary Evidence for Macedonian Speech," *Historia* 43: 131–42.

Hammond, N. G. L. 1995a. "Alexander's Order during the Cleitus Episode," *AHB* 9: 111–16.

Hammond, N. G. L. 1995b. "Did Alexander Use One or Two Seals?" *Chiron* 25: 199–203.

Hammond, N. G. L. 1995c. "Philip's Innovations in Macedonian Economy," *SO* 70: 22–9.

Hammond, N. G. L. 1996. "Some Passages in Polyaenus *Stratagems* concerning Alexander," *GRBS* 37: 23–53.

Hammond, N. G. L. and G. T. Griffith. 1979. *A History of Macedonia II: 550–336 BC.* Oxford: Clarendon Press.

Hammond, N. G. L. and F. W. Walbank. 1988. *A History of Macedonia III: 336–167 BC*. Oxford: Clarendon Press.

Hanson, V. D. 1999. *The Wars of the Ancient Greeks and their Invention of Western Military Culture*. London: Cassell.

Harding, P. 1985. *Translated Documents of Greece and Rome, Vol. 2: From the End of the Peloponnesian War to the Battle of Ipsos*. Cambridge: Cambridge University Press.

Hauben, H. 1970. "The King of the Sidonians and the Persian Imperial Fleet," *Anc. Soc.* 1: 1–8.

Heckel, W. 1977. "The Conspiracy *against* Philotas," *Phoenix* 31: 9–21.

Heckel, W. 1979. "Philip II, Kleopatra and Karanos," *RFIC* 107: 385–93.

Heckel, W. 1980. "Alexander at the Persian Gates," *Athenaeum* 58: 168–74.

Heckel, W. 1981a. "Philip and Olympias (337/6 BC)," in G. S. Shrimpton and D. J. McCargar (eds.), *Classical Contributions: Studies in Honour of Malcolm Francis McGregor*. Locust Valley, NY: J. J. Augustin, 51–7.

Heckel, W. 1981b. "Polyxena, the Mother of Alexander the Great," *Chiron* 11: 79–86.

Heckel, W. 1981c. "Two Doctors from Kos?" *Mnemosyne* 34: 396–8.

Heckel, W. 1983–4. "Kynanne the Illyrian," *RSA* 13–14: 193–200.

Heckel, W. 1986. "*Somatophylakia*, a Macedonian *cursus honorum*," *Phoenix* 40: 279–94.

Heckel, W. 1988. *The Last Days and Testament of Alexander the Great: A Prosopographic Study*. Historia Einzelschriften, Heft 56. Stuttgart: Franz Steiner.

Heckel, W. 1992a. *The Marshals of Alexander's Empire*. London: Routledge.

Heckel, W. 1992b. "Doryphoroe in Curtius 3.3.15 Again," *RhM* 135: 191–2.

Heckel, W. 1994. "Notes on Q. Curtius Rufus' *History of Alexander*," *AC* 37: 67–78.

Heckel, W. 1997. "Resistance to Alexander the Great," in L. A. Tritle (ed.), *The Greek World in the Fourth Century: From the Fall of the Athenian Empire to the Successors of Alexander*. London: Routledge, 189–227.

Heckel, W. 2002a. *The Wars of Alexander the Great: 336–323 BC*. Oxford: Osprey.

Heckel, W. 2002b. "The Case of the Missing Phrourarch: Arrian 3.16.6–9," *AHB* 16: 57–60.

Heckel, W. 2003. "King and Companions: Observations on the Nature of Power in the Reign of Alexander," in J. Roisman (ed.), *Brill's Companion to Alexander the Great*. Leiden: E. J. Brill, 197–225.

Heisserer, A. J. 1980. *Alexander the Great and the Greeks: The Epigraphic Evidence*. Norman: University of Oklahoma Press.

Heskel, J. 1988. "The Political Background of the Arybbas Decree," *GRBS* 29: 185–96.

Hoffmann, O. 1906. *Die Makedonen: ihre Sprache und ihr Volkstum*. Göttingen: Vandenhoeck and Ruprecht; reprinted Georg Olms 1974.

Holt, F. L. 1982. "The Hyphasis 'Mutiny': A Source Study," *AncW* 5: 33–59.

Holt, F. L. 1986. "Alexander's Settlements in Central Asia," *AM* 4: 315–18.

Holt, F. L. 1988. *Alexander the Great and Bactria: The Formation of a Greek Frontier in Central Asia*. Supplements to Mnemosyne 104. Leiden: E. J. Brill.

Holt, F. L. 2000. "The Death of Coenus: Another Study in Method," *AHB* 14: 49–55.

Hornblower, J. 1981. *Hieronymus of Cardia*. Oxford: Clarendon Press.

Jaschinski, S. 1981. *Alexander und Griechenland unter dem Eindruck der Flucht des Harpalos*. Bonn: Peter Lang.

Kienast, D. 1973. *Philipp II. und das Reich der Achaimeniden*. Munich: Beck.

Kiilerich, B. 1988. "Physiognomics and the Iconography of Alexander," *SO* 63: 51–66.

Kiilerich, B. 1993. "The Public Image of Alexander the Great," in J. Carlsen et al. (eds.), *Alexander the Great: Reality and Myth*. Rome: 85–93.

Kingsley, B. 1986. "Harpalos in the Megarid (333–331 BC) and the Grain Shipments from Cyrene," *ZPE* 66: 165–77.

Konstan, D. 1997. *Friendship in the Classical World*. Cambridge: Cambridge University Press.

Krentz, P. and E. Wheeler. 1994. *Polyaenus: Stratagems of War*, 2 vols. Chicago, IL: Ares Press.

Kuhrt, A. 1987. "Usurpation, Conquest, and Ceremonial: From Babylonia to Persia," in D. Cannadine and S. Price (eds.), *Rituals of Royalty: Power and Ceremonial in Traditional Societies*. Cambridge: Cambridge University Press, 20–55.

Lane Fox, R. 1973. *Alexander the Great*. London: Allen Lane.

Lane Fox, R. 1996. "Text and Image: Alexander the Great, Coins and Elephants," *BICS* 41: 87–108.

Lane Fox, R. 1997. "The Itinerary of Alexander: Constantius to Julian," *CQ* 47: 239–52.

Larsen, A. O. 1932a. "Alexander and the Oracle of Ammon," *CPh* 27: 70–5.

Larsen, A. O. 1932b. "An Additional Note at the Oracle of Ammon," *CPh* 27: 274–5.

Lauter, H. 1988. "Alexanders wahres Gesicht," in W. Will (ed.), *Zu Alexander dem Grossen*, vol. 2. Amsterdam: Hakkert, 717–43.

Lock, R. 1972. "The Date of Agis III's War in Greece," *Antichthon* 6: 10–27.

Lock, R. 1977a. "The Macedonian Army Assembly in the Time of Alexander the Great," *CPh* 72: 91–107.

Lock, R. 1977b. "The Origins of the Argyraspids," *Historia* 26: 373–8.

McCoy, W. J. 1989. "Memnon of Rhodes at the Granicus," *AJPh* 110: 413–33.

MacDermot, B. C. and K. Schippmann. 1999. "Alexander's March from Susa to Persepolis," *IA* 34: 283–308.

Mack, John E. 1998. *A Prince of our Disorder: The Life of T. E. Lawrence*. Cambridge, MA: Harvard University Press.

McKechnie, P. 1995. "Diodorus Siculus and Hephaestion's Pyre," *CQ* 45: 418–32.

McQueen, E. I. 1967. "Quintus Curtius Rufus," in T. A. Dorey (ed.), *Latin Biography*. London: 17 ff.

McQueen, E. I. 1978. "Some Notes on the Anti-Macedonian Movement in the Peloponnese in 331 BC," *Historia* 27: 40–64.

Macurdy, G. H. 1930. "The Refusal of Callisthenes to Drink to the Health of Alexander," *JHS* 50: 294–7.

Macurdy, G. H. 1932. *Hellenistic Queens: A Study of Woman-Power in Macedonia, Seleucid Syria and Ptolemaic Egypt*. Johns Hopkins University Studies in Archaeology, no. 14. Baltimore, MD: Johns Hopkins University Press.

Manti, P. A. 1983. "The Cavalry Sarissa," *AncW* 8: 73–80.

Markle, M. M. 1977. "The Macedonian Sarissa, Spear, and Related Armour," *AJA* 81: 323–39.

Markle, M. M. 1978. "Use of the Sarissa by Philip and Alexander of Macedon," *AJA* 82: 483–97.

Markle, M. M. 1982. "Macedonian Arms and Tactics under Alexander the Great," *Macedonia and Greece in Late Classical and Early Hellenistic Times*. Studies in the History of Art, no. 10. Washington: 87–111.

Marsden, E. W. 1964. *The Campaign of Gaugamela*. Liverpool.

Mederer, E. 1936. *Die Alexanderlegenden bei den ältesten Alexanderhistorikern*. Stuttgart.

Milns, R. D. 1967. "Philip II and the Hypaspists," *Historia* 16: 509–12.

Milns, R. D. 1968. *Alexander the Great*. London.

Milns, R. D. 1971. "The Hypaspists of Alexander III – Some Problems," *Historia* 20: 186–95.

Milns, R. D. 1976. "The Army of Alexander the Great," in E. Badian (ed.), *Alexandre le grand: image et réalité*. Fondations Hardt. Entretiens 22. Geneva: 87–136.

Miltner, F. 1933. "Alexanders Strategie bei Issos," *JÖAI* 28: 69–78.

Montgomery, H. 1985. "The Economic Revolution of Philip II – Myth or Reality?" *SO* 60: 37–47.

Munn, M. 1997. "Thebes and Central Greece," in L. A. Tritle (ed.), *The Greek World in the Fourth Century: From the Fall of the Athenian Empire to the Successors of Alexander*. London: Routledge, 66–106.

Murison, C. L. 1972. "Darius III and the Battle of Issus," *Historia* 21: 399–423.

Nielsen, A. M. 1993. "The Mirage of Alexander – A Minimalist View," in J. Carlsen et al. (eds.), *Alexander the Great: Reality and Myth*. Rome: 137–44.

Nylander, C. 1993. "Darius III – the Coward King: Points and Counterpoints," in J. Carlsen et al. (eds.), *Alexander the Great: Reality and Myth*. Rome: 145–59.

O'Brien, J. M. 1980. "Alexander and Dionysus: The Invisible Enemy," *Annals of Scholarship* 1: 83–105.

O'Brien, J. M. 1992. *Alexander the Great: The Invisible Enemy*. New York: Routledge.

Ogden, D. 1999. *Polygamy, Prostitutes and Death: The Hellenistic Dynasties*. London: Duckworth.

Olmstead, A. T. 1948. *History of the Persian Empire*. Chicago, IL: University of Chicago Press.

Parke, H. W. and D. E. W. Wormell. 1956. *The Delphic Oracle II: The Oracular Responses*. Oxford: Blackwell.

Parsons, P. J. 1979. "The Burial of Philip II," *AJAH* 4: 97–101.

Pearson, L. 1960. *The Lost Histories of Alexander the Great*. New York: American Philological Association.

Perrin, B. 1895. "Genesis and Growth of an Alexander-Myth," *TAPhA* 26: 56–68.

Pollitt, J. J. 1990. *The Art of Ancient Greece: Sources and Documents*. Cambridge: Cambridge University Press.

Polo, M. P. 1993. "La terminologia sobre las asembleas macedonias en Quinto Curcio y Justino," *Athenaeum* 81: 264–9.

Powell, J. E. 1939. "The Sources of Plutarch's Alexander," *JHS* 59: 229–40.

Prandi, L. 1998. "A Few Remarks on the Amyntas 'Conspiracy'," in W. Will (ed.), *Alexander der Grosse: Eine Welteroberung und ihr Hintergrund*. Bonn: 91–102.

Prentice, W. K. 1923. "Callisthenes, the Original Historian of Alexander," *TAPhA* 54: 74–85.

Reames-Zimmerman, J. 1999. "An Atypical Affair? Alexander the Great, Hephaistion Amyntoros and the Nature of their Relationship," *AHB* 13: 81–96.

Reames-Zimmerman, J. 2001. "The Mourning of Alexander the Great," *Syllecta Classica* 12: 98–145.

Renard, M. and J. Servais. 1955. "A propos du mariage d'Alexandre et de Roxane," *L'Antiquité Classique* 24: 29–50.

Roisman, J. 1984. "Ptolemy and his Rivals in his History of Alexander," *CQ* 34: 373–85.

Roller, L. E. 1984. "Midas and the Gordian Knot," *CA* 3: 256–71.

Romane, J. P. 1987. "Alexander's Siege of Tyre," *AncW* 16: 79–90.

Ross Taylor, L. 1927. "The 'Proskynesis' and the Hellenistic Ruler-Cult," *JHS* 47: 53–62.

Rubinsohn, Z. 1977. "The 'Philotas Affair' – A Reconsideration," *AM* 2: 409–20.

Ruzicka, S. 1997. "The Eastern Greek World," in L. A. Tritle (ed.), *The Greek World in the Fourth Century* BC. London: Routledge, 107–66.

Sage, M. 1996. *Warfare in Ancient Greece: A Sourcebook.* London: Routledge.

Sancisi-Weerdenburg, H. 1993. "Alexander and Persepolis," in J. Carlsen et al. (eds.), *Alexander the Great: Reality and Myth.* Rome: 177–88.

Schachermeyr, F. 1973. *Alexander der Grosse: Das Problem seiner Persönlichkeit und seines Wirkens.* Vienna.

Schepens, G. 1971. "Arrian's View of his Task as Alexander Historian," *Anc. Soc.* 2: 254–68.

Schmidt, E. 1953–70. *Persepolis*, 3 vols. Chicago.

Schubert, R. 1898. "Der Tod des Kleitos," *RhM* 53: 98–117.

Schwarzenberg, E. von. 1976. "The Portraiture of Alexander," in E. Badian (ed.), *Alexandre le grand: image et réalité.* Fondation Hardt. Entretiens Hardt 22. Geneva: 223–78.

Seibert, J. 1967. *Historische Beiträge zu den dynastischen Verbindungen in hellenistischer Zeit*, Historia Einzelschriften, Heft 10. Wiesbaden.

Seibert, J. 1972. *Alexander der Grosse*, Erträge der Forschung, no. 10. Darmstadt: Wissenschaftliche Buchgesellschaft.

Seibert, J. 1985. *Die Eroberung des Perserreiches durch Alexander den Großen auf kartographischer Grundlage.* TAVO Beiheft, Reihe B, no. 68. Wiesbaden.

Seibert, J. 1987. "Dareios III," in W. Will (ed.), *Zu Alex. d. Gr.* Amsterdam: 437–56.

Sekunda, N. and S. Chew. 1992. *The Persian Army: 560–330* BC. Elite Series 42. Oxford: Osprey.

Snell, B. 1964. *Scenes from Greek Drama.* Berkeley: University of California Press.

Spann, Philip O. 1999. "Alexander at the Beas: Fox in a Lion's Skin," in F. B. Titchener and R. F. Moorton, Jr. (eds.), *The Eye Expanded: Life and the Arts in Graeco-Roman Antiquity.* Berkeley: University of California Press, 62–74.

Speck, H. 2002. *Alexander at the Persian Gates: A Study in Historiography and Topography*, *AJAH* n.s. 1.1: 1–234.

Stein, A. 1929. *On Alexander's Track to the Indus.* London.

Stein, A. 1932. "The Site of Alexander's Passage of the Hydaspes and the Battle with Porus," *GJ* 80: 31–46.

Stein, A. 1938. "An Archaeological Journey in Western Iran," *GJ* 92: 313–42.

Stein, A. 1940. *Old Routes of Western Iran.* London.

Stewart, A. 1993. *Faces of Power: Alexander's Image and Hellenistic Politics.* Berkeley: University of California Press.

Stoneman, R. (ed. and trans.) 1991. *The Greek Alexander Romance.* Harmondsworth: Penguin Books.

Stoneman, R. (ed. and trans.) 1994. *Legends of Alexander the Great.* London: Everyman.

Stoneman, R. 1997. *Alexander the Great.* Lancaster Pamphlets. London: Routledge.

Strasburger, H. 1934. *Ptolemaios und Alexander.* Leipzig.

Tabacco, R. 2000. *Itinerarium Alexandri. Testo, apparato critico, introduzione, traduzione e commento.* Turin: Leo S. Olschki.

Tarn, W. W. 1913. *Antigonos Gonatas.* Oxford: Clarendon Press.

Tarn, W. W. 1921a. "Heracles, Son of Barsine," *JHS* 41: 18–28.

Tarn, W. W. 1921b. "Alexander's *Hypomnemata* and the World Kingdom," *JHS* 41: 3–17.

Tarn, W. W. 1948. *Alexander the Great*, 2 vols. Cambridge: Cambridge University Press.

Thomas, C. G. 1974. "Alexander's Garrisons: A Clue to his Administrative Plans?" *Antichthon* 8: 11–20.

Tod, M. N. (1948). *A Selection of Greek Historical Inscriptions*. Oxford: Clarendon Press.

Tritle, L. A. (ed.) 1998. *Balkan Currents: Studies in the History, Culture and Society of a Divided Land*. Claremont, CA: Regina Books.

Tronson, A. 1984. "Satyrus the Peripatetic and the Marriages of Philip II," *JHS* 104: 116–26.

Tucci, G. 1977. "On Swat: The Dards and Connected Problems," *East and West* 27: 9–85.

Tyrrell, W. B. 1984. *Amazons: A Study in Athenian Mythmaking*. Baltimore, MD: Johns Hopkins University Press.

Unz, R. 1985. "Alexander's Brothers," *JHS* 105: 171–4.

Vlasidis, V. and V. Karakostanoglou. 1995. "Recycling Propaganda: Remarks on Recent Reports on Greece's 'Slav–Macedonian Minority'," *Balkan Studies* 36: 150–70.

von Gaertringen, F. H. 1906. *Inschriften von Priene*. Berlin.

Walbank, F. W. 1972. *Polybius*. Berkeley: University of California Press.

Warmington, B. H. 1969. *Nero: Reality and Legend*. London.

Warry, J. 1991. *Alexander 334–323 BC: Conquest of the Persian Empire*. Campaign Series 7. Oxford: Osprey.

Welles, C. B. 1963. *Diodorus of Sicily*. Loeb Classical Library, vol. 8. Cambridge, MA: Harvard University Press.

Wheatley, P. V. 1998. "The Date of Polyperchon's Invasion of Macedonia and the Murder of Heracles," *Antichthon* 32: 12–23.

Wilcken, U. 1967. *Alexander the Great*, trans. G. C. Richards, introduction and notes by E. N. Borza. New York: Norton.

Wood, M. 1997. *In the Footsteps of Alexander the Great*. Berkeley: University of California Press.

Worthington, I. 1984. "The First Flight of Harpalus Reconsidered," *G & R* 31: 161–9.

Worthington, I. 1986. "The Chronology of the Harpalus Affair," *SO* 61: 63–76.

Worthington, I. 1992. *A Historical Commentary on Dinarchus*. Ann Arbor: University of Michigan Press.

Worthington, I. 1994a. "The Harpalus Affair and the Greek Response to Macedonian Hegemony," in I. Worthington (ed.), *Ventures into Greek History*. Oxford: Clarendon Press, 307–30.

Worthington, I. 1994b. "Alexander and Athens in 324/3 BC: On the Greek Attitude to the Macedonian Hegemony," *Mediterranean Archaeology* 7: 45–51.

Yardley, J. C. (trans.) 1984. *Quintus Curtius Rufus: The History of Alexander*, introduction, notes, and appendixes by W. Heckel. Harmondsworth: Penguin Books.

Yardley, J. C. and W. Heckel. 1997. *Justin, Epitome of the Philippic History of Pompeius Trogus, Vol. 1: Books 11–12: Alexander the Great*. Clarendon Ancient History Series. Oxford: Clarendon Press.

Ziegler, K. 1936. "Plutarchstudien," *RhM* 84: 369–90.

Index

CPSIA information can be obtained at www.ICGtesting.com
Printed in the USA
BVOW09s2049160315

391964BV00007B/36/P

9 780631 228219